*The Vulnerability of Integrity
in Early Confucian Thought*

The Vulnerability of Integrity in Early Confucian Thought

MICHAEL D. K. ING

OXFORD
UNIVERSITY PRESS

OXFORD
UNIVERSITY PRESS

Oxford University Press is a department of the University of Oxford. It furthers
the University's objective of excellence in research, scholarship, and education
by publishing worldwide. Oxford is a registered trade mark of Oxford University
Press in the UK and certain other countries.

Published in the United States of America by Oxford University Press
198 Madison Avenue, New York, NY 10016, United States of America.

CIP data is on file at the Library of Congress
ISBN 978-0-19-067911-8

1 3 5 7 9 8 6 4 2
Printed by Sheridan Books, Inc., United States of America

To Michael Puett

Mentor, friend, and junzi 君子

Water of the utmost purity is sure to have no fish.

水至清即無魚

(*Kongzi Jiayu* 《孔子家語》 21/42/7)

Contents

Acknowledgments

THIS PROJECT WOULD not have been possible without the generous support of many people. I have benefited greatly from my colleagues at Indiana University. The Ethics, Philosophy, and Politics group, as well as our Chinese reading group, have been invaluable. More specifically I would like to thank Aaron Stalnaker, Richard Miller, Cheryl Cottine, Zhang Meng, Bharat Ranganathan, Winnifred Sullivan, Constance Furey, Lisa Sideris, Richard Nance, Fan Rui, Susan Blake, Hong Hao, He Ruilin, and Hsu Nai-yi. Aaron in particular has endured long discussions about this book and has read through much of the manuscript. I have also benefited greatly from conversations with David Haberman, Kevin Jaques, Alexus McLeod, Newell Ann Van Auken, Benjamin Huff, Tobias Zuern, Lu Jing, Youngsun Back, and Derik Goatson. I am deeply indebted to my colleagues in the Enhancing Life Project for encouraging me to think in new ways, especially Bill Schweiker and Günter Thomas.

I presented portions of this work over the past four years at the Midwest Conference on Chinese Thought and shared many parts of it with my students. These people have contributed in innumerable ways. Huang Yong and the editors at *Dao* have been gracious in allowing me to republish parts of "Born of Resentment: *Yuan* 怨 in Early Confucian Thought," *Dao: A Journal of Comparative Philosophy* 15.1 (March 2016): 19–33. I have also used parts of "Two Virtuous Actions Cannot Both Be Completed: Rethinking Value Conflicts in Early Confucian Thought," which was published in *The Journal of Religious Ethics* 44.4 (October 2016): 659–684.

Cynthia Read and the editorial team at Oxford University Press have been a pleasure to work with, and I am grateful for the insights offered by the anonymous readers of the manuscript version of this book.

My family has been my biggest inspiration. Lalea, Kai'ava and Sherene make everyday meaningful, and I am forever grateful for all my father and mother have done for me.

The John Templeton Foundation (via the Enhancing Life Project), Indiana University, and the Chiang Ching-kuo Foundation for International Scholarly Exchange provided extensive financial support to begin and complete this project. The opinions expressed in this book are my own and do not necessarily reflect the views of these organizations.

Conventions

I EMPLOY THE *Pinyin* system of Romanization throughout this book except for the names of contemporary authors whose work is published under alternative forms of Romanization (e.g., Tu Weiming). If a system other than *Pinyin* was used in a quotation, I converted the terms into *Pinyin* and often added Chinese characters. I also converted the names of figures or texts used in quotations into forms that are uniform throughout this book (e.g., "Confucius" to "Kongzi"). I use the traditional script form of Chinese characters except when citing an article or book composed in simplified characters.

When referencing East Asian scholars I follow the custom of referring to them by their last name first, although in the bibliography I follow the guidelines set forth in the recent edition of *The Chicago Manual of Style*. I also follow the custom of using "Kongzi" instead of "Confucius" and "Mengzi" instead of "Mencius" in order to maintain uniformity in referring to early Chinese figures.

For the sake of clarity I use single quotation marks to designate technical terms; and I use double quotation marks in their standard grammatical sense—to designate the words or terms of others. When words are italicized they are either foreign words or words I wish to stress in a given sentence.

For primary sources from than Han dynasty and earlier I follow the Institute of Chinese Studies' *Ancient Chinese Text Concordance Series* 《香港中文大學中國文化研究所先秦兩漢古籍逐字索引叢刊》, unless noted in the endnotes. Full citation for each concordance is found in the bibliography rather than the endnotes (to keep the endnotes to a minimum). In citing the texts, I follow the practice of "chapter/page/line," with the exception of the *Analects* and *Mengzi*, where I follow the common citation style of "chapter.passage" or "chapter-division-passage." Occasionally I modify the punctuation as found in the *Ancient Chinese Text Concordance Series*. In studying the texts, I also rely on digital editions including the Chinese University of Hong Kong's Ancient Chinese Texts Database (www.chant.org), The Chinese Text Project (www.ctext.org), and the Digital Heritage Publishing Company's (迪志文化出版社) *Sikuquanshu* 《文淵閣四庫全書電子版》.

Introduction

The times are filthy, foul, and nowhere near clean;
the age is brutal, chaotic, and far from illustrious.
[How I] long for acceptance, and wait for the right time;
but with great fear [I see] the years passing by.
If only [I] could bend the rules and follow along with the tide;
[yet my] heart holds fast [to them] without reprieve.

時溷濁猶未清兮，世殽亂猶未察。
欲容與以俟時兮，懼年歲之既晏。
顧屈節以從流兮，心鞿羈而不夷。

("YUANSI" 怨思, *Chuci* 《楚辭》)[1]

THE "LUN RU" 論儒 chapter of the *Yantielun* 《鹽鐵論》 purports to record a debate between Confucian scholars and Han dynasty government officials (c. 81 BCE) about the efficacy of Confucianism and the extent to which Confucians are willing to go to in order to be efficacious.[2] At one point, the officials charge that many of the supposedly great Confucians were willing to "demean the Way in order to seek the acceptance [of the ruling class who would employ them]" 貶道以求容.[3] The Confucians respond,

> An illustrious ruler is concerned when the world is not at peace or when the various states of his kingdom are not tranquil. Sages and worthies are concerned when there is no king on the throne and no head of the royal clans serving beneath the king, or when the world is disarrayed and chaotic. This is why Yao worried about the floods and Yi Yin worried about the people. Guan Zhong submitted to arrest and Kongzi (Confucius) wandered around [seeking employment] because they worried about the misfortunes of the people and longed to calm their fears. [The great figures of the past] shouldered vessels and stands [i.e., took responsibilities beneath their station], suffered imprisonment, and [tired themselves to the point of] crawling along the ground in order to save the people.

The point is that when one chases after someone fleeing, he runs fast; and when one saves someone drowning, he gets wet. Now, it seems that the people of the kingdom have fallen in a filthy ditch. Even if one wanted to be without stain [in saving them], how could it be otherwise?

天下不平，庶國不寧，明王之憂也。上無天子，下無方伯，天下煩亂，賢聖之憂也。是以堯憂洪水，伊尹憂民，管仲束縛，孔子周流，憂百姓之禍而欲安其危也。是以負鼎俎、囚拘、匍匐以救之。故追亡者趨，拯溺者濡。今民陷溝壑，雖欲無濡，豈得已哉？ 4

The "Lun Ru" chapter then concludes by saying that the government officials were left speechless. Many of the specifics of the figures mentioned in this passage are discussed throughout this book. The point worth noting here, however, is the author's claim regarding the necessity of "getting wet" in accomplishing some great, yet difficult, task.

This imagery of getting wet, or even sullying oneself, in complex moral situations is a reoccurring theme in many early Confucian texts. The *Xinxu* 《新序》 and the *Han Shi Waizhuan* 《韓詩外傳》, for instance, tell of Shentu Di 申徒狄 (c. 1600 BCE), an advisor who drowned himself in a river rather than accept an illegitimate position in the government of his time. Before jumping in the river, Cui Jia 崔嘉, a fellow advisor, counseled Shentu Di as he stood by the river and criticized him for planning to drown himself instead of saving the people of the kingdom, who, in Cui's view, were figuratively "drowning" in the difficulties of the day. He questioned Shentu's actions, stating, "The sages and humane scholars of the world are like mothers and fathers to the people. Do you think it permissible to refrain from saving the drowning on the basis of not wanting to get [your] feet wet" 聖人仁士之於天地之間，民之父母也，今為濡足之故，不救溺人，可乎？ 5 The *Yantielun* also describes Kongzi as one "born in a chaotic age. He reflected on the Way of Yao and Shun, traveled around the kingdom until his head was sun-burnt and his feet were wet, hoping to enlighten the rulers of his day" 孔子生於亂世，思堯、舜之道，東西南北，灼頭濡足，庶幾世主之悟. 6 More mainstream texts such as the *Mengzi* 《孟子》 employ similar themes in passages such as 4A17 where Mengzi endorses breaking the rules of propriety (*li* 禮) in order to save one's drowning sister-in-law. The *Analects* 《論語》 also draws on a similar motif in passages such as 18.6 when Kongzi and his disciples, looking for a safe place to cross a river, confront Jie Ni 桀溺, literally one who is "steadfast in drowning seas," and Chang Ju 長沮, one who has been "pulling [people] out for a long time." This motif is repeated in other early Chinese texts as well. 7

The purpose of this book is to explore what the authors of these early Confucian texts might have meant by claiming that some situations require moral agents to get wet, or even dirty, while saving the drowning or suffering. Stated more broadly, I explore the degree to which early Confucian texts argue that the integrity of the moral agent is vulnerable to unfortunate, and even tragic, circumstances. I show that a variety of positions emerge within early Confucianism. Some positions restrict the degree to which the moral agent is compromised. In these cases, the moral agent (often depicted in terms of a sage; *shengren* 聖人), encounters situations where values appear to conflict with each other or appear threatened. In these situations, the moral agent harmonizes conflicting values or focuses on the internal goods of the Confucian Way, and by doing this he renders his integrity invulnerable to misfortune. The moral agent may even grieve over the pain inflicted on others because of his choices. However, he does not feel regret. In other words, while the moral agent may sorrow over misfortune or harm, he does not wish that he acted in some alternative way. Other positions, however, argue for a more robust form of moral distress. In these views not even the most paradigmatic of moral agents can emerge from complex situations with his integrity fully intact. The way in which his self is composed and connected to others is vulnerable to tragic circumstances.

One of the larger claims this book will reveal is that the preference of many contemporary scholars to rely on texts such as the *Mengzi, Xunzi* 《荀子》, and the *Analects* in developing and describing Confucian ethics has obscured other readings of early Confucianism. While notions of invulnerability can indeed be found in the Confucian tradition, they emerge through debate. This book investigates this debate and suggests that even well-known texts such as the *Analects* and the *Mengzi* exhibit tragic tendencies when read in light of the larger discourse. In this way, I bring a series of neglected texts to bear on these issues. These include texts such as the *Han Shi Waizhuan*, the *Kongzi Jiayu* 《孔子家語》, the *Kong Congzi* 《孔叢子》, and the *Liji* 《禮記》. These texts yield new insight into questions of vulnerability and encourage a rereading of more popular texts. They are also particularly relevant given recent archeological finds that push the dating of texts such as the *Kongzi Jiayu* closer to the composition of texts such as the *Analects*.[8] While most issues of textual composition lay beyond the purview of this book, I hope to open the way for further discussion about what constitutes Confucian thought and which texts are worthy of investigation.

In its broadest sense, this book is about the necessity and even the value of vulnerability in human experience. While I focus on early Confucianism, my hope is to provide space and a vocabulary for cross-cultural reflection on similar issues. I aim to participate in a dialogue about the ways in which meaningful things are vulnerable to powers beyond our control and, more specifically, to explore the ways in which relationships with meaningful others might compel tragic actions. In a general sense, vulnerability is often understood as a category of the

disenfranchised—a descriptor for the young, the old, and others too weak to protect themselves. Vulnerability, in this light, is an undesirable state—something
that individuals and institutions work to resist, overcome, or deny.[9] While I recognize the need for adopting strategies of resistance in various situations, I strive
to demonstrate that vulnerability is far more enduring in human experience and
that it enables values such as morality, trust, and maturity. Vulnerability also
highlights the need for care (care for oneself and for others). The possibility of
tragic loss stresses the difficulty of offering and receiving care and thereby fosters
compassion for others as we strive to care for each other. Tragedy, in the form
of irresolvable value conflicts, means that vulnerability runs deep. The possibility that we can be held accountable for harming or neglecting significant values
despite how well we perform means that we cannot construct an invulnerable
moral world. Vulnerability, in this sense, cannot be eliminated and must be coped
with. At the same time, vulnerability is worthy of appreciation in that it enables
aspects of a good life.

This book is structured to explore the plurality of Confucian thought as it
relates to the vulnerability of integrity. The first two chapters describe traditional
and contemporary views that argue for the invulnerability of integrity in early
Confucian thought. The remaining five chapters investigate alternative views. In
particular these later chapters give attention to neglected voices in the tradition,
which argue that our concern for others can, and even should, lead to us compromise our integrity. In these cases we are compelled to do something transgressive
for the sake of others, and in these situations our integrity is jeopardized in the
transgressive act. The conclusion of this book explains the value of vulnerability
from a Confucian perspective.

Vulnerability, Integrity, and Early Confucian Thought

The major terms in the title of this book are "vulnerability," "integrity," and "early
Confucian thought." Chapter 7 explores integrity in more detail, and the conclusion elaborates on a particularly Confucian theory of vulnerability. Nevertheless,
it will be helpful to provide a description of these terms at the outset so that readers will properly understand them, as they appear before chapter 7.

Vulnerability

Etymologically speaking, "vulnerability" comes from the Latin word *vulnerare*,
which means "to wound" or "to hurt," and is often associated with susceptibility to harm. While this way of understanding vulnerability captures significant

aspects of the concept, it also tends to leave insufficient room for understanding the value of vulnerability in human experience. I aim to build on the work of contemporary scholars in the field of vulnerability studies that highlights the value of maintaining vulnerability in various facets of life.

Vulnerability has become a significant concept of analysis in fields of study or disciplines such as ethics, theology, public health (and policy), risk management, and social work. Within ethics, the discourse of vulnerability largely emerged from the work of scholars such as Judith Butler, Robert Goodin, Martha Fineman, Alasdair MacIntyre, and Martha Nussbaum. In recent years, scholars of ethics and religion have focused more explicitly on vulnerability. In 2010, for instance, Jonathan Schofer published *Confronting Vulnerability: The Body and the Divine in Rabbinic Ethics,* and Kristine Culp published *Vulnerability and Glory: A Theological Account.*[10] From 2013 through 2014 four edited volumes emerged on the topic of vulnerability; one volume included two articles on Confucian views of vulnerability.[11] And in 2014, Erinn Gilson published *The Ethics of Vulnerability: A Feminist Analysis of Social Life and Practice,* which is the most in-depth account of vulnerability from a philosophical perspective to date. Much of this work seeks to rehabilitate the notion of vulnerability—showing how vulnerability serves as a source for the obligations we have to at-risk groups or advocating a more universal notion of vulnerability where vulnerability enables aspects of human flourishing. These are attempts to rehabilitate vulnerability in the sense of recognizing the necessity or benefits of vulnerability in human experience, instead of treating vulnerability as something largely negative. Gilson's account of vulnerability is particularly relevant since it provides an interpretation of vulnerability that is thoroughly tuned in to contemporary conversations on the topic; it also shares many affinities with the Confucian account of vulnerability I provide in the conclusion of this book.

Gilson describes vulnerability in terms of potential. Vulnerability, on her account, is not pain, joy, or other feelings or experiences that result from being vulnerable. Rather, vulnerability is an experience distinct from the conditions that it brings about.[12] Gilson explains that vulnerability "is an ambivalent condition of potential in the sense that it may produce results of uncertain value—harm or sustenance, affection or aggression, change or re-entrenchment."[13] According to Gilson, vulnerability is a state of being that could have positive or negative results, and the results themselves are not the feelings of vulnerability. Gilson explains, "[V]ulnerability is defined by openness and affectivity, and such openness entails the inability to predict, control, and fully know that to which we are open and how it will affect us."[14] In short, vulnerability is the experience of openness.

Gilson also explains vulnerability in terms of receptivity to change. Gilson says, "In its more fundamental sense vulnerability may be understood as an

openness to being altered and more specifically, being altered in ways that desta-
bilize a previously stable, or seemingly stable, state."[15] Vulnerability is an openness
to being changed by someone or something other than oneself. It entails a dis-
placement of agency or a partial loss of self-determination. While Gilson notes
the passive nature of vulnerability, she stresses that vulnerability is not simply susceptibility to change. She states, "Passivity, therefore, is not a mode of weakness
or even just susceptibility to the impressions coming from the world and others.
Rather, it is an opening and a capacity for taking in, intertwining with, and connecting with other bodies."[16] Vulnerability is thus understood as a capacity to
engage and experience rather than as a submission to external forces. Borrowing
from Hélène Cixous, Gilson explains that vulnerability is a kind of "force in . . .
fragility."[17] In this light, Gilson concludes that vulnerability is "that openness that
allows us to move forward, to change, to experience something new, to pass from
what we take ourselves to be to what we are becoming, and so perhaps learn."[18]

   Part of what Gilson is doing is critiquing views that understand vulnerability
solely in its etymological sense of susceptibility to harm. Even though many of
those who employ such a definition aim to highlight the positive aspects of vulnerability, such a construal is limited in its capacity to rehabilitate the concept.
Gilson notes several problems with such a definition. For one, it tends to con-
flate harm with vulnerability itself, or, at the very least, it highlights one aspect of
vulnerability to the detriment of others. In talking about the experience of love,
for instance, Gilson explains that "what renders one uniquely vulnerable in the
experience of love is not the possibility of loss but the exceptional openness that
characterizes the relationship and, indeed, the expectation that one will change
in unforeseen ways in relation to the loved one. In relationships between intimates, the unpredictability and uncontrollability of other beings has a heightened effect on the self; one is more vulnerable because one is more open to this
other. Vulnerability, thus, may include being affected by loss, but this particular
kind of event is not the constitutive dimension of vulnerability."[19] Thus vulnerability is not simply about the threat of harm but is also about the sheer fact of
the unknown. When we love another we open ourselves up to being changed,
and while this includes the prospect of being harmed, such a prospect does not
fully explain the openness entailed in love. In more general terms, vulnerability
understood as susceptibility to harm promotes an incomplete assessment of our
fears with regard to vulnerability—what we fear is not only the prospect of harm
"but the ambiguity and uncertainty that define vulnerability."[20] In other words,
the trepidation associated with vulnerability is not just a fear of being harmed but
is a broader apprehensiveness of the unknown.

   Gilson also notes that understanding vulnerability simply as susceptibility to harm tends to obscure the universal nature of vulnerability. Rather than

recognizing our own vulnerability, we see "vulnerable groups" that are distinct from, or "other than," the groups we belong to. Or, if we see ourselves as vulnerable, we tend to treat our condition as a temporary state we seek to rectify. Gilson explains, "Vulnerability, [understood this way], is the condition of the very young and very old, and those who are physically or mentally disabled, and constitutes a distinct departure from our normal mode of functioning. Thus, it is consigned to the borders of human experience rather than the center, considered a marginal condition rather than a central one that must be taken into account for adequate theorizing."[21] When vulnerability is associated solely with susceptibility to harm, we tend to associate the vulnerable with the marginalized, the neglected, or the weak—groups that need to be protected by stronger groups. These other groups are set apart or distanced from other supposedly stronger groups. In this light, our obligations to others stem from our power over others, instead of a relationship of shared vulnerability.

When vulnerability is seen as belonging to the margins of life, we limit the ways in which we might learn from others. Gilson states, "Yet, if we continue to regard old age, disability, illness, and injury solely as conditions of weakness and limitation, conditions we are lucky to avoid, then we persist in perceiving them simply as negative states and fail to imagine how we might find different perspectives, experiences, and modes of strength and capacity in these conditions."[22] In Gilson's view we cannot treat vulnerability as a condition akin to being sick—something we do not want to be. When vulnerability is conceptualized in terms of misfortune or even reluctance, we limit our opportunities for self-development, and in a worse-case scenario we reinforce the conditions of marginalization by reaffirming the distinct categories of the vulnerable and the invulnerable.

This is not to deny that some groups are more vulnerable than others or to assert that susceptibility to harm is an insignificant aspect of vulnerability. Indeed, in many regards this book focuses on the ways in which integrity is susceptible to irresolvable value conflicts, and so, in many senses, I foreground vulnerability as the potential for harm. Rather Gilson's point is that vulnerability is more pervasive and empowering than we tend to recognize.

We come into the world as vulnerable beings, and as we grow we gain an awareness of our vulnerability. We naturally feel anxious about the unknown, and so we spend significant portions of our lives managing our vulnerability.[23] This process of management entails determining when and how we remain open to others and, more fundamentally, if we can in fact control our degree of openness. The anxieties associated with vulnerability tempt us to strive for minimizing our openness, and, as such, invulnerability is often seen as an optimal state. In many cases, total invulnerability is not possible, but that does not mean that human beings will not work to transform vulnerability, gloss over it, or deny it.

Vulnerability as an intrinsic condition is pliable inasmuch as human beings are capable of eliminating that which harms meaningful things, strengthening that which is vulnerable, or assigning meaning only to those things that can be protected with certainty.[24] In the right circumstances these strategies enable human flourishing. In the wrong circumstances they ignore a condition basic to human existence.

Vulnerability is also relational—it is experienced in relationships—and since relationships are construed, experienced, and enacted in different ways, the experience of vulnerability is not uniform. Gilson notes that vulnerability is universal in certain senses yet unique in others. She states, "If vulnerability is this univocal form of potential—a fundamental openness that is said of all in the same way—it is quite clear that it is not actualized for all equally or in the same way; we do not all live our vulnerability in the same ways. It is only as an ontological condition that vulnerability is univocal."[25] Vulnerability is unique in that human beings are uniquely situated and shaped by distinctive relationships. Vulnerability, therefore, is multifaceted and resists simplistic classifications, yet at the same time the experiences of vulnerability can be rendered sufficiently relatable across time and space. As such, while being human entails being vulnerable, there are still radically different ways of being vulnerable and many vulnerabilities that should be shored up, if not eliminated. Furthermore, it is worth noting that human beings are never vulnerable *simpliciter* but rather are vulnerable in certain respects while invulnerable in other respects, and this changes over time.

Vulnerability entails a three-part relationship—a person, an object (tangible or intangible) deemed valuable by the person, and an entity that challenges the person's ability to control the object. Throughout human history, people have found various things meaningful. In an early Confucian context, these meaningful things included one's health and life, one's social standing, one's reputation passed down to future generations, one's relationships with other people, the lives and health of other people, one's cultivation of virtue, and many other things. Confucians, for instance, believed that attaining a position in society that could bring about broad social change depended on encountering the right political circumstances. Kongzi was never able to fully implement his teachings because he never found a ruler who was willing to give him an appropriate position. His social standing (*wei* 位), as such, was vulnerable to powers beyond his control. In describing a Confucian perspective on vulnerability, concepts such as *ren* 仁, *ai* 愛, *xin* 信, and *li* 禮 are significant. I explore this broader perspective of vulnerability in the conclusion of this book. Most of the book, however, focuses on one specific aspect of vulnerability—it investigates how early Confucians saw their integrity as susceptible or insusceptible to forces outside their control.

Vulnerability is an undertheorized concept in Confucian studies. While many scholars indirectly address issues related to vulnerability, there is relatively little scholarship that approaches Confucianism from a perspective of vulnerability.[26] This lacuna in scholarship highlights an opportunity for the language of vulnerability to play an important role in understanding Confucian thought. This book foregrounds a perspective of vulnerability. It raises questions such as: What vulnerabilities are inherent to the human condition? Is the process of self-cultivation vulnerable to agents other than the self? In what ways does the sage or moral agent render himself invulnerable to other things in the world? How is vulnerability a valuable part of the human experience?

I address aspects of these questions by examining a concept that is not usually understood in terms of vulnerability. This allows me to explore a variety of intellectual positions within early Confucianism and among contemporary interpreters while aiming for a rereading of Confucianism that challenges dominant paradigms. The concept I am interested in is integrity, which I understand as confidence in maintaining commitments that affirm one's moral standing. Adpating this for an early Confucian context, integrity also refers to one's ability to foster desire in others to fulfill obligations that arise from relationships.

Integrity

"Integrity" is often understood in terms of purity, coherence, and/or soundness. Someone who stays uncorrupted or firmly holds to his or her commitments in difficult circumstances is said to be someone of integrity. Integrity is a relational term such that it expresses a personal confidence one has in relation to one's commitments as well as a relationship between the individual and the communities that evaluate the individual's moral standing. Integrity, as such, is about integration. It is about bringing the self into a state of wholeness, where wholeness occurs on the personal level and the communal level. In a Confucian context, the communal level is particularly important since the self is often conceptualized socially. Roger Ames, in speaking about the importance of relationships in Confucianism, explains, "To begin with, we are not separate 'I' entities that then come into 'we' relationships. As relationally constituted persons, 'we' is the starting point, and we grow our lives significantly only through the extension and amplification of those relations that we already share as mother and wife and neighbor."[27] In this view, a concept such as integrity is understood first as a social relation and second as a personal one. The work of integration is about tending to the network of relationships that one finds oneself in, as well as plugging into new networks that foster further self-cultivation.

In Chinese, integrity is represented by terms such as *de* 德, *xing* 行, *yi* 義, *jie* 節, *qing* 清, and *lian* 廉. *De* 德 is particularly important for understanding integrity. In English the term *de* 德 is translated as "virtue," "integrity," "generosity," or sometimes "power." In many cases *de* 德 is a moral power accumulated by individuals who demonstrate their commitment to specific people they form relationships with or specific virtues embedded in relationships. The *Xiaojing* 《孝經》, for instance, explains that filial care—the virtue associated with the younger generation caring for the older generation—is the root of *de* 德 (*fuxiao dezhibenye* 夫孝，德之本也).[28] Contemporary scholar Robert H. Gassmann provides a significant interpretation of *de* 德, suggesting that *de* 德 refers to a "power to obligate."[29] In other words, Gassmann argues that *de* 德 is a compelling force of attraction generated when someone does something for someone else. Confucians often understand this in a moral context. Gassmann explains, "*[De* 德] is the establishment of a dependency between two parties, the obligee and the obligor."[30] Simply put, *de* 德 entails the obligor fostering a desire in the obligee to fulfill obligations that arise from the relationship. In this light, Gassmann explains *de* 德 by using the language of "a socially accepted debt," and David Nivison calls it a "gratitude credit."[31] What this means is that *de* 德 is something accumulated as we perform our roles in relationships. The more *de* 德 we accumulate, the greater confidence we have in our moral standing in our communities. While *de* 德 does not simply equate with integrity as I have defined it here, it works to highlight notions of confidence, commitment, and moral standing.

Integrity, in this light, is related to connections or relationships between people, and these relationships serve as nodes where one's accumulated *de* 德 fosters meaningful interaction that leads to human flourishing. Coincidentally, the term *jie* 節, which is often translated as "purity," "chastity," or "integrity," literally refers to nodes or divisions of a bamboo plant. Similar to the way in which sections of a bamboo plant are divided and connected by *jie* 節, people are likewise divided and connected by their relationships. Staying within the proper boundaries (*jie* 節) of each relationship maintains one's purity. As this book unfolds we will see that the vulnerability of integrity is very much about the penetration of these boundaries.

It is worth noting that "integrity," as I use it in this book, functions more as an organizing framework to bring these terms into contemporary discussions of Confucian thought rather than a term with one-to-one correspondence in Chinese. As such, "integrity" plays an interpretive role. It works to not only accurately describe the texts but also to render them intelligible within contemporary discourses of Confucian thought. I am writing *about* early Confucianism but *for* an audience of contemporary interpreters. My hope is to demonstrate a kind of dialogical relationship between the text and the interpreter where the text shapes the questions we ask as much as the questions we ask shape our readings of the texts. In other words, I do not believe that the term "integrity" as I have described it here is necessarily found as a readily translatable term in early Confucian texts. I do, however, believe that the authors or editors of these texts could think of their ideas in the conceptual framework of integrity. As such, integrity serves to frame native terms in a way that should not misconstrue them and yet rearticulates them in such a way that I produce new understandings of early Confucianism that engage contemporary debates. I say more about this process later in this introduction.

Early Confucian Thought

As far as "early Confucian" is concerned, the term "early" is admittedly vague. Most Sinologists use terms like "Pre-Qin" (*xianqin* 先秦) and "Han" (*han* 漢/ *lianghan* 兩漢) to talk about the period I am calling "early." This would roughly correspond to the fifth century BCE through the third century CE. My interests, however, are primarily in interpreting texts and only secondarily in reconstructing the thought of actual persons and their contexts. In other words, rather than trying to describe a particular time period, I aim to describe texts constructed and embedded in particular time periods. History, as such, informs my interpretation, but the goal of this book is not necessarily to produce descriptions of past events. Additionally, issues of textual composition in this period are quite complicated. Many of the texts from the Pre-Qin era were significantly redacted through the Han, and many texts that purport to include material from before the Qin dynasty, which were long thought to be Han creations, have now proven to include Pre-Qin material. As such, the vagueness of "early" in "early Confucian" appropriately reflects the ambiguities associated with textual composition.

While my decision to focus on texts through the Han is partially pragmatic (i.e., one can only closely read so many texts), I am primarily interested in narratives concerned with reproducing the words or actions of paradigmatic figures such as Kongzi in situations where values are harmed or left unfulfilled. In other words, I am interested in narratives of conflict or difficulty involving figures later Confucians took as exemplary. These narratives may or may not be fictitious. My interests, however, are literary and philosophical, which means that I focus on how and why these stories are employed and brought into dialogue with other texts.

Narrative texts are particularly good at dramatizing conflict. Amy Olberding, in an article titled "Confucius' Complaints and the *Analects*' Account of the Good Life," demonstrates what happens when we give priority to the narrative portions of the *Analects* over its explicitly doctrinal statements.[32] Olberding's approach highlights the fact that the passages we choose to start an interpretation shape our larger readings of the text and tradition. With regard to the vulnerability of integrity, this means that while there clearly was a tradition within early Confucianism that argued for the invulnerability of integrity, taking this tradition as representative of early Confucian thought tends to downplay or even neglect other early Confucian traditions. Part of what I strive to accomplish is to explore what happens when we begin our interpretation with another set of passages or at least allow alternative passages a larger voice in the conversation. Indeed, texts that make generous use of narratives such as the commentaries on the *Chunqiu* tend to portray a different set of human experiences than texts such as the *Xunzi*, which utilizes more doctrinal essays.

Heiner Roetz, in his work on early Confucian thought, notes a relevant tension in the *Xunzi*. When talking about the way in which Xunzi advocates "bending and straightening" according to the circumstance, Roetz explains that Xunzi's design is to achieve an "uncorrupted flexibility."[33] Roetz then questions the degree to which those depicted in the *Xunzi* actually achieve such flexibility. He states,

> Too many things which we heard about its protagonists [i.e., the main characters in the *Xunzi*]—their toying with the idea of leaving society, their conquering their self, their nearly coquettish sentiment of being misjudged, their groaning under the burden of duty—reveal Xunzi's elegant art of bending and straightening as a hardly achievable ideal. In an immoral world, a moral actor may even have to confront much greater obstacles than those discussed among the ancient Confucians. Nevertheless, they suffer enough from the discrepancy between their goals and the compulsions of reality. The deepest of the aporias they have to cope with is perhaps that "humaneness" (*ren* 仁) transcends the very limits which in the given world of inequality and group interest are strictly drawn everywhere.[34]

For Roetz, there is a sharp tension between Xunzi's teachings and the figures depicted in the text. While I personally do not see as strong a tension in the *Xunzi* as Roetz, Roetz does highlight the strain between the theoretical or doctrinal aspects of Confucianism on the one hand and its narrative or lived dimensions on the other. In this light, texts such as the *Kongzi Jiayu* can even be seen as an alternative voice criticizing the idealistic voices. In short, these texts are sometimes voices of internal dissent. When we listen to them, we discover significant differences in the Confucian tradition, and when we reread the canonical texts with these voices in mind, we discover surprising similarities as well.

I use "Confucian" largely as a functional rather than a substantive term. In other words, I am not so much arguing for the existence of any particular tradition or school as much as I am using the term for the purpose of participating in contemporary discussions about texts and ideas. At the same time, there certainly were traditions that looked to Kongzi as someone who understood how best to order the world (and Kongzi himself claimed to pass this on from earlier figures). This tradition came to be known as the *ru* 儒 in East Asian discourse and as "Confucian" in the English discourse.[35] While both terms are anachronistic in different ways, there is no need to discard them for the purposes of this book. As such, "Confucian" is shorthand for those authors and editors who saw themselves as faithful interpreters of Kongzi's program of self-cultivation, which included the development of social roles as well as virtues including humaneness (*ren* 仁), ritual propriety (*li* 禮), and family care (*xiao* 孝). Confucians are a self-conscious group of individuals who share the commitment of bettering themselves, their societies, and the extra-human world by means of Kongzi's teachings.[36]

Practically speaking, this book examines passages from texts including the *Analects*, the *Mengzi*, the *Kongzi Jiayu*, the *Han Shi Waizhuan*, and others. Where relevant I also reference non-Confucian or quasi-Confucian texts such as the *Zhuangzi* 《莊子》, the *Hanfeizi* 《韓非子》, or the *Lüshi Chunqiu* 《呂氏春秋》.

Assumptions and Approach

Since I consider such a large number of texts, my reading is necessarily selective. This means that my organization of the material creates a kind of systematic response to questions of vulnerability that may not reflect one specific voice or text within the tradition. Nonetheless, I do believe the voices I choose from these texts would subscribe to my reading. In short, there are constructive and reconstructive dimensions to this book. It is constructive in the sense that I situate passages alongside texts that they originally may not have been in dialogue with. In this regard I am emending the early Confucian tradition by coordinating passages that share ideological features but may not share a strict historical connection.[37] I do this in part because exploring issues of vulnerability in early Confucian thought necessitates reorganizing textual material in accordance with a nonnative concept or theme. Indeed, vulnerability is not a native Confucian concept, and therefore there are no focused expositions on the topic in the early literature. However, I believe this approach is justified in part by the heterogeneous nature of the texts.

Most early Confucian texts were composed by many hands over many years, and attempts to create a systematic answer to a question—particularly a question the texts do not explicitly aim to address—leads to highlighting certain passages over others. My work emphasizes a number of neglected passages against the backdrop of contemporary scholars who stress other passages. Said differently, by framing the issue in terms of vulnerability, I necessarily highlight certain aspects of early Confucianism while downplaying other aspects. In some sense, this is inevitable in any interpretation, and so I strive to demonstrate an awareness of the obscurities and shortcomings entailed in my analysis. For instance, I realize that creating a coherent argument about vulnerability and integrity often entails presuming a strong sense of continuity between material separated by time and authorship. This means that I am likely imposing more coherence between the texts than may have existed in their original settings; however, I modify my reading where the evidence of textual composition dictates otherwise. Indeed, Confucianism is a diverse tradition with internal disagreements and interpretational complexities. By paying attention to broadly shared themes across texts, I risk glossing over disagreements between passages, yet this is a risk necessary for a book with constructive dimensions such as this one.

At the same time, this book is reconstructive in the sense that it provides accurate interpretations of passages within their contexts. In other words, each reading I provide for any passage is defended by Sinological standards of interpreting early Chinese texts. As such, at the micro level I provide valid readings of individual passages, while at the macro level I construct an "early Confucian view" of vulnerability informed by contemporary discourses. This is not to say that the questions I bring to the texts are necessarily foreign to them. Rather, these questions about vulnerability and integrity are shaped by my prolonged study of early Confucian texts and the history of Chinese culture. Because of this, I believe that the authors or redactors of early Confucian texts are invested in these issues even if they may not have articulated them as explicitly as I do. This means that engaging these questions entails going beyond a reading that strives to recover original meanings and instead emphasizes the act of interpretation.

My work of interpretation places these early Confucian texts in somewhat unfamiliar discourses (discourses shaped by contemporary concerns, assumptions, and terminology, ones we might call religious ethics or Chinese philosophy). Yet these discourses are only "somewhat unfamiliar" because I believe that the authors and editors of these texts understood their projects in terms that are conceptually relevant to these discourses. They did not author a single treatise on a topic such as vulnerability and may not even have a single term that translates to "vulnerability"; however, they were certainly interested in similar concepts such that their terms, narratives, and texts provide sufficient resources to form a voice in these discourses. As such, vulnerability functions along the lines of what Aaron Stalnaker calls a "bridge concept," a fluid expression that allows diverse groups of people to define a term in culturally specific ways for the sake of comparison. Bridge concepts are designed with elasticity such that a term like "vulnerability" can be understood many different ways, and at the same time the term remains a recognizable concept from the perspectives of those internal to the group.[38]

In this light, interpretation is built on the hope that human beings can speak to each other in ways that we come to (perhaps not fully, but largely) understand each other's perspectives, feelings, and motivations. This is of course easier for those living in the same time, speaking the same language, and meeting face to face, but if carefully done this might extend to people living in other areas, speaking other languages, and even living in different times.

This act of interpretation extends diachronically in terms of including those within a tradition carrying on a shared conversation but also spatially in terms of sharing a conversation with those culturally removed from the tradition. If done properly, it creates a grey area between the native and the foreign where the bridge concept cannot be untangled from either category. Yet, at the same time, this approach strives to recognize and maintain real differences—differences found within the tradition and differences between the goals of the texts and goals of contemporary interpreters. The result, I hope, demonstrates that, conceptually speaking, the discourses of religious ethics and early Confucianism are capable of conversation, even if I exercise a directing role in facilitating such a conversation.

In the end, my aim is to present a strong reading of early Confucian texts, where "strong" means adhering to Sinological standards of interpreting Chinese material, as well as representing the texts in ways that are compelling to those living at this time and able to read this book.[39]

Chapter Summaries

Chapter 1 looks at arguments for the invulnerability of integrity as articulated by early Confucians and later Confucian interpreters. It begins by sketching out a tension found throughout the early literature: namely, a conflict between desiring to transform society and desiring to maintain one's integrity. This conflict occurs in situations where transforming society entails colluding with immoral leaders in government or otherwise violating standards of ethical action. The texts and interpreters argue that only highly cultivated moral agents, or sages, are able to effectively navigate these situations such that they maintain their integrity but also act on their desire to transform society. Sages "balance" these difficult situations by means of moral deliberation, or *quan* 權. This chapter details two theories of moral deliberation made by Confucian interpreters in order to show how arguments for the invulnerability of integrity developed within the tradition.

Chapter 2 examines arguments for invulnerability made by contemporary interpreters working with Confucian material. It begins by situating discourses of invulnerability within the broader field of philosophical ethics. In these discussions, the vulnerability or invulnerability of integrity often falls under the rubric of value conflicts, moral remainder (or residue or distress), and dirty hands. This chapter begins with an overview of this discourse, which serves as a backdrop for discussing how contemporary scholars of Confucian ethics discuss the invulnerability of integrity. The majority of chapter 2 explores the scholarship of these contemporary interpreters, and highlights an approach to invulnerability called the "harmony thesis." I demonstrate the ways in which the harmony thesis dovetails with the arguments for invulnerability described in chapter 1, and then I suggest one fruitful way of continuing to develop the harmony thesis in contemporary philosophical terms that are at the same time supported by early Confucian texts. Finally, at the end of this chapter I explore three shortcomings of the harmony thesis.

Chapters 3 and 4 describe the role of regret in early Confucian moral thought. In light of the previous two chapters, I demonstrate that moral distress in early Confucian texts is best understood in terms of regret. I begin chapter 3 by characterizing regret with regard to sorrow, resentment, and a longing for things to be otherwise, and then I demonstrate the ways in which the moral agent sorrows over his inability to tend to values in difficult situations. More specifically, I examine portrayals of Kongzi as he strives (and fails) to bring about the Confucian *dao* 道. After discussing the Confucian Way in light of contemporary scholars' notions of "external goods," I explore an event purported to have taken place toward the end of Kongzi's life—the discovery of a mythical animal called a *lin* 麟, which represents Kongzi's unique potential to transform the world. I examine Kongzi's connection to this animal as well as his reaction to its discovery and death.

Chapter 4 builds on the previous chapter by further exploring regret as it relates to resentment and transgression. Specifically, in this chapter I challenge the dominant understanding of resentment in Confucian thought. I argue that, from an early Confucian perspective, resentment is a sign that we require the care of significant others and that we are vulnerable to their concern or neglect. I then connect resentment with frustrated desire and the production of literature designed to channel this desire to future others who might realize the Confucian *dao* 道. I show that this act of releasing pent up desire is often associated with the transgression of social norms, as in the case of Kongzi composing the *Chunqiu* 《春秋》. In short, I demonstrate that early Confucians saw these kinds of transgressions as valid responses to value conflicts.

Chapter 5, "Irresolvable Value Conflicts in a Conflictual World," reveals that early Confucians saw irresolvable value conflicts as real possibilities. It starts with an overview of the ways in which contemporary scholars have described Confucianism in terms of harmony and the lack of tragedy. It then challenges these narratives by looking at several vignettes that depict moral agents confronting irresolvable value conflicts. In this chapter I also analyze the notion of tragedy in an early Confucian worldview to show that early Confucians did not see values as *necessarily* conflicting with each other, although they accepted the *possibility* of tragic conflict.

Chapter 6 explores irresolvable value conflicts with regard to sages. It begins with portrayals of early sages such as Yao and Shun as compromised figures in a broad array of early Chinese texts. This serves as a context for understanding how early Confucians stressed the virtuous nature of sages on the one hand and accepted portions of the broader discourse of compromise on the other. To illustrate this I look more closely at the case of Wu Wang 武王 and show that early Confucian texts were ambivalent about his violent overthrow of the Shang dynasty. This chapter also looks at Kongzi and builds off the notion of transgression discussed in chapter 4 to show that he was also understood as a conflicted figure.

Chapter 7 examines the vulnerability of integrity more closely. It begins with a description of the Confucian self, understood as interconnected and communal, and then discusses the porous nature of this self with regard to the connections and boundaries that are seen to exist between the individual and others. The majority of this chapter focuses on integrity, which I explain in terms of *de* 德. The notion of *de* 德 highlights the charismatic aspects of integrity such that integrity in an early Confucian context is understood as a power to motivate others to perform their roles in relationships. This power is obstructed or weakened in situations of irresolvable value conflict. *De* 德 is a social value associated with the way in which moral actions enable the realization of the self, which is partially constituted by relationships. Integrity, as such, is vulnerable to irresolvable value conflicts and unfortunate situations because in those circumstances moral action is impeded such that meaningful relations cannot be maintained.

Finally, in the conclusion I discuss the value of vulnerability. Expanding on the description of vulnerability provided in the introduction, I articulate a Confucian account of vulnerability that adds to the conversation in three ways:

1. It foregrounds the notion of vulnerability as an essential characteristic of human beings.
2. It stresses that vulnerability is good in instrumental and intrinsic ways—instrumentally it enables values such as morality, trust, and maturity. Intrinsically, vulnerability is a kind of caring *about* things. To be vulnerable is to be in a state of care—a condition of caring about people or things.
3. It provides a robust notion of self-cultivation designed to foster an optimal degree of vulnerability by means of ritual practice.

The majority of the conclusion explores the instrumental and intrinsic values of vulnerability.

Implications for the Study of Confucian Thought

I hope that this book will create space for further discussion about Confucian thought. More specifically, I aim to expand the canon of contemporary scholarship beyond the *Analects*, the *Mengzi*, and the *Xunzi* by encouraging interest in other early Confucian texts. Despite the problems with dating some of these texts, they still present material that should be philosophically interesting to contemporary scholars. Taken together, this broader collection of early Confucian texts demonstrate that there is no one Confucian approach to value conflicts. Stated more generally, including more voices in conversations about early Confucianism will add to the richness of early Confucian thought and even encourage contemporary scholars to rethink what constitutes "Confucianism."

While the voices in the noncanonical texts are themselves diverse, they contribute to what might be called "Lived Confucianism" (*rensheng rujia* 人生儒家). As opposed to a Confucianism that emphasizes learning from sages (or sagely learning, *shengxue* 聖學), Lived Confucianism stresses the applied features of being moral in real situations.[40] Lived Confucianism is "lived" in the sense of being rooted in experiences that are firmly within human possibility. Rather than framing paradigmatic human experience with the lives and teachings of near-perfect sages, Lived Confucianism seeks to frame paradigmatic human experience with those human beings still learning what it means to be paradigmatically human (i.e., those human beings in the midst of learning to be human, *xuezuoren* 學做人). These figures are not necessarily models of perfect virtue, but they remain in the mix of things—struggling to confront the complexities of life.[41] They possess moral fortitude such that they persist in the discovery of meaning even when discovery entails grief or pain. In other words, a person worthy of admiration is one who recognizes value in the world, realizes that he or she may not be able to fulfill all values, may even need to harm some value, and yet acts under the weight of the situation. Such a person is marked by his or her engagement with others and their attendant values, wherein he or she finds meaning.

In his translation of the first ten chapters of the *Kongzi Jiayu* R. P. Kramers explains that the *Jiayu* reveals "a somewhat different Kongzi: a Kongzi to whom perhaps less wonderful qualities are attributed than usually accorded to him by Chinese tradition, but also a Kongzi who precisely because of this appeals more to us by his human touch."[42] Coincidentally, Li Ling 李零, a professor of Chinese literature at Peking University, borrows an image from the *Jiayu* for the title of his book on the *Analects*—*Sangjiagou: Wo Du Lunyu* 《丧家狗：我读论语》 (*A Homeless Dog: My Reading of the* Analects).[43] Li uses the description of Kongzi as a homeless dog for a point of departure in reading the *Analects*. What emerges is indeed a different Kongzi—one who has sparked controversy and led

to Li Ling's latest book, *Qu Sheng Naide Zhen Kongzi: Lunyu Zonghengdu*
《去圣乃得真孔子：论语纵横读》(*Get Rid of the Sage and Then [You'll]
Find the Real Kongzi: A Horizontal and Vertical Reading of the* Analects).[44]
While there are parts of Li Ling's work that I do not agree with, I sympathize
with his attempt to add more of a human touch to Kongzi and to create a kind
of Lived Confucianism.

In 2009 Carine Defoort dedicated an entire issue of *Contemporary Chinese
Thought* to the work of Li Ling. In the introduction Defoort states,

> The Kongzi described by Li Ling is authoritative in his impossible con-
> victions, charismatic in his frustrations, and inexplicably happy in his sor-
> rows. These paradoxes seem to express a homelessness in which we are all
> at home, a somewhat awkward but familiar feeling. Perhaps this tension
> is well caught in the German idea of *das unheimliche* (the un-homely),
> which is commonly rendered in English as "the uncanny." This translation,
> however, only expresses its dominant sense of disquieting strangeness and
> mild fear. Another and less obvious meaning of the German term is almost
> the opposite, namely the "un-secretive" and hence the very familiar.[45]

In this view, Kongzi is a misfit—his aspirations for transforming the world are
incongruous with his experience in the world, and in this he represents a common human experience. As such, by telling about Kongzi's mismatch between his
hopes and his experiences, it opens the possibility for us, his readers, to explore
the (sometimes tragic) gap between our hopes and our experiences.

Kramers and Li Ling are not alone in their attempts to portray a more
human Kongzi. Scholars such as Amy Olberding read the *Analects* in this light.
Olberding explains, "As a first gesture toward treating Kongzi's deviant aspects
as infelicities in performance, we can grant the importance of recognizing his
humanity. He too can get things wrong, and this fact about him preserves rather
than undermines our incentives to emulate him. Eliding his imperfections does
not, under my interpretation, merely create an interpretive strain. It also threatens to render him less potent as a model for emulation, for it is through his fallible humanity that a necessary kinship with him is achieved."[46] Olberding also
describes Kongzi's fallible humanity as a "hook" that binds his readers to his
story.[47] Following Olberding, part of what motivates people to be like Kongzi is
his fallibility. Olberding continues, "Indeed, the Kongzi of the *Analects* appears in
some measure to defy the later tradition's 'Kongzi,' a cleaned up sage scrubbed of
those features that do not conform to pristine moral heroism. While the *Analects*
unambiguously does heroicize Kongzi, it does so while leaving him something of
his humanity. In it, he is not yet an *idea* or *ideal*, but still a man."[48] Building on

this, we might say that Kongzi is admirable not because he is a model of perfect virtue but because he aspires to virtue and models deep and genuine connection with other people. His life is admirable in the sense of encouraging us to imitate his devotion despite his frustration. What this view of Kongzi reveals is that the life devoted to relationships and virtues is not so much an investigated life as much as it is a life invested in remaining sensitive to the needs of others even when these relationships and virtues often lay beyond our power to control. It is partially Kongzi's recognition of the contextualized significance of people and things—in other words an appropriate degree of vulnerability to that which is meaningful—that makes him admirable.

Notes

1. Fu Xiren 傅錫壬, ed. *Xinyi Chuci Duben* 《新譯楚辭讀本》 (Taibei 臺北: Sanmin Shuju 三民書局, 2011), 295.
2. For more background on the Yantielun see pages 1–28 in Lu Liehong 盧烈紅, ed. *Xinyi Yantielun* 《新譯鹽鐵論》 (Taibei 臺北: Sanmin Shuju 三民書局, 1995); and Esson M. Gale, trans., *Discourses on Salt and Iron: A Debate on State Control of Commerce and Industry in Ancient China* (Taipei: Ch'eng-wen Publishing Company, 1967), xv–xli.
3. *Yantielun* 2.5/16/3–4.
4. *Yantielun* 2.5/16/6–9.
5. *Xinxu* 7.23/41/16–17. See also *Han Shi Waizhuan* 1.26/6/5–6. *Xunzi* 3/8/20–3/9/1 also criticizes Shentu Di, explaining that his act is not esteemed because it "does not accord with ritual propriety and rightness" 非禮義之中也. A similar phrase appears in *Han Shi Waizhuan* 3.33/24/12–13.
6. *Yantielun* 10.4/75/28.
7. See, for instance, *Huainanzi* 20/218/1–8; *Kongcongzi* 5.2/52/20–30; *Xunzi* 8/32/7–14; *Shuoyuan* 5.1/31/19–5.2/32/5; *Lüshi Chunqiu* 19.8/127/23–25; and Ma Teying 馬特盈, ed., *Shiji Jinzhu* 《史記今註》 (Taibei 台北: Taiwan Shangwu yinshuguan 臺灣商務印書館, 1987), 2508. *Zhuangzi* 19/51/27–52/2 is particularly interesting because it depicts Kongzi and his disciples trying to save someone from drowning, only to have them discover that the man is not actually drowning. Passages such as these are critiques of Confucian impulses to save the world when, in fact, from the perspective of texts such as the *Zhuangzi*, they misunderstand the nature of the world. Later texts such as the *Lunheng* (1/1/3–8) depict the sages as muddied or filthy. The *Hou Hanshu* 《後漢書》 describes the exemplary person (*junzi* 君子) as one who "takes action such that his feet get wet and he endures disgrace" 故其行也，則濡足蒙垢. Fan Ye 范曄, ed., *Hou Hanshu* 《後漢書》 (Beijing 北京: Zhonghua Shuju 中華書局, 1965–1973), 1739.

8. On the dating of the *Analects* see Mark Csikszentmihalyi and Tae Hun Kim, "History and Formation of the *Analects*," in *Dao Companion to the* Analects, edited by Amy Olberding (New York: Springer, 2014), 21–36; and Michael Hunter, "Sayings of Confucius, Deselected" (PhD diss., Princeton University, 2012).

9. Erinn Gilson explores this in *The Ethics of Vulnerability: A Feminist Analysis of Social Life and Practice* (New York: Routledge, 2014), 73–124.

10. Jonathan Wyn Schofer, *Confronting Vulnerability: The Body and the Divine in Rabbinic Ethics* (Chicago: University of Chicago Press, 2010). Kristine A. Culp, *Vulnerability and Glory: A Theological Account* (Louisville, KY: Westminster John Knox Press, 2010). See also Marina McCoy, *Wounded Heroes: Vulnerability as a Virtue in Ancient Greek Literature and Philosophy* (Oxford: Oxford University Press, 2013); and Elizabeth O'Donnell Gandolfo, *The Power and Vulnerability of Love* (Minneapolis: Fortress Press, 2015).

11. Amanda Russell Beattie and Kate Schick, eds., *The Vulnerable Subject: Beyond Rationalism in International Relations* (New York: Palgrave Macmillan: 2013); Martha Fineman and Anna Grear, eds., *Vulnerability: Reflections on a New Ethical Foundation for Law and Politics* (Burlington, VT: Ashgate, 2013); Catriona Mackenzie, Wendy Rogers, and Susan Dodds, eds., *Vulnerability: New Essays in Ethics and Feminist Philosophy* (New York: Oxford University Press, 2014); and Joseph Tham et al., eds., *Religious Perspectives on Human Vulnerability in Bioethics* (New York: Springer, 2014). The articles on Confucian views of vulnerability can be found in Tham et al., Jonathan Keung Lap Chan, "Health Care and Human Vulnerability: A Confucian Perspective," 153–164; and Ping Cheung Lo, "Family as First Bulwark for the Vulnerable: Confucian Perspectives on the Anthropology and Ethics of Human Vulnerability," 61–77. In 2008 Emory University, under the direction of Martha Fineman, also started the Vulnerability and the Human Condition Initiative.

12. On page 136 Gilson, *Ethics of Vulnerability,* states, "If we imagine, for instance, times at which we have felt particularly emotionally vulnerable—fragile even—we find that we cannot reduce that particular feeling to the pain or joy that may ultimately have come from it. Vulnerability itself is a distinctive experience."

13. Gilson, *Ethics of Vulnerability,* 138.

14. Gilson, *Ethics of Vulnerability,* 127.

15. Gilson, *Ethics of Vulnerability,* 64.

16. Gilson, *Ethics of Vulnerability,* 133.

17. Gilson, *Ethics of Vulnerability,* 144.

18. Gilson, *Ethics of Vulnerability,* 179.

19. Gilson, *Ethics of Vulnerability,* 65.

20. Gilson, *Ethics of Vulnerability,* 146.

21. Gilson, *Ethics of Vulnerability,* 16.

22. Gilson, *Ethics of Vulnerability,* 24.

23. On the relationship between anxiety and vulnerability see Gandolfo, *Power and Vulnerability*, 119–124.

24. Mackenzie et al., in *Vulnerability*, employ the language of vulnerability as intrinsic to the human condition on pages 7–8. See those same pages for a taxonomy of vulnerability.

25. Gilson, *Ethics of Vulnerability*, 137.

26. Besides the articles by Chan and Lo in Joseph Tham et al.'s *Religious Perspectives*, G. E. R. Lloyd also touches on it in *The Delusions of Invulnerability: Wisdom and Morality in Ancient Greece, China and Today* (London: Duckworth, 2005).

27. Roger T. Ames, *Confucian Role Ethics: A Vocabulary* (Honolulu: University of Hawai'i Press, 2011), 98. While I endorse Ames's view on this point, I do not go all the way with him in defining the self as one's roles: "That is, there is no 'self,' no 'soul,' no discrete 'individual' behind our complex and dynamic habits of conduct. Each of us is irreducibly social as the sum of the roles we *live*—not *play*—in or relationships and transactions with others." *Confucian Role Ethics*, 96.

28. Li, Xueqin 李學勤, ed., *Xiaojing Zhushu* 《孝經注疏》, *Shisanjing Zhushu* 《十三經注疏》 Vol. 26 (Beijing北京: Beijing daxue chubanshe 北京大學出版社, 2000), 3.

29. Robert H. Gassmann, "Coming to Terms with *De* 德: The Deconstruction of 'Virtue' and an Exercise in Scientific Morality," in *How Should One Live?: Comparing Ethics in Ancient China and Greco-Roman Antiquity*, edited by Richard A. H. King and Dennis Schilling (Boston: Walter de Gruyter, 2011), 117.

30. Gassman, "Coming to Terms with *De* 德," 107.

31. Gassman, "Coming to Terms with *De* 德," 107; and David S. Nivison, *The Ways of Confucianism: Investigations in Chinese Philosophy* (Chicago: Open Court, 1996), 32.

32. Amy Olberding, "Confucius' Complaints and the *Analects'* Account of the Good Life," *Dao: A Journal of Comparative Philosophy* 12.4 (2013): 417–440.

33. Heiner Roetz, *Confucian Ethics of the Axial Age: A Reconstruction Under the Aspect of the Breakthrough Toward Postconventional Thinking* (Albany: State University of New York Press, 1993), 191. Italics removed.

34. Roetz, *Confucian Ethics of the Axial Age*, 191.

35. For more on this see Nicolas Zufferey, *To the Origins of Confucianism: The "Ru" in Pre-Qin Times and During the Early Han Dynasty* (New York: Peter Lang, 2003).

36. I adapted this from Aaron Stalnaker's notion of "philosophical dialogue" as found in *Overcoming Our Evil: Human Nature and Spiritual Exercises In Xunzi and Augustine* (Washington, DC: Georgetown University Press, 2006), 186.

37. I adapt the language of "emending" from Lee H. Yearley, "Confucianism and Genre: Presentation and Persuasion in Early Confucian Thought," in *Confucianism in Dialogue Today: West, Christianity & Judaism*, eds. John Berthrong, Shu-Hsien Liu, and Leonard Swidler (Philadelphia: Ecumenical Press, 2004), 139.

38. Stalnaker, *Overcoming Our Evil*, 18.

39. In *The Dysfunction of Ritual in Early Confucianism* (New York: Oxford University Press, 2012), 15–16, I describe this as a "discursively informed description" of early Confucian texts. See also Stephen Angle's discussion of "interpretive" and "dialogical" modes of reading the *Analects* in "The *Analects* and Moral Theory," in *Dao Companion to the* Analects, edited by Amy Olberding, (New York: Springer, 2014), 229.

40. Huang Yushun 黄玉顺 develops a not entirely unrelated notion of "living Confucianism" 生活儒學 in *Ruxue yu Shenghuo: "Shenghuo Ruxue" Lungao* 《儒学与生活—『生活儒学』论稿》 (Chengdu 成都: Sichuan Daxue Chubanshe 四川大学出版社, 2009).

41. Parts of this sentence draw from Amy Olberding, *Moral Exemplars in the* Analects: *The Good Person is* That (New York: Routledge, 2011), 18.

42. R. P. Kramers, trans., *K'ung Tzu Chia Yu: The School Sayings of Confucius* (Leiden: Brill, 1950), 1.

43. Li Ling 李零, *Sangjiagou: Wo Du Lunyu* 《丧家狗：我读论语》 (Shanxi 山西: *Shanxi Renmin Chubanshe* 山西人民出版社, 2007).

44. Li Ling 李零, *Qu Sheng Naide Zhen Kongzi: Lunyu Zonghengdu* 《去圣乃得真孔子：论语纵横读》 (Beijing 北京: Sanlian Shudian 三联书店, 2008).

45. Carine Defoort, "A Homeless Dog: Li Ling's Understanding of Confucius," *Contemporary Chinese Thought* 41.2 (Winter 2009–2010), 10.

46. Olberding, *Moral Exemplars*, 130.

47. Olberding, *Moral Exemplars*, 128.

48. Olberding, *Moral Exemplars*, 106.

I

The Invulnerability of Integrity

EARLY TEXTS AND COMMENTATORS

The exemplary person is able to make [himself] valuable, [but he] cannot make others value him. [He] is able to make [himself] employable, [but he] cannot make others employ him.

君子能為可貴，不能使人必貴己；能為可用，
不能使人必用己。

(*XUNZI* 6/24/12–13)

THIS CHAPTER AIMS to explore passages in texts such as the *Analects* and the *Mengzi* 《孟子》 that argue for the invulnerability of integrity. In doing so I draw from later Confucian interpreters of these texts to show how they built on these passages to develop various theories of invulnerability. I look at two theories in particular, in the hopes of demonstrating that the early texts did not put forth a single or clear theory of invulnerability and that no uniform consensus emerged within the tradition as to how a moral agent renders his integrity invulnerable to difficult circumstances. This chapter sets the stage for the next chapter, which examines arguments for the invulnerability of integrity made by contemporary scholars of Confucian ethics. Taken together these two chapters reveal that the invulnerability of integrity is a dominant claim within the tradition itself and within the academic community studying the tradition. At the same time, later chapters of this book will show that these questions are far from settled.

The seventeenth chapter in the *Analects* contains several instances of Kongzi's disciples dissuading him from seeking employment from immoral or corrupt leaders of their time. In the seventh passage, Zilu 子路 objects to Kongzi meeting with Bi Xi 佛肸 on the grounds that "the exemplary person does not enter a situation where those he will be close with do not do good" 親於其身為不善者，君子不入也。[1] Kongzi, in part, replies, "Is it not said, '[If something is] truly hard, then scraping will not penetrate [it]; and [if something is] truly white, then dyeing will not stain [it]'" 不曰堅乎，磨而不磷；不曰白乎，涅而不緇?[2] The conversation as presented in the *Analects* ends here. Most traditional commentators take *Analects* 17.7 as Kongzi "analogizing the way in which the exemplary person, while residing in filth and chaos, does not allow [himself] to be polluted by the filth and chaos" 喻君子雖在濁亂，濁亂不能污.³ In this reading, the character of an exemplary person such as Kongzi cannot be marred by the impurities that surround him, even if he is directly involved with those who are otherwise corrupt. Some traditional commentators, such as Zhu Xi 朱熹 (1130–1200), stress the difficulty of emerging untainted in these situations and further explicate this passage by invoking *Analects* 18.8.⁴

In 18.8 Kongzi lists three groups of people that those of his time admired— one group starved to death rather than disgrace themselves by serving an illegitimate political regime; another group degraded themselves by serving in corrupt governments but did this in hopes of transforming society; and a third group removed themselves from politics by becoming recluses, thereby preserving their purity. In speaking about them, Kongzi comments, "I am different from all of these. There is no [course of action] that I am necessarily for or against" 我則異 於是，無可無不可. When taken together, these two passages from the *Analects* and the interpretations of traditional commentators make several important points. For one, they recognize that moral agents desire to keep themselves pure and also desire to transform others into better people. They assume that serving in the government is the most effective way to bring about a transformation but that gaining appointment in the government entails appealing to those in power. Unfortunately, some of those in power are not good people, and serving them may entail making compromises. As such, these passages acknowledge that some situations bring the desire to remain pure in conflict with the desire to transform society. The moral agent wishes to make the world a better place but so doing requires dealing with immoral rulers. Involving oneself with these individuals might taint oneself (although exactly what is tainted is not entirely clear). Some moral agents respond to this scenario by following their desire for purity. They remove themselves from the situation—either by death or withdrawal. Others follow their desire to help society and subject themselves to degradation by serving in the government. For some, the truly "hard" or "white," however, there exists a way of remaining pure while participating in a corrupt regime. In a sense these profound people follow their desire to maintain their integrity as well as their desire to serve society.

The Sage and Moral Deliberation

Many commentators claim that only highly cultivated individuals can maintain their purity in complex moral situations. These highly cultivated individuals, or sages (*shengren* 聖人), are the rare few who have reached the pinnacle of moral attainment. Huang Kan 皇侃 (b. 488), in commenting on *Analects* 17.7, for instance, explains, "For 'worthies' on down [i.e., those cultivated individuals who have not yet reached the level of a sage], it is easy to be defiled. This is why it is not permissible for them to enter into [these situations]. If it is permissible for anyone, it is the sage. The sage is not harmed or defiled by the filth of the times because he is like a thing that is extremely hard and extremely white" 賢人以下易染。故不許入也。若許入者是聖人。聖人不為世俗染累，如至堅至白之物也.[5] Following this line of thought, the sage is uniquely able to maintain his purity in what would for others be morally compromising situations. While worthies are paradigmatic individuals—more virtuous than most people will ever be—even they cannot encounter complex circumstances and emerge untainted.[6]

The sage, we learn, is able to preserve his integrity by exercising a form of moral deliberation such that he recognizes when following the *dao* 道 (the method of flourishing where all people in the world maximize their potential for growth and development) entails varying from the normal course of ethical action. As such he remains aloof from any fixed course of action. In early Confucian texts, this act of deliberation is often referred to as *quan* 權, a notion contemporary scholars understand as "moral balance," "moral discretion," or "deliberation" and often translate as "expediency" or "exigency."[7] A paradigmatic usage of *quan* 權 occurs in *Mengzi* 7A26 where Mengzi contrasts three views on the relationship between caring for oneself and caring for society (a tension similar to the one that appears in *Analects* 17.7 and 18.8). The first view is represented by Yangzi 揚子, a figure Mengzi sees as being self-concerned (*weiwo* 為我): "If removing one hair of his body would benefit the world, he would not do it" 拔一毛而利天下，不為也. The second view is represented by Mozi 墨子, who advocated an impartial love of others (*jianai* 兼愛): "If plucking every hair from head to foot would benefit the world, he would do it" 摩頂放踵利天下，為之. The third view, taken up by Zimo 子莫, occupies the middle ground between the positions of Yangzi and Mozi. Mengzi, it seems, agrees with Zimo that one should find a balance between caring for oneself and caring for society but then adds a caution: "Holding to the middle point without a sense of discretion [*quan* 權], is just like holding to one extreme. The reason I despise holding to one extreme is because it harms the *dao* 道. It raises up one [value] while casting aside a hundred others" 執中無權，猶執一也。所惡執一者，為其賊道也，舉一而廢百也.[8] What we see in *Mengzi* 7A26 is a call for context sensitivity such that the moral agent does not hold fast to one value while neglecting others.

Further passages in early Confucian texts stress that only highly cultivated individuals fully possess the capacity to *quan* 權. *Analects* 9.30 is significant in this regard. In this rather abstruse passage Kongzi states, "While there might be [people] fitting to study with, [they] may not be fitting to travel with on the Way.

While there might be [people] fitting to travel with on the Way, [they] many not be fitting to establish their character alongside [oneself]. While there might be [people] fitting to establish their character alongside [oneself], [they] may not be fitting to join [oneself] in employing discretion" 可與共學 , 未可與適道 ; 可與適道 , 未可與立 ; 可與立 , 未可與權.[9] While there are other ways of translating this passage, most commentators take it in the sense rendered here— the ability to "employ discretion" is limited to a select group.[10] In commenting on passage 9.30, traditional interpreters make an explicit connection between the sage and moral deliberation. Cheng Yi 程頤, an important eleventh-century interpreter, for instance, claimed, "To be a sage is simply to deliberate and balance" 聖人則是權衡也; and Zhu Xi stated, "One must be a sage; and only then is it fitting to join in employing discretion" 然須是聖人方可與權.[11] These interpretations establish a specific connection between *quan* 權 and the sage by arguing that only someone as great as a sage is able to employ moral discretion.

These same commentaries also go on to relate *quan* 權 with the capacity of the sage (or in some instances a *great* worthy—*daxian* 大賢) to preserve his integrity in morally complex circumstances. Zhu Xi, immediately after the previous quote, continues his thought by tying in *Analects* 17.7: "[The passage says], 'Scraped but not penetrated. Dyed but not stained.' But when the character of those today is scraped, it is penetrated; and when dyed, it is stained. How is it even possible to speak of moral discretion? This is why it is said, 'Before one learns to run, he must first learn to walk'" 「磨而不磷 , 涅而不緇。」 而今人才磨便磷 , 才涅便緇 , 如何更說權變?所謂 「未學行 , 先學走」 也.[12] Hu Guang 胡廣 (1369–1418), also commenting on *Analects* 9.30, explains, "While most people will encounter the changing times of unfortunate situations and attempt to handle them by means of moral deliberation, only a great worthy will not lose his upright character" 而眾人亦可能至扵遭事之變 , 而處以權 , 則惟大賢能不失其正.[13] The ability to employ moral discretion, these commentaries suggest, is the capacity of highly cultivated individuals to remain untainted in difficult times.

Quan 權

The early texts do not provide a detailed explanation of how *quan* 權 works (in the *Analects*, for instance, the term only appears three times).[14] Later commentators, while elaborating on the term, do not construct a systematic exposition of how the sage is able to deliberate. Nevertheless, taking what is provided in the early texts, and synthesizing various commentaries—Zhu Xi's and Chen Tianxiang's 陳天祥 (1230–1316) in particular—we might provide the following description of moral deliberation. Literally the character *quan* 權 refers to the actions and implements involved in weighing objects (e.g., the weights and various kinds of scales).[15] In early Chinese discourses these actions and objects were taken as metaphors for determining an appropriate course of action in complicated circumstances. When a sage encountered a situation where different values competed for his attention, he would "weigh" (*quan* 權) the various facets of the situation in order to determine an appropriate course of action.

Authors of early texts and their interpreters do not only employ one metaphor when discussing *quan* 權; rather, they make use of a few different metaphors.[16] Sometimes authors or interpreters speak about *quan* 權 as choosing between two courses of action, similar to the way one might compare the weight of two objects with a scale. Other times they speak of *quan* 權 as the sense of discretion employed when choosing the appropriate course of action among the many possible courses of action, similar to the way in which one moves the counterpoise along the arm of a steelyard to bring the arm into balance. Commentators such as Zhu Xi tend to employ *quan* 權 as a variation of the steelyard metaphor. *Quan* 權, in this view, is kind of moral deliberation involved when current standards fail to provide sufficient action guidance in value conflicts. In these situations, one temporarily reorients the standards such that the value conflict is resolved, similar to the way one might shift the fulcrum of a steelyard toward the object being weighed to allow the arm to have greater length for the counterpoise to leverage.[17] In other words, a steelyard tends to have a standard spot for its fulcrum. This allows one to weigh most objects one might need to weigh in day-to-day affairs; however, if one needs to weigh a particularly heavy (or light) object, one cannot weigh it without moving the fulcrum. Moving the fulcrum reorients the ability of the steelyard to weigh by providing additional (or less) room to move the counterpoise along the arm. It also shifts the values of the unit markings along the arm—rendering the normal markings inapplicable in weighing the new object.

Morally speaking, authors and interpreters such as Zhu Xi claim that the sage tends to accord with a standard set of norms (*chang* 常 or *jing* 經) when taking action. However, when confronted with a complex situation, the sage might need to reorient these standards (*bian* 變 or *quan* 權)—rendering them temporarily inapplicable in determining proper action but also creating the opportunity for an alternative mode of action that deals effectively with the situation. In these cases, the sage may even perform actions that seem to go far beyond the standard. To illustrate this, authors and commentators often refer to the military expeditions of Tang 湯 and Wu 武—each of whom overthrew (and killed) an evil ruler in order to establish a new dynasty. In this context, the standard course of action is for subjects to serve their rulers. Tang and Wu, however, varied from the standard and even went so far as to kill their rulers. Nonetheless, the commentators stress, they did what was appropriate for their situations.

These authors and commentators also stress that after the sage deals with an exigent situation, he returns to the normal way of managing moral affairs. Interpreters such as Zhu Xi emphasize the temporary nature of employing *quan* 權. In responding to a question about moral deliberation, he states, "In the end, *quan* 權 should be temporary and not permanent. Yao and Shun abdicated the throne, and Tang and Wu embarked in military expeditions and punished [the wicked]. As for these cases of *quan* 權, how could they be done all the time" 畢竟權則可暫而不可常。如堯舜揖遜，湯武征誅，此是權也，豈可常行乎？[18] Zhu Xi also notes that people will rarely encounter situations that require this kind of extreme response. He stated several times, for instance, "If one frequently employed [*quan* 權], what kind of world would [it] create" 若日日時時用之，則成甚世界了？[19] In other instances he notes that the actions of Tang and Wu only occur as appropriate actions once every 600 or 700 years.[20] While this kind of extreme is rarely called for, in other places Zhu Xi distinguished between a "heavy" (*zhong* 重) and a "light" (*qing* 輕) form of *quan* 權, where the latter is employed in more general circumstances.[21]

Authors of early Confucian texts and commentators tend to contrast exigent situations where moral balancing is necessary with a standard way of handling moral affairs. They do this by using the terms *jing* 經 and *quan* 權 (or *chang* 常 and *bian* 變).[22] The character *jing* 經 literally refers to the "warp" or "the main thread" in a piece of a cloth.[23] Early Chinese glossographies also refer to *jing* 經 as a "pathway" or a "foundation."[24] The third century glossography, *Shiming* 《釋名》, for instance, defines *jing* 經 as "pathways" (*jing* 徑) and then explains, "Like pathways and roads that reach in all directions, [they] can be constantly used" 如徑路無所不通，可常用也.[25] *Jing* 經 in this sense are the normal paths one takes to reach a destination. Zhu Xi often defined *jing* 經 in a way that fits with the *Shiming*'s gloss. He claimed, for instance, "*Jing* 經 are the normal/constant paths of action for all generations" 經是萬世常行之道.[26] In a more abstract sense, *jing* 經 refers to the norms moral agents follow in the process of self-cultivation. *Quan* 權, in contrast to *jing* 經, are those moments when varying from the norm becomes necessary. Commentators often discuss *quan* 權 in this light as "varying from *jing* 經 in order to accord with the *dao* 道" 反經而合道.

The relationship between *jing* 經 and *quan* 權 is a subject of debate in the commentaries (much less is said about them as a pair in early Confucian texts). A dominant position in this debate is that *jing* 經 and *quan* 權 represent different aspects of the *dao* 道. Zhu Xi, for instance, states, "*Jing* 經 are the constant (or normal) aspects of the *dao* 道. *Quan* 權 are the shifting (or changing) aspects of the *dao* 道. The *dao* 道 is a unifying framework; [it] strings together *jing* 經 and *quan* 權" 經者，道之常也；權者，道之變也。道是箇統體，貫乎經與權.[27] Similarly, many commentators discuss *jing* 經 and *quan* 權 as different modes of *yi* 義, a term usually translated as "justice," "righteousness," or "rightness," but in general refers to a moral sense that determines appropriate courses of action.[28] Drawing from Zhu Xi again, we learn, "When it is right (*yi* 義) to hold to *jing* 經, one holds to 經. When it is right to employ *quan* 權, one employs *quan* 權. This is what is meant by the saying, 'Rightness can include both *jing* 經 and *quan* 權'" 義當守經，則守經；義當用權，則用權，所以謂義可以總括得經、權。[29] In this view, one's sense of rightness evaluates situations and determines when one should act in accordance with the norm and when one should act with exigency. Rightness, as such, means more than simply following the standard or the norm. One can vary from what is otherwise appropriate and still be right. To be *yi* 義, in this view, is to accord with the *dao* 道, and according with the *dao* 道 may or may not entail following standard ethical action.

Commentators such as Zhu Xi go to great lengths to stress the interrelated nature of *jing* 經 and *quan* 權. While they seem to be separate, they are actually united in the *dao* 道 and even dependent on each other. Zhu Xi explains this as follows:

> The standard is indeed the standard; and the exigent is indeed the exigent. However, while one might depart from the standard in order to accord with the *dao* 道, this by no means entails turning one's back on the standard. It's similar to people having two feet. The left foot is indeed the left foot; and the right foot is indeed the right foot. [But] when walking, one foot must go first and the other foot must go second. They depend on each other in the act of walking; and only as such can one actually begin to walk. [You] cannot replace the left foot with the right, nor the right foot with the left.

> 經自是經，權自是權。但是雖反經而能合道，卻無背於經。如人兩腳相似，左腳自是左腳，右腳自是右腳，行時須一腳先，一腳後，相待而行，方始行得。不可將左腳便喚做右腳，右腳便喚做左腳。[30]

In this view, *jing* 經 and *quan* 權 are mutually supporting aspects of the *dao* 道; both are actually necessary for "walking" (*xing* 行) on, or acting in accordance with, the *dao* 道. When a moral agent employs *quan* 權, as such, he does not overtly go against standard ethical action; rather he operates in conjunction with the standards.

Zhu Xi further stresses the relationship between *jing* 經 and *quan* 權 by explaining moral discretion as the subtle or refined aspects of standard ethical action. Only highly cultivated individuals are capable of understanding these subtle aspects. He states, for instance, "*Quan* 權 are the profound, subtle, and reserved recesses of *jing* 經. If one does not see the refined, reserved, penetrating, and pure patterns of the *dao* 道, [he] is not qualified as one with which to discuss *quan* 權" 權乃經之要妙微密處。非見道理之精密、透徹、純熟者，不足以語權也.[31] Zhu Xi does not provide many more details about "the subtle aspects of standard ethical action," but he does make it clear that *jing* 經 and *quan* 權 should not be thought of as completely separate forms of ethical action.[32] The significance of this, for our purposes, is that when moral agents employ *quan* 權 they are not rebelling against or totally straying from standard ethical action; rather, they are actually engaging in a more subtle form of standard ethical action.[33] In other words, to take exigent action is to accord with the *dao* 道—it is to accord with standard ethical action in a more profound way. While the specifics of how this occurs are not readily available from the texts or commentaries, this move allows authors or interpreters to argue for a kind of invulnerability. A moral agent who deliberates properly may appear to stray from standard ethical action, but he is "right" 義, and never actually leaves behind the *dao* 道.

In other places, Zhu Xi also connects *quan* 權 with the ability to respond appropriately to various circumstances (*shizhong* 時中), to follow the patterns of the cosmos (*tianli* 天理), or to ensure that one's heart is "receptive, illuminated, pure, and singular" 心虛明純一.[34]

Comparing Two Theories of Quan 權

The Yuan Dynasty commentator Chen Tianxiang 陳天祥 builds on these accounts and provides a somewhat clearer explanation of how the sage might "go against standard ethical action" (*fanjing* 反經) while maintaining his integrity. Much of his discussion on this topic occurs in his commentary on passages such as *Mengzi* 4A17 where Mengzi is asked if he would save his sister-in-law were she drowning. What makes this a complicated situation, from the perspective of Mengzi's inquisitor, is that the rules of propriety limit male and female interaction. In the case of a drowning sister-in-law, one would likely have to make physical contact with her in order to pull her out of the water, and this goes beyond what is permitted in normal circumstances. Confronted with this scenario Mengzi explains, "Only a wolf would let his sister-in-law drown and not help her. For men and women not to touch when exchanging things accords with ritual propriety, [but] to extend a hand to assist one's drowning sister-in-law is a case of moral discretion (*quan* 權)" 嫂溺不援，是豺狼也。男女授受不親，禮也；嫂溺援之以手者，權也. With reference to this passage, Chen Tianxiang explains, "If [the moral agent] encounters an abnormal circumstance, [he] makes a distinction between the internal and the external. Internally, [he] holds to the upright; externally, [he] goes against the standard. Only then is [he] able to accomplish the work of saving things [from harm]" 若遇非常之事則有內外之分。內則守正，外須反經。然後能成濟物之功.[35] Later in his commentary he adds, "While externally [the moral agent] temporarily goes against the standard of not touching when [males and females] exchange things, internally [he] holds fast to the fact that [he] is saving someone from death. Can anyone say that in employing moral discretion [one] cannot still hold to the upright way" 外雖暫反授受不親之經，內則主於救人一身之死。孰謂從權則不可以守正道哉?[36] There are several things in these two comments that are worth noting in regard to Chen's account of going against standard ethical action. Most relevant is the notion that when the moral agent encounters an unusual circumstance, he takes action that is counter to standard ethical action. Internally, however, he holds fast to what is upright, which in this case is saving his sister-in-law from death. While Chen does not tell his readers what constitutes an abnormal circumstance, he is at least clear that things other than external guides for action should be taken into consideration when determining proper behavior.

In this light, *Mengzi* 4A17 shares several affinities with passage 6B1 where Mengzi explains that other considerations can occasionally outweigh the demand for acting in accordance with ritual. The analogy used in 6B1 is that of metal and feathers. Mengzi points out that while we tend to instinctively think that metal is heavier than feathers, a wagon-load of feathers might actually outweigh a small portion of metal.[37] Employing this analogy, Mengzi explains that considerations such as starving to death, or leaving no posterity, can sometimes trump considerations of eating in accordance with ritual or following the ritual script for a wedding ceremony. These are situations, following the analogy, where feathers outweigh metal. Similarly, encountering one's drowning sister-in-law is a situation where her life outweighs the demands of ritually prohibited interaction.[38]

Building on 4A17 and 6B1, we might infer that abnormal situations are those circumstances where the good of breaking from standard ethical action far exceeds the good of following standard ethical action, where "good" refers to preserving life or fostering a social order that fulfills relationships and virtues. So while letting one's sister-in-law drown (on the basis of following ritual) continues to encourage the social order established by tradition, this good is not as significant as preserving her life. The implication here is that in most situations standard ethical action will maximize the goods of life, relationships, and virtues, but there are occasions where they fail to maximize one or more of these goods.[39] As such, in these situations, the moral agent should vary from standard ethical action in order to take action that realizes the good at risk or perhaps avoids harming it in a significant way.

In his commentary, Chen suggests that "internally holding to the upright" is predicated on fostering internal states that remain constant in changing circumstances. He asserts,

> [One] should make a distinction between "establishing one's character"'
> and "employing discretion" [in *Analects* 9.30]. To establish one's character
> is to complete oneself; and to employ discretion is to complete [external]
> things. When people are able to correct and focus their minds—not allow-
> ing [themselves] to be tempted by external things, nor distracted by riches
> and honors, nor disturbed by hardship and poverty, nor bothered by
> violent threats and war—this is what it means to "establish one's character."

> 立與權又當分辨。立以成己；權以成物。人能正定其心，
> 不使外物可奪，富貴不能淫，貧賤不能移，威武不能屈，
> 是之所謂立也。[40]

From this passage we learn that people "complete themselves" when they focus their mind such that they remain unperturbed in any situation. Their heart or mind remains firmly attached to the correct way of living (*zhengdao* 正道) regardless of whether they encounter situations of poverty, honor, or wealth.[41] The moral agent achieves a state where he is internally fixed on following the *dao* 道. "Establishing one's character," as such, means strengthening one's commitment to correct principles, where we might infer that correct principles lead to the cultivation of life, relationships, and virtues. According to Chen, cultivating a firm commitment to correct principles means to establish one's character. It is a precondition for taking exigent action. At the same time, however, it is not a sufficient condition for taking exigent action.

Unfortunately, Chen does not specify how the moral agent moves from establishing his character to employing discretion. But one way to systematize his thinking is to draw from passages such as *Mengzi* 5B1, which discuss themes of adjusting to circumstances (*shi* 時), sageliness (*sheng* 聖), and a qualitative distinction between Kongzi and other great figures who have achieved aspects of sagehood but still remain fixed on one course of action. As we have already seen, these tend to be reoccurring themes in discussions of *quan* 權 (and coincidentally three of the four figures discussed in *Mengzi* 5B1 also appear in *Analects* 18.8).

In *Mengzi* 5B1, Mengzi lists four figures and their different responses to serving in governmental office. Bo Yi 伯夷, Mengzi explains, is a sage of purity (*qing* 清)—he would not look or listen to anything he deemed bad; neither would he change his loyalty to serve another ruler or associate with anyone that might tarnish his purity. Yi Yin 伊尹 is a sage of devotion (*ren* 任)—he served in situations of order and chaos, taking responsibility such that if there were those who suffered, "it was as if he had pushed them into a ditch himself" 若己推而內之溝中. Liuxia Hui 柳下惠 is a sage of harmony (*he* 和)—he was not ashamed to serve a corrupt ruler or associate with those of questionable character. Mengzi quotes him stating, "You are you, and I am I. Even if you stood at my side bearbacked and naked, how would you tarnish me" 爾為爾，我為我。雖袒裼裸裎於我側，爾焉能浼我哉? [42] Finally, Kongzi is a sage of timeliness (*shi* 時)—when it was proper to take office, he took office; and when it was proper to go into retirement, he went into retirement. Mengzi calls Kongzi, "one who collected the great accomplishments [of others]" 集大成者, meaning that Kongzi could be pure, devoted, or harmonious depending on the circumstance. Given that in passage 2A9 Mengzi invokes much of the same language as in 5B1 and concludes by criticizing Bo Yi for being obstinate (*ai* 隘), and Liuxia Hui for being impudent (*bugong* 不恭), it seems that Mengzi admires all these figures but also sees the first three as lacking in some important sense.[43] So Mengzi regards Bo Yi, Yi Yin, and Liuxia Hui as sages, but they are not timely sages like Kongzi.[44] Rather they each highlight one aspect of sagehood. When taken in this light, 5B1 is an explanation of why Kongzi is superior to Bo Yi, Yi Yin, and Liuxia Hui. He is the one able to adapt to various situations, perhaps by employing some kind of discretion when taking action.

In 5B1 Mengzi defines the ability to vary according to the situation as *zhi* 智, which I understand as a kind of practical knowledge or skillful wisdom.[45] Toward the end of the passage, Mengzi distinguishes between skillful wisdom and sageliness (*sheng* 聖). *Zhi* 智 he likens to the skill or aim (*qiao* 巧) needed to hit a target in archery. *Sheng* 聖 is the strength (*li* 力) required for the arrow to reach the target. "If the arrow reaches the target," Mengzi explains, "it is because of one's strength. If it hits the target, [however,] it is not due to one's strength" 其至，爾力也。其中，非爾力也. Hitting the target, it seems, is also a matter of proper skill. As such, sagliness without skillful wisdom is insufficient to hit the mark in every occasion (as is skillful wisdom without sagliness). Said less metaphorically, one can cultivate himself to a high degree, or, following *Analects* 9.30, one can establish his character, but if one lacks skillful wisdom—a sense of discretion in determining which attributes to bring to bear in particular circumstances—he will not respond properly in every situation. In other words, the timely moral agent, in addition to cultivating a variety of virtues, must also foster skillful wisdom if he is to render himself effective in every situation. *Quan* 權, I suggest, is the application of skillful wisdom in situations of apparent value conflict.[46]

What we get from synthesizing these passages in the *Mengzi* with Chen Tianxiang's commentary is the following: A refined moral agent is one who has established his character and possesses skillful wisdom. When he encounters a situation where the good of going against standard ethical action clearly out-weighs the good of following standard ethical action, he exercises moral discre-tion. This entails inwardly holding to correct principles while externally taking action contrary to standard ethical action. The result is a situation-specific perfor-mance that maximizes goods such as life, relationships, and virtues.

While there are significant differences between Chen's external-internal interpretation of *jing* 經 and *quan* 權 and what we might call Zhu Xi's mutu-ally dependent interpretation of *jing* 經 and *quan* 權, there are also a number of important similarities between the two interpretations. For one, Chen and Zhu agree that exigent action must be done with a sense of reluctance. The moral agent must feel that he has no other choice in light of the disastrous alternative. Zhu Xi repeatedly stresses that "*quan* 權 is something done only when compelled" 權是不得已而用之.[47] The phrase I translate as "compelled," *budeyi* 不得已, implies a desire to do otherwise.[48] One desires, in these cases, to follow standard ethical action; however, the situation dictates over-riding, or perhaps realigning, this desire for the sake of according with the *dao* 道.[49] Taking exigent action, as such, entails navigating impulses that the moral agent has cultivated over his lifetime. In these cases, the moral agent has spent years refining a constant desire to accord with standard ethical action, but now the moral agent must stray from standard ethical action in order to do what is right. I suspect that this is why both Zhu and Chen stressed that only the most adept of moral agents are capable of taking exigent action.

Second, personal benefit should not be the primary motive for taking exigent action. Instead, the central motivation is a concern for others.[50] Most Confucian texts claim that early sages demonstrated a deep concern (*you* 憂) for people in the kingdom. On this note, Mengzi recounts that the sages Yu 禹 and Ji 稷 passed the door to their homes several times but did not enter because they considered the work of saving the kingdom to be so urgent (*ji* 急). He explains, "Yu reflected in such a way that if there were any people drowning in the king-dom, it was as if he had drown them himself. Ji reflected in such as way that if there were any people starving in the kingdom, it was as if he had starved them himself. Such was their sense of urgency." 禹思天下有溺者，由己溺之也；稷思天下有飢者，由己飢之也，是以如是其急也.[51] Other early Confucian texts stress that communal rightness or public justice (*gongyi* 公義) should often trump personal desires (*siyu* 私欲).[52] Chen Tianxiang ties several of these elements together in his commentary on *Mengzi* 4A17. He states,

> Tang overthrew Jie, Wu Wang attacked Zhou 紂, Yi Yin banished Tai Jia, and Zhou Gong 周公 punished Guan Shu. These actions are not the con-stant patterns of relation between a ruler and minister or an older brother

and younger brother. In confronting these situations, [however], the sage is compelled to do as they did. I have yet to hear that ordering one's family and state, or pacifying all under heaven, cannot accord with the *dao* 道. It is just like the situation of extending one's hand if one's sister-in-law were drowning. Look into the reasons one does it—one extends one's hand to one's sister-in-law, and with an attitude of humble sincerity one goes against the standard of [males and females] not touching even when exchanging things. Investigate how one does it—one does it by using one's humanity to preserve one's heart; and by focusing on saving this panic-stricken person who is drowning from death. How is this not able to accord with the *dao* 道?

如湯征桀，武王伐紂，伊尹放太甲，周公誅管叔，皆非君臣，兄弟之常理。聖人於此不得已而爲之。然後家國治而天下平；未聞不能合道也。只如嫂溺援之之事，視其所以，乃是以手援嫂，誠爲反其授受不親之經；察其所安，乃是以仁存心，期在救其逡巡溺者之死。斯豈不能合道哉？[53]

What we see here is a reluctance to do things that go against standard ethical action but also the realization that there are compelling reasons for taking an alternative course of action. Exigent action is done for the sake of ordering the state and bringing peace to the kingdom. One's focus when taking exigent action is on saving others from death and preserving one's heart.

Remarkably, neither the early texts nor commentaries quoted here mention any kind of negative feelings lingering on the part of the sage after taking exigent action. Instead, they argue that the sage acts out of concern for the well-being of the kingdom, and it seems reasonable to assume that this concern for the people continues even after the sage confronts a complex moral situation inasmuch as the people have further unmet needs.[54] At the same time, the fact that the sage's concern continues after taking exigent action does not stem from any guilt or regret in going against standard ethical action; rather it stems from the realization that there are further obstacles hindering the well-being of the kingdom. We might imagine that if the sage could take exigent action such that the entire world was properly aligned with the *dao* 道, the sage would then have no more concern. In other words, the sage's concern is tied to the problems facing humanity, and not to the rules or norms he may have transgressed in addressing these problems.

The third, and perhaps most important, similarity between Zhu and Chen's theories is that both come to the conclusion that the moral agent is able to render his integrity invulnerable to unfortunate circumstances. Chen might see this attained through an inner commitment, and Zhu Xi might see this attained through a realization of the subtle profundities of standard ethical action, but both agree that taking exigent action is taking right (*yi* 義) action and entails according with the *dao* 道. As such, there is no talk of lingering negative feelings in either of their views because to properly deliberate is to act in accordance with the *dao* 道, and when one acts in accordance with the *dao* 道 there is no need for remorse.

This idea of invulnerability is summed up rather well in *Mengzi* 5A7 where Mengzi is asked whether Yi Yin served as a cook in order to attract the attention of the king at the time and thereby put himself in a place to become a counselor. Mengzi replies that Yi Yin actually did farm the fields of the ruling family, but he did not become a cook, and neither did Yi Yin farm the fields in the hope of attracting the king's attention. Instead, the king sought him out. Yi Yin accepted the position because he "reflected on the people in the kingdom—[all] the men and women—who had not received the care of Yao and Shun; and [considered it] as if he, himself, had pushed [them] into the midst of a filthy ditch" 思天下之民匹夫匹婦有不被堯舜之澤者，若己推而內之溝中. Mengzi continues, "This is the degree to which Yi Yin undertook the heavy responsibility of the kingdom" 其自任以之重如此. For Mengzi, though, it is important that Yi Yin did this in the right way. He did not debase himself by becoming a cook (i.e., someone in charge of killing animals, which Mengzi sees as harmful to humaneness in 1A7), nor by farming the fields to get in good with the king. Only after he was properly summoned did he accept the role of counselor, and his primary concern in accepting the role was not his status but the interest of the people in the kingdom. In short, Mengzi denies the idea that sages might debase themselves in seeking to save the people. In this light, Mengzi concludes, "I have never heard of one who bends himself in order to straighten others; so how would [I hear] of one who demeans himself in order to straighten the world? The sages did different things—some traveled far, some stayed near, some left [official positions], some did not leave [official positions]—but [they all] returned with pure selves" 吾未聞枉己而正人者也，況辱己以正天下者乎？聖人之行不同也，或遠或近，或去或不去，歸潔其身而已矣.[55]

Conclusion

A larger summary of this chapter is as follows. Some portions of early Confucian texts as well as commentators such as Zhu Xi and Chen Tianxiang argue that moral agents desire to both maintain their integrity and transform society such that it accords with the *dao* 道. They recognize that sometimes these desires can appear to conflict with each other. This is particularly true in situations where aligning society with the *dao* 道 involves colluding with immoral leaders in government or otherwise violating standards of ethical action. Only highly cultivated moral agents, called sages, are able to effectively navigate these situations such that they maintain their integrity but also act on their desire to transform society. Sages "balance" these difficult situations by means of moral deliberation, or *quan* 權. *Quan* 權 is a process of rendering normal standards temporarily inapplicable and engaging in exigent action. While it seems that taking exigent action involves straying from standard ethical action (*fanjing* 反經), it actually entails according with the *dao* 道 and exercising one's sense of rightness to abide by the subtle profundities of standard ethical action. Alternatively, *quan* 權 entails externally varying from standard ethical action while internally holding to correct principles. Either way, *quan* 權 leaves no lingering feelings in the form of blame or guilt because instead of the moral agent engaging in wrong or improper action, he alternatively engages in right or appropriate action that does not actually deviate from the *dao* 道. In taking exigent action, the sage is motivated by concern for the people in the kingdom. This concern persists as long as there are further obstacles preventing society from operating in accordance with the *dao* 道. If these obstacles were eliminated, even if eliminated by means of exigent action, the sage, it seems, would have no lingering concern. As such, the sage is able to render his integrity invulnerable to complex moral situations by means of a context sensitivity that allows him to always do what is right.

The following chapter shows how contemporary scholars of Confucian ethics borrow from the account provide here and develop alternative accounts in interesting and relevant ways. I will also suggest several areas where contemporary scholars might emend their theories, and I will outline the way in which a broader reading of Confucian texts challenges these theories.

Notes

1. Bi Xi was a dignitary from the state of Jin 晉 who aided an enemy of the state, thereby displaying his disloyalty to the state.

2. Similar themes occur in *Analects* 18.2 and *Mengzi* 5A7. See also *Lüshi Chunqiu* 2.4/9/21–22, 2.4/9/24–26, and 12.4/60/11–13.

3. Li Xueqin 李學勤, ed., *Lunyu Zhushu* 《論語注疏》, Vol. 2 (Taibei 台北: Taiwan Shufang 台灣書房, 2001), 268.

4. Zhu Xi 朱熹, *Sishu Zhangju Jizhu* 《四書章句集注》 (Beijing 北京: Zhonghua Shuju 中華書局, 2005), 177.

5. He Yan 何晏, ed., *Lunyu Jijieyishu* 《論語集解義疏》. *Wenyuange Sikuquanshu Dianziban* 《文淵閣四庫全書電子版》 (Hong Kong: Digital Heritage Publishing Limited, accessed September 17, 2014), 9.8.

6. Robert Ashmore discusses this point and provides related interpretations of the *Analects* in *The Transport of Reading: Text and Understanding in the World of Tao*

Qian (365–427) (Cambridge, MA: Harvard University Press, 2010), 141–144. He quotes Shen Linshi 沈鱗士 (419–503): "When the age is chaotic it is fitting for the worthy to hideaway and preserve his life; [however,] it is fitting for the sage to emerge and fulfill [all] things" 世亂，賢者宜隱而全生；聖人宜出以弘物. Translation is my own.

7. *Quan* 權 can also be translated as "authority" in other contexts; although for the purposes of this project, I discuss *quan* 權 only as "authority" when it relates to the argument at hand. *Quan* 權 as authority is likely tied to *quan* 權 as "weighing" in the sense of having authority to determine standards, in this case, standards of measurement. Chenyang Li poses an alternative explanation: "We may understand the derivative meaning of *quan* 權 as power [i.e., authority] in this way: from the meaning of the weight in the weighing instrument comes the meaning of carrying weight; if someone carries weight, he controls the force of *quan* 權, or power." Chenyang Li, *The Confucian Philosophy of Harmony* (New York: Routledge, 2014), 132.

8. A quote in the *Mingru Xuean* 《明儒學案》 presents a useful explanation of this passage. It states, "Zimo holds to the balancing point—desiring to take up a position between self-concern and impartial love; however, he misunderstood that self-concern and impartial love could also be balancing points. If it is fitting for the times to be self-concerned, then the balancing point is with Yangzi. Yanzi [Confucius's favorite disciple], for instance, lived in a narrow lane and closed his window [to the outside world]. [On the other hand], if it is fitting for the times to love impartially, then the balancing point is with Mozi. The sage Yu, for instance, passed the door to his own home [while managing floods] and did not enter in [to check on his family]. As such, the balancing point has no fixed form; rather, discretion (*quan* 權) is its form. And discretion has no fixed point of implementation; instead, the *dao* 道 is simply its point of implementation. Discretion is the principle one's mindful heart naturally possesses. All one must do is be 'cautious and careful about the unseen' and 'fearful and apprehensive over the unheard' [quoting the *Zhongyong*]; and then in whatever circumstances he finds himself in, he will be able to hit the balancing point. He will transform and change, following the *dao* 道, and will always assert himself with natural ease" 子莫執中，蓋欲擇為我兼愛之中而執之，而不知為我兼愛皆中也。時當為我，則中在楊子；陋巷閉戶，顏子是也。時當兼愛，則中在墨子；過門不入，禹是也。蓋中無定體，惟權是體，權無定用，惟道是用。權也者，吾心天然自有之則，惟戒慎不睹、恐懼不聞，然後能發無不中，變易從道，莫非自然之用. Huang Zongxi 黃宗羲, ed., *Mingru Xuean* 《明儒學案》, *Wenyuange Sikuquanshu Dianziban* 《文淵閣四庫全書電子版》 (Hong Kong: Digital Heritage Publishing, accessed February 3, 2015), 17.38–39.

9. After translating this passage, Edward Slingerland adds, "'Discretion' thus refers to a kind of cognitive flexibility that allows one to amend or bend the rules in response to changing or unique circumstances." Edward Slingerland, trans. *Confucius: Analects* (Indianapolis: Hackett Publishing Company, 2003), 97.

10. Another way of reading this passage is to take it as a list of different, but not lesser, characteristics of various groups of people.

11. Li Jingde 黎靖德, ed. *Zhuzi Yulei* 《朱子語類》 (Beijing 北京: Zhonghua Shuju 中華書局, 1999), 987. Hereafter, *Zhuzi Yulei*. On the same page Zhu is asked about who has the ability to *quan* 權 and he says, "Great worthies and above [i.e., those that surpass great worthies in moral cultivation, or sages]" 大賢已上. He also states, "When it comes to *jing* 經 [i.e., the standard set of norms or rules], most people, including learners, are able to follow it; but when it comes to *quan* 權, if not a sage or worthy, [one] is not able to do it" 所謂經，眾人與學者皆能循之；至於權，則非聖賢不能行也.

12. *Zhuzi Yulei*, 987.

13. Hu Guang 胡廣, ed., *Sishu Daquan* 《四書大全》, *Wenyuange Sikuquanshu Dianziban* 《文淵閣四庫全書電子版》 (Hong Kong: Digital Heritage Publishing, accessed September 25, 2014), 9.40. A similar phrase also appears in the *Yijing* 《易經》: "Only a sage knows how to advance or retreat, or to pre-serve [something] or destroy [it], without losing his upright character" 知進退存亡而不失其正者，其唯聖人乎. Guo Jianxun 郭建勳, ed. *Xinyi Yijing Duben* 《新譯易經讀本》 (Taibei Shi 臺北市: Sanmin shuju 三民書局, 1996), 21.

14. The earliest substantive discussion of *quan* 權 is in the "Quanmou" 權謀 chap-ter of the *Shuoyuan* 《說苑》 (compiled by Liu Xiang 劉向 [77–6 BCE]), which is more descriptive than analytical. See *Shuoyuan* 13/101-111. The *Mozi* 《墨子》 also makes an important statement about *quan* 權. It remarks, "*Quan* 權 is when 'wrong' becomes 'right'; [it] is not to take 'wrong' as 'wrong.' To *quan* 權 is to rectify [i.e., make something right]" 權，非為是也；非，非為非也。權，正也. *Mozi* 11.1/92/17–18. For a broader overview of *quan* 權across early Chinese texts see Lu Ruirong 盧瑞容, *Zhongguo Gudai "Xiangdui Guanxi" Siwei Tantao: "Shi," "He," "Quan," Ququ," Gainian Suyuan Fenxi* 《中國古代「相對關係」思維探討—「勢」「和」「權」「屈曲」概念溯源分析》 (Taibei 台北: Shangding Wenhua Chubanshe商鼎文化出版社, 2004), 222–299.

15. For a more in depth discussion of *quan* 權 in early China see Griet Vankeerberghen, "Choosing Balance: Weighing (*Quan* 權) as a Metaphor for Action in Early Chinese Texts." *Early China* 30 (2005): 47–89. Other than the sources cited by Vankeerberghen and those cited in this chapter, see also John H. Berthrong, "Weighing the Way: Metaphoric Balances in *Analects* 9:30," in *Interpretation and Intellectual Change: Chinese Hermeneutics in Historical Perspective*, ed. Ching-I Tu, (New Brunswick, NJ: Transaction, 2005), 3–18; Paul R. Goldin, "The Theme of the Primacy of the Situation in Classical Chinese Philosophy and Rhetoric," *Asia Major* 18.2 (2005): 18–23; and Gregory Smits, "The Intersection of Politics and Thought in Ryukyuan Confucianism: Sai On's Uses of *Quan*," *Harvard Journal of Asiatic Studies* 56.2 (December 1996): 443–477.

16. Vankeerberghen notes three uses of the scale metaphor: "[As] an instrument that can determine whether a given entity measures up to a standard, as an

instrument that can facilitate choice between two mutually exclusive options and, third, as an instrument that can help find one the 'mysterious' point of balance." Vankeerberghen, "Choosing Balance," 65.

17. "Leverage" is also one of the early meanings of *quan* 權. It is additionally worth noting that Vankeerberghen argues against the existence of scales with shifting fulcrums in early China (Vankeerberghen, "Choosing Balance," 52). While it is possible that instead of moving the fulcrum, one would move the object weighed to a different place along the arm, the notion of a moving fulcrum tends to be the best way to make sense of the metaphor in many Confucian texts.

18. *Zhuzi Yulei*, 990.

19. *Zhuzi Yulei*, 989–990.

20. *Zhuzi Yulei*, 990. Contemporary ethicists working in the Western philosophical tradition also worry about the problem of normalizing moral breaches. See, for instance, Paul Rynard and David P. Shugarman, eds., *Cruelty & Deception: The Controversy Over Dirty Hands in Politics* (New York: Broadview Press, 2000), 137.

21. *Zhuzi Yulei*, 1331.

22. Pairing *jing* 經 and *quan* 權 together becomes more common by the time of the *Chunqiu Fanlu* 《春秋繁露》 (c. second century BCE–fourth century CE). One of the earliest pairings occurs in a passage from the *Han Shi Waizhuan* 《韓詩外轉》, which claims to quote Mengzi: "The Way has two [aspects]; the constant is called *jing* 經, [and] the changing is called *quan* 權. Embrace the constant Way, hold fast to its changing exigencies, and thereby obtain the status of a worthy" 夫道二：常之謂經，變之謂權。懷其常道，而挾其變權，乃得為賢. *Han Shi Waizhuan* 2.3/7/24.

23. The *Shuowen Jiezi* 《說文解字》 also defines *jing* 經 as the act of "weaving," or *zhi* 織. Xu, Shen 許慎. *Shuowen Jiezi* 《說文解字》 (Beijing 北京: Zhonghua Shuju 中華書局, 2004), 271.

24. Guan Xihua 管錫华, ed., *Erya* 《尔雅》 (Beijing 北京: Zhonghua Shuju 中华書局, 2014), 189.

25. *Shiming* 6.3/70/20.

26. *Zhuzi Yulei*, 989–990.

27. *Zhuzi Yulei*, 989; see also page 995.

28. For more on *yi* 義 see Chung-ying Cheng, *New Dimensions of Confucian and Neo-Confucian Philosophy* (Albany: State University of New York Press, 1991), 233–245; David L. Hall and Roger T. Ames, *Thinking Through Confucius* (Albany: State University of New York Press, 1987), 89–110; Kwong-Loi Shun, *Mencius and Early Chinese Thought* (Stanford, CA: Stanford University Press, 1997), 84–135; Jinhua Jia and Pang-Fei Kwok, "From Clan Manners to Ethical Obligation and Righteousness: A New Interpretation of the Term *yi* 義," *Journal of the Royal Asiatic Society* 17.1 (January 2007): 33–42; and Michael D. K. Ing, *The Dysfunction of Ritual in Early Confucianism* (New York: Oxford University Press, 2012), 57–71. Bryan W. Van Norden makes a relevant point with regard to *yi* 義: "Although *yi* 義

will sometimes involve obligations and other times prohibitions, my sense is that it is overall more like an agent-relative *prohibition* to avoid certain kinds of conduct. (In contrast, *ren* 仁, when used in its narrow sense as benevolence, is primarily an agent-relative *obligation* to benefit others.)" *Virtue Ethics and Consequentialism in Early Chinese Philosophy* (New York: Cambridge University Press, 2007), 118. Throughout this book I translate *yi* 義 as "justice," "rightness," "righteousness," or "right," depending on the context.

29. *Zhuzi Yulei*, 990. On page 995 he also says, "The notion of *yi* 義 unifies *jing* 經 and *quan* 權, employing them both" 『義』字兼經、權而用之.

30. *Zhuzi Yulei*, 995. Zhu Xi also uses the metaphor of an unusually warm day in winter, where instead of wearing a coat it would be appropriate to use a fan, on pages 988–989.

31. *Zhuzi Yulei*, 992; see also page 989: "*Jing* 經 is *quan* 權 that has already been settled; and *quan* 權 is *jing* 經 that is yet to be settled" 經是已定之權，權是未定之經. Antonio Cua explains this as *jing* 經 being the determinate form of *quan* 權 in *Moral Vision and Tradition: Essays In Chinese Ethics* (Washington, DC: Catholic University of America Press, 1998), 263.

32. In *Zhuzi Yulei*, 992, for instance, he states, "Although [they] have differences, in reality *quan* 權 does not leave behind *jing* 經" 雖有異，而權實不離乎經也. See also page 990 and the other passages on page 992.

33. Vankeerberghen makes a similar point on page 77 of her article: "[*Quan* 權] allows the agent, under certain special circumstances, to act at his own discretion without necessarily being guilty of transgressing the norm. With *quan* 權, the theorists thus recognize that real action can involve a complex process of negotiating rules and norms with the unique features of time and place in which the agent operates."

34. *Zhuzi Yulei*, 202, 988, and 989.

35. Chen Tianxiang 陳天祥, *Sishubianyi* 《四書辨疑》, *Wenyuange Sikuquanshu Dianziban* 《文淵閣四庫全書電子版》 (Hong Kong: Digital Heritage Publishing, accessed September 17, 2014), 5.21.

36. Chen, *Sishubianyi*, 11.20.

37. After translating this passage Bryan W. Van Norden adds, "This chapter is an illustration of the need for 'discretion' in applying propriety and righteousness (4A17). One must be willing to adapt to particular circumstances, as when Shun ignores the ritual of informing his parents when taking a wife (5A2), but one must not compromise what is important, so Mengzi refuses to sacrifice his integrity to take an official position (3B1)." Bryan W. Van Norden, trans., *Mengzi: With Selections from Traditional Commentaries* (Indianapolis: Hackett Publishing, 2008), 159.

38. Mark Csikszentmihalyi interprets this differently: "In the *Mengzi*'s examples, the comparison is not unconnected to the external situation, but neither is it a calculation of the relative consequences of actions. Instead, it is a weighing of internal reactions to the alternative." On the same page, he continues, "While an 'exigency' is action justified by an end, these examples describe an internal weighing

of cultivated dispositions." *Material Virtue: Ethics and the Body in Early China* (Boston: Brill, 2004), 124.

39. The "Wudi Benji" 五帝本紀 chapter in the *Shiji* 《史記》 contains a more explicit example of weighing values in the context of *quan* 權 (discussed in chapter 6). In this passage Yao deliberates between giving the throne to his immoral son (but rightful heir) and giving the throne to Shun, an unrelated but morally upright person. The goods that come into play in this circumstance are not exactly the same as those in passages such as *Mengzi* 4A17; however, this passage illustrates the notion of weighing something like the livelihood of other people against the livelihood of one's family or the tradition of passing the throne on to one's son.

This may not fit squarely with any form of consequentialism in the Western philosophical tradition, but a few scholars have argued for the relevance of consequentialism in early Confucian thought. Philip Ivanhoe discusses "character consequentialism" in "Character Consequentialism: An Early Confucian Contribution to Contemporary Ethical Theory," *Journal of Religious Ethics* 19.1 (1991): 55–70. For a critique of this position see Manyul Im, "Mencius as Consequentialist," in *Ethics in Early China: An Anthology*, edited by Chris Fraser, Dan Robins, and Timothy O'Leary (Hong Kong: Hong Kong University Press, 2011), 41–63. Im argues for what he calls "objective act consequentialism" in the *Mengzi*.

For a relevant discussion of this in the Western philosophical discourse see C. A. J. Coady, *Messy Morality: The Challenge of Politics* (Oxford: Oxford University Press, 2008), 80–81.

40. Chen, *Sishubianyi*, 5.22.

41. This is reminiscent of the discussion of *budongzhixin* 不動之心 in *Mengzi* 2A2.

42. Fredrick Mote speaks about Lou Shide 婁師德 (630–699), who took a similar stand: "Lou Shide of the Tang was a man whose forbearance was so great that he did not approve of a man's so much as flickering an eyelid if someone spat in his face. When someone asked him, 'Do you mean you would just wipe it off and nothing more?' he replied that he would not even bother to wipe it off; he would be so unmoved that he would let the spittle dry by itself." Frederick W. Mote, "Confucian Eremitism in the Yuan Period," in *The Confucian Persuasion*, edited by Arthur F. Wright (Stanford, CA: Stanford University Press, 1960), 226.

43. In commenting on this passage Cheng Yi 程頤 states, "Bo Yi understood the constant [principles] of ritual propriety, but did not understand the changing [principles] of the sages" 伯夷知常禮而不知聖人之變. Zhu Xi 朱熹, ed., *Lun–Meng Jingyi* 《論孟精義》, *Lunyu Jingyi* 《論語精義》, *Wenyuange Sikuquanshu Dianziban* 《文淵閣四庫全書電子版》 (Hong Kong: Digital Heritage Publishing, accessed February 3, 2015), 3A.35. In the subcommentary of the *Sishumengyin* 《四書蒙引》, *bian* 變 ("changing") in this phrase is glossed as *yongquan* 用權 ("employing discretion"). Cai Qing 蔡清, ed., *Sishumengyin* 《四書蒙引》, *Wenyuange Sikuquanshu Dianziban* 《文淵閣四庫全書電子版》 (Hong Kong: Digital Heritage Publishing, accessed February 3, 2015), 20.32.

In other words, according to Cheng Yi, Bo Yi understood standard action but did not understand how to employ discretion. In translating this passage in the *Mengzi*, Van Norden adds, "Bo Yi's disdain to do what is wrong is a manifestation of the heart of righteousness. Consequently, he is highly commendable. However, he has extended his heart too far." Van Norden, *Mengzi*, 49. Mote quotes an alternative opinion expressed in poetry by later Confucians: "Bo Yi looked upon the whole world/ And wished that all men might stand with him. / I say that it was Liuxia Hui who was narrow-minded; / Let the reader himself find my reasons for saying so." Mote, "Confucian Eremitism," 226.

44. This suggests a weak theory of virtue interentailment.

45. Van Norden defines *zhi* 智 as, "A virtue that consists of understanding the other virtues, being a good judge of the character of others, and skill at means-end deliberation." Van Norden, *Mengzi*, 207. Edward Slingerland explains it in part as "an ability to accurately perceive situations." Slingerland, *Analects*, 243.

46. The *Shuoyuan* explicitly ties the terms together: "One who is skillfully wise measures those in authority and weighs the circumstances" 智者度君權時 (9.1/67/ 22); as does the "Sangfu Sizhi" 喪服四制 chapter of the *Liji* 《禮記》: "*Quan* 權 is skillful wisdom" 權者知也. The character *zhi* 知 is often used interchangeably with *zhi* 智; and the "Sangfu Sizhi" chapter actually switches between both. See *Liji* 50.2/174/22. Kwong-loi Shun also provides a useful discussion of *zhi* 智 in *Mencius and Early Chinese Thought*, 66–71. Shun explains that *zhi* 智 is about developing proper aims or directions (*zhi* 志) in the heart, which are then maintained in situationally sensitive ways. This aligns quite closely with Chen Tianxiang's theory where internally the moral agent is fixed on the Way, and externally he adapts to circumstances. Lee Yearley talks about *zhi* 智 as "intelligent awareness" and explains, "People who fully manifest intelligent awareness operate neither from rules, habits, nor temperamental dispositions. Rather they operate from a delicate appreciation of and judgment upon the particular circumstances they face." Lee H. Yearley, *Mencius and Aquinas: Theories of Virtue and Conceptions of Courage* (Albany: State University of New York Press, 1990), 71. The idea of hitting the mark (*zhong* 中), which appears in *Mengzi* 5B1, is also commonly used in talking about *quan* 權. For instance, Zhu Xi says, "*Quan* 權 is to hit the mark in every situation. If [one] does not hit the mark, then he did not employ *quan* 權" 權是時中，不中，則無以為權矣. *Zhuzi Yulei*, 989.

47. *Zhuzi Yulei*, 989–990.

48. Cross reference *Mengzi* 4A9, 2B12, and *Liji* 4.34/26.

49. *Mengzi* 3B9, discussed in chapter 4, is an excellent example of this.

50. Wang Chong 王充 (27–c. 100 CE) in the "Daning" 答佞 chapter of the *Lunheng* 《論衡》 makes a relevant comment: "The worthy has [his version of] *quan* 權; and the sophist has [his version of] *quan* 權. After the worthy employs *quan* 權, there is proper accord. When the sophist employs *quan* 權, [he] also goes against the standard, [however] afterwards there is iniquity. This is because the worthy's

quan 權 is done for the sake of serving [a ruler] or for the sake of the state, while the sophist's *quan* 權 is done for the sake of himself or for the sake of his clan" 賢者有權，佞者有權。賢者之有權，後有應；佞人之有權，亦反經，後有惡。故賢人之權，為事為國；佞人之權，為身為家. *Lunheng* 33/163/12–14.

51. *Mengzi* 4B29. Note the familiar theme of drowning.

52. A similar passage in the *Kongcongzi* 《孔叢子》 (2.3/12/27) states that Shun and Yu "believed the minuteness of their own sentiment to be incomparable to the greatness of communal rightness" 以為私情之細，不如公義之大. See also *Xunzi*, 2/8/16: "The exemplary person enables communal rightness to trump personal desire" 君子之能以公義勝私欲也.

53. Chen, *Sishubianyi*, 5.21–22. The *Shuoyuan* (5.2/31/29–32/1) also makes a related point: "The virtuous teaching of the humane person is as follows: [When] sincerity and commiseration take shape internally, [and when] the utmost compassion forms within, [it] cannot stop at one's heart; because of this, in ordering the world, one [acts] as if saving someone from drowning" 仁人之德教也，誠惻隱於中，悃愊於內，不能已於其心；故其治天下也，如救溺人.

54. Contemporary Chinese intellectuals sometimes describe this continuing commitment as *youhuan yishi* 憂患意識, or "concern consciousness." See, for instance, Peimin Ni, "Practical Humanism of Xu Fuguan," in *Contemporary Chinese Philosophy*, ed. Chung-ying Cheng and Nicholas Bunnin (Malden, MA: Blackwell, 2002), 281–304.

55. Zhu Xi, in part, comments on 5A7 saying, "If Yi Yin sought out Tang by cooking he would have certainly disgraced himself; [and so] how would he have rectified the world" 若伊尹以割烹要湯，辱己甚矣，何以正天下乎? *Sishu Zhangju Jizhu*, 311. *Mengzi* 5A8 and 5A9 are similar stories about Kongzi and Boli Xi not humiliating themselves. In commenting on 5A9, Zhu Xi quotes a previous scholar, "When the ancient sages and worthies had yet to encounter the right times they engaged in lowly and debased occupations, and had no shame in doing it" 古之聖賢未遇之時，鄙賤之事，不恥為之. *Sishu Zhangju Jizhu*, 313. Mengzi makes the point in 5B5 that one can take a lowly position if one needs to get by but that it should not be done for the sake of hoping to go beyond that station.

2

The Invulnerability of Integrity

CONTEMPORARY SCHOLARSHIP

[He] who lets himself in for politics, that is, for power and force as means, contracts with diabolical powers and for his action it is not true that good can follow only from good and evil only from evil, but that often the opposite is true.

(MAX WEBER, *Politics as a Vocation*)[1]

IN THE PREVIOUS chapter, I articulated several views about the invulnerability of integrity as found in early Confucian texts and in commentaries written by interpreters of early Confucian texts. I demonstrated that commentators such as Zhu Xi 朱熹 (1130–1200) argued for invulnerability on the basis of the *dao* 道 encompassing both standard ethical action and exigent action. The purpose of this chapter is to situate the vulnerability of integrity within contemporary discourses on ethics. I begin by examining the vulnerability of integrity within the broader field of philosophical ethics. In these discussions, the vulnerability of integrity often falls under the rubric of value conflicts, moral remainder (residue or distress), and dirty hands. This chapter begins with an overview of this discourse and serves as a backdrop for discussing how contemporary scholars of Confucian ethics discuss the vulnerability of integrity. The second part of this chapter explores the scholarship of contemporary interpreters working with Confucian material. In this section I highlight approaches that argue for the invulnerability of integrity, in particular an approach called the "harmony thesis." I demonstrate the ways in which the harmony thesis dovetails on the arguments for invulnerability described in chapter 1, and I suggest at least one fruitful way of continuing to develop the harmony thesis in contemporary philosophical terms that are supported by early Confucian texts. In short, I suggest that contemporary scholars can develop this position by arguing for a distinction between "responsibility to others" and "responsibility for acts," where sages remain responsible *to* people, especially those they harm, but are not responsible *for* the unfortunate results of value conflicts. Finally, I explore three shortcomings of the harmony thesis and outline the ways in which subsequent chapters of this book explore these shortcomings.

Value Conflicts, Moral Remainder, and Dirty Hands

Value conflicts occur when two or more meaningful aspects of a situation appear incompatible to a moral agent who feels compelled to tend to each aspect. Said differently, value conflicts are circumstances where two or more meaningful things are threatened and a moral agent fears he or she may not be able to tend to each value. The value conflicts I am particularly interested in occur when a moral agent can tend to some values but only at the expense of others and when the values at stake are seen by the moral agent to be worthy of great concern.

Value conflicts are not necessarily dilemmas (although some scholars use the terms interchangeably). Dilemmas are situations where no one course of action emerges as the best or least bad course of action. In dilemmas, the moral agent is left without sufficient action guidance to suggest one course of action over another course of action. Dilemmas might be seen as one kind of value conflict or as being distinct from value conflicts. Taking them as distinct, the key difference between dilemmas and value conflicts is that a moral agent finds sufficient action guidance in value conflicts, despite the fact that the result of his action entails harming some value or leaving some value unfulfilled. For some time, scholars have debated the existence of dilemmas.[2] Since the early Confucian texts tend to deal with value conflicts rather than dilemmas, I do not explore the contours of the debate about the possibility of dilemmas, except to mention that early Confucian texts do not explicitly rule out the possibility of dilemmas. Instead, I discuss two significant distinctions as they relate to value conflicts.

The first distinction is between epistemic and ontological value conflicts. With ontological value conflicts, the situation is such that the moral agent cannot realize or refrain from harming one or more values involved in the situation, despite his skill in moral reasoning or his attainment of virtue. In ontological value conflicts, the conflict is, ultimately speaking, irresolvable because the world exists in a way that does not rule out value conflicts. Epistemic value conflicts are irresolvable only because the moral agent lacks the necessary skills or virtues to adjudicate between competing values (although, practically speaking, a moral agent may find an epistemic value conflict is actually an ontological value conflict once he or she gains the necessary skills or virtues to grapple with the conflict). Many contemporary scholars of Confucian ethics argue for the existence of epistemic value conflicts and against the existence of ontological value conflicts.[3] As such, any value conflict is only an "apparent" value conflict. Said another way, all value conflicts are resolvable. If one could reason through the situation more effectively, or respond to a situation the way a sage would respond, the value conflict would be resolved (although some resolutions may still entail a moral remainder, as discussed later).

A second significant distinction with regard to value conflicts is the distinction between action guidance and agent assessment. Action guidance refers to the cues a system of ethics provides a moral agent in determining what he or she should do in a given situation. Agent assessment refers to how the moral agent should evaluate himself in light of how he responded to a situation (including not only a judgment about the rightness of his actions but also a judgment about the appropriateness of his feelings during and after the situation). Since, for the purposes of this project, dilemmas are less relevant than value conflicts, action guidance is also less significant than agent assessment. In other words, the authors of early Confucian texts, for the most part, assume that their systems of ethics provide sufficient action guidance in value conflicts. In the views represented in these texts, there is an appropriate thing to do in just about any circumstance (even if the appropriate thing might entail doing something bad or leaving another value unfulfilled). The problem I am concerned with is assessing the moral standing of the agent involved in a conflict.

At the same time, contemporary scholars, as we will see, argue for a variety of positions. Some see no meaningful distinction between action guidance and agent assessment. In these views, as long as the agent operated in accordance with the actions recommended by the ethical system, the agent's moral standing was not compromised. For others, action guidance and agent assessment can sometimes come unhitched. The moral agent may recognize the right thing to do but assess himself as doing something worthy of regret or even guilt.[4] Both positions agree about action guidance but disagree on agent assessment.

It is also worth noting that even if value conflicts are resolvable, many scholars agree that there may still be some kind of lingering feelings associated with the difficulty of resolving the conflict. In irresolvable value conflicts, these lingering feelings are more intense.[5] Ethicists refer to these feelings as moral "remainder," "residue," or "distress."[6] The problem that value conflicts create, in terms of agent assessment, is determining how much, if any, distress a moral agent should feel. Put simply, the views of contemporary scholars can be put on a spectrum that depicts the appropriate degree of moral residue and ranges from no moral distress to a great deal of moral distress. For the purposes of this chapter, I depict two points along this spectrum—one that calls for a lesser degree of distress and another that calls for a greater degree of distress. A useful way of conceptualizing these views is to discuss the former in terms of "grief" and the latter in terms of "guilt."

Some scholars argue that grief is the only remainder a skilled moral agent should feel after confronting a value conflict. In this view, once all values are taken into consideration and a decision is made, a conscientious moral agent will take the right course of action. The moral agent might feel some grief in leaving an obligation undone, not fulfilling all values, or harming some value, but in these cases there are no "violations" of morality.[7] The action is seen as unequivocally right in ethical theories that reduce all values to a common value (as in most forms of consequentialism). Nonetheless, these scholars tend to recognize the appropriateness of feeling grief, especially in situations where one's actions harm other people. Kai Nielsen, for instance, describes the status of the moral agent who is compelled to choose the lesser of two evils. He explains,

> Where whatever we do or fail to do leads to the occurrence of evil or sustains it, we do not do wrong by doing the lesser evil. Indeed, we do what, everything considered, is the right thing to do: the thing we ought—through and through ought—in this circumstance, to do. In doing what we ought to do, we cannot . . . do wrong. We may do things that in normal circumstances would be horribly wrong, but in these circumstances . . . they are not, everything considered, wrong.[8]

According to Nielsen, the moral agent who chooses among the best of his bad options does the right thing. He does what he "through and through ought" to do. Nielsen does not stop his analysis here, however. He recognizes that the conscientious moral agent will feel troubled by making a difficult decision. Nielsen even says that the moral agent will go beyond feeling "merely saddened."[9] Nielsen describes moral distress as feelings of "anguish" and "remorse," and he adds that, "psychologically speaking, it is perhaps inevitable that [the moral agent] will feel guilty."[10] Importantly, though, Nielsen adds this qualification: "But to *feel* guilty is not necessarily to *be* guilty."[11] The distinction between feeling guilty and being guilty is significant. In Nielsen's view, value conflicts inevitably give rise to feelings such as guilt. However, as far as agent assessment is concerned, although a conscientious moral agent should perhaps feel some kind of anguish, he should not see his course of action entailing any wrong, and as such he is not actually guilty. C. A. J. Coady, borrowing from Frances Kamm, suggests the language of "acting wrongly" versus "wronging someone" in making sense of this distinction.[12] A conscientious moral agent who confronts a value conflict that can only be resolved by wronging someone should in fact feel anguish over the harm entailed in the situation. In short, he has wronged someone. At the same time, when all things are taken into consideration, he did not act wrongly. Indeed, he did the best he could. As such, he should still feel something for the harm entailed in the situation even if he did not act wrongly. As Thomas Hill astutely notes, feelings of sorrow in value conflicts are to be "expected in moral agents who have the aims, attitudes, commitments, and value judgments that they should have."[13] In other words, the values of a moral agent are reflected in the moral agent's sensitivity to someone else's harm.

In explaining these situations, Nielsen uses the language of "feeling guilty."[14] My sense, though, is that views such as Nielsen's are better represented with the language of "grief." Grief, in short, is the anguish that one should feel when some value is harmed or unfulfilled. So one can, and should, grieve when someone else is wronged, for instance, particularly if one was personally involved in wronging someone. However, in this view, one should not feel guilty if the decision was made conscientiously. Guilt, in these circumstances, is an inappropriate feeling because one is in fact not guilty and cannot be guilty if one has done the right thing. Grief, in this sense, is appropriate moral distress, but guilt is not appropriate moral distress.

On the end of the spectrum that calls for a greater degree of moral distress are the views of scholars that argue that the conscientious moral agent, after confronting a value conflict, should feel guilt or regret.[15] One of the more prominent advocates of this position is Michael Walzer. In 1973 Walzer wrote an article titled "Political Action: The Problem of Dirty Hands."[16] In the article, Walzer argues that involvement in politics entails confronting value conflicts.[17] Adjudicating between values requires making compromises, and while most compromises can be understood in terms of mutual concessions interested parties make in order to further some common good, other situations are more extreme. These situations call for compromise in the sense of harming or demeaning something valuable. Walzer explains these "dirty hands" situations, using the example of a moral politician making a backroom deal with a dishonest ward boss, as follows:

> We know [the moral politician] is doing right when he makes the deal [with a dishonest ward boss] because he knows he is doing wrong. I don't mean merely that he will feel badly or even very badly after he makes the deal. If he is the good man I am imagining him to be, he will feel guilty, that is, he will believe himself to be guilty. That is what it means to have dirty hands.[18]

There are several things worth noting in Walzer's description of dirty hands. For one, Walzer stresses the contradictory element involved with dirty hands situations—the moral agent does the right thing by knowingly doing wrong. In later work elaborating on the concept, Walzer describes ambivalent feelings such as "hesitation" associated with dirty hands, as well as the "paradoxical" nature of such action.[19] Indeed, Walzer wants to go beyond even assessing different aspects of the moral agent and claim that it is possible for the same action to be right and wrong at the same time. In this light, while the moral agent might conscientiously choose the best or least worst among his options, he must also acknowledge that he has done wrong.

Perhaps more relevant is Walzer's assessment of the moral agent. In his view, the moral agent will not only *feel* guilty but will also see himself *as* guilty. The moral agent, as such, will have to "repent and do penance" for the wrongdoings.[20] Walzer goes on to say that "we want a record of his anguish."[21] In this theory of moral distress, the moral agent should not simply feel grief for the harm brought about by the situation. Instead, the moral agent should actually feel guilt.

Walzer's notion of dirty hands seems the most applicable to value conflicts where one must choose between bad and worse. An argument can be made, however, for the appropriateness of guilt, or an associated feeling like regret or remorse, in a broader set of value conflicts. Where one is compelled to choose between good and better, for instance, leaving some good unfulfilled, or one is compelled to choose between obligations, leaving some obligation undone, one can still assess oneself as guilty of doing something not quite right. Bernard Williams discussed the latter in terms of the "ought that is not acted upon."[22] According to Williams, the moral agent should feel the need to take "reparatory action" in situations where he is unable to meet all obligations.[23] This is particularly true in situations where the moral agent's past actions led to the value conflict. Williams draws on this idea in developing his notion of "agent-regret." In short, agent-regret is a first-person desire for a situation to have been otherwise (where "first-person" entails the feeling of regret arising because of one's causal role in the situation; an external observer might feel regret but not agent-regret).[24] Agent-regret is an inevitable part of value conflicts, even in unfortunate situations where one's past actions did not generate the conflict. Sharon Bishop makes a point similar to Williams, noting that "morality does not turn off once one decides which claim is more pressing at the moment."[25] Following Bishop, guilt is particularly appropriate to feel in situations where the values in conflict are directly connected to people rather than abstract entities.[26]

For Walzer, Williams, and Bishop, feeling guilt or regret in value conflicts is a marker of a conscientious moral agent. The moral agent, in other words, does what is right by choosing the best of his options; however, utilizing a phrase developed by Margaret Urban Walker, a conscientious moral agent understands that his "responsibility outruns control."[27] In other words, the moral agent realizes that he is responsible for the unfortunate results of his choices. Walzer explains this in the case of a moral politician: "[The moral politician's] willingness to acknowledge and bear . . . his guilt is evidence, and it is the only evidence he can offer us, both that he is not too good for politics and that he is good enough."[28] If the moral politician did not feel guilty, then he would not be a conscientious moral agent. His recognition of his wrongs enables him to fittingly perform the role of a politician. He makes hard decisions and accepts responsibility for the wrong they bring about, and if unwilling to accept that responsibility he would neither be a good politician nor a conscientious moral agent. With reference to Walzer's moral politician, Bishop states, "I suspect that we prefer having politicians who have the capacity to dirty their hands, but who also have the capacity to recognize and acknowledge that they have done wrong, and that this acknowledgement transforms them so that they take their duties more seriously."[29] For Bishop, feeling guilt is a marker of the seriousness with which the politician performs his role. Harming values one might have otherwise protected is cause for serious penance, and the possibility of "redemption," according to Bishop, can serve as a strong motivator to continue to appropriately perform one's role.[30]

To make sense of the conflicting nature of doing right while doing wrong, Coady suggests the notion of "noble corruption." An act made in an irresolvable value conflict is noble because "its motivation is not private benefit" and given the circumstance it is the appropriate thing to do; however, it is also corrupting because it compromises the integrity of the moral agent.[31] In this view, the intent of the moral agent is preserved while other aspects of the agent are marred.

Contemporary Scholars of Confucianism on Value Conflicts and Moral Distress

Contemporary scholars of Confucianism take a variety of positions regarding value conflicts and moral distress in Confucian texts. Unfortunately, relatively few scholars describe their position in much detail. Nonetheless, a dominant paradigm among scholars is that value conflicts are only epistemic and that the only appropriate remainder is grief. Stephen Angle, while speaking primarily about Confucianism in the twelfth to sixteenth centuries, articulates this view most clearly. Angle, in short, argues for the "situation-specific harmonization of all values in a manner that honors the importance of each distinct value."[32] To explain his view, which is shared by several other contemporary scholars, I employ the term "harmony thesis."[33]

In contrast to views that reduce all values to a common value when adjudicating value conflicts, or views that create a ranking of values—trading off the less significant values for the more significant ones—the harmony thesis advocates maximizing each value "relative to the possibilities afforded by the situation."[34] In articulating this, Angle uses a metaphor of making soup. He explains,

> It is certainly true that a cook needs to take into account the amounts of pepper, broth, and so on in his soup as he decides how much salt to add.

His goal, though, is an appropriate saltiness—the perfect contribution to the overall harmony—rather than maximizing the amount of salt he can put into the soup without compromising the other ingredients. Once he finds the harmony, we are not tempted to say that some saltiness was sacrificed in order to preserve the right amount of pepper.[35]

According to Angle, the skilled cook does not exhaust every possible ingredient when making soup. Rather he brings some of each ingredient together in order to cook the best soup possible. In terms of value conflicts, the moral agent, like the cook, realizes some of each value in creating a harmonious solution. While a situation may limit the possible ways of realizing values, the agent with a creative "moral imagination" will find ways to "maximally realize all relevant values."[36] Angle illustrates this with passage 5A3 in *Mengzi* 《孟子》.

In 5A3, Mengzi is asked why the sage-king Shun 舜 appointed his morally defunct brother, Xiang 象, ruler of an area in the kingdom. Mengzi's inquisitor is particularly troubled because Shun had punished other people (some by death) for engaging in activity similar to the activity of Xiang. Perplexed by Shun's actions, Mengzi's inquisitor asks, "Is this indeed how a humane person behaves? When it comes to others he punishes them, but when it comes to his brother he makes him ruler" 仁人固如是乎？在他人則誅之，在弟則封之？ In response, Mengzi explains how a humane person will love his brother, adding that if the humane person were in the position of king, he would in fact seek to give his brother a noble position in the kingdom. Mengzi does not stop there, however. He goes on to explain that Xiang's position, while noble, was actually constricted by the officials Shun arranged to assist Xiang. Xiang had no real power in his position to harm the people living in the area. Xiang's enfeoffment (*feng* 封) was also a banishment (*fang* 放); Shun's gift of love was at the same time a punishment. In Angle's view, Shun's solution is harmonious because it honors each of the values at stake in the situation—the treatment of one's brother, the treatment of criminals, and the king's concern for the people in the kingdom. Angle goes on say that the value conflicts involved in the situation were "imaginatively resolved without regret and without the perceived forgoing of any genuine value."[37]

It is worth noting that Angle's interpretation is well supported by several traditional commentators. In remarking on *Mengzi* 5A3, for instance, Zhu Xi quotes an earlier commentator, stating, "[This passage] explains how the sage does not cast aside familial kindness for the sake of public justice, and [how the sage] does not harm public justice for the sake of familial kindness. In Shun's treatment of Xiang, [we see] the utmost humanity and the consummation of justice" 言聖人不以公義廢私恩，亦不以私恩害公義。舜之於象，仁之至，義之盡也.[38]

Following interpreters such as Zhu Xi, neither public justice nor familial kindness are sacrificed or traded off; humanity and justice are each tended to and realized.

While Angle recognizes that moral remainder is seldom mentioned in the passages he interprets, he stresses the role of grief in tending to certain value conflicts. A harmonious solution, in Angle's view, may still involve pain, specifically in situations of suffering or loss.[39] As such, even the sage will, and should, feel grief. The world is such a place that suffering and loss are inevitable. The sage may find himself in unfortunate situations where maximizing the relevant values entails some kind of harm to himself or others (Angle uses the example of having to choose between feeding one's elderly parents or feeding a stranger, for instance). In these situations the sage does the right thing and is grieved by the pain entailed in the situation. Angle endorses negative emotions such as grief and sadness as long as they are not assessments of the agent.[40] In other words, the sage never "regrets" his choices.[41] He does the right thing given the context and does not wish he had acted in some alternative way. In Angle's view the sage is never marred. Stated most directly, "For sages, there are no tragic dilemmas."[42]

Several other contemporary scholars subscribe to versions of this harmony thesis.[43] Kam-por Yu, for instance, reads the *Zhongyong* 《中庸》 as advocating a kind of value "pluralism." Yu contrasts this view with "moderatism" and "internalism."[44] Moderatism takes right action as the middle point between extremes. Internalism calls for a correct internal state, which then ensures proper external conduct. Pluralism, on the other hand, "sees ethical thinking not only as a choice between good and evil, but also a choice among various goods."[45] While Yu is not clear about the degree to which these are mutually exclusive ways of dealing with value conflicts, he does see value pluralism as the superior mode of dealing with value conflicts in the Confucian tradition. Similar to Angle, Yu argues that multiple values exist and that these values cannot be reduced to each other. He also argues that the sage gives each value "due recognition."[46] As such, Yu explains that the sage finds a way of doing the right thing without violating any "moral constraints."[47] In this light, the sage should never feel guilty.[48] Henry Rosemont states the issue in stronger terms. In discussing value conflicts in early Confucian thought, he explains, "[It] is not simply that the early Confucians explicitly *denied* that there were any actual moral dilemmas. On the contrary, the textual evidence all goes to show that they never even *entertained* the idea of genuine conflict involving moral questions, and we must therefore conclude that the concept of moral dilemmas does not play a role in the Confucian moral theory of human action."[49]

In a recently published article, Sungmoon Kim addresses the problem of dirty hands in an early Confucian context. Through a reading of *Mengzi* and

Xunzi 《荀子》, Kim argues that dirty hands problems such as those articulated by Walzer are precluded from early Confucian thought. This is in part because early Confucians did not distinguish between ethical virtues and political virtues. Kim states, "[No] early Confucian was persuaded that a political leader must sometimes do the wrong thing in order to do the right thing. In their minds, if the political actor is a truly moral person, he can never do genuine wrongdoing even in the critical political moment."[50] In building this argument, Kim describes a kind of "Dao absolutism" where paradigmatic figures bend the rules in exigent situations, but they do this in accord with the *dao* 道 and for the sake of upholding the *dao* 道. As such, while their actions may seem problematic, given their motives and their capacity for moral discretion (or *quan* 權), their actions are not in fact wrong. Kim uses the example of Zhou Gong's 周公 seemingly inappropriate behavior in governing the Zhou dynasty. In applying his theory of *dao* 道 absolutism Kim concludes, "Therefore, even when Zhou Gong was bending the rules of ritual propriety, his hands were never made dirty. In the end, his moral integrity remained untarnished."[51] According to Kim, when confronted with difficult moral situations, sages and paradigmatic figures such as Zhou Gong are virtuosos who do not "engage in internal struggle."[52]

All of the theories advocated by these contemporary scholars claim that value conflicts are only apparent or epistemic. Ultimately speaking, values do not conflict. Yet only sages can reason through difficult situations. Those who have not attained sagehood might occasionally, or even often, get things right, but non-sages lack the moral imagination of the sage. The sage exercises his moral imagination by taking into account each value at stake in a situation and by realizing the constraints a situation places on each value. The sage harmonizes a plurality of relatable, but not reducible, values in doing the right thing. Like Shun, he gives honor to each value. At the same time, grief and sadness are real possibilities for a sage. Pain is an inevitable experience of life, and sometimes moral decision-making should leave behind a feeling of grief. This grief, however, should not extend to regret. A sage does not wish he had acted in some alternative way or second-guess his decision. In light of the broader philosophical discourse mentioned earlier, the harmony thesis fits comfortably among theories advocated by scholars such as Kai Nielsen. The conscientious moral agent should feel sad in the right circumstances, but he is not guilty. He should feel grief, but he should not feel remorse. The harmony thesis denies a gap between action guidance and agent assessment in the sense that if one does the right thing he should then assess himself as being right. The harmony thesis is also in contrast with dirty hands theorists such as Michael Walzer who argue that value conflicts can lead to situations where doing the right thing can mar the moral agent such that he not only feels guilty but is in fact guilty.

When we compare the harmony thesis with theories of invulnerability discussed in the previous chapter, we see several similarities and differences. Like Zhu Xi and Chen Tianxiang 陳天祥 (1230–1316), the harmony thesis portrays a sage whose integrity is invulnerable to value conflicts. The sage is one who reasons properly, and even in difficult situations the sage emerges untainted. While all theories remain open to the possibility of (or even actively encourage) grief, the sage, in these views, should never feel guilt or regret. At the same time, within these similarities there are also significant differences between the theories advocated by Zhu, Chen, and Angle. Angle argues for invulnerability based on the creative imagination of the sage to find innovative ways of maximizing all relevant values in a given situation. Chen argues for invulnerability based on establishing a firm internal commitment to remain upright, thereby allowing for actions that externally seem to deviate from the standard. In this regard, Chen fits into Kampor Yu's internalist category (and it is also worth noting that Zimo 子莫 in *Mengzi* 7A26 fits into Yu's moderatist category).[53] Finally, Zhu advocates invulnerability based on the mutually dependent nature of the standard (*jing* 經) and exigent (*quan* 權). In Zhu's view, the standard and the exigent are like a person's left and right foot—both are necessary for following the correct path, or *dao* 道.

In some regards, the variation between traditional theories of invulnerability and the harmony thesis is based on different conceptions of *quan* 權. For Chen and Zhu, *quan* 權 is about determining situation-specific actions that deviate, or at least seem to deviate, from the accepted standard but still accord with the *dao* 道. For Angle, *quan* 權 is about balancing the plurality values involved in the situation. In short, traditional interpreters tend to foreground their concern with the normative force of their rules or social conventions (i.e., *li* 禮), while harmony theorists tend to see this concern as one of the many that come into play when confronting difficult scenarios. Yet despite these differences, there is room for synthesis. The notion of according with the *dao* 道, stressed by traditional interpreters, can certainly be understood in terms of harmonizing the many values that come into play when confronted with a difficult moral situation. The harmony thesis, as such, can largely accommodate Zhu Xi and Chen Tianxiang's theories. Additionally, the harmony thesis can be adjusted to recognize the higher value placed on following social conventions. In this light, the harmony thesis provides a theory consistent with traditional interpretations but cast in contemporarily relevant philosophical terminology.

Developing the Harmony Thesis

The harmony thesis can be developed by more fully exploring the nature of grief as the sage's moral distress in apparent value conflicts. In this regard, the philosopher Mark Wilson provides a useful distinction between "responsibility *to* others" and "responsibility *for* acts."[54] Wilson, speaking primarily about unfortunate situations where the moral agent unintentionally harms someone, suggests that we reconceptualize the notion of responsibility as it relates to culpability. Rather than seeing responsibility simply as culpability we can also see responsibility as a concern engendered by a causal relationship. In other words, when we unintentionally harm someone we should not assess ourselves as responsible *for* an unethical act, but we should see ourselves as responsible *to* the person suffering. Wilson explains this as follows: "If the question is, can we be held *accountable*, praised or blamed, for involuntary or accidental acts, the answer is an unequivocal no. . . . But if the question is, on the other hand, are we *responsible to* such acts and events, and more importantly to the others who are affected by these acts, the answer is an unequivocal yes."[55] Stated in general terms, we have obligations to tend to the suffering of others.

Wilson, however, stresses that the responsibility we have to those who we unintentionally harm extends beyond our prima facie obligations to tend to the suffering of others. Our actions have placed us in a special relationship with those now suffering; if we had done things differently, this person or these people would not be hurting. While we should not blame ourselves for having done something morally wrong, we cannot simply tend to, or grieve for, the suffering of these people as we would normally tend to, or grieve for, the suffering of others whose suffering we did not cause. In describing this relationship Wilson states, "To say, in response to any action, 'I did not mean to,' implies 'But *I did*.' . . . The 'I did' reveals acutely the relationship between the agent and the action in question, a relationship that cannot be washed away by the qualification that one 'did not mean to.'"[56] The "I" involved in the phrase "I did not mean to" is significant for Wilson. We cannot distance ourselves from the ill effects of our actions simply because we did not intend to harm someone. Instead, we should see ourselves involved in a new relationship, one that "demands emotional and reflective action."[57]

The kind of emotional and reflective action called for by the new relationship will vary according to the circumstance. Slightly modifying one of the examples Wilson uses, we might examine a professional baseball player who hits a fly ball only to have it land on a young child in the stands, harming the child such that he needs to go to the hospital. Such a baseball player may have previously hit hundreds of fly balls without hurting anyone. But this time, there happened to be a child where the ball fell. In Wilson's view, this baseball player should not be judged as having done anything unethical in hurting the child (it is not as if he hit the ball with the intent of harming the child). At the same time, however, a virtuous baseball player would feel bad about causing the injury. This feeling of grief comes, not because of culpability in an unethical act, nor simply because the baseball player has a duty to care for those who are suffering, rather it springs from the causal relationship that the baseball player has with the now-suffering child. In looking at this closer we might see that everyone who witnessed the event has some (however minor) obligation to tend to the child (this might involve calling the paramedics, providing first aid, trying to calm the child down, sitting quietly so others can do their job, etc.), but the baseball player has an additional set of obligations born of the unfortunate act. Practically speaking, fulfilling these obligations might entail a sincere note or gift sent to the child, or perhaps a visit to the hospital. Indeed, these are obligations that are fitting for someone in this special relationship but not necessarily fitting for those who happen to simply witness the event.

Wilson goes on to explain that we should even find something lacking in an agent who does not grieve nor feel an extra set of obligations to care for someone whose suffering he caused. This judgment, though, does not stem from an evaluation of the action that caused the suffering; instead it stems from what Wilson calls "the character of response."[58] In other words, an agent that unintentionally causes someone harm should have the kind of character that recognizes his responsibility to those he has harmed. An agent who does not tend to these responsibilities is blameworthy for being an unresponsive, and irresponsible, agent. He is still not, however, blamed for the harmful act.

Before discussing the applicability of Wilson's distinction in terms of the harmony thesis, I should note that Wilson does not employ his distinction in the context of value conflicts. In other words, Wilson's primary concern is with situations of bad moral luck where an agent unintentionally harms some other person or people. Value conflicts, as I have discussed them here, involve intentionality.[59] The baseball player that hits a fly ball into the stands only to have the ball strike a young child is quite different for Wilson than someone having to choose between harming their father and harming a stranger's child. In the latter case the agent is largely aware of the results of his actions before the moment of choice, whereas in the former case the agent discovers the ill-effects of his choice as his actions unfold. Since Wilson does not explore value conflicts, it is difficult to say whether or not he would see his distinction applicable in these cases; nevertheless, given the harmony thesis articulated by contemporary scholars of Confucianism, Wilson's distinction between responsibility *to* others versus responsibility *for* acts seems quite fitting.

The root of the word "responsible" is "to respond," and in many respects Confucian ethics is about a character of response.[60] Human beings are partially constituted by a complex web of relationships, and a moral person will strive to cultivate these relationships. A central part of the process of cultivation is learning to respond to those others related to oneself. The idea of harmony (*he*和) discussed in the early texts often appears in a context of response.[61] The

Yijing 《易經》, for instance, utilizes imagery of birds finding their young at night by describing how cranes cry out in order to get their young to "respond" (*he* 和) to them (*ming he zai yin qizi hezhi* 鳴鶴在陰，其子和之). Xu Shen 許慎 (ca. 58 CE–147 CE), in one of the earliest Chinese dictionaries called the *Shuowen Jiezi* 《說文解字》, simply glosses *he* 和 as "answering each other" 相應也.[62] In this light, and in a very practical sense, harmony is about an appropriate response to one's surrounding relations.

Texts such as the *Zuo Zhuan* 《左傳》 stress that harmony is not about dissolving differences for the sake of unity; rather, harmony entails maintaining difference and even opposition in the context of response. The annals from the twentieth year of the reign of Zhao Gong 昭公 (522 BCE) recount how a minister named Yanzi 宴子 explained the difference between harmony and conformity (*tong* 同) when ministers respond to their superiors:

[Qi] Gong said, "Only Ju, [a minister,] harmonizes (*he* 和) with me."

公曰，唯據與我和夫。

Yanzi responded, "Ju conforms to you; but how does he harmonize with you?"

晏子對曰，據亦同也，焉得為和。

[Qi] Gong asked, "Is there a difference between harmony and conformity?"

公曰，和與同異乎。

Yanzi responded, "There is. Harmony is like a thick soup. Water, fire, vinegar, meat-paste, salt, and plum seasoning are used to cook the meats. It is brought to stew with firewood, with the cook blending each part. [He] brings the ingredients together by taste—adding where insufficient and thinning it out where excessive. The ruler eats it, and it calms his mind.

The relationship between the ruler and his ministers is like this. If the ruler considers something permissible, but there are impermissible aspects, the minister presents him with these impermissible aspects and thereby creates a permissible [action]. If the ruler considers something impermissible, but there are permissible aspects, the minister presents the ruler with the permissible aspects, and removes that which is impermissible. As such, the process of governing is peaceable and the people are not disturbed, leaving them without a mind to contend [with each other].

. . . But [your minister] Ju is not like this. If you consider something permissible, Ju simply says it is permissible. If you consider something impermissible, Ju simply says it is impermissible. This is like using water to add to [the flavor] of water; who would be able to enjoy such a dish? Or if the Qin and Se zithers only played one note, who would be able to enjoy such sound? The improper nature of conformity is precisely like this.

對曰異。和如羹焉。水火醯醢鹽梅，以烹魚肉。燀之以薪，宰夫和之。齊之以味，濟其不及，以洩其過。君子食之，以平其心。君臣亦然。君所謂可，而有否焉，臣獻其否，以成其可。君所謂否，而有可焉，臣獻其可，以去其否。是以政平而不干民、無爭心。。。今據不然。君所謂可，據亦曰可。君所謂否，據亦曰否。若以水濟水，誰能食之？若琴瑟之專壹，誰能聽之？同之不可也如是。[63]

In this passage, Yanzi explains that proper response is a kind of harmony. Rather than always agreeing with one's superior, the appropriate thing to do is to sometimes critique one's superior for the sake of arguing for a more permissible form of action. What we learn from this passage is that harmony is about ministers appropriately responding to the actions and ideas of their superiors. We might also surmise that from the perspective of the ruler, harmony entails heeding the criticism of a minister when offered appropriately.[64] Stated in more general terms, harmony is about each person properly responding to each other in their particular role. The minister's role is to respond to his ruler. When those actions and ideas are good, he responds with affirmation; when they are not good, he responds with criticism. The ruler's role, in relation to his ministers, is to be receptive to criticism. From this passage we also learn that harmony is about bringing different things together by means of what one contemporary scholar calls "cooperative opposition." As opposed to "antagonistic opposition," cooperative opposition entails an openness to conflicting views rather than a suppression of conflict.[65] Difference, in terms of cooperative opposition, is viewed as an asset that enables the cooking of soup rather than "using water to add to [the flavor] of water" or having all musical instruments play the same note. With regard to the harmony thesis, there are several parallels between it and this passage. For instance, they both advocate the preservation of differences (either preserving the expression of different views or different values), they give each difference due attention, and they both argue that differences can be brought together to contribute to an ideal outcome. Indeed, Angle constructs his soup metaphor from the imagery of this passage in the *Zuo Zhuan*.[66]

Other early Confucian texts stress the notion of proper response and harmony in the context of ritual (*li* 禮) and musical performances (*yue* 樂). One of the first passages in the *Liji* 《禮記》, for instance, emphasizes, "Without ritual the relations between rulers and ministers, higher-ranking and lower-ranking officers, fathers and sons, as well as older brothers and younger brothers will

not be settled" 君臣、上下、父子、兄弟，非禮不定.[67] And in the open-
ing chapter of the *Analects* (1.12), Kongzi's disciple You Ruo 有若 explains, "Of
the functions of ritual, harmony is most highly valued" 禮之用，和為貴. The
"Yueji" 《樂記》 chapter of the *Liji* argues that good musical performances are
essential in educating people in proper interaction. At one point it states,

> Music is played in the ancestral temples because when rulers and ministers
> as well as well as higher-ranking and lower-ranking officers hear it there
> are none that will not then be harmonious and reverent. When the old
> and young hear it in village and clan gatherings there are none that will
> not then be harmonious and concordant. When fathers and sons, as well
> as older brothers and younger brothers, hear it at home there are none that
> will not then be harmonious and devoted to each other.

> 是故樂在宗廟之中，君臣上下同聽之則莫不和敬；在族長鄉里
> 之中，長幼同聽之則莫不和順；在閨門之內，父子兄弟同聽之
> 則莫不和親。[68]

Passages such as this one stress the importance of music in role performance.
When people hear good music they are inclined to perform their roles appropriately; they harmonize and accord with each other. This happens in part, the
"Yueji" explains, because people, like musical instruments, are agents of response.
When one string of a lute is plucked, other similarly tuned strings vibrate in
response. Similarly, when we come into contact with something or someone, we
are stirred to response. The "Yueji" explains that musical performances are rooted
in these responses. Its opening lines state,

> The origins of musical sound stem from the mindful hearts of people.
> When this mindful heart is moved, it is because external things cause it
> to be so. When external things agitate it to the point of movement, [this
> movement] then takes shape in the form of vocalized sound. Sounds
> respond to each other and generate variations in sound. When these varia-
> tions are organized they are called musical sound. When musical sound is
> taken and theatrical instruments such as spears, shields, plumes, and ban-
> ners are added, it becomes musical performances.

> 凡音之起，由人心生也。人心之動，物使之然也。感於物而
> 動，故形於聲。聲相應，故生變；變成方，謂之音；比音而樂
> 之，及干戚羽旄，謂之樂。[69]

Musical performances can inspire people to be good or bad. "This is why," the
"Yueji" goes on to explain, "the early kings were careful with what agitated

them" 是故先王慎所以感之者.[70] According to the "Yueji," the musical performances that inspire people to be bad are rooted in interactions that generate bad
responses. The "Yueji" states, "Decadent sounds agitate people and their rebellious *qi* 氣 responds to it. Their rebellious *qi* 氣 then takes shape, and licentious
musical performances arise" 凡姦聲感人，而逆氣應之；逆氣成象，而淫
樂興焉. Conversely, good musical performances are rooted in positive interactions. "Upstanding sounds agitate people and their cooperative *qi* 氣 responds.
Their cooperative *qi* 氣 then takes shape, and harmonious musical performances
arise" 正聲感人，而順氣應之；順氣成象，而和樂興焉.[71] These musical
performances then lead to situations within countries that are either ordered (*zhi*
治) or chaotic (*luan* 亂). In a more general sense, the "Yueji" goes on to claim that
this notion of response is a part of the larger nature of the world. It states, "With
sound and response there is interaction. The perverse, the wicked, the crooked,
and the upright; each tends toward its corresponding group. In looking at the
patterning of all things in the world, each reacts in accordance with its category"
倡和有應。回邪曲直，各歸其分；而萬物之理，各以其類相動也.[72]
Response, in the view of the "Yueji," is a natural part of the world.

The notion of *ren* 仁, arguably the cardinal virtue of Confucianism, is also
about relatedness and response. *Mengzi* 2A6 explains that all human beings have
innate responses when confronted with the suffering of others. When we see someone about to be harmed, Mengzi explains, we "all have a heart that [feels] alarm
and compassion" 皆有怵惕惻隱之心. Good people cultivate these responses,
and bad people stamp them out. Indeed, one way of explaining the character 仁
is as an ideograph that combines the characters 二 (two) and 人 (person), giving
the character 仁 the meaning of "two people," or, in more interpretive terms, "the
connection that exists between two people."[73] *Ren* 仁, as such, is entailed in being
human, and it is in this light that several early texts play on the semantic relationship between *ren* 仁 and "human being" (*ren* 人), since both characters share the
same pronunciation from at least the late Han (c. first century CE).[74] For these and
other reasons some modern-day scholars translate *ren* 仁 as "humanity."

What we find in these examples is that many of the central concepts of early
Confucianism are about response in the context of relationships. We learn to
appropriately respond to other people and other things in a world where being
human means living in a situation of constant interaction. We are responsible to
others in several senses. At a minimum, we, human beings cannot but react to
things that "agitate" (*gan* 感) us. Normatively speaking, our relationships will
determine the kind of response we should offer. Practices such as rituals and good
musical performances teach us of our response-abilities within our relationships.
They train us to make appropriate responses, and they teach us to be responsible
to other people and other things in the world. In short, from an early Confucian

perspective, being "responsible to" someone or something is about learning to "respond to" that other person or thing.

Passage 4B29 in the *Mengzi* summarizes these ideas nicely. It also highlights the way in which early Confucian texts argue that our relationships will determine the kind of responsibilities we have to other people. In this passage, Mengzi explains the difference between the actions of early sage-kings such as Yu 禹 and Ji 稷 in comparison with the actions of Yan Hui 顏回. Yu is purported to have lived in a time of great floods, and Ji is purported to have lived in an era of famine. Both labored so intensively for the kingdom that they barely spent any time at home. Yan Hui was Kongzi's most advanced disciple. In contrast to Yu and Ji, Yan Hui largely removed himself from society and kept to his studies. Mengzi explains why both groups of people, despite such different actions, are worthy of admiration.

> Yu and Ji lived in an orderly age. They walked past the doors to their homes several times without entering [because they were hard at work]. Kongzi praised them as worthies. Yan Hui lived in a chaotic age. He lived in a narrow alley, had only one bowl to eat with, and one cup to drink with. Most people could not endure his worries, [yet] Yan Hui did not alter his [path to] joy. Kongzi [likewise] praised him as a worthy. Mengzi added, "Yu, Ji, and Yan Hui [followed] the same *dao* 道. When Yu reflected on those drowning in the world, it was as if he drowned them himself. When Ji reflected on those starving in the world, it was as if he starved them himself. This is why they were so concerned. If Yu, Ji, and Yan Hui were to switch places, they would each have responded in the same manner.

> So now, if people from the same household [as yourself] were fighting, [you should] stop the fight. It is permissible to stop the fight even if [your] hair was down and hat was not firmly tied. But if people from the same village [as yourself, but not from the same household,] were fighting, [and you were to] run out with [your] hair down and cap untied to stop the fight, this is to confuse [your roles]. Even if you were to close your window, [effectively ignoring the argument,] it would be permissible.

> 禹、稷當平世。三過其門而不入。孔子賢之。顏子當亂世。
> 居於陋巷。一簞食，一瓢飲。人不堪其憂，顏子不改其樂。
> 孔子賢之。孟子曰：「禹、稷、顏回同道。禹思天下有溺者，由
> 己溺之也；稷思天下有飢者，由己飢之也，是以如是其急也。
> 禹、稷、顏子易地則皆然。今有同室之人鬬者，救之，雖被髮纓
> 冠而救之，可也。鄉鄰有鬬者，被髮纓冠而往救之，則惑也。
> 雖閉戶，可也。」

There are several significant things worth noting in this passage. First, Yu's concern for the people was such that if any were drowning, it was as if he had drown them himself. Ji's concern was similar for those starving. Yu and Ji see themselves as responsible to others in a way similar to someone who had actually caused the suffering themselves.[75] They worked to save the people as if they had brought about the problem. This passage demonstrates the extent to which, in an early Confucian view, people are responsible to each other. Even though Yu and Ji had no personal role in causing the floods or famine, they labored to save the people as if they did. In considering these responsibilities with regard to Yan Hui, we see that Yu and Ji's responsibilities depended on their role. Yan Hui was not a ruler. He had no position of authority in the government. He lacked a role that called for responses similar to those of Yu and Ji. Indeed, Yan Hui responded to his situation very differently. *Mengzi* 4B29 demonstrates that an appropriate response depends on one's role. Said differently, our responsibilities to others are determined by the relationships we have with them. The responsibilities are "special" in the sense of being particular to the roles we find ourselves occupying in various circumstances. In the case of Yu, he found himself in the role of king, responsible to the entire kingdom. In the case of Yan Hui, he found himself in the role of a disenfranchised scholar, responsible for his own learning. In the case of someone overhearing a fight between two people from his household, he finds himself with the responsibility to stop the fight, even if it entails him rushing out before being properly dressed. However, in the case of someone overhearing a fight between two people not from his household, he does not find himself with the responsibility to rush out and stop the fight. While there are undoubtedly a number of historical factors required for justifying the latter response, Mengzi's point seems to be that each relationship has its own set of responsibilities special to it. In other words, our responses to others should be determined by our relationship with them. Context determines the ways in which our particular responsibilities emerge as special responses in relationships.

Mengzi 4B29 does not explicitly extend the idea of special responsibilities to situations of moral remainder. While Mengzi does assume that someone who harms others has extra responsibilities to respond to that harm, he does not, for instance, say that Yu and Ji grieved over the fact that they could not stop at home while working to order the kingdom. The *Shangshu* 《尚書》, coincidentally, depicts Yu, explaining that he even heard his child crying but did not tend to him because he was so busy laboring to stop the floods.[76] In the context of moral distress, we might think that Yu was faced with a difficult decision but that he made the right choice. In the context of a distinction between "responsibility to" and "responsibility for" we might go on to think that he was still responsible to tend to the unfortunate aspects of his choice. Did Yu grieve over his inability to tend to his family? Did he do anything in response to the harm brought on his family? Mengzi is silent on this point, although his silence may be largely due to the fact that his primary purpose in the dialogue was to stress the range of responses sages take in various situations and not to investigate the ways in which Yu might have harmonized competing values. Taking a closer look at the passage, we see that Yu certainly cared about his family. Mengzi mentions him passing his home to stress the degree to which he dedicated himself. We might also imagine that Yu, in some respects, wanted to stop at home each time he passed. Perhaps Mengzi simply does not mention Yu's imaginative way of resolving this apparent value conflict or his grief in being unable to stop at home. Certainly Mengzi does not preclude such resolutions.[77]

Other passages in early Confucian texts more explicitly take up the issue of moral distress in situations where we have responsibilities to those others we have harmed. Passage 13.18 in the *Analects* raises the issue of how values appear to conflict with each other when one's father steals a sheep. This situation presents a tension primarily between values of filial care (*xiao* 孝) and moral rectitude or uprightness (*zhi* 直, spoken about more generally as justice, or *yi* 義, in related passages). A son should take care of his father, but he should also work to create an upright world. Traditionally it has raised questions about whether or not family members should cover up for each other or report each other to the authorities when unjust acts are done.[78] At first glance *Analects* 13.18 does not seem to address the issue of moral distress, but several other passages in dialogue with it take up the issue in more detail. *Analects* 13.18 reads,

> She Gong said to Kongzi, "In my village there is a person known as Upright Gong. His father illicitly acquired a sheep, and he reported the incident."
>
> 葉公語孔子曰：「吾黨有直躬者，其父攘羊，而子證之。」
>
> Kongzi responded, "My village's notion of uprightness is different from this. Fathers cover up for their sons and sons cover up for their fathers. Uprightness is found in the midst of this."
>
> 孔子曰：「吾黨之直者異於是。父為子隱，子為父隱。直在其中矣。」

Kongzi's response to She Gong is that uprightness is found in the midst of fathers and sons covering up for each other. Indeed, Kongzi seems to reason that covering up for family members is the right thing to do, at least in these kinds of situations. Following this line of thought, several traditional commentators justify Kongzi's position on the basis of *quan* 權, which as we have seen entails a breach of norms or standards that still manage to accord with the *dao* 道.[79] Other commentators explain uprightness on the basis of filial care and mercy (*ci* 慈). Fan Zuyu范祖禹 (1041–1098), for instance, states, "When fathers cover up for sons it is because of mercy; and when sons cover up for fathers it is because of filial care. Merciful fathers and filial sons are the [fundamental] uprightness of the world" 父為子隱則慈。子為父隱則孝。父慈、子孝天下之直也。[80] In this view, uprightness is attained by means of mercy and filial care. As such, neither filial care nor uprightness is lost when family members cover up for each other, because being filial is being upright.

While commentators such as Fan Zuyu do not address precisely how values such as uprightness or justice are tended to, passages from texts such as the *Han Shi Waizhuan* 《韓詩外傳》 address this more directly. At one point, the *Han Shi Waizhuan* states, "If sons cover up for their parents then justice does not attain its rightful place. If rulers punish the unjust then humaneness does not attain its acceptable place. Despite contravening humaneness and harming justice, the model to follow lies in between the two" 子為親隱，義不得正；君誅不義，仁不得受。 雖違仁害義，法在其中矣。[81] This passage, unfortunately, does not say more (other than quoting a line from the *Shijing* 《詩經》). In chapter 5 I explore the ways in which this passage might challenge aspects of the harmony thesis, but, for our purposes here, it serves as an example of early Confucians recognizing that the value of justice is not necessarily attained when sons cover up for their parents. There is some kind of distress involved when people cover up for each other. Justice does not attain its rightful place when sons cover up for their fathers. Interestingly, the *Lüshi Chunqiu* 《呂氏春秋》, usually taken by scholars as a syncretic text, provides a more detailed account of Upright Gong and the way in which the values at stake in this situation might be harmonized. The "Dangwu" 《當務》 chapter recounts,

> In the state of Chu there was someone known as Upright Gong. His father stole a sheep and he reported his father to the authorities. The authorities captured his father and were about to punish him. Upright Gong asked to take his place. As they were about to punish Upright Gong [in place of his father] he told the attendant, "When my father stole a sheep, I reported it; isn't that being trustworthy? When my father was about to be punished, I took his place; isn't this offering filial care? If the trustworthy and filial people of the state are punished, would there be anyone in the state not worthy of punishment?"

> 楚有直躬者。其父竊羊而謁之上。上執而將誅之。直躬者請代之； 將誅矣，告吏曰：「父竊羊而謁之，不亦信乎？父誅而代之，不亦孝乎？信且孝而誅之，國將有不誅者乎？」

> The ruler of Jing heard this, and did not punish him. When Kongzi heard about this he remarked, "Isn't it odd how Upright Gong became trustworthy?

He used his father to make a name for himself." This is why the trustworthiness of Upright Gong is not as good as [simply] being without trust.

荊王聞之，乃不誅也。孔子聞之曰：「異哉直躬之為信也，一父而載取名焉。」故直躬之信，不若無信。[82]

Momentarily bracketing Kongzi's negative judgment of Upright Gong, what we see here is the attempt of Upright Gong to provide an imaginative solution to a complex situation.[83] He reports his father, thereby maintaining his trustworthiness as someone, we might imagine, committed to a sense of justice (*yi* 義). He then takes his father's place as a sign of his filial piety. While Kongzi is critical of the way in which Upright Gong used his father to make a name for himself, we might suspect that Upright Gong took a real risk in taking his father's place. He certainly could have been punished for his father's crime. The significance of this passage is that it demonstrates the ways in which some authors of early texts were attentive to the responsibilities engendered by special relationships created in complex situations. Here we see a son committed to uprightness and filial care.

The fact that Kongzi has a problem with this solution is also worth noting. Should Upright Gong not have reported his father to the authorities? Does Kongzi see an alternative way of tending to the situation—one that involves a harmonious solution where values such as justice are given due attention? A recently discovered text, called the *Nei Li* 《內禮》 suggests an alternative solution. The *Nei Li* parallels portions of early Confucian texts such as the *Da Dai Liji* 《大戴禮記》 and the *Liji* 《禮記》, but it also includes several variations. One portion of the text stresses the way in which sons should serve their parents. It reads,

> In serving [his] parents, the exemplary person [i.e., the filial son] is without personal delights and without personal anxieties. [Rather, if his] parents delight in something, [he] delights in it. [If his] parents are anxious about something, [he] is anxious about it. [If his parents] do what is good, [he] follows it. [If his parents] do what is not good, [he] stops it. [If he] is unable to stop it, [he then] covers up [for his parents] and takes responsibility for the act as if [it] originated with him.

> 君子事父母，無私樂，無私憂。父母所樂，樂之；父母所憂，憂之。善則從之，不善則止之。止之而不可，隱而任之，如從己起。[84]

The final line is the most relevant for our purposes. If the filial son is unable to stop his parents from doing something wrong, he covers up for them and takes responsibility for the act. As such, the son remains filial by protecting his parents, but he also tends to the value of justice. In the context of the *Lüshi Chunqiu's* description of Upright Gong, the problem that Kongzi has with Upright Gong is that his imaginative solution does not properly tend to the value of filial care. Instead of covering up for his father, he turns his father over to the authorities. What if the authorities did not permit Upright Gong to take his father's place? Indeed, he may have taken a real risk in turning his father in, and even if Upright Gong knew he would be allowed to take his father's place, it still seems that Kongzi has a problem with him turning his father in for the sake of establishing his reputation. Perhaps from Kongzi's perspective there was another way to be trustworthy. In light of the *Nei Li*, a more harmonious solution would be for the son to take responsibility for the act and compensate the owner of the sheep or perhaps turn himself in to the authorities of the state.

Not entirely unlike the value conflicts discussed earlier in this chapter, the filial son of a sheep thief finds himself in the unfortunate position of having a special relationship created where he did not want one to be created.[85] He must take care of his relationship with his father, but he must also take care of his new relationship with the wronged party. He takes care of his relationship with his father by covering up for him; at the same time, however, he recognizes the moral distress associated with his actions. He recognizes that he is responsible to the unfortunate results of his choosing to cover up for his father. While he is not guilty of theft himself, he turns himself in as the thief in order to tend to the remaining values entailed in the situation. This kind of son is exemplary (a *junzi* 君子) in the sense of successfully harmonizing the multitude of values at play in the situation. Stated succinctly, the exemplary son accepts responsibility for his father's actions in order to demonstrate his responsibility to the values left lingering when he covers up for his father.

The solution suggested by the *Nei Li* is not without its problems. Does letting the father go unpunished, for instance, truly harmonize all values at stake in the situation? What if the father's actions were worse than steeling a sheep; should a son still cover up for his father?[86] The answers to these questions fall beyond the scope of this chapter. At the same time, however, they are not questions left unconsidered by Confucians. Other early Confucian texts and commentators have dealt with them in a variety of places. For our purposes, these passages demonstrate that the harmony thesis can be used to interpret early Confucian texts and that these texts, or at least portions of them, are amenable to a distinction between responsibility for wrongdoings and responsibility to others harmed by unfortunate acts; that a distinction between grief and guilt is an effective way of making sense of the texts; and that something like a conception of responsibilities born of special relationships can be seen operating in the texts. They do not go so far as to demonstrate that early Confucian thinkers articulated these distinctions or conceptions themselves. A developed version of the harmony thesis is also a continued development of Confucian thought. It provides an explanatory framework for early Confucian thought articulated in a contemporary philosophical sensibility.

The harmony thesis highlights aspects of Confucian thought that stress the kinds of responsibilities we have to each other. In this view, Confucianism is about an art of response, where our responses are determined by the roles we find ourselves occupying in various circumstances. Occasionally we find ourselves confronted with a complex situation. In these situations we employ our moral imagination to harmonize the conflicting values. An imaginative moral agent will be able to reconcile every value, leaving him without any guilt in having done something wrong. This does not mean, however, that the moral agent will not grieve over the harms involved in the difficult decision. This is not because the situation ambiguously suggests a course of right action; rather, taking right action may entail harming some other person or party. The imaginative moral agent sees the grief caused by the harms as not just a sadness born from confronting the harms but as a sorrow born of situations that engender special relationships. The grief, as such, is a moral distress that spurs the moral agent to tend to these special relationships. The moral agent responds to them and cares *for* those he harms even if he is not responsible, morally speaking, for the harms.

A Critique of The Harmony Thesis

While the harmony thesis captures certain aspects of Confucian thought, it neglects other aspects. In this section I raise three points of criticism for the harmony thesis. I briefly expand each point and explain how the following chapters of the book pursue these criticisms in more detail. The first point of criticism is that moral distress is not uniformly portrayed as grief in early Confucian texts. It sometimes extends into regret, where regret means a kind of sorrowful longing for things to be otherwise. Second, early Confucian texts do not consistently adhere to a notion of value harmony. Put in the language of contemporary philosophical discourse, value conflicts, in some early Confucian views, are not simply epistemic; they can also be ontological.[87] Third, since values cannot always be brought into harmony with each other, tragic situations are real possibilities. In other words, early Confucians wrote about moral agents who confronted situations where competing values could not be reconciled. In these circumstances, the integrity of the moral agent is vulnerable to misfortune. Said differently, in tragic situations, the moral agent is compelled to harm some value or leave some value unfulfilled. He may not be guilty of doing something wrong, in a strict sense, but he is forever tied to the unfortunate act. He is connected to it, and it has become a part of him. His integrity, or the way in which his self is composed and connected to others, is vulnerable to tragic circumstances.

Regret can be tied to a feeling of sorrow and a desire that one had done something differently. If, for instance, Upright Gong, as described in the *Lüshi Chunqiu*, had not been allowed to take his father's place, Upright Gong would likely have regretted turning his father in to the authorities. Confucians believe that people should feel regret in situations where they have done something wrong. The sage, according to the harmony thesis, always does what is right. As such, he never wishes that he had taken a different course of action. Following Angle, "[S]ages' reactions never lead to regret."[88]

We might expand the definition of regret, however, beyond a desire to have done things differently. This is to go beyond what we might call a "contrition" model of regret. In line with a broader meaning of the term, regret can also entail a feeling of disappointment and a desire for things to have been otherwise. Regret, in this sense, is not wishing one had performed differently but instead is a frustration or disappointment that the world is such a place that tough choices have to be made and that these choices partially shape the self. We might call this a "lamentation" model of regret. I explore this notion of regret in the next two chapters by investigating accounts of sorrow (*bei* 悲 or *ai* 哀), frustration (*fen* 憤), and resentment (*yuan* 怨) across several early Confucian texts.

I believe that a lamentation model of regret is different from grief as described in the harmony thesis in at least three respects. First, it provides added depth to the sorrow associated with grief. Regret certainly conveys a sorrow over the fact of harm entailed in a difficult situation, and because of one's special role in caus-ing the harm it also recognizes a sense of sorrow that goes beyond a prima facie reaction to another's pain. At the same time, this lamentation model of regret realizes that one's self has been transformed by the unfortunate act. This transfor-mation may (or may not) extend to the realm of guilt, but after these acts the self is never the same.

Second, regret in this sense is a lament that the world is such a place that diffi-cult decisions need to be made. It captures a sense of complaint, frustration, and even protest about the condition of the world. Last, regret keeps the door open for the possibility of contrition. Since very few moral agents are actually sages, decisions are made from perspectives with greater degrees of ambiguity. Regret, in this sense must be a real possibility at least for all non-sages.

In short, the harmony thesis gives up on the language of regret too soon. Stated in the terms developed in this chapter, the harmony thesis does not account for the ambivalence associated with agent assessment. Angle, for instance, states, "[C]lassic Confucian treatments of moral conflicts say little or nothing about the agent's mixed emotions or difficulties."[89] Yet I will show that the many portions of the early texts present moral agents who are quite conflicted. Said somewhat differently, the harmony thesis, with its demand on resolvable dilemmas, can actually create a kind of guilt in its efforts to avoid it. We might call this "under-achiever's guilt" where the possibility of harmony puts inhuman demands on the moral agent.[90]

My second point of criticism with regard to the harmony thesis is that values, as described in some early Confucian texts, are not always harmonizeable. There are situations where regardless of one's moral imagination there are no harmonious solutions. The *Han Shi Waizhuan*, for instance, tells of Shen Ming 申鳴 (fl. 480 BCE), who was known for his filial piety and his ability to manage government affairs. After declining several requests to serve in the government, his father encouraged him to accept a position. He accepts, and excels at, his new role as a leader of the state of Chu's 楚 military forces. When a competing state learns that Shen Ming is a leader of the Chu army, however, they capture his father and threaten to kill him unless Shen Ming defects from Chu and joins forces with them. Shen Ming weeps bitterly before commanding the Chu forces to destroy their enemies. As a result of his choice, his father is killed. While the ruler of Chu rewards Shen Ming for the victory, Shen Ming laments that he could not be both loyal (*zhong* 忠) to the state of Chu and filial (*xiao* 孝) to his father. Shen Ming sorrows over the fact that his actions could not fulfill both values (*xing buliangquan*行不兩全), and then he kills himself. The narrator of the story (Han Ying 韓嬰 c. 200–c. 130 BCE) concludes with a quote from the *Shijing* 《詩經》: "Whether advancing or retreating, there is only obstruction" 進退惟谷."[91] The notion of being in a hard place such that one cannot attend to all relevant values is repeated in other vignettes and other texts. I explore these and other kinds of value conflicts in chapter 5. In chapter 6 I also examine the way in which value conflicts are real for sages and not just those who might lack the moral imagination of the sage.

My final critique of the harmony thesis is that it fails to capture the vulnerability of integrity as described in early Confucian texts. Since values, according to the harmony thesis, are always capable of being harmonized, there is always a solution to every value conflict. A shortcoming, in this sense, is a shortcoming of the moral agent's imagination in harmonizing conflicting values. A cultivated moral agent is consistently able to render himself invulnerable to moral distress beyond grief. As such, one's integrity is always capable of being protected. In contrast with this, I discuss a notion of tragic conflict in chapter 5. In tragic situations the moral agent's sense of self-determination is compromised. In these circumstances, the moral agent cannot emerge without being transformed, and he cannot control the way in which he is transformed. His sense of self, or his character and relations to things around him, is determined by forces beyond his control.

His integrity, as such, is vulnerable to situations where values cannot be harmonized. Yet despite the susceptibility of integrity to tragic circumstances, vulnerability serves to create a more meaningful life and to enrich moral performance. As such, I discuss the value of vulnerability in the final chapter of this book.

Notes

1. Max Weber, *Politics as a Vocation*, translated by H. H. Gerth and C. Wright Mills (Philadelphia: Fortress Press, 1968), 49.
2. In addition to H. E. Mason, ed., *Moral Dilemmas and Moral Theory* (New York: Oxford University Press, 1996), see also Christopher W. Gowans, ed., *Moral Dilemmas* (New York: Oxford University Press, 1987); and Lisa Tessman, *Moral Failure: On the Impossible Demands of Morality* (New York: Oxford University Press, 2015).
3. For an alternative categorization of value conflicts in early Confucian thought see César Guarde-Paz, "Moral Dilemmas in Chinese Philosophy: A Case Study of the *Lienü Zhuan*," *Dao: A Journal of Comparative Philosophy* 15.1 (January 2016): 81–90.
4. For an example of action guidance and agent assessment coming unhitched see Lisa Tessman, *Burdened Virtues: Virtue Ethics for Liberatory Struggles* (New York: Oxford University Press, 2005), 162.
5. These feelings will also differ if the conflict is self-imposed rather than imposed by the conditions of the world.
6. On these terms see Bernard Williams, "Ethical Consistency," in Gowans, *Moral Dilemmas*, 115–137; Ruth Barcan Marcus, "Moral Dilemmas and Consistency," in Gowans, *Moral Dilemmas*, 188–204; Terrance C. McConnell, "Moral Residue and Dilemmas" in Mason, *Moral Dilemmas*, 36–47; and Christopher W. Gowans, *Innocence Lost: An Examination of Inescapable Moral Wrongdoing* (New York: Oxford University Press, 1994), 19, 95.
7. C. A. J. Coady describes a similar position in more detail in *Messy Morality: The Challenge of Politics*. (Oxford: Clarendon Press, 2008), 80.
8. Kai Nielsen, "There is No Dilemma of Dirty Hands," in *Cruelty & Deception: The Controversy Over Dirty Hands in Politics*, edited by Paul Rynard and David P. Shugarman (New York: Broadview Press, 2000), 140–141, italics removed.
9. Nielsen, "There is No Dilemma of Dirty Hands," 139.
10. See Nielsen, "There is No Dilemma of Dirty Hands," page 139 for the language of remorse and anguish; for the remaining quote see page 140.
11. Nielsen, "There is No Dilemmas of Dirty Hands," 140.
12. Coady, *Messy Morality*, 83–84.
13. See Thomas E. Hill Jr., "Moral Dilemmas, Gaps, and Residues: A Kantian Perspective," in Mason, *Moral Dilemmas and Moral Theory*, 189.
14. On a related note, Hill states, "The argument, in sum, is that *feeling bad* about what one has done does not amount to *feeling guilty* in the fullest sense unless it reflects

the *judgment* that one *is guilty*, and Kantians should not judge that conscientious agents who act in practical dilemmas are in fact guilty." "Moral Dilemmas, Gaps, and Residues," in Mason, *Moral Dilemmas*, 187.

15. Some scholars use "regret" the way that I use "grief." Agent regret as discussed by Williams, for instance, seems to be closer to what I am calling grief. Ruth Barcan Marcus, D. Z. Phillips, and H. O. Mounce also use the language of guilt; as cited in Gowans, *Innocence Lost*, 95. Gowans uses the language of culpability: "The morally distressed agent is not only pained at having failed to fulfill a moral responsibility to someone. The agent also feels a sense of culpability, or blameworthiness, for this failure. This feeling is different, of course, from the sense of culpability that arises from the recognition of having failed to do what, all things considered, ought to have been done (on account of maliciousness, weakness, negligence, and the like). But it is a feeling of culpability nonetheless. . . . To sum up, when I speak henceforth of the agents being 'morally distressed' or 'morally disturbed,' I will mean that they are feeling some measure of mental pain in response to the recognition that they have done something morally wrong—not necessarily in the sense of having violated the correct conclusion of moral deliberation but in the sense of having transgressed some moral value, in particular a moral responsibility to someone— and that they feel the need to in some way apologize or compensate to the person for this wrongdoing." *Innocence Lost*, 97.

16. *Philosophy and Public Affairs* 2.2 (1973): 160–180.

17. Walzer actually makes a much stronger claim: "No one succeeds in politics without getting his hands dirty." "Political Action," 164. Then, "It is easy to get one's hands dirty in politics and it is often right to do so," 174.

18. Walzer, "Political Action," 166.

19. Michael Walzer, *Just and Unjust Wars: A Moral Argument with Historical Illustrations* (New York: Basic Books, 1977), 254; Michael Walzer, *Arguing about War* (New Haven, CT: Yale University Press, 2004), 33.

20. Walzer, "Political Action," 167.

21. Walzer, "Political Action," 176.

22. Bernard Williams, *Problems of the Self* (New York: Cambridge University Press, 1973), 175.

23. Bernard Williams, *Moral Luck* (New York: Cambridge University Press, 1981), 74.

24. Williams, *Moral Luck*, 27–29.

25. Sharon Bishop, "Connections and Guilt," *Hypatia* 2.1 (Winter, 1987): 12. Gowans makes a similar point in *Innocence Lost*, 18: "moral demand does not simply disappear every time a more compelling moral consideration comes into conflict with it. A responsibility overridden in deliberation about what to do remains a responsibility."

26. Gowans makes an insightful point in this regard: "A principal though generally unstated reason why opponents of inescapable moral wrongdoing have resisted this idea is that they believe that our ultimate moral responsibility is not to specific persons at all, but to something that in comparison with concrete persons is an

abstraction." He continues, "For example, though it might be thought that Kant, with his emphasis on respecting persons as ends in themselves, would be immune to this objection, he is quite clear that our ultimate moral responsibility is not to persons as such, but to the moral law." *Innocence Lost*, 20–21.

27. Margaret Urban Walker, "Moral Luck and the Virtues of Impure Agency," in *Moral Luck*, edited by Daniel Statman (Albany: State University of New York Press, 1993), 241. Italics removed.

28. Walzer, "Political Action," 167–168.

29. Bishop, "Connections and Guilt," 14.

30. Bishop states, "Redemption is not merely something that transforms the agent and relieves her of guilt, it also gives evidence that a person takes the lives and interests of others seriously and feels badly when he or she has to do something that injures them." "Connections and Guilt," 14.

31. Coady, *Messy Morality*, 91. The notion of "noble cause corruption" is also discussed in police ethics where it is almost always a negative term. See, for instance, John P. Crank and Michael A. Caldero, *Police Ethics: The Corruption of Noble Cause* (Cincinnati: Anderson Publishing, 2000).

32. Stephen C. Angle, "No Supreme Principle: Confucianism's Harmonization of Multiple Values," *Dao: A Journal of Comparative Philosophy* 7.1 (2008): 35–36. He details this view in *Sagehood: The Contemporary Significance of Neo-Confucian Philosophy* (New York: Oxford University Press, 2009), 93–111.

33. My use of "harmony thesis" is different from the view of harmony (where all values are reduced to an ur-value) that Angle critiques in *Sagehood*, 95. For a more in depth discussion on this issue see Lisa Tessman, *Moral Failure*, 31–44. One relevant portion (42–43), drawing on the work of Martha Nussbaum and Christopher Gowans, reads, "To combine Gowans's and Nussbaum's insights, one could say that if the value of an overriding moral requirement can either *substitute* or *compensate* for the value of the overridden moral requirement, then the overridden moral requirement can be fully eliminated; it does not become an impossible moral requirement, and it leaves no moral remainder. When one value *substitutes* for another, there is no unique loss; when one value *compensates* for another, there may be a loss of something unique and irreplaceable, but such a loss is a cost that is to be borne."

34. Angle, *Sagehood*, 99. On page 97, Angle states, "When faced with conflict, one's reaction should never be to simply weigh the value of the opposed values and choose the greater; instead, imagination should lead to a harmonious solution in which all values are honored."

35. Angle, *Sagehood*, 99.

36. Angle, *Sagehood*, 100. For a critique of the idea that it is always possible to find a more creative solution to a value conflict (from a perspective within the Western philosophical tradition) see Thomas E. Hill, "Moral Purity and the Lesser Evil," *The Monist* 66.2 (1983): 216: "Often, no doubt, a wise and diligent search will turn up other options and the apparent problem will disappear. But to suppose that this is

always possible is, I think, an act of faith rather than an inference from observation." Several individuals within the Western philosophical tradition have developed the notion of moral imagination in ways that differ from Angle's use of the term. See, for instance, Mark Johnson, *Moral Imagination: Implications of Cognitive Science for Ethics* (Chicago: University of Chicago Press, 1993).

37. Angle, *Sagehood*, 96.

38. Zhu Xi 朱熹, *Sishu Zhangju Jizhu* 《四書章句集注》 (Beijing 北京: Zhonghua Shuju 中華書局, 2005), 305. Notably, *Xunzi* 《荀子》 2/8/16 takes a different route, stating that public justice should trump personal concerns.

39. In *Sagehood*, page 98, Angle states, "In a manner I will discuss more fully later, when the world is structured in such a way that even the most harmonious possible solution is still one that leaves behind a residue of grief, sages (and the rest of us) should rely on this grief as a spur to imagining ways in which the world can be different—even if the grief is something that we can bear, given the way the world is today."

40. In *Sagehood*, page 247 note 26, Angle quotes Jason Swedene with regard to moral dilemmas: "negative self-assessing emotions ought to be discouraged in favor of emotions such as grief and sadness, which are negative and self-conscious, but not self-assessing."

41. Angle, *Sagehood*, 103.

42. Angle, *Sagehood*, 105–106.

43. In addition to the scholars discussed below see also Robert Eno, *The Confucian Creation of Heaven: Philosophy and the Defense of Ritual Mastery* (Albany: State University of New York Press, 1990), 175–177; David Keightley, "Early Civilization in China: Reflections on How It Became Chinese," in *Heritage of China: Contemporary Perspectives on Chinese Civilization*, edited by Paul S. Ropp (Berkeley: University of California Press, 1990), 21, 32, and 51; and Joseph Chan, "Confucian Attitudes Toward Ethical Pluralism," in *Confucian Political Ethics*, edited by Daniel A. Bell (Princeton, NJ: Princeton University Press, 2008), 115.

44. Kam-por Yu, "The Handling of Multiple Values in Confucian Ethics," in *Taking Confucian Ethics Seriously: Contemporary Theories and Applications*, edited by Kam-por Yu, Julia Tao, and Philip J. Ivanhoe (Albany: State University of New York Press, 2010), 27.

45. Yu, "The Handling of Multiple Values," 28.

46. Yu, "The Handling of Multiple Values," 29.

47. Yu, "The Handling of Multiple Values," 32.

48. It is worth noting that Yu's theory has problems in terms of action guidance. On "The Handling of Multiple Values," page 46, Yu states, "However, I don't expect that those who are seriously interested in solving ethical problems will be entirely happy with the account that I have presented. No clear explanation has been given regarding how we can strike the right balance among multiple views. To this I reply, following Aristotle, by saying that ethics is an art, not a science. We cannot demand greater precision than the nature of the subject allows."

49. Henry Rosemont, "Notes from a Confucian Perspective: Which Human Acts are Moral Acts?" *International Philosophical Quarterly* 16.1 (1976): 57.

50. Sungmoon Kim, "Achieving the Way: Confucian Virtue Politics and the Problem of Dirty Hands," *Philosophy East and West* 66.1 (January 2016): 154.

51. Kim, "Achieving the Way," 166.

52. Kim, "Achieving the Way," 154.

53. For a more contemporary internalist account see Kwong-loi Shun, "Ethical Self-Commitment and Ethical Self-Indulgence," in *The Philosophical Challenge from China*, edited by Brian Bruya (Cambridge, MA: MIT Press, 2015), 185.

54. Mark A. Wilson, "The Emotion of Regret in an Ethics of Response" (PhD dissertation, Indiana University, 2007), 8.

55. Wilson, "The Emotion of Regret," 107–108.

56. Wilson, "The Emotion of Regret," 51–52.

57. Wilson, "The Emotion of Regret," 5.

58. Wilson, "The Emotion of Regret," 107.

59. See Wilson, "The Emotion of Regret," 13.

60. "Responsible," *Oxford English Dictionary*, http://dictionary.oed.com (accessed January 2, 2015).

61. "Harmony" understood as *he* 和 does not necessarily equate with "harmony" in the harmony thesis. For different notions of harmony in Confucian thought see Alan K. L. Chan, "Harmony as a Contested Metaphor and Conceptions of Rightness (*yi*) in Early Confucian Ethics," in *How Should One Live? Comparing Ethics in Ancient China and Greco-Roman Antiquity*, edited by R. A. H. King and Dennis Schilling (Boston: De Gruyter, 2011), 37–62. Li Chenyang has done the most extensive work on *he* 和 in Confucian thought. See *The Confucian Philosophy of Harmony* (New York: Routledge, 2014).

62. *Yijing* 65/78/11. Xu Shen 許慎, *Shuowen Jiezi* 《說文解字》 (Beijing 北京: Zhonghua Shuju 中華書局, 2004), 32. I first saw these passages used in Chenyang Li, "The Confucian Ideal of Harmony," *Philosophy East and West* 56.4 (2006): 583–603.

63. Yang Bojun 楊伯峻, ed., *Chunqiu Zuo Zhuan zhu* 《春秋左傳注》 (Beijing 北京: Zhonghua Shuju 中華書局, 2000), 1419–1420. Hereafter, *Zuo Zhuan*.

64. Harmony often appears in terms of a response, which implies something or someone first performing an action that that generates a response. In this sense, harmony often appears explicitly linked to those in lower-ranked positions responding to those in higher-ranked positions. Those in higher-ranked positions perform actions, which generate responses.

65. Li, "The Confucian Ideal of Harmony," 591.

66. Besides its popularity in discussions about Confucian perceptions of harmony, Angle also quotes it in *Sagehood*, 62–63.

67. *Liji* 1.6/1/16–17.

68. *Liji* 19.28/104/24–25.

69. *Liji* 19.1/98/12–13.

70. *Liji* 19.1/98/16.

71. *Liji* 19.13/101/9–10. Xunzi makes a similar point in *Xunzi* 20/100/4–5.

72. *Liji* 19.13/101/10–11.

73. In the Guodian 郭店 manuscripts the character *ren* 仁 is written as *shen* 身 over *xin* 心; providing an alternative understanding of the character.

74. Axel Schuessler, *ABC Etymological Dictionary of Old Chinese* (Honolulu: University of Hawai'i Press, 2007), 440–441. See also *Liji* 33.7/148/22; 32.14/144/26; and *Kongzi Jiayu* 17.1/34/15.

75. Some commentaries explicitly invoke the language of responsibility by using terms such as *ren* 任, *zhi* 職, and *ze* 責 to explain this passage. See for instance, Hu Guang 胡廣, ed, *Sishu Daquan* 《四書大全》, *Mengzi Jizhu Daquan* 《孟子集註大全》, *Wenyuange Sikuquanshu Dianziban* 《文淵閣四庫全書電子版》 (Hong Kong: Digital Heritage Publishing, accessed September 25, 2014), 8.44.

76. Sun Xingyan 孫星衍, ed., *Shangshu Jinguwen Zhushu* 《尚書今古文注疏》 (Beijing 北京: Zhonghua Shuju 中華書局, 2004), 111–122. Anne Birrell also quotes from the *Shizi* 《尸子》: "For ten years [Yu] did not visit his home, and no nails grew on his hands, no hair grew on his shanks. He caught an illness that made his body shrivel in half, so that when he walked he could not lift one leg past the other, and people called it 'the Yu walk.'" *Chinese Mythology: An Introduction* (Baltimore: Johns Hopkins University Press, 1993), 83.

77. One way later commentators have dealt with this situation is to explain that in tending to the floods, Yu was serving his family. See, for instance, See Hu Guang 胡廣, *Mengzi Jizhu Daquan* 《孟子集註大全》, 8.413–414.

78. On this particular issue see Lijun Bi and Fred D'Agostino, "The Doctrine of Filial Piety: A Philosophical Analysis of the Concealment Case," *The Journal of Chinese Philosophy* 31.4 (December 2004): 451–467; *Dao: A Journal of Comparative Philosophy* 6.1 (March 2007); Tao Liang, "Thinking Through the Notion of 'Relatives Covering for Each Other' in Comparison with 'Covering and Taking Responsibility for Their Faults,'" *Contemporary Chinese Thought* 56.3 (May 2015): 40–66; and Erin M. Cline, *Confucius, Rawls, and the Sense of Justice* (New York: Fordham University Press, 2013), 157–163.

79. See Hu Guang 胡廣, ed., *Sishu Daquan* 《四書大全》, *Lunyu Jizhu Daquan* 《論語集註大全》, 13.23: "Fathers covering up for sons, and sons covering up for fathers is moral discretion" 父為子隱，子為父隱，權也. Wang Huaiyu develops the notion of *quan* 權 in interpreting *Analects* 13.18 in "Piety and Individuality Through a Convoluted Path of Rightness: Exploring the Confuican Art of Moral Discretion via *Analects* 13.18," *Asian Philosophy* 21.4 (November 2011): 411–414.

80. Zhu Xi 朱熹, ed., *Lun-Meng Jingyi* 《論孟精義》, *Lunyu Jingyi* 《論語精義》. *Wenyuange Sikuquanshu Dianziban* 《文淵閣四庫全書電子版》 (Hong Kong: Digital Heritage Publishing, accessed September 25, 2014), 7A24. Greg Whitlock suggests something similar to this as possible Confucian responses to

the situation. See Greg Whitlock, "Concealing the Misconduct of One's Own Father: Confucius and Plato on a Question of Filial Piety," *Journal of Chinese Philosophy* 21 (1994): 118–119. Whitlock abandons these positions for what he calls "Chinese clan rule" as the best justification of *Analects* 13.18. In Chinese clan rule the entire family would handle the matter and would be particularly harsh in situations where an individual's repeated infractions threatened familial and social harmony. See Whitlock, "Concealing the Misconduct," 124–126.

81. *Han Shi Waizhuan* 4.17/30/10.

82. *Lüshi Chunqiu* 11.4/56/6–9. On the relationship between this passage and *Analects* 13.18 see Oliver Weingarten, "Delinquent Fathers and Philology in *Lun Yu* 13.18 and Related Texts," *Early China* 37.1 (December 2014): 221–258.

83. Wang Huaiyu points out that this passage also reveals that the punishment for thievery is death, which may impact how one feels about reporting one's father to the state. Wang, "Piety and Invividuality," 398–399.

84. For the *Nei Li* see Ma Chengyuan 馬承源, ed., *Shanghai Bowuguancang Zhanguo Chu Zhushu (Si)* 《上海博物館藏戰國楚竹書(四)》 (Shanghai 上海: Shanghai Guji Chubanshe 上海古籍出版社, 2004), 219–229. I follow Liang Tao's reading of the text, which entails taking strip eight immediately after strip six; as discussed in Liang, " 'Relatives Cover for Each Other.' "

85. The *Baihutong* 《白虎通》 explains how this relationship extends to the son. In describing the unique relationship between fathers and sons it states, "Rulers do not cover up for their ministers, so why is it that only fathers [should] cover up for their sons? It is because fathers and sons are one body, so their share of glory and shame fall on each other. This is why the *Analects* says, 'Fathers cover up for their sons and sons cover up for their fathers. Uprightness is found in the midst of this' " 君不為臣隱，父獨為子隱何？以為父子一體，而分榮恥相及，故《論語》曰：「父為子隱，子為父隱，直在其中矣」(12/33/16–17; see also 12/32/12–15). In light of this passage, a son is able to take responsibility for his father's misdeed because his father's misdeed is also his misdeed. The son of a sheep thief, as such, is drawn into a special relationship with the owner of the sheep because of his relationship with his own father. Alternatively, Whitlock highlights "the problem of complicity" and suggests that public disclosure by the son would diminish the ability of the father beyond the family. Whitlock, "Concealing the Misconduct," 116.

86. Coincidentally, many commentators downplay the father's crime by claiming that the character *rang* 攘 refers to a theft where the sheep wondered into the family's fold, so the father's crime was one of omission.

87. "Ontological" in this sense does not mean that values inherently conflict. I discuss this in detail in chapter 5.

88. Angle, *Sagehood*, 103.

89. Angle, *Sagehood*, 95.

90. I would like to thank Alexus McLeod for this idea. The term "underachiever's guilt" is my own. Angle recognizes a related problem in *Sagehood*, 17–18.

91. *Han Shi Waizhuan* 10.24/78/6–16.

3

The Sorrow of Regret

*[Kongzi] then cried, saying, "As the lin 麟 is among animals,
I am among humans. The lin 麟 appeared, and then died.
My path (dao 道) has reached [its] end!"*

遂泣曰：「予之於人，猶麟之於獸也。麟出而死，
吾道窮矣。」

*Thereupon [Kongzi] sang out,
"In the era of Yao and Shun, lins 麟 and phoenixes freely
roamed.
But now is not that time; what did [you] come seeking?
Oh lin 麟, oh lin 麟; my heart is aggrieved."*

乃歌曰：「唐虞世兮麟鳳遊，今非其時來何求，
麟兮麟兮我心憂。」

(*KONGCONGZI* 《孔叢子》 2.2/11/15–17)

THE PURPOSE OF this chapter and the next is to describe the role of regret in early Confucian thought. In light of the previous two chapters, I demonstrate that from the perspectives of early Confucian texts, moral distress is best understood in terms of regret. Regret, as I describe it, may or may not entail guilt, but regret is a more apt description of early Confucian views of moral distress than the term grief. While grief is involved in regret, it fails to capture aspects of moral distress such as disappointment and frustration. Regret, as mentioned in the previous chapter, also preserves the possibility of moral agents feeling guilty, which should not be ruled out as a valid feeling, at least for all people who are not yet sages, in early Confucian thought.

In these chapters I am not only concerned with situations previously described as value conflicts. Additionally, I am concerned with situations I refer to as "value defeats." Value defeats are similar to value conflicts such that some value is harmed or left unfulfilled. Value defeats are different from value conflicts, however, because in value defeats the moral agent is not the party choosing which value is harmed or left unfulfilled. Instead, in value defeats a second party (including other human beings or aspects of the natural world), which the moral agent cannot control, determines the situation. In these cases some value either cannot be realized or is harmed despite the effort, hope, or even the expectation of the moral agent. The distinction between value conflicts and value defeats is not as significant as the fact that regret is relevant to both situations. As such, these chapters are about more than an appropriate description of moral distress. Regret, as I discuss it, is applicable to value conflicts, both epistemic and ontological, as well as to value defeats. Regret, from an early Confucian view, is an appropriate feeling when things that we value are harmed.

I begin this chapter by exploring various definitions of the English word "regret" and then situate these definitions in an early Confucian context. I am particularly interested in regret understood as lamenting misfortune or as a response to frustrated desire for the world to be a place were more values might be realized. Regret in this sense entails frustration, sorrow, and resentment. The majority of this chapter explores the frustration and sorrow associated with regret, leaving resentment for the next chapter.

This chapter focuses on Kongzi's attitude toward external goods. I demonstrate that Kongzi is more concerned with external goods than many interpreters realize. He is particularly concerned with gaining a position in society that would allow him to implement broad social change, as well as with establishing a reputation that others in the future might rely on to enact the Confucian *dao* 道. Sorrow over external goods is especially appropriate in situations where external goods benefit people other than oneself.

I spend most of this chapter looking at Kongzi's sorrow as his righteous desires are frustrated. In particular I examine Kongzi's encounter with a *lin* 麟—a mythical deer with a flesh-like horn, sometimes translated as "unicorn" by contemporary interpreters. In early Confucian literature *lin*s 麟 are auspicious signs that good things have happened or are about to happen. A number of texts, for instance, explain that a properly ordered state will have *lin*s 麟 freely residing in its boundaries.[1] *Lin*s 麟, as such, represent the achievement, or the anticipated achievement, of the Confucian *dao* 道. *Lin*s 麟, in this light, are seen as incredibly rare and incredibly desirable animals. Virtuous leaders should want *lin*s 麟 to appear, and, of course, virtuous leaders would not kill a *lin* 麟. In Kongzi's context, however, he finds a dead *lin* 麟; and he sees the death of the *lin* 麟 as a sign that his *dao* 道 has reached its end.

Before concluding this chapter I also build on the accounts of Kongzi encountering a *lin* 麟 to discuss two other vignettes where Kongzi expresses similar sorrow and frustration. These vignettes reveal the ways in which self-realization is predicated on the recognition of others. External goods such as one's position in society and reputation are not only vulnerable to one's circumstances, but they are also worthy of deep sorrow when not achieved.

Characterizing Regret

The English word "regret" originates from notions of mourning and sorrow. More broadly speaking, regret involves feelings of disappointment and a desire for a situation to have a different outcome. From as early as the fourteenth century (in a European context), it entailed disappointment at the death of someone meaningful coupled with a desire for the deceased to remain alive. In a more contemporary context it often involves disappointment in one's own moral failure and a desire to have done otherwise. Regret, in this latter sense, is often linked with contrition. One might regret taking a wrong course of action and thereby feel sorrow and seek to make amends. Regret, in this light, is tied to self-reflection, feelings of guilt (or shame in a Confucian context), and reparation. Early Confucians can be said to advocate a contrition model of regret in situations of moral failure, although these models may vary within the tradition and may be radically different from models found in non-Confucian contexts.[2] If an agent does something wrong he *should* feel sorrow and work to remedy the situation. Kongzi in the *Zhongyong* 《中庸》, for instance, likens the moral agent to the archer, who "upon failing to hit [his] target turns inward and seeks the cause of the failure within himself" 失諸正鵠，反求諸其身.[3] In the *Analects* Kongzi bemoans, "Alas, I have yet to see someone who, upon seeing their faults, is able to turn inward and reproach himself" 已矣乎！吾未見能見其過而內自訟者也.[4] Kongzi's point is not that few people advocate a kind of contrition but rather that few people thoroughly engage in such self-reflection. Here, Kongzi stresses the seriousness with which reproach should be performed. The character *song* 訟, translated in the passage as "reproach," also means "to litigate" in other contexts. There is a way in which the moral agent is able to criticize as well as judge himself and even make amends in the pursuit of something resembling justice.[5]

In addition to regret as contrition, regret can also be understood as a kind of lamentation. It can be a disappointment over the outcome of a situation or a frustration in light of one's inability to realize some value. Regret, in this light, is not necessarily about the disappointment of the moral agent over his performance; rather the moral agent laments the unfortunate results of a situation. Regret expresses a disappointment over the gap between the moral agent's wishes and his experience. It should occur when one's moral expectations are thwarted, particularly when one's expectation of how moral norms should function are not realized.[6]

Regret, in this sense, is used similarly to the way it is employed in contemporary forms of correspondence in parts of American culture. One is invited to an event, where the inability to attend is marked by one's "regret." Some invitations use the form of "regrets only," where the event planner is expecting invitees to attend unless they notify the event planner otherwise. In these cases, assuming one wants to attend the event, regret does not mean wishing that one had done otherwise (although one may certainly come to regret not attending the event in this sense). Rather, regret entails wishing that one *could* do otherwise. It is about wishing that there were in fact another option, or, stated in more ambitious terms, it is about wishing that the world were such a place where one could realize all the values at stake. It is a desire for things to be arranged differently such that another outcome is possible. When one expresses regret in not being able to attend an event, therefore, it is not about a desire to have performed differently. Indeed, these regrets are usually expressed prospectively rather than retrospectively. Stated differently, at the point of responding to the invitation, it is not too late to rearrange things such that one could actually attend the event in question. Regret, however, as used in this light, is about wishing that one could actually attend but recognizing that there are obstacles preventing one from attending (perhaps there are more pressing matters one chooses to attend to, for instance). Regret, as such, is an acknowledgment of misfortune, a recognition that we live in a world where good desires cannot always be realized.

Similarly, in parts of contemporary America, regret is often used to express a kind of sorrow over unfortunate ends. An official announcement from an employer to an employee might in part read, "We regret to inform you that as of the end of the month your employment here will be terminated." Such a statement does not necessarily reflect the employer's remorse over poor choices he or she may have made leading to the employee's termination. Rather, the statement can be read as a kind of wish that they could do otherwise. The employers can be understood as expressing their sorrow over having to fire the employee. They could in essence be saying, "We wish we didn't have to do this, but since the situation is beyond our control, we are left with no better option but to terminate your employment." Assuming the situation to be largely out of their control—perhaps the entire company is going out of business due to circumstances they did not contribute to—regret, in this sense, has a strong social and conciliatory function. It reinforces the value of social norms—that good workers should be gainfully employed—and commiserates with those harmed. Regret, as such, sends a message saying, " I too understand that this should not happen, and I sorrow with you."

Applying this notion of regret to value conflicts and value defeats means that regret is a sorrow and disappointment one feels when things valued are harmed or when values are left unfulfilled. One wishes the world were such a place that one did not have to choose between values or witness the harm of something valued. It entails the frustration of a desire to attend to things of worth. We might continue to expand the notion of regret in the context of correspondence etiquette.

Similar to the way one might regret one's inability to *attend* an event, one might regret one's inability to *attend to* something of significance. In both cases, the moral agent laments his inability to provide the attention due to some other worthy person or thing. His desire to realize something of value is frustrated. To utilize a more colloquial saying, the moral agent is unable to *pay attention*; he is unable to be present or to provide care.

Regret also involves anger and resentment. When a moral agent regrets witnessing the harm of something valuable, he is indignant over the harm. Following Margaret Urban Walker, resentment is an "accusing anger."[7] To the offender it states, "You should know better." To one's peers it invites communal solidarity such that it reaffirms the "boundaries norms define, boundaries that offer protection against harm or affront, as well as the security of membership and reliable expectations in a community of shared normative judgment."[8] As such, resentment is multivocal; it expresses a variety of hopes and feelings to a variety of audiences.

In situations that call for regret, the offender can be other human agents responsible for creating the unfortunate situation or, as is sometimes the case in Confucianism, the divine power that establishes moral norms (usually referred to as *Tian* 天).[9] Regret is a sorrowful complaint that one's righteous expectations were thwarted. It can also be a complaint in the sense of dissatisfaction with the enforcement of moral norms. When significant things are supposed to be protected from harm but turn out to be vulnerable, the moral agent will feel let down, frustrated, and even disillusioned. Regret, as such, is about reexamining the grounds of trust and a search for reassurance that one properly identified moral norms and adequately understood how those norms are enforced.[10] Failing to find sufficient sources of power to enforce moral norms, regret becomes a means of commiserating with others who share similar frustrations. This commiseration extends beyond the event via texts that invite readers to become "literary witnesses" to the misfortune.[11] These stories are meant to invite readers to take part in the outrage and to become a member of the commiserating community. It allows this community to extend itself temporally and spatially.

Regret entails a stronger sense of moral exploration than grief. Whereas grief involves contemplating the value of the loss, regret additionally involves reevaluating one's expectations of how values are protected and how moral norms are enforced. In more extreme cases it may even lead to questioning the validity of norms themselves. Additionally, while grief and regret involve communities, regret involves others not only in the process of mourning but also in the process of reevaluation and understanding. Those feeling regret turn to the community for solace, for reaffirmation that something of value was harmed, and for the space to explore the gap between expectation and experience.

In contemporary Chinese, regret is translated a number of different ways including *wanxi* 惋惜, *yihan* 遺憾, and *houhui* 後悔. These terms capture a range of feelings that fit under general definitions of regret. *Houhui* 後悔, for instance, might literally be understood as remorse (*hui* 悔) one feels after (*hou* 後) an inappropriate act. As such, *houhui* 後悔 fits a contrition model of regret. *Wanxi* 惋惜, on the other hand, might literally be understood as a sorrowful sigh (*wan* 惋) one makes at having to part with something cherished (*xi* 惜). This falls in line with a lamentation model of regret. In early Confucian discourse regret as lamentation is often expressed by terms such as *yuan* 怨, *fen* 憤, *you* 憂, *sang* 喪, *ai* 哀, *bei* 悲, and others.

Sorrowing Over the External Goods of the Confucian Way

Analects 15.19 and 15.20 appear to be in tension with each other. In 15.19 Kongzi states, "The exemplary person is concerned with lacking ability; [he] is not concerned with others not recognizing him" 君子病無能焉，不病人之不己知也. In a general sense, the moral agent should worry about his abilities and not about others appreciating his abilities. This language is repeated in several other passages in the *Analects* including 1.16, 4.14, and 14.30.[12] Passages such as these have led contemporary commentators to argue that Kongzi emphasized cultivating the "internal goods of the Confucian Way." Edward Slingerland, in explaining 4.14 for instance, notes, "Again we see a distaste for self-assertion, self-aggrandizement, and contention for external goods. The gentleman focuses solely upon achieving the internal goods of the Confucian Way. External recognition should and may follow, but is subject to the vagaries of fate and is not inevitable (especially in a disordered or corrupt age), and in any case is not a worthy object of concern."[13] In the view of interpreters such as Slingerland, the moral agent cultivates himself such that he is "indifferent to externalities."[14]

In seeming contrast to this, Kongzi in *Analects* 15.20 states, "The exemplary person worries that he will leave this generation without his name being praised" 君子疾沒世而名不稱焉. When compared with 15.19, this passage argues for a concern over what, in Slingerland's view, are external goods such as the way in which one is perceived by other people. Indeed, the idea of *ming* 名 can be understood as a "reputation" or as "a name," in the sense of "making a name for oneself." In more interpretive terms, *ming* 名 can be understood as the way in which one is remembered—a kind of historical or cultural memory of an individual. While I say more later about the moral agent's motives in being concerned with his *ming* 名, it is worth noting here that one's reputation is dependent on factors beyond one's control. In other words, whether or not the moral agent is remembered is contingent on others recognizing him and creating a means by which he can be remembered (often done through the act of writing or passing on his writings). It is also worth noting that Kongzi assigns value to things dependent on agents other than oneself. Passages such as these challenge Slingerland's assertions about the way in which the moral agent is indifferent to external goods and should lead interpreters to reexamine instances where Kongzi or other paradigmatic figures lament the loss of these values.

Benjamin Schwartz, notably, defines the Confucian *dao* 道 as "nothing less than the total normative sociopolitical order with its networks of proper familial and proper sociopolitical roles, statuses, and ranks, as well as the 'objective' prescriptions of proper behavior—ritual, ceremonial, and ethical—that govern the relationships among these roles."[15] While other contemporary interpreters may not stress the "objective" aspects of the *dao* 道 to the same degree as Schwartz, the notion that the *dao* 道 is connected with factors beyond the internal virtues of the individual is not controversial. The *dao* 道, as such, is vulnerable to a variety of forces. Creating the normative sociopolitical order is predicated on one not only understanding the *dao* 道 but also having a context where it can be realized. Mengzi likened this unto skilled artisans and their tools:

> Mengzi said, "[Even with] the insightful vision of Li Lou or the craftsmanship of Gongshuzi, without using the compass and square, one could not create squares and circles. [Even with] the keen ear of Master Kuang, without using the six pitch pipes, one could not standardize the five notes. . . . This is why it is said that skill alone is insufficient to govern, and model institutions alone cannot enact [government] by themselves.
>
> 孟子曰：「離婁之明，公輸子之巧，不以規矩，不能成方員：師曠之聰，不以六律，不能正五音。。。。故曰，徒善不足以為政，徒法不能以自行。」[16]

According to Mengzi, one needs craftsmanship and tools to construct good objects, and one needs skill and institutional regulations to enact good government. Stated in more relevant terms, Mengzi argues that one needs moral knowledge and governmental authority to bring about the Confucian *dao* 道.[17] If one lacked moral knowledge but had a position of authority in the government, then one would likely create a disorganized society. If one had moral knowledge but lacked a position of authority in the government, then one should not regulate society despite its need to be regulated. In *Analects* 8.14 Kongzi remarks, "[If one] is not in a position of authority, [one] does not make plans to govern" 不在其位，不謀其政. The idea here is that the moral agent should not step beyond the proper bounds of his role. He should not regulate society without authority granted by the state.

Mengzi and Kongzi spoke about these roles, or positions of authority, in terms of *wei* 位. W*ei* 位, for my purposes, are offices in the governing structures of the times granted by those in power. Mengzi and Kongzi traveled to various states in early China seeking an office of authority. Their hope was to gain a post that would allow them to bring about the Confucian *dao* 道. They aimed to first establish the proper sociopolitical order in an area under their authority, and then eventually the rest of the kingdom would see the virtue of their plan and would want it spread to the rest of the kingdom. Kongzi and Mengzi, as described in early Confucian texts, never attain such a position. Several early texts, coincidentally, depict Kongzi's response to these rejections. In one form or another he states, "My *dao* 道 has reached [its] end" 吾道窮矣![18] Indeed, not only is the Confucian Way concerned with external goods, but bringing it to fruition is predicated on a number of external factors. Kongzi, Mengzi, and other early Confucians often lamented their inability to realize the *dao* 道.

They also hoped that if they were unable to transform society in their generation, they might at least be remembered by later generations because of their reputation, or *ming* 名. In this light, later generations would be able to implement the *dao* 道 because of their examples. At the same time, however, these figures also understood that this cultural memory was contingent on factors beyond their control.[19]

Reconciling the tension between passages such as 15.19 and 15.20 is central to making sense of regret and vulnerability. On the one hand Kongzi advocates not seeking after the praise of others. On the other hand he realizes that valuable things are predicated on the actions and attitudes of others. Interestingly, these two passages occur in succession in the *Analects*. For quite some time, traditional commentators have read these passages in light of each other. Hu Guang 胡廣 (1369–1418), for instance, cites several comments that explain 15.19 as expressing a proper concern for one's own self-development and 15.20 as expressing proper concern for the development of others.[20] In other words, the tension between the passages is resolved by explaining the way in which the moral agent seeks a name, not for himself, but for the benefit of other people. In this view, one's *ming* 名 is not simply the way in which one is esteemed by others; additionally, and perhaps more importantly, one's *ming* 名 serves as an example for others to utilize in the process of enacting the Confucian Way. Kongzi in 15.20, therefore, explains that the moral agent is concerned with his *ming* 名 because without it people will lack an example to use in implementing the *dao* 道. As such, there is no conflict between worrying about one's abilities in 15.19 and worrying about establishing a reputation in 15.20.

Building on this, we might see Kongzi's concern with not being remembered as precipitating a kind of grief. In other words, even if we adopt the language of internal and external goods, when things of value are harmed the moral agent ought to feel sorrow. At the same time, however, the sorrow of the moral agent is not a self-centered sorrow. He does not sorrow over the fact that he cannot make a name for himself; rather, he sorrows over the fact that he cannot leave behind a legacy to guide others on the Way. He is motivated, as we saw in chapter 1, out of a concern for others.

In the *Shiji* 《史記》 Sima Qian 司馬遷 (c. 145–86 BCE) builds on the ideas found in *Analects* 15.20 and highlights themes of recognition, disappointment, and frustration. In depicting the later years of Kongzi's life, Sima Qian details Kongzi's sorrow as he realizes he will not be able to implement the *dao* 道.

> The Master remarked, "Alas! Alas! The exemplary person worries that he will leave this generation without his name being praised. [If] my *dao* 道 will not be enacted, how will I reveal myself to later generations?" As such, [Kongzi] used [various] historical records to compose the *Chunqiu*.

> 子曰：「弗乎弗乎，君子病沒世而名不稱焉。吾道不行矣，吾何以自見於後世哉？」乃因史記作《春秋》 21

I discuss the significance of Kongzi composing the *Chunqiu* in the next chapter, but my reason for citing this passage here is that it ties together several of the themes already mentioned. Kongzi's concern with his reputation is set in the context of implementing his *dao* 道 and preserving a model for future generations. He also precedes his remark with a lament.

Interestingly, shortly before this lament, Sima Qian records similar expressions. One of those is purported to occur around 481 BCE when the aristocracy from the state of Lu sponsored a hunt at Daye 大野 (literally, "Great Countryside"). While cutting firewood, one of the participants captured (and killed) an animal that no one recognized. Upon returning from the hunt, Kongzi identified the animal as a *lin* 麟. Sima Qian explains that Kongzi, finding the body of the *lin* 麟, picked it up and remarked, "I am finished" 吾已矣夫!22 He then went on to lament, "My path has reached [its] end" 吾道窮矣! The fate of Kongzi, it seems, is somehow tied to the fate of the *lin* 麟. Several early texts describe the capture of the *lin* 麟 as a significant event in Kongzi's life. Indeed, Kongzi's reaction gives us a window on the notion of regret in early Confucian discourse as it depicts sorrow, frustration, and disappointment in light of Kongzi's righteous expectations. It also leads to Kongzi composing the *Chunqiu*, which, as we will see, involves Kongzi working through a conflict between respect for the authority of the state and leaving a *ming* 名 that future generations can use to bring about the Confucian *dao* 道.

The Capture of the Lin 麟 *and Kongzi's Rejection*

The *Kongzi Jiayu* 《孔子家語》 and the *Kongcongzi* 《孔叢子》 provide the most detailed narratives of the capture of the *lin* 麟.[23] Both accounts situate the story around the year 481 BCE when Shusun, head of one of the powerful families illegitimately controlling the state of Lu, participated in a hunt.[24] The *Kongzi Jiayu* recounts,

> A charioteer of the Shusun clan named Zi Chushang, was chopping firewood in Daye and captured a *lin* 麟. He severed its left front foot, put it in the chariot and brought it back. Shusun considered [the animal] inauspicious, [so he] dumped it outside the city wall and sent men to inform Kongzi saying, "What do you make of a river-deer with a horn?"
>
> 叔孫氏之車士，曰子鉏商，採薪於大野，獲麟焉；折其前左足，載以歸。叔孫以為不祥，棄之於郭外，使人告孔子曰：「有麕而角者何也？」
>
> Kongzi went to see it and said, "It's a *lin* 麟. Why did [it] come? Why did [it] come?" [He then] turned over his sleeve and wiped his face. [He] wept and sobbed until his lapel was wet. Shusun heard about this, and went and retrieved the *lin* 麟.
>
> 孔子往觀之，曰：「麟也。胡為來哉？胡為來哉？」反袂拭面，涕泣沾衿。叔孫聞之，然後取之。
>
> Zigong asked, "Master, why do you cry?"
>
> 子貢問曰：「夫子何泣爾？」
>
> Kongzi replied, "When a *lin* 麟 comes, it is because of a brilliant king. [Yet] this *lin* 麟 appeared at the wrong time and was harmed. I am painfully sorrowed because of it."
>
> 孔子曰：「麟之至，為明王也。出非其時而見害，吾是以傷焉。」[25]

The *Kongcongzi* tells a similar story, but adds a number of significant features. It states,

> One of the soldiers from the Shusun clan's chariot-team reported [to the court], "While Zi Chushang was gathering firewood in the countryside he captured an animal. No one recognized it, but [they] thought it inauspicious, and dumped it at Wufu road."

叔孫氏之車卒曰：「子鉏商樵於野而獲獸焉。眾莫之識，以
為不祥，棄之五父之衢。」

Ran You reported it to the Master, saying, "There is an odd deer with a
flesh-like horn. Is this an ill-omen from *Tian* 天?"

冉有告夫子曰：「有麕而肉角，豈天之妖乎？」

The Master said, "Where is it now? I would like to see it."

夫子曰：「今何在？吾將觀焉。」

So he went; [and while traveling he] spoke with the driver of his chariot,
Gao Chai, saying, "According to Qiu's [i.e., Ran You] report, this must
be a *lin* 麟." When they arrived, he looked at it, and indeed [Ran You's
report] was correct.

遂往，謂其御高柴曰：「若求之言，其必麟乎！」到視之，果信。

Yan Yan asked, "Among flying animals, the phoenix is revered; and among
crawling animals, the *lin* 麟 is revered. This is because they rarely come
around. But since we now see a *lin* 麟, may [I] ask who corresponds with it?"

言偃問曰：「飛者宗鳳，走者宗麟，為其難致也。敢問今見其
誰應之？」

The Master said, "When the king spreads virtue, he brings about an era of
great peace. *Lin*s 麟, phoenixes, turtles, and dragons appear beforehand
as auspicious omens. But now the line of the Zhou is nearly extinct, and
there is no ruler in the world. So who did [it] come for?" [He] then wept,
saying, "As the *lin* 麟 is among animals, I am among humans. The *lin* 麟
appeared, and then died. My path [*dao* 道] has reached [its] end!"
Thereupon [Kongzi] sang out,
"In the era of Tang [Yao] and Yu [Shun], *lin*s 麟 and phoenixes freely
    roamed.
But now is not that time; what did [you] come seeking?
Oh *lin* 麟, oh *lin* 麟; my heart is aggrieved."

子曰：「天子布德，將致太平，則麟鳳龜龍先為之祥。今周宗
將滅，天下無主，孰為來哉？」遂泣曰：「予之於人，猶麟之
於獸也。麟出而死，吾道窮矣。」乃歌曰：「唐虞世兮，麟鳳
遊；今非其時，來何求；麟兮麟兮，我心憂。」[26]

While there are a few conflicting aspects of these stories, they highlight several
similar themes. A *lin* 麟 was captured by someone from the Shusun clan. The

animal was at least severely harmed, if not killed, and then dumped somewhere near the city. At first no one could recognize the animal, including Kongzi's disciples, and Shusun, a person of power in the state of Lu, even considered it inauspicious. Kongzi, however, properly recognized the animal as a *lin* 麟. He laments its harm and feels a personal connection to it.

The *lin* 麟, of course, represents Kongzi. He is the auspicious animal come to usher in the Confucian *dao* 道. Yet no one recognizes his significance. Many of the reigning powers of the time consider him inauspicious. They reject him, and some even try to kill him. The *Kongzi Jiayu* version interestingly recounts that Shusun retrieved the body of the *lin* 麟 after Kongzi identified it. We might read this as the author's attempt to demonstrate the way in which Kongzi will only be recognized after his death.[27]

The *Kongcongzi* telling of the story states that the body of the *lin* 麟 was dumped at Wufu road. Interestingly, one of the few other appearances of Wufu road occurs in the "Tangong Shang" 檀弓上 chapter of the *Liji* 《禮記》 where Kongzi holds part of the funerary rites for his mother at Wufu road. The passage states,

> While young, Kongzi was left fatherless; [and he] did not know the location of his father's tomb. He performed the coffining rites [for his mother] at Wufu road. When people saw this, they all thought he was performing the burial rites. But Kongzi was cautious, using only the implements for the coffining rites. He asked the mother of Manfu, who was from Zou, [about the location of his father's tomb]. [He was] thereby able to perform a joint burial [for his parents] at Fang.

> 孔子少孤，不知其墓。殯於五父之衢。人之見之者，皆以為葬也。其慎也，蓋殯也。問於郰曼父之母，然後得合葬於防。[28]

The *Kongzi Jiayu* and *Kongcongzi* recount a similar story, with the *Kongcongzi* specifically mentioning the rites performed at Wufu road.[29] This story and the story of the *lin* 麟 share a number of commonalities. In both vignettes, something that Kongzi values lies dead in Wufu road. The people come to see it, and they misrecognize what they see.

A passage earlier in the "Tangong Shang" chapter explains that joint burials were not practiced in antiquity (*hezang feiguye* 合葬非古也).[30] In performing a joint burial, it seems, Kongzi is transgressing the norms of antiquity.[31] As I discuss in the next chapter, after the death of the *lin* 麟, Kongzi transgresses social norms by composing the *Chunqiu*. So in these passages we see a theme that occurs at least twice in the literary life of Kongzi—he experiences the loss of something meaningful in the midst of other people who do not fully understand what is going on, and he then does something transgressive; in the case of his mother's burial he violates the norms of antiquity, and in the case of the *lin* 麟 he contravenes the role of a minister. Coinciding with the etymology of regret, Wufu road is the scene of death, mourning, and disappointment.

Shusun, as mentioned, is a usurper of authority. He is not a rightful governor of the state of Lu. This makes his discovery of the *lin* 麟 all the more out of place. *Lin*s 麟 should be seen by good governors. Kongzi states that the *lin* 麟 appeared at an inopportune time (*chu feiqishi* 出非其時). Kongzi, likewise, appeared at a time that was not fitting for someone of his ability. He explains that the *lin* 麟 encountered harm (*jianhai* 見害), and that he hurts (*shang* 傷) too. Kongzi's pain should be understood as a connection he shares with the *lin* 麟. He hurts not only because a wonderful creature has suffered pain but also because he realizes that his fate is connected to the creature's fate—he too will go unrecognized in his life and will even be abused. The *Gongyang Zhuan* 《公羊傳》 goes so far as to connect Kongzi's reaction to the death of the *lin* 麟 to his reaction to the deaths of Yan Hui 顏回 and Zilu 子路. In discussing the capture of the *lin* 麟 it states, "When Yan Yuan died the Master said, 'Alas! *Tian* 天 has forsaken me.' When Zilu died the Master said, 'Alas! *Tian* 天 has cursed me.' When a *lin* 麟 was captured during a hunt in the west Kongzi said, 'My path has reached [its] end!'" 顏淵死，子曰：「噫！天喪予。」子路死，子曰：「噫！天祝予。」西狩獲麟，孔子曰：「吾道窮矣！」[32] The *Gongyang Zhuan* depicts a similar sorrow felt in each situation. It reveals that Kongzi hoped his *dao* 道 would be implemented—either by Yan Hui, Zilu, or himself. Yet in each of these cases his hope was thwarted. His disciples die before gaining the necessary social positions to enact the *dao* 道, and the capture of the *lin* 麟 is a sign of his own impending defeat.[33] Indeed, the *lin* 麟 seems to be a central indication that his *dao* 道 will not prevail, at least not during his lifetime.

In the *Gongyang* telling of the event, death, sorrow, and frustration are tied to *Tian* 天, which in early Confucian texts is often connected to the times, or *shi* 時.[34] The idea of the times or timeliness in early Confucian texts is complicated, and the texts do not present a uniform view. In a general sense *shi* 時, when used as a noun, can be understood as a context for performance.[35] It is often used similar to the way the term "season" is used in English. Each year can be divided into four seasons, for instance, where certain things are done or are not done according to the differences in the times. Most crops are planted in spring, of course, and people tend to wear more clothing in winter.[36] We might build on these basic observations by examining the colloquial phrase "everything has its season." The notion that everything has its season suggests that different contexts (temporal contexts in the case of the four seasons) necessitate different responses. Most crops should not be planted in winter, for instance, and lighter clothing should be worn in summer. Failure to perform according to the season could bring about minor misfortune (feeling uncomfortably hot when wearing winter clothes in the heat) or life-threatening disaster (less food to eat when crops do not grow in the cold).

Coincidentally, several texts state that the *lin* 麟 was captured in the spring of 481 BCE. The hunt (*shou* 狩), sponsored by the Shusun clan, was actually the kind of hunt that should only take place during the winter.[37] Hence, Shusun's insensitivity to the season contributed to the death of the *lin* 麟. While much more could be said about Shusun's untimely performance, the point worth stressing here is that human beings are capable of unseasonal action, and unseasonal action leads to misfortune.

"Everything has its season" can also be applied to situations other than the changing times of the natural world. In a contemporary American context, we might use the phrase, for instance, in speaking about sporting events (e.g., football season), employment (e.g., seasonal jobs), or even clothing style (e.g., this season's fashion). Similarly, *shi* 時 can be broadened to a variety of temporal situations. In early Chinese texts *shi* 時 is often connected with *shi* 世 (one's generation) or *ming* 命 (one's allocated lifespan as well as an allotment of other potential that can be developed throughout one's life).[38] These temporal situations extend from the immediate context one finds oneself in to the entirety of one's life (and in some cases the term has implications beyond one's life). *Shi* 時, as such, is spoken about in immediate as well as long-term senses.

At the same time, it is worth noting that *shi* 時, as suggested by the term "context," also entails a spatial dimension where appropriate action is understood as the recognition of the possibilities afforded by one's location in space as well as time. People living near the ocean have a context different from people living in the mountains even if it can be said that they share the same time. Preparations for winter and the kind of crops that can be planted will vary according to place. More relevant to the discussion here, we might summarize this by saying that *shi* 時 involves a number of factors and varies (sometimes significantly) from time to time, place to place, and even person to person.

Another way of conceptualizing *shi* 時 is in terms of boundaries. *Shi* 時 highlights the limitations or boundaries that curb action in a given situation. Said differently, it highlights the restrictions placed on the kinds of things one can bring about throughout one's life. In this light, early Confucian texts often use *shi* 時 as a descriptive term, where the moral agent who is *shi* 時 is able to recognize the limitations that a situation presents.[39]

The "Xueji" 學記 chapter of the *Liji* casts *shi* 時 in this light by discussing teacher-student interaction. It defines *shi* 時 as teachers providing instruction "in accordance with the student's abilities" 當其可.[40] Following this line of thought, the teacher presents situations that match the potential of a particular learner. The goal of such instruction is not only to create a context where the student maximizes his potential but also a context where the student comes to learn the boundaries of his abilities across a variety of circumstances.

In other texts, the term *zhong* 中 is connected with *shi* 時 where the moral agent who is *zhong* 中 is able to perform appropriately such that he realizes the potential of a given situation.[41] The "Zhongyong" 中庸 chapter of the *Liji* explains that the exemplary person is able to *shizhong* 時中, or to "hit the mark in any situation."[42] He is able to perform according to the dynamics of the circumstances, continually bringing his potential to bear in accordance with the limitations of the times. The title, "Zhongyong," we might even extrapolate as "realizing one's potential in the daily situations of life." The exemplary person, in this view, is one who is sensitive to context and "matches" each situation such that "in situations of wealth and honor, [he] performs in accordance with wealth and honor; and in situations of poverty and debasement, [he] performs in accordance with poverty and debasement" 素富貴，行乎富貴；素貧賤，行乎貧賤.[43] In the view of the authors of the "Zhongyong," the moral agent is able to recognize the possibilities afforded by his contexts and bring himself to bear in those contexts such that the unique possibilities of each circumstance are realized. The grand result, conceptualized in texts such as the "Zhongyong," is that human beings "form a triad with the heavens and the earth" 與天地參; in other words, human beings participate in the creative process of the cosmos by bringing to completion the activities begun by the heavens and the earth (*tiandi shengzhi shengren chengzhi* 天地生之，聖人成之).[44]

Mengzi 5B1, as discussed in chapter 1, lists several profound people of the past that Mengzi viewed as sages. Each one is ascribed a particular characteristic of sageliness. Bo Yi 伯夷, for instance, is "the pure one of the sages" 聖之清者, and Yi Yin 伊尹 is "the dutiful one of the sages" 聖之任者. Kongzi, according to *Mengzi* 5B1, is "the timely one of the sages" 聖之時者, meaning that he is able to take up the characteristics of the others according to the context. Kongzi recognizes the contours of a situation and responds in accordance with the possibilities afforded by his station. Coincidentally, the *Han Shi Waizhuan* 《韓詩外轉》 retelling of this passage casts Kongzi as "the *zhong* 中 one of the sages" 聖人之中者也, thereby highlighting the synonymous usage of *shi* 時 and *zhong* 中 in early Confucian texts.[45] In other places, particularly within the commentarial tradition, *shi* 時 and *zhong* 中 are connected with *quan* 權, which as we saw in chapter 1 involves assessing a situation to determine proper action and often entails breaking with perceived norms. Rooted in the metaphor of weighing objects, these three terms might be systematized such that *shi* 時 is taken as the object in need of being weighed, *zhong* 中 is the spot that brings the fulcrum to balance, and *quan* 權 is the skill of identifying the balancing spot. Cheng Yi 程頤 (1033–1107), quoted in the *Jinsilu* 《近思錄》, employs a similar systemization in discussing the "Zhongyong." He states,

[If you] desire to comprehend the "Zhongyong," there is nothing as [import-
ant] as *quan* 權. [*Quan* 權] entails finding the balancing point (*zhong* 中)
when encountering a situation. However, finding the middle point between
"callusing [one's] hands and feet" and "shutting the door and not going out"
is not [necessarily] the balancing point. If [you] ought to [work to the point
of] callusing [your] hands and feet then this is the balancing point. [If you]
ought to shut the door and not go out then this is the balancing point. In
explaining *quan* 權, it simply means to weigh and balance. What objects are
weighed? Rightness (*yi* 義) and the situation (*shi* 時).

欲知《中庸》，無如權，須是時而爲中。若以手足胼胝，閉
戶不出，二者之間取中，便不是中。若當手足胼胝，則於此爲
中。當閉戶不出，則於此爲中。權之爲言，秤錘之義也。何物
爲權？義也，時也。[46]

According to Cheng Yi, *shi* 時, *zhong* 中, and *quan* 權 (as well as *yi* 義) come
together to produce the appropriate response to a variety of life's situations. The
moral agent is able to weigh the various facets of a situation to determine the
proper balancing point—a point that may entail working so hard for the public good that one's hands and feet become callused (as in the case of Yu 禹) or
closing the door to one's home and shutting oneself off from the outside world
(as in the case of the person hearing people fighting in *Mengzi* 4B29—discussed
in chapter 2). Understanding the "Zhongyong" entails understanding *quan* 權
and these other concepts. In a broader context, we might say that human beings
are presented with a variety of circumstances (*shi* 時). Finding the appropriate
response (*zhong* 中) to the circumstance is predicated on our ability to take into
account the contours of the situation (*quan* 權). While early Confucian texts
rarely employ this degree of systematicity, we can reasonably conclude that all
three terms, as used in the early Confucian texts, involve some kind of recognition or reading of one's context in the act of moral reasoning.

　　Shi 時, *zhong* 中, and *quan* 權 entail an awareness of each circumstance's
boundaries where the moral agent is able to make the most of each situation,
even if it calls for some kind of transgression (*quan* 權). In a sense then, these
terms highlight the descriptive and normative boundaries of a situation.[47] They
draw attention to the possibilities afforded to the moral agent (i.e., the descriptive boundaries) as well as the restrictions a moral agent ought to consider when
taking action (i.e., the normative boundaries). For instance, due to the limits of
Kongzi's time, he was unable to gain a position in society where he could implement the Confucian *dao* 道. There is nothing he could have done differently that
would have yielded a different result because of the limitations of his time.

In speaking normatively, one's situation is informed by guidelines that direct human beings in appropriately relating themselves to each other and to their surroundings. These guidelines are often referred to as ritual (*li* 禮). Agents can choose to perform in accordance with ritual or not in accordance with ritual. When human beings do not perform in accordance with ritual, the result is usually misfortune that ranges from minor inconvenience to utter catastrophe. The "Yueling" 月令 chapter of the *Liji*, for instance, explains what happens when ritual regulations are followed at the wrong time.

> If, in the early month of spring, the summer regulations are followed, the rain will not fall in its proper time, the [leaves on] shrubs and trees will wither and fall to the ground, and [the people in] the state will be in constant fear. If the autumn regulations are followed, there will be pestilence among the people, violent winds will rage, heavy rains will fall incessantly, and various wild shrubs will arise. If the winter regulations are followed, reservoirs will fail to hold the [increasing] water; snow and frost will be severe, and seeds will be unable to be planted.

> 孟春行夏令，則雨水不時，草木蚤落，國時有恐。行秋令則其民大疫，猋風暴雨總至， 藜、莠、蓬、蒿並興。行冬令則水潦為敗，雪霜大摯，首種不入。⁴⁸

While it is worth noting that not all early Confucian texts see such a responsive cosmos, what we see in this passage are the results of transgressing the normative boundaries marked by ritual regulations and determined by the times. Misfortune occurs when normative boundaries are disregarded.

The relationship between the descriptive and the normative boundaries of a situation are significant. Transgressing the normative boundaries affect the descriptive boundaries such that the violation of ritually prescribed actions limit the possibilities afforded by the current situation or future situations. We saw that Kongzi, for example, was limited in his ability to realize the Confucian *dao* 道 because people in power, such as Shusun, violated the rituals appropriate for their stations and their times. Traditional commentators often refer to Kongzi's time as an era where "the ritual system had collapsed, and musical performances were destitute" 禮崩樂壞. In such a time, it was possible for Kongzi to fully comprehend his *dao* 道, but it was impossible for him to actually implement it.

In this light, these passages about the *lin* 麟 are significant for several reasons. For one, they show that someone else's disregard for the normative boundaries of a situation can impact the descriptive boundaries for other people. Those violating ritual norms in Kongzi's time restricted the kinds of things Kongzi could bring about. Kongzi is a timely sage though, because he recognized the possibilities his situation afforded and maximized the values relevant to the circumstance. On the other hand, Kongzi laments the fact that he appeared at an inopportune time (*chu feiqishi* 出非其時).[49]

These passages also show that a moral agent's desire to realize certain values may extend beyond the descriptive possibilities allowed by his circumstance. Kongzi appearing at an inopportune time means that he found himself in a situation where he had the potential to realize more values than the situation allowed. Indeed, he could not bring his full potential to bear. To draw from the imagery of chapter 2, Kongzi is not like a cook who is satisfied with using a limited amount of each ingredient to make his soup. His righteous desires extend beyond the descriptive possibilities of the situation, and so he laments his misfortune. If the descriptive boundaries were different, he would be able to usher in the Confucian Way. We might see Kongzi working through this sorrow by exercising his moral imagination in composing the *Chunqiu*. As such, he finds a way to tend to those lingering values.[50]

Harmony theorists might advocate that Kongzi comes to find satisfaction in this strategy. He understands that the Confucian *dao* 道 will not be realized in his time, but he has faith that it will be realized in later generations. While this line of thought provides a certain degree of explanatory power, it does not fully capture all facets of Kongzi's sorrow. For instance, it disregards the personal nature of his crisis due to the fact that neither he, nor the people he knows and cares about, will live in an ordered age. Additionally, this view does not recognize the ambivalent nature of some early Confucian forms of faith—that while Kongzi may hope that the Confucian Way will be implemented in the future, at the same time he has good reasons to question his faith. As we will see in the chapters 5 and 6, early Confucians recognized the contingent nature of such success. Numerous early texts stress that the sage waits for the right time (characters for "wait" such as *dai* 待 and *deng* 等 are graphically related to *shi* 時).[51] Yet the passages about the *lin* 麟 reveal that waiting can also be frustrating, especially when one will not live to see the end of the wait.

The full *Shiji* account of the capture of the *lin* 麟 provides a useful summary of this discussion by tying together and highlighting many of the issues raised throughout this section. The text reads,

> In the spring of the 14th year of the reign of Duke Ai in the state of Lu there was a hunt at Daye. A charioteer from the Shusun clan named Zi Chushang captured an animal, and considered it inauspicious. Zhongni [i.e., Kongzi] saw it and said, "It's a *lin* 麟." [He] picked it up and said, "The Yellow River does not send forth its map, and the Luo River does

not send forth its writing. I am finished!" When Yan Yuan died Kongzi remarked, "*Tian* 天 has forsaken me!" So when this hunt was held in the west and [he] saw the *lin* 麟 he said, "My path has reached [its] end!"

魯哀公十四年春，狩大野。叔孫氏車子鉏商獲獸，以為不祥。仲尼視之，曰：「麟也。」取之。曰：「河不出圖，雒不出書，吾已矣夫！」顏淵死，孔子曰：「天喪予！」及西狩見麟，曰：「吾道窮矣！」

[In an earlier context, Kongzi] sighed and then lamented, "No one understands me!" Zigong responded, "Why do you say that no one understands you?" The Master replied, "[I] do not resent *Tian* 天, nor do [I] blame people. [I] learn from those below [*Tian* 天,] and [I] strive to attain to what is above [human beings]. Only *Tian* 天 understands me!"

喟然嘆曰：「莫知我夫！」子貢曰：「何為莫知子？」子曰：「不怨天，不尤人，下學而上達，知我者其天乎！」

[Kongzi also previously remarked,] "Among those who would not lower their ambition nor shame themselves were Bo Yi and Shu Qi." [He] said, "Liuxia Hui and Shao Lian lowered their ambitions and shamed themselves." [He then] said, "Yu Zhong and Yi Yi lived in seclusion, [but] freely shared their teachings. Their actions hit the mark of purity, and in banishing [themselves but still teaching they] hit the point of balance (*quan* 權). I am different from these, [however,] there is no position [that I necessarily take] as being permissible or impermissible."

「不降其志，不辱其身，伯夷、叔齊乎！」謂「柳下惠、少連降志辱身矣」。謂「虞仲、夷逸隱居放言，行中清，廢中權」。「我則異於是，無可無不可。」

The Master remarked, "Alas! Alas! The exemplary person worries that he will leave this generation without his name being praised. [If] my *dao* 道 will not be enacted, how will I reveal myself to later generations?" As such, [Kongzi] used [various] historical records to compose the *Chunqiu*.

子曰：「弗乎弗乎，君子病沒世而名不稱焉。吾道不行矣，吾何以自見於後世哉？」乃因史記作春秋。[52]

The *Shiji* version of the capture of the *lin* 麟 begins with a condensed description of the capture followed by a series of laments Kongzi made at various points of his life. It then culminates in Kongzi creating the *Chunqiu*.[53] The movement from the capture to the creation is worth noting. Like Sima Qian (or Sima Tan 司馬談)

does elsewhere, the passage is constructed largely from quotations of other texts. In this case, most of the quotations come from what is now the *Analects*. In the first two quotations Kongzi laments the irresponsive nature of the cosmos ("The Yellow River does not send forth its map") and the death of Yan Hui ("*Tian* 天 has forsaken me"). In the third quote Kongzi stresses that he does not resent *Tian* 天, and that *Tian* 天 alone understands him. The fourth quote highlights Kongzi's flexibility in the context of terms such as *zhong* 中 and *quan* 權, and the final quote expresses Kongzi's concern about establishing a name for himself. Interestingly, the final quote as it appears in the *Shiji* differs from the way it appears in *Analects* by adding the question, "[If] my *dao* 道 will not be enacted, how will I reveal myself to later generations?" The *Shiji* version of the passage ties Kongzi's concern with recognition explicitly to his desire to reveal his Way to later generations. This allows the narrator of the *Shiji* to weave the composition of the *Chunqiu* into his story. Kongzi composes the *Chunqiu* because of his desire to assist later generations.

Sima Qian's style, in particular the minimal narration he provides, makes it difficult to construct a systematic interpretation of the discovery of the *lin* 麟 as depicted in the *Shiji*.[54] Nevertheless, the following explanation is one way to aim for coherency: In confronting the death of the *lin* 麟, Kongzi is reminded of other similar sorrows and frustrations. He previously thought, for instance, that *Tian* 天 would provide signs of the imminent success of the Confucian Way, yet no signs appeared. He thought that Yan Hui was such a sign, but then he died. It is as if *Tian* 天 had forsaken him. Yet he did not resent *Tian* 天, because he knew it understood his righteous desires and that, in the long run, it would help fulfill them. Unlike the model people of the past who deemed only one particular way of achieving their righteous desires to be appropriate, Kongzi had no fixed way. Therefore, when concerned with providing an example for future generations, Kongzi exercised his timely ability to properly assess the situation and composed the *Chunqiu*. This narrative, then, is about Kongzi's sorrow in confronting his inability to realize his desire to reform society but also about his creative response and continued hope in the eventual fulfillment of the Confucian Way.

In his retelling of Kongzi's life Sima Qian stresses the theme of recognition.[55] Kongzi is not only depicted as someone able to identify the *lin* 麟 but also as someone able to identify and explain an odd sheep found buried in a pot, bones from an animal much larger than any known at that time, and a foreign arrow. In most cases he provides not only a name for these things but also a context. The arrow, for instance, Kongzi explains as originating in a series of gifts made by barbarian tribes long before his time. His ability to recognize and interpret is contrasted with the inability of those he encounters to properly recognize and name or interpret things—in particular their inability to recognize the greatness of Kongzi. The irony the text presents to its readers also manifests itself in Kongzi's ability to name things, in contrast with his inability to make a name for himself. Kongzi can name the *lin* 麟 and the sheep, thereby revealing their significance within their contexts; however, Kongzi is unable to disclose his own significance. In his own words, no one recognizes him; only *Tian* 天 understands him. He lacks the kind of deep companionship that allows for full self-disclosure. Kongzi's sorrow is tied to this irony—to the incongruence between his ability to give meaning to various situations and his inability to render himself meaningful even in those situations.

Expressions of Sorrow

The *Kongcongzi* prefaces the story of the *lin* 麟 with several other stories that depict Kongzi's sorrow and frustration in not being recognized and therefore not being able to implement the Confucian Way. In this section I use the two vignettes that immediately precede the vignette of the *lin* 麟 to elaborate on the nature of Kongzi's sorrow. These vignettes demonstrate the heartache, despair, and even agony associated with the moral agent's inability to realize the "external goods" of the Confucian Way. Contrary to the views of scholars such as Jiyuan Yu, who argue that the cultivated person is without complaint, these passages express the intimate complaints of the paradigmatic good person—Kongzi.[56]

Both of these stories follow a similar pattern: Kongzi is given reason to believe that he will gain an influential position (*wei* 位) in the government where he would be able to implement his *dao* 道, only to have that hope dashed by powers beyond his control. In both stories, Kongzi responds to rejection by reciting or composing poetry. These passages take part in a larger tradition of lamenting one's misfit with the times by means of song or poetry. Early Confucians such as Xunzi 荀子 (313–238 BCE) also composed a number poems on the theme of "not encountering the [right] times" 不遇時.[57] Later, figures such as Sima Qian, Dong Zhongshu 董仲舒 (179–104 BCE), and Tao Yuanming 陶淵明 (c. 365–427) composed lengthy poems on the topic with titles such as "A Lament for the Scholar not Encountering [the Right Times]" 悲士不遇 and "Stirred [to Sorrow] for the Scholar not Encountering [the Right Times]" 感士不遇. Similar themes also appear throughout Qu Yuan's 屈原 (c. 340–278 BCE) "Lisao" 離騷 and the *Chuci* 《楚辭》 as a whole. In each of these cases the author grieves over his incongruence with his circumstance. The next chapter of this book explores the relationship between regret and literary production in more detail, but the general point worth mentioning here is that poetry can provide a glimpse into grief.[58]

In the first vignette, Ai Gong 哀公, ruler of Kongzi's home state of Lu, courts Kongzi by sending him a gift. The implication is that Ai Gong has a found a place for Kongzi to serve in his court. Since Kongzi is well known by the aristocracy at this point in his life, this is likely no minor position; rather, Kongzi is to be given a great deal of authority in the state. The situation, however, takes a turn for the worse. The text explains,

> Ai Gong sent a gift to Wei to greet the Master. However, it turned out that [Ai Gong] could not employ [Kongzi]. This is why the Master wrote "The Song of the Hill," which says:

> [I] climb this hill; its slopes are long and steep.
> The *dao* 道 of humaneness is near; but when seeking it, [it] seems so far.
> At once [I] am lost, and cannot return.
> I am encircled by hardships and difficulties; [and so I] sigh and look back
>   at [my] path.
> Before [me] is Mount Tai; luxuriant and firm with its majesty.
> [Yet] Mount Liangfu is tortuous and winding; and thistles fill its roads.
> [I] ascend it, but there is no route to follow.
> [I] would cut a trail, but have no axe.
> [My] afflictions, like these vines, spread in all directions.
> [I] can only let out a long sigh, and cry sorrowfully until [my] tears flow
>   like streams.

> 哀公使以幣如衛迎夫子，而卒不能當。故夫子作《丘陵之歌》，
> 曰：「登彼丘陵，峛崺其阪。仁道在邇，求之若遠。遂迷不復，
> 自嬰屯蹇，喟然回慮。題彼泰山，鬱確其高，梁甫回連，
> 枳棘充路。陟之無緣，將伐無柯，患茲蔓延，惟以永歎，涕霣潺
> 湲。」59

Commentators agree that Mount Tai represents Lu, or more specifically, an idealized version of Lu where it serves as the respository for the consummate features of Zhou dynasty culture. In other words, it represents the Confucian *dao* 道. To reach Mount Tai, travelers coming from certain directions must first cross Mount Liangfu. Yü Ying-shih argues that by the Han, and possibly earlier, Mount Tai represented the domain of the ruler, whereas Liangfu represented the domain of those serving the ruler.60 As such, Kongzi in this poem is cut off from the ruler, and the path over Liangfu is figurative of his difficulties in gaining a fitting position in the government that would allow him to realize the consummate features of Zhou dynasty culture. He finds himself encircled with problems and following a path that continues to disappear. All the while, Mount Tai, in its full splendor, looms in the background. It is as if he can see his goal—he knows how to realize the *dao* 道, but, similar to *Mengzi* 4A1 discussed earlier in this chapter, he lacks the tools (i.e., the position, *wei* 位) to cut a path to his destination. In the end, all he can do is agonize over how close he is to his goal and weep over his misfortune. The image of Kongzi weeping is a fairly common trope. It appears at least a dozen times in the early texts. This stands in contrast to depictions of Kongzi as achieving a state of equanimity or contentment when confronted by challenges.[61] Amy Olberding astutely notes this tension in her article titled, "Confucius' Complaints and the *Analects'* Account of the Good Life." She, in part, explains Kongzi's sorrows in terms of "moral maturity." Following Olberding, moral maturity "consists most basically in having the perspicacity and existential honesty to acknowledge a series of home truths, truths that are as unpleasant as they are basic: We do not get all we wish; circumstances constrain our possibilities; seeking to fulfill some of our desires entails leaving others behind."[62] Kongzi's life, as such, is admirable but not desirable. In other words, we might esteem the kind of person described in the texts and embodied by Kongzi; however, this does not mean that we desire to live his life. Olberding stresses that not even Kongzi would choose to live the life he is given. She continues, "Kongzi's complaints appear to reinforce rather than alleviate the suspicion that while virtue may, as the cliché would have it, be its own reward, its rewards can nonetheless experientially register as rather spare or even mean."[63] In this light, Kongzi is the morally mature agent whose sorrows are a poignant reflection of him coming to terms with the limitations of his times.

The title of the song is also worth noting. The term *qiuling* 丘陵 means "hill," but these characters suggest other readings as well. For one, Kongzi's given name is Qiu 丘, and *ling* 陵, besides referring to a hill, can additionally mean to wane, to collapse, or to enter a state of disorder. *Qiuling zhige* 丘陵之歌, therefore, at once means "The Song of the Hill" as well as "The Song of Kongzi's Decline." It is poetry that on the one hand uses a hill as a metaphor for Kongzi's trials—an object that gives him perspective on his goal, but also obstructs him from achieving it. On the other hand, the hill represents him in a more personal sense. The opening lines can also be translated as, "[They] trample on this waning mound, with its steep sides all around. The *dao* 道 of humaneness is near; [yet they] seek it as if [it] is far."[64] Kongzi, in this reading, is the mound. He stands upright, ready to serve, but those in positions of power do not recognize him. Instead they trample and step over him, looking for something beyond the mark.

Qiuling 丘陵 can also mean "tomb" or "grave mound."[65] In this light, *qiuling zhige* 丘陵之歌 can be understood as "The Song of the Grave." Here, we again see the appearance of death in the context of desire and disappointment. While the image of the tomb might evoke Kongzi's personal death or demise, it is also possible that the tomb represents something else, especially if we read the poem with Kongzi as the narrator. In this reading, the tomb represents the achievements of those in the past—the accomplishments of the sages in creating an ordered world. People stand on these achievements, gaining perspective, yet unfortunately they continue to seek for the Way of humaneness somewhere else, and so the author of the poem states, "Although lost, [they] do not return" 遂迷不復.[66]

In the second vignette, the ruler of the state of Chu planned to give Kongzi control over a small portion of his state, which Kongzi could then use as a model for other parts of the state to follow. However, a competing minister in the court was able to over turn the ruler's plan.[67] The vignette begins with a description of the gifts sent to Kongzi as an expression of the ruler's intentions. Kongzi's disciples rush to inform him about the gift, and in doing so they ask about two individuals that lived long before Kongzi—Taigong 太公 and Xuyou 許由. Taigong lived in the Shang dynasty, and in his old age he became the counselor of Wen Wang 文王, who at the time was conspiring to overthrow the Shang king. Xuyou lived in the time of Yao 堯 and had the reputation of a worthy. Before giving the throne to Shun 舜, Yao tried to give the throne to Xuyou. Xuyou, however, refused to accept the throne because he was not a descendent of Yao. He then spent the rest of his days living in seclusion. In asking about Taigong and Xuyou, Kongzi's disciples are wondering if Kongzi will accept the ruler's offer like Taigong or reject it like Xuyou.[68]

The ruler of Chu sent an envoy to present gifts of gold and silk to the Master. Zai Yu and Ran You remarked, "This certainly means that the Master's *dao* 道 will be implemented!"

楚王使使奉金帛聘夫子。宰予冉有曰：「夫子之道於是行矣。」

They immediately sought an audience with the Master, and asked, "Taigong wore himself out, [and despite how] hard it was, [he clung to his] ambition. Only when [he] was 80 years old did he finally meet Wen Wang. Who is more worthy, [Taigong] or Xuyou?"

遂請見，問夫子曰：「太公勤身苦志，八十而遇文王，孰與許由之賢？」

The Master replied, "Xuyou only bettered himself; [but] Taigong united and benefited the world. However, in this age there is no ruler like Wen Wang. Even if there was [someone like] Taigong, who would recognize him?"

夫子曰：「許由，獨善其身者也。太公，兼利天下者也。然今世無文王之君也，雖有太公，孰能識之？」

[He] then sang out,
"When the Great Way became obscure; ritual became the [only] foundation [of society].
The worthies in hiding; waited for the right moment.
[But now] the world is all the same; [so] where should [I] desire to go?"

乃歌曰：「大道隱兮，禮為基；賢人竄兮，將待時；天下如一，欲何之。」[69]

Kongzi's response to his disciples is that he sides with Taigong. He would take a post if there were a ruler like Wen Wang who recognized Taigong. Unfortunately for Kongzi, there were no such rulers in his time. The parallel between Taigong and Kongzi is worth noting. According to several early texts, Wen Wang met Taigong while on a hunt. The *Liutao* 《六韜》, for instance, even mentions that Wen Wang divined (*bu* 卜) before the hunt, where he was told that rather than catching a dragon or tiger, he would find a teacher sent from *Tian* 天 (*tianqian rushi* 天遺汝師).[70] Wen Wang, in contrast to the leaders of Kongzi's day, recognized the metaphorical *lin* 麟. He identified the creature sent to help usher in the *dao* 道, and understood how to employ it.

Similar to the first vignette, this vignette also draws on the theme of recognition. Taigong was recognized by Wen Wang, but Kongzi lacked someone to recognize him. The contemporary scholar, Eric Henry, writes about recognition in early China. He explains, "In the world of early Chinese narrative, to be 'known,' that is, valued at one's true worth, is the only bliss; to be 'unknown'—misunderstood, unappreciated, falsely blamed—is the only torture."[71] While Henry, in my opinion, overstates the singularity of the bliss and torture associated with recognition, he does get at the significance of recognition in many early Confucian texts. Indeed, Henry goes on to explain that from the perspectives of these texts, to know another is to bestow upon the one known an awareness of life without which life is simply less meaningful. In short, no one can fully live until known by another.[72] Full self-expression, in this light, is contingent on being recognized by someone else, and failing to find someone that allows for full self-expression is certainly worthy of sorrow. Kongzi's search for an employer, for someone who will pay the right price for him (to use the imagery of *Analects* 9.13), can be conceptualized as a search for someone who recognizes his desires or appreciates his worth, and his sorrow expressed in these two vignettes can be taken as a kind of grief associated with not being able to find such a person. The bliss predicated on finding this other person, and the pain associated with failing to find him reveal the vulnerable nature of living a full life. Indeed, as both of these vignettes demonstrate, a treasure is most valuable when treasured.

Conclusion

In several early Confucian texts Kongzi is likened to a homeless dog (*sangjia zhi gou* 喪家之狗).[73] Commentators have divergent opinions about the meaning of this phrase because of the ambiguity of the character *sang* 喪—meaning "to lose" as well as "to mourn."[74] Kongzi is clearly "homeless" 喪家 in the sense of lacking a base from where he can pursue his righteous desires. In the *Han Shi Waizhuan* account of this story, Kongzi explains the notion of *sangjia zhi gou* 喪家之狗 in the context of mourning. He states, "While [the deceased] is being clothed and coffined, and the ritual implements are laid out for the sacrifices, [the dog] furtively looks around, fully hoping to serve someone, but no one is there" 既斂而槨，布器而祭，顧望無人，意欲施之. Kongzi then goes on to liken this to the disorder of his time, proclaiming, "In the highest position of leadership there is no illustrious ruler; and in lower positions of leadership there are no worthy scholars or ministers. The Way of the kings has declined, [and good] government and education have been tossed aside. The strong abuse the weak, and the many oppress the few. The people have given free reign to [the desires of their] hearts; and none have fixed standards" 上無明王，下無賢士方伯，王道衰，政教失，強陵弱，眾暴寡，百姓縱心，莫之綱紀. In this version of the event, Kongzi is like a dog that has lost his master. Despite his desire to serve, there is no one whom he can serve. When taken together, these passages seem to purposefully play on the various meaning of the term *sang* 喪. Kongzi has not only "lost" his home, but his loss is a kind of death worthy of grief and sorrow. Part of the sorrow, explicitly stated in this passage and implied in the passages mentioned throughout this chapter, comes because of a desire for the world to be a different place—a place where more values can be realized, or a place where the *dao* 道 can be enacted. Stated succinctly, Kongzi regrets the world he finds himself living in.[75]

The purpose of this chapter was to introduce the notion of regret in an early Confucian context and to characterize the sorrow associated with regret. The harmony thesis, detailed in chapter 2, likewise accounts for grief or sorrow, and this chapter has largely been an attempt to flesh out the nature of such sorrow. The next chapter begins a more sustained critique of the harmony thesis by exploring regret in light of Confucian accounts of frustration, resentment, and transgression.

Notes

1. See, for instance, *Liji* 9.36/64/10–12; *Kongzi Jiayu* 10.1/16/23–27, 22.2/42/29–22.2/43/5, 32/57/27–28; and *Mengzi* 2A2.

2. For models of regret and contrition in Western philosophical literature see Margaret Urban Walker, *Moral Repair: Reconstructing Moral Relations after Wrongdoing* (New York: Cambridge University Press, 2006), 136–148; and Nick Smith, *I was Wrong: The Meanings of Apologies* (Cambridge, UK: Cambridge University Press, 2008).

3. *Liji* 32.9/143/29. A similar metaphor is used in *Liji* 47.11/172/1–3 and *Mengzi* 2A7.

4. *Analects* 5.27; see also 15.30, 19.21, and 12.4. See also *Dadai Liji* 4.3/29/14.

5. See, for instance, *Mengzi* 4A4, 4B29, *Shuoyuan* 19.44/172/19–173/2, and *Han Shi Waizhuan* 9.3/6516–22. On the notion of justice in Confucianism see Erin M. Cline, *Confucius, Rawls, and the Sense of Justice* (New York: Fordham University Press, 2013). For a more developed model of regret as contrition in a Confucian context (in this case the *Analects*) see Amy Olberding, "Regret and Moral Maturity: A Response to Michael Ing and Manyul Im," *Dao: A Journal of Comparative Philosophy* 14.4 (December 2015): 579–587.

6. Regret, as I employ it, is meant in a normative sense. While there are situations where one might conceive of an inappropriate notion of regret, my primary concern in this chapter is with regret as experienced by the paradigmatic moral agent.

7. Walker, *Moral Repair*, 114.

8. Walker, *Moral Repair*, 114–115.

9. *Xunzi* is a significant exception in this case.

10. This is building on Walker, *Moral Repair*, 133–134. On page 26 Walker also notes, "Resentment and indignation arise as responses to behavior that contravenes normative expectations. Among our normative expectations are expectations that others, with whom we think we are playing by rules, not only play by them, but also rise to the reiteration and enforcement of those rules when someone goes out of bounds. *Normative confirmation* and enforcement is something we usually feel we have a right to expect of each other in addition to the behavior that specific rules require. When we express and direct our resentment or indignation at a norm violator, we demand some rectifying response from the one who is perceived as out of bounds. When we express our resentment to others, we invite confirmation from others that we have competently judged a normative violation and that others share our interest in affirming the norms we hold, in showing disapproval of conduct out of bounds, and perhaps in seeking redress of violations. Most fundamentally, we seek confirmation that these norms are meant to include and protect *us*; that we are recognized by others and that our dignity is valued by others. All the more so when the violation is a serious one, a cause of harm, indignity, or insult that is apt to be seen as moral matter."

11. Walker, *Moral Repair*, 143.

12. The language of focusing on the internal is also used in *Xunzi* 《荀子》 2/6/12–14, 6/24/12–15, 8/9/22–30/2, and 29/143/14–16. Perhaps the strongest statement is found in *Kongcongzi* 《孔叢子》 3.3/20/30–3.3/21/3, where Zisi encourages his interlocutor not to weep over the decadent condition of the world. He, in part, states, "This is [like] worrying about the muddy water of a river and using [one's] tears to clean it.... One can only discuss the Way with others who do not worry about the chaos of [their] age, and are instead concerned with the disorderliness of themselves" 是憂河水之濁而泣清之也。。。。唯能不憂世之亂而患身之不治者，可與言道矣. Similar themes occur in *Qiongda*

Yishi 《窮達以時》 from Guodian; see Scott Cook, *The Bamboo Texts of Guodian: A Study and Complete Translation* (Ithaca, NY: Cornell University East Asia Program, 2012), 429–464.

13. Edward Slingerland, trans. *Confucius: Analects* (Indianapolis: Hackett, 2003), 34.

14. Slingerland, *Analects*, 56. On page 71 he states, "We see here again the idea that the unselfconscious joy derived from the internal goods of the Confucian Way renders one indifferent to externalities." See also pages 68 and 127. For a sustained critique of this view see Michael D. K. Ing, *The Dysfunction of Ritual in Early Confucianism* (New York: Oxford University Press, 2012), 74–78.

15. Benjamin I. Schwartz, *The World of Thought in Ancient China* (Cambridge, MA: Harvard University Press, 1985), 62.

16. *Mengzi* 4A1. Nafsika Athanassoulis makes a relevant comment with regard to moral luck: "In cases of bad situational luck, the virtuous person will make the best he can out of a bad lot, in the same way that a good craftsman will make the best use of substandard material. The virtuous agent cannot be held responsible for elements of the situation which are not under his control, but should be praised for performing the best possible action, under the circumstances." *Morality, Moral Luck and Responsibility: Fortune's Web* (New York: Palgrave Macmillan, 2005), 52. Joachim Gentz elaborates on the kind of metaphor used in *Mengzi* 4A1 in "Can We be in Time to Lead a Good Life? Discourses on the Human Ability to Lead a Good Life Through Timely Action in Early Chinese Thought," unpublished manuscript.

17. Xunzi makes this point most clearly in *Xunzi* 8/32.

18. *Kongcongzi* 2.2/11/16, Xue Ke 雪克, ed., *Xinyi Gongyang Zhuan* 《新譯公羊傳》 (Taibei 台北: Sanmin Shuju 三民書局, 2008), 535 ("Ai Gong" 哀公 14); hereafter, *Gongyang Zhuan*. Ma Teying 馬特盈, ed., *Shiji Jinzhu* 《史記今註》 (Taibei 台北: Taiwan Shangwu yinshuguan 臺灣商務印書館, 1987), 1993 and 3141; hereafter, *Shiji*.

19. In interpreting the *Shiji* Stephen Durrant makes the point that the "preservation of one's name within the canon might be partly a matter of chance." *The Cloudy Mirror: Tension and Conflict in the Writings of Sima Qian* (Albany: State University of New York Press, 1995), 21. Durrant goes on to say, "Thus, many deserving gentlemen, confined to a period of time or to a situation where there is little chance to display great merit, labor and die in obscurity. No one, it seems, can count on fame." *The Cloudy Mirror*, 24.

20. Hu, Guang 胡廣. ed. *Sishu Daquan* 《四書大全》, *Lunyu Jizhu Daquan* 《論語集註大全》. *Wenyuange Sikuquanshu Dianziban* 《文淵閣四庫全書電子版》 (Hong Kong: Digital Heritage Publishing, accessed September 25, 2014), 15.28.

21. *Shiji*, 1994. For the sake of convenience I refer to Sima Qian as the author of the *Shiji*; and where necessary I discuss his father's role in composing the text.

22. *Shiji*, 1992.

23. For a textual history of the *Kongzi Jiayu* see R. P. Kramers, trans., *K'ung Tzu Chia Yu: The School Sayings of Confucius* (Leiden: Brill, 1950), 1–198. For a textual history of the *Kongcongzi* see Yoav Ariel, trans., *K'ung-ts'ung-tzu: The K'ung Family Masters' Anthology* (Princeton, NJ: Princeton University Press, 1989), 3–69. Coincidentally both texts have been discounted as authentic representations of Kongzi for quite some time. However, recent archeological discoveries have pushed the dating of at least portions of the *Kongzi Jiayu* back into the Warring States. On this see Li Xueqin 李学勤, "Zhujian *Jiayu* yu Han-Wei Kongshijia Xue" 竹简〈家语〉与汉魏孔氏家学, *Kongzi Yanjiu* 《孔子研究》 (1987.2), 60–64; and Liao Mingchun 廖明春 and Zhang Yan 张岩, "Cong Shangbojian *Minzhi Fumu* 'Wuzhi' Shuolun *Kongzi Jiayu Lunli* de Zhenwei" 从上博简〈民之父母〉"五至"说论〈孔子家语·论礼〉的真伪, *Xian-Qin, Qin-Hanshi* 《先秦，秦漢史》 (2006.1), 54–59. For a more background on the *Jiayu* see Yang Chaoming 楊朝明 and Song Lilin 宋立林, eds., *Kongzi Jiayu Tongjie* 《孔子家語通解》 (Jinan 濟南: Qilu Shushe 齊魯書社, 2013).

24. Shusun in these passages refers to the head of the clan, which would technically be the grandson of the original Shusun.

25. *Kongzi Jiayu* 16.10/34/6–9. See also *Shuoyuan* 5.1/31/19–5.2/32/4 where Kongzi's desire to save the world from drowning is associated with his weeping after finding the *lin* 麟.

26. *Kongcongzi* 2.2/11/11–17.

27. On the connection between recognition and the *lin* 麟 see Wei-yee Li, *The Readability of the Past in Early Chinese Historiography* (Cambridge, MA: Harvard University Press, 2007), 416. Piotr Gibas states, "Confucius discloses the identity of the unicorn, but at the same time the *lin* 麟 also confirms that of the Sage. In other words, the *lin* 麟 is not just a passive object of recognition, but also an effective agent." "Waiting for the Unicorn: Perception of Time and History in Early Chinese Writings" (PhD diss., University of California, Berkeley, 2009), 33.

28. *Liji* 3.10/11/30–31. For an explanation of the character *shen* 慎 in connection to ritual implements see Jiang Yihua 姜義華, *Xinyi Liji Duben* 《新譯禮記讀本》 (Taibei Shi 臺北市: Sanmin shuju 三民書局, 1997), 75.

29. *Kongcongzi* 5.1/52/20–30; and *Kongzi Jiayu* 44.3/89/18–25.

30. *Liji* 3.3/11/6.

31. On the transgressive nature of joint burial see Michael D.K. Ing, "The Ancients did not Fix Their Graves: Failure in Early Confucian Ritual," *Philosophy East and West* 62.2 (April 2012): 223–245.

32. *Gongyang Zhuan*, 535 ("Ai Gong" 哀公 14).

33. See also Li, *The Readability of the Past*, 413.

34. Joachim Gentz makes the following statement with regard to the recently discovered text, *Qiongda Yishi* 《窮達以時》 : "Neither virtue nor merit are sufficient to generate success, the efficacy of any human action depends on the right time which

is something that lies entirely with Heaven [Tian 天], not with man." "Can We Be in Time to Lead a Good Life?," 6.

35. In his work on *shi* 時, James D. Sellman states, "Time, generally speaking for the pre-Qin world, is basically waiting for the opportune moment to take action." *Timing and Rulership in Master Lü's Spring and Autmn Annals (Lüshi chunqiu)* (Albany: State University of New York Press, 2002), 195.

36. The *Lüshi Chunqiu* 《呂氏春秋》 uses these two metaphors in 14.3/72/25–14.3/73/4 and 14.5/74/17–23.

37. This is according to the *Zuo Zhuan*, "Yin Gong" 隱公 5; Yang Bojun 楊伯峻, ed., *Chunqiu Zuo Zhuan Zhu* 《春秋左傳注》 (Beijing 北京: Zhonghua Shuju 中華書局, 2000), 42.

38. On the notion of *ming* 命 see Christopher Lupke, ed., *The Magnitude of Ming: Command, Allotment, and Fate in Chinese Culture* (Honolulu: University of Hawai'i Press, 2005). David Hall and Roger Ames also provide an insightful definition of *ming* 命: "As the causal conditions defining a particular event, *ming* 命 is both its possibilities and its limitations. *Ming* is a possible future negotiated within the limitations of the sponsoring circumstances." *Thinking Through Confucius* (Albany: State University of New York Press, 1987), 209. On page 210 they add, "That is, *ming* 命 might be compared to a notion such as *shi* 勢, 'conditions or circumstances,' in that both can describe a calculus of existing conditions—physical, moral, environmental—that constitute the matrix for a given event."

39. See, for instance, *Mengzi* 5B1. Other texts will sometimes speak of this in terms of *zhishi* 知時 or *zhiming* 知命. See, for instance, *Analects* 20.3; *Mengzi* 7A2; *Shuoyuan* 17.40/148/4–5, 13.1/101/3–13; and *Kongzi Jiayu* 15.17/31/11–13.

40. *Liji* 18.4/97/3.

41. See, for instance, *Mengzi* 5B1.

42. *Liji* 32.2/146/26.

43. *Liji* 32.8/143/24–25.

44. *Liji* 32.20/145/29; and *Xunzi* 10/44/8.

45. *Han Shi Waizhuan* 3.34/24/25.

46. Zhu Xi 朱熹 and Lü Zuqian 呂祖謙, eds., *Jinsilu* 《近思錄》, *Wenyuange Sikuquanshu Dianziban* 《文淵閣四庫全書電子版》 (Hong Kong: Digital Heritage Publishing, accessed February 3, 2015), 3.24–25. In *Sishu Daquan* 9.38 Hu Guang presents a slightly different explanation: "To weigh (*quan* 權) is to use one's sense of rightness (*yi* 義) to seek after the balancing point (*zhong* 中). . . . In using rightness to weigh something and find the balancing point, rightness is like the counterpoise of the steelyard. To weigh is to take this counterpoise and determine the heaviness [of an object]. The balancing point is when the object being weighed is brought to its even point" 權是用那義底問中。。。以義權之，而後得中，義似秤，權是將這秤去稱量，中是物得其平處.

47. This distinction is largely heuristic; meaning that it is not necessarily found in the texts.

48. *Liji* 6.12/39/21–22.

49. See also *Xunzi* 28/141/3–8.

50. It is also worth forecasting a discussion that I will elaborate on in chapter four. Namely, in Kongzi's case, tending to lingering values entailed going beyond the normative boundaries of his context. In other words, when confronted with a situation where his potential could not be fully realized, Kongzi's response was to breach the boundaries appropriate for his station. This demonstrates that transgressing the normative boundaries of a situation can also increase the descriptive possibilities of the situation (or future situations). Kongzi's creation of the *Chuqiu*, an act appropriate only for the king, enables people in the future to be able to implement his Way. Only by transgressing the normative boundaries of his situation can he broaden the descriptive boundaries of future situations such that they allow for the realization of the Confucian *dao* 道.

51. See, for instance, *Xunzi* 25/121/2–5 and *Kongzi Jiayu* 5/6/6–7.

52. *Shiji*, 1992–1994.

53. This point is reinforced in the "Rulin Liezhuan" 儒林列傳 chapter; *Shiji*, 3141–3158. Later scholars would even refer to the *Chunqiu* as the *Linjing* 《麟經》.

54. More specifically, it is not easy to relate Kongzi's lament over *Tian* 天 (at the death of Yan Hui) with his statement that he does not resent *Tian* 天—going so far as to say that only *Tian* 天 understands him. While the next chapter explores the nature of resentment, it is worth mentioning here that while on the one hand the *Shiji* often seeks to represent the incoherent and complex nature of the world, on the other hand these passages may represent Kongzi's struggle to not resent *Tian* 天 in spite of experiences that push him in that direction.

55. I borrow this idea from Li, *The Readability of the Past in Early Chinese Historiography*, 413–421.

56. Jiyuan Yu, *The Ethics of Confucius and Aristotle: Mirrors of Virtue* (New York: Routledge, 2007), 187. Yu explains that the virtuous person's "goal is *ren* 仁, which is up to him to grab. If he gets it, he should not have any complaints."

57. See, for instance, *Xunzi* 25/121/7–122/10. For a philosophical exploration of this poem see David W. Pankenier, "'The Scholar's Frustration' Reconsidered: Melancholia or Credo?" *Journal of the American Oriental Society* 110.3 (1990): 434–459.

58. Steven Van Zoeren makes the following point in *Poetry and Personality: Reading, Exegesis, and Hermeneutics in Traditional China* (Stanford, CA: Stanford University Press, 1991), 14: "Like the music they were associated with, the Odes were thought to elicit in a particular direct, unmediated way in the student the feelings and impulses that originally gave rise to their composition; they thereby provided a privileged means to the project of mobilizing the emotions in the service of Confucian norms."

59. *Kongcongzi* 2.2/11/1–4.

60. Ying-shih Yü, "'O Soul, Come Back!' A Study in the Changing Conceptions of the Soul and Afterlife in Pre-Buddhist China," *Harvard Journal of Asiatic Studies* 47.2 (December 1987): 388–391. Yü is talking specifically about conceptions of the afterlife in this regard, which coincidentally fits some of the imagery in the poem as discussed below. He also notes on page 391 that in "Han popular culture, Mount Tai itself, especially its peak, was a symbol of life and immortality whereas Liangfu was that of death." I take 梁父 and 梁甫 to refer to the same mountain.

61. This kind of Kongzi emerges in descriptions of the conflict between the states of Chen 陳 and Cai 蔡 (*kunyu chencai zhijian* 困於陳蔡之間) for instance.

62. Amy Olberding, "Confucius' Complaints and the *Analects*' Account of the Good Life," *Dao: A Journal of Comparative Philosophy* 12 (2013): 427.

63. Olberding, "Confucius' Complaints," 434.

64. Coincidentally, in places such as the *Shiji* Kongzi is described as having this physical characteristic, and being named for it (i.e., Qiu 丘). *Shiji*, 1952.

65. I would like to thank Jue Guo and Charles Sanft for this insight.

66. The second vignette more strongly suggests a motif of looking to the past by drawing on imagery used in the "Liyun" 禮運 chapter of the *Liji*.

67. For more background on this see Fu Yashu 傅亞庶, ed., *Kongconzi Jiaoyi* 《孔叢子校釋》 (Beijing 北京: Zhonghua Shuju 中華書局, 2011), 105 fn. 50.

68. A similar strategy for gauging Kongzi's response to a situation occurs in *Analects* 7.15.

69. *Kongcongzi* 2.2/11/6–9. Admittedly, the phrase *dushan qishen* 獨善其身 does not need to be read negatively; and later Confucians use it in a positive light. See, for instance, *Mengzi* 7A9. In this reading, *du* 獨 means something like "alone" and hence, in reclusion.

70. A similar account appears in *Shiji*, 1502–1503. This notion of Taigong appearing as an omen of *Tian* 天 interestingly parallels the *Kongcongzi* account of the *lin* 麟 appearing as an omen of *Tian* 天.

71. Eric Henry, "The Motif of Recognition in Early China Author," *Harvard Journal of Asiatic Studies* 47.1 (June 1987): 8. The notion of lacking recognition is also what drives Qu Yuan's attempts to leave the world in the *Lisao*.

72. Henry, "The Motif of Recognition," 9.

73. See *Kongzi Jiayu* 22.8/44/5–8; *Shiji*, 1969; and *Han Shi Waizhuan* 9.18/68/28–9.18/69/9. The *Kongzi Jiayu*, for instance, recounts,

> While traveling to Zheng, Kongzi was separated from his disciples. He stood by himself outside the eastern gate [of the city]. Some approached Zigong saying, "Outside the eastern gate there is a person. His height is nine *chi* 尺 and six *cun* 寸. [His] eyes are long like a river; [and he has] a high forehead. His head is like Yao's. His neck is like Gao Yao's. His shoulders are like Zi Chan's. From the

waist below he is three *cun* 寸 shorter than Yu. And he is emaciated like a dog who has lost its home."

孔子適鄭，與弟子相失，獨立東郭門外，或人謂子貢曰：「東門外有一人焉，其長九尺有六寸，河目隆顙，其頭似堯，其頸似皋繇，其肩似子產，然自腰以下，不及禹者三寸，纍然如喪家之狗。」

Zigong then [went and found Kongzi], and reported [what he had heard]. Kongzi was delighted, but then sighed, saying, "My body and form are not quite there, [but] being like a dog that has lost its home is so true, so true."

子貢以告。孔子欣然而歎曰：「形狀未也，如喪家之狗，然乎哉！然乎哉！」

74. For the contemporary debate see See Zhang Yunfei 张云飞, "Shengzhe Qinghuai—Sangjia zhi Gou Shijie" 圣者情怀——"丧家之狗"试解, *Kongzi Yanjiu* 《孔子研究》 4 (2010): 40–48; Zhao Wu 赵武, Sangjiagou Shuojie "丧家狗"说解, *Renwen Zazhi* 《人文杂志》 3 (2013): 19–25; and Carine Defoort, ed., *Contemporary Chinese Thought: Translations and Studies* 41.2 (2009–2010); especially pages 43–53.

75. Robert Ashmore provides a related reading of Book 10 in the *Analects*, which contains a stream of passages detailing the minutiae of Kongzi's conduct. Ashmore states, "Taken locally, [these passages] show the capacity of perfect and timely response. In the broader sense of the age in which Kongzi lived, however, such traces remind us precisely of the lack of fit between Kongzi as an embodier of the way and a world in which that way was destined never to be realized." *The Transport of Reading: Text and Understanding in the World of Tao Qian (365–427)* (Cambridge, MA: Harvard University Press, 2010), 134.

4

Regret, Resentment, and Transgression

You trust slander as readily as raising a glass to a guest's toast.
You are not caring; refraining from thoroughly investigating
   accusations.
When cutting trees down, one pulls to the side; when split-
   ting firewood, one follows the grain.
[But you] release those who are guilty; and [instead] attri-
   bute it to me.

君子信讒，如或醻之。
君子不惠，不舒究之。
伐木掎矣，析薪杝矣。
舍彼有罪，予之佗矣。

("xiaopan" 小弁, *Shijing* 《詩經》)[1]

THE PREVIOUS CHAPTER began a discussion about regret and highlighted the role of sorrow and frustration with regard to regret. This chapter builds on the previous chapter by further exploring regret as it relates to resentment. I argue that from an early Confucian perspective, resentment is a result of frustrated desire for affection. Said differently, resentment is a frustration or anger that occurs when those close to us withhold their care or when they otherwise injure us. It is a sign that we require the care of significant others and that we are vulnerable to their concern or neglect. When understood positively, resentment signals genuine recognition of meaningful relationships; it is a sign that we are affected by those who ought to matter to us. These "significant others" (*qin* 親) are often our family members but also include those with obligations to support the fulfillment of our righteous desires. For many early Confucians this includes *Tian* 天.

Importantly, resentment has a creative dimension in that it can lead to the production of literature aimed to channel frustrated desire toward realizing the Confucian *dao* 道. These texts work to connect the author's resentment with the reader's possibility of remaking the world in a way desired by the author. Sometimes, this act of releasing frustrated desire is associated with the transgression of social norms, as in the case of Kongzi composing the *Chunqiu* 《春秋》. In this chapter I discuss transgression as it relates to regret. I show that early Confucians saw these kinds of transgressions as valid responses to value conflicts or value defeats. However, I set aside the question of how these transgressions might impact the integrity of the moral agent for later chapters.

In exploring these arguments, I begin with a general overview of the term *yuan* 怨, which I interpret as "resentment." I focus on its positive portrayal in passages such as *Mengzi* 《孟子》 6B3 and 5A1. Then I situate these positive accounts of resentment in a broader context of passages that discourage resentment. In the last two sections of this chapter I connect resentment with the production of literary texts, and then I show how Kongzi's production of the *Chunqiu*, which was created on the basis of him resenting his circumstances, violates the norms of social order. This chapter, in combination with chapter 3, provides a thorough account of how early Confucians expressed regret with regard to unfortunate circumstances.

Resentment

The character *yuan* 怨 is often translated as "anger," "complaint," "frustration," "grief," or "resentment." The second-century dictionary, *Shuowen Jiezi* 《說文解字》, glosses *yuan* 怨 as *hui* 恚, "indignant" or "bearing a grudge." Xu Shen 許慎, the author of the *Shuowen Jiezi*, also uses *yuan* 怨 to gloss terms such as *xie* 懈 ("enmity"), *dui* 懟 ("anger"), and *hen* 恨 ("hatred").[2] Occasionally *yuan* 怨 is a loan-character for *yun* 蘊, which means "to store up" or "to accumulate." Contemporary scholars also note that *yuan* 怨 is linguistically associated with *yuan* 苑 ("an enclosure for animals") and *yuan* 宛 ("to pile up").[3] Notably, *yuan* 怨 is associated with feelings of anger and frustration, as well as concepts of restriction and accumulation. For the purposes of this project I translate *yuan* 怨 as "resentment," where resentment entails pent-up frustration and leads to grief, anger, as well as discontent.

Generally speaking, resentment is not encouraged in early Confucian texts. The *Analects* state that the filial son serves his parents without resentment (*lao er buyuan* 勞而不怨).[4] The *Kongzi Jiayu* 《孔子家語》 says that the exemplary person does not have a resentful heart (*xinbuyuan* 心不怨).[5] And the *Xunzi* 《荀子》 explains, "Those who understand themselves do not resent others. Those who understand their lot in life do not resent *Tian* 天. Those who resent others are destitute. Those who resent *Tian* 天 lack commitment. [While] the shortcoming lies within themselves, [they] attribute it to others. Indeed, how could [such a person] not be perverse" 自知者不怨人，知命者不怨天；怨人者窮，怨天者無志。失之己，反之人，豈不迂乎哉.[6]

There are many other passages in early Confucian texts that discourage resent-ment, but *Analects* 14.35 is particularly significant because of its influence on later authors (I employed Sima Qian's 司馬遷 usage of it in the previous chapter, for instance).[7] The passage reads, "The Master stated, 'No one understands me!' Zigong inquired, 'Why do you say that no one understands you?' The Master replied, '[I] do not resent *Tian*天, nor do [I] blame people. [I] learn from those below [*Tian*天,] and [I] strive to attain to what is above [human beings]. Only *Tian* 天 understands me'" 子曰：「莫我知也夫！」子貢曰：「何為其莫知子也？」子曰：「不怨天，不尤人。下學而上達。知我者，其天乎！」 In this somewhat cryptic passage Kongzi laments not being under-stood or recognized, yet he does not resent *Tian* 天 or blame others for that fact. Indeed, in this circumstance, Kongzi strives to take comfort in the notion that *Tian* 天 understands him. Passages such as these highlight the notion that the exemplary person should not be resentful; more particularly, he should not begrudge *Tian* 天 or his parents.

Contemporary scholars tend to emphasize these passages in explaining resent-ment. One of the more in-depth accounts of resentment is in Eric Nelson's arti-cle "Recognition and Resentment in the Confucian *Analects*."[8] Nelson primarily understands resentment as a negative sentiment to be eliminated, stating that, according to the *Analects*, resentment must be "reduced," "undone," "dismantled," and "overcome."[9] He explains that the exemplary person ought not respond to others with resentment. Nelson states, "Based on these and related expressions, we can conclude that even if others act in a way that would produce negative emotions like resentment in yourself, becoming ethically realized as a *junzi* 君子 entails not having reactive feelings by working on and adjusting your emotions and by acting non-symmetrically and non-interchangeabley with humane benev-olence toward them."[10]

At the same time, Nelson recognizes that resentment can function positively such as in cases where the moral agent resents injustice; however, Nelson qualifies his endorsement by stating that feelings such as resentment "primarily damage oth-ers and the persons whose comportment and attitudes are shaped by them."[11] As such, resentment is to be avoided or eliminated such that it does not harm the moral agent. Nelson's account of resentment represents a dominant view in the field.[12]

In contrast to these views of resentment, there are a handful of passages that endorse *yuan* 怨. One of these is *Mengzi* 6B3. In this passage, Gongsun Chou 公孫丑, a disciple of Mengzi, asks about a poem titled "Xiaopan" 小弁, which was apparently a widely known poem among educated groups of the time (a received version can be found in the *Shijing*). In the poem, Yijiu 宜臼 (c. 781 BCE–720 BCE), the oldest son of the ruler, describes his feelings when his father chose a younger son (from a favored concubine) to be the heir to the throne.[13] Given the practice of passing the throne on to the oldest son, Yijiu is quite disappointed with his father's decision. Gongsun Chou asks Mengzi about the poem because other people were criticizing it on the basis that Yijiu resents his father's decision.

> Gongsun Chou stated, "Gaozi says that the 'Xiaopan' poem is the poem of an uncultivated person."

公孫丑問曰：「高子曰：『《小弁》，小人之詩也。』」

> Mengzi asked, "Why does [he] say this?"

孟子曰：「何以言之？」

> [Gongsun Chou] responded, "[Because the poem expresses] resentment."

曰：「怨。」

> [Mengzi] said, "Gaozi is so superficial when it comes to [interpreting] poetry! Let's say that there was a man who encountered a person from the state of Yue. This person from Yue grabbed a bow and arrow and shot at him. Later, the man would be able to recount the experience with great verbosity and laughter for no other reason than the fact that this person was not closely related to him. However, if his older brother were to take up a bow and arrow and shoot at him, he would recount the story while crying with his head hung low. [This] is for no other reason than his close relation with his brother. The resentment in the 'Xiaopan' poem is [a result of] family members being closely related to each other. Humaneness occurs when family members [truly] act as kin. Indeed, Gaozi is so superficial when it comes to [interpreting] poetry!"

曰：「固哉，高叟之為詩也！有人於此，越人關弓而射之，則己談笑而道之；無他，疏之也。其兄關弓而射之，則己垂涕泣而道之；無他，戚之也。《小弁》之怨，親親也。親親，仁也。固矣夫，高叟之為詩也！」

> [Gongsun Chou] asked, "Why doesn't the 'Kaifeng' poem [express] resentment?"

曰：「《凱風》何以不怨？」

> [Mengzi] replied, "In the 'Kaifeng' poem, the faults of the parent are minor; [whereas] in the 'Xiaopan' poem, the faults of the parent are major. To be without resentment when [one's] parent's faults are major is to [consider one's parents] too distantly related. To be resentful when [one's] parent's faults are minor is to be easily provoked. [Considering them] too distantly related is unfilial; and being easily provoked is also

unfilial. Kongzi said, 'Shun is the utmost filial. At 50 he was still yearning for affection.'"

曰：「《凱風》，親之過小者也；《小弁》，親之過大者也。親之過大而不怨，是愈疏也；親之過小而怨，是不可磯也。愈疏，不孝也；不可磯，亦不孝也。孔子曰：『舜其至孝矣，五十而慕。』」

In this passage Mengzi provides a defense of *yuan* 怨. Gaozi apparently believes that any expression of resentment is inappropriate; however, Mengzi argues otherwise. Resentment is appropriate in familial relationships. If one's brother shot an arrow at oneself, one should certainly grieve it. The resentment in the "Xiaopan" poem is the result of family members being harmed by those closest to themselves. Translating the term *qinqin* 親親 more literally, resentment is born of circumstances where family members should have been familial.

A closer look at the "Xiaopan" poem (assuming the received version is roughly the same as the version Mengzi talks about) also reveals that resentment goes beyond grief or sadness felt when a family member fails to be familial. The poem begins with the author explaining that he has suffered "deep misfortune" 獨于罹. "How have I offended *Tian* 天," he asks, "What is my crime" 何辜于天，我罪伊何? The refrain used several times in the poem states, "[My] heart is aggrieved" 心之憂矣. After setting the stage with his sorrow and then explaining the importance of a father and mother, the author goes on to question the timing that *Tian* 天 used in creating him (*Tian zhi sheng wo, wo chen an zai* 天之生我，我辰安在). The next two stanzas are particularly relevant:

Look at that captured rabbit; even a stranger stumbling upon it [will
    release it].
There is a dead person on the side of the road; even a stranger will bury him.
[Yet] the heart you hold, it mercilessly forbears [bestowing pity].
[My] heart is aggrieved; [and my] tears fall on and on.

相彼投兔，尚或先之。
行有死人，尚或墐之。
君子秉心，維其忍之。
心之憂矣，涕既隕之。

You trust slander, as readily as raising a glass to a guest's toast.
You are not caring; refraining from thoroughly investigating accusations
    [against me].
When cutting trees down, one pulls to the side; when splitting firewood,
    one follows the grain.

[But you] release those who are guilty; and [instead] attribute it to me.

君子信讒，如或醻之。
君子不惠，不舒究之。
伐木掎矣，析薪杝矣。
舍彼有罪，予之佗矣。[14]

The poem continues on to more fully express the author's dejection. What we see in the "Xiaopan" poem is not only sorrow associated with misfortune but also frustration associated with one's parents, one's ruler (which in this case is his father) and *Tian* 天 (which is described as a kind of parental figure). Even a stranger will show pity on a dead body discovered on the side of the road, but the author's ruler will show no mercy to his own son. Instead, the ruler trusts in slander, withholds his favor, and blames his son for the mistakes of others. The author does not simply lament coming into the world in a time where his value will go unrecognized (themes already seen in the previous chapter); in addition he is perturbed and accusatory. His righteous desires were thwarted, but he does more than sorrow over his misfortune. Indeed, he wishes the world were different. He wishes his father were caring; he wishes that his father might stop attributing to him the guilt of others, and he questions the timing of *Tian* 天. What we see in this poem is someone holding others responsible for his difficulties—others who are close to him. So instead of blaming himself for failing to understand the timing of *Tian* 天, or blaming himself for failing to court the care of his father, the author incriminates them in the unfortunate act. These are people (or forces in the world) that should have known better. Yet rather than aiding the author in realizing his righteous desires they obstruct and frustrate him. In short, the resentment of the "Xiaopan" poem is discontent with harm caused by those who are supposed to care.[15]

Mengzi 6B3 does not only discuss the "Xiaopan" poem. Gongsun Chou also asks about another poem titled "Kaifeng." The background of the "Kaifeng" poem is less clear, but it is set in the voice of several sons who have been wronged by their mother.[16] Discussing this poem allows Mengzi to narrow the scope of proper resentment. *Yuan* 怨, we learn, is only appropriate when family members commit significant offenses. To resent them for minor offenses is to be too easily provoked. Although Mengzi does not distinguish between significant and minor offenses (other than providing examples of attempting to take a brother's life or passing over the oldest son in naming an heir), he does connect resentment with filial care (*xiao* 孝). To fail to be resentful when family members commit significant offenses is to treat them as distant relatives, and treating them as distant relatives is not the way to offer filial care. As such, Mengzi suggests that resentment is related to offering proper familial care.

It is also worth noting that *qin* 親, which I have been translating as "parents" or "family," can also refer to those nonfamilial people with whom one is close (as in *Analects* 17.7, which is discussed in chapter 1). As such, while most of the examples under discussion draw on familial relationships, resentment, as we will see, can also be an appropriate expression of discontent in relationships where people have become *like family*. In other words, when we depend on the care of others for our sense of self (i.e., our physical, psychological, or social well-being), we draw others in to a family-like situation where we render ourselves vulnerable to their concern or neglect. Resentment serves as an appropriate response to their neglect.

Earlier in the passage Mengzi also connects resentment with treating family members familially (*qinqin* 親親) as well as humaneness (*ren* 仁), both concepts that are related to filial care in a variety of early Confucian texts. Interestingly, we see here that proper resentment is associated with some of the most central Confucian concepts. In this light, if humaneness, in a general sense, is a sensitivity to care for others, and filial care is humaneness as it begins within the family (per *Analects* 1.2), resentment occurs when offense is dulled out in the place of care. Using the language of "offense," or *guo* 過 more literally to mean "exceeding proper boundaries," resentment happens when those close to us significantly breach the norms of offering proper care. Or, said differently, resentment occurs when those close to us take advantage of the vulnerability necessary for entering into meaningful relationships rooted in care.

In 6B3 Mengzi justifies resentment, but he does not describe it in much detail. Fortunately, the concluding line of the passage ties in with another passage in the *Mengzi* that also endorses resentment while providing a significant description of *yuan* 怨. In *Mengzi* 5A1, Wan Zhang 萬章, a disciple of Mengzi, asks Mengzi about an episode in Shun's life where he fled to the forest and began farming the land after his father, stepmother, and brother tried to kill him. Once there, Shun shed tears and called upon *Tian* 天. Wan Zhang asks what it meant for Shun to cry and call out to *Tian* 天. Mengzi's response is two characters: *yuanmu* 怨慕, which might be translated as, "[He was] resentful while yearning."[17] In other words, Shun resented his family's attempts to take his life, but he still yearned for their affection. His wailing expressed his frustration, and his calling out to *Tian* 天 expressed his desire to gain the affection of his family.

Understanding *mu* 慕 will shed some light on resentment. Kong Yingda 孔穎達 (574–648), in commenting on a passage from the *Liji* 《禮記》, uses a helpful analogy to explicate *mu* 慕. He states, "[*Mu* 慕] can be said [to describe a situation] where a father and mother are ahead [of their young child on the road]; and the young child is lagging behind, afraid that [he] will not catch up to them. So [he] cries out from behind while chasing after them" 謂父母在前，嬰兒在後，恐不及之，故在後啼呼而隨之.[18] *Mu* 慕, in this sense, is a fear of losing the attention of one's parents. A child left alone is vulnerable to all sorts of misfortunes, so he seeks after the security of those he knows best. *Mu* 慕 is therefore associated with protection, safeguard, and comfort. In a broader context, *mu* 慕 is about desiring appropriate care. A child lagging behind his parents longs for the safety guaranteed by his parents—a kind of safety that goes beyond merely preventing physical harm to include dependably offering concern for a wider array of personal development. As far as *Mengzi* 5A1 is concerned, *mu* 慕 is best understood as "yearning for affection" or "desiring care." In other words, Shun yearned for a situation such that he would be able to gain the constant care of his family.[19] While I say more about *yuan* 怨 later, we might briefly build on Kong Yingda's analogy to suggest that *yuan* 怨 is the feeling of frustration and hurt that children feel when their parents uniformly disregard their cries for comfort or when parents harm their children rather than creating a circumstance of constant care. In a larger sense, *yuan* 怨 occurs when those whose care we desire withhold their care or when they injure us in ways that cause us to question their concern for us. Stated succinctly, *yuan* 怨 occurs when those we are close with neglect our vulnerability.

In 5A1 Wan Zhang goes on to question how Shun could be resentful; after all, Wan Zhang explains, even if "[your] father and mother detest you, [you should still] labor to serve [them] without resentment" 父母惡之，勞而不怨. Mengzi responds by stating that a filial son desires the love (*ai* 愛) of his parents and that even the reward of running the kingdom would be insufficient to "relieve [a filial son's] distress" 解憂. Indeed, without reconciling with his family, Shun is (and should continue to be) distressed. Mengzi then explicates the relationship between resentment and desire for affection. He states, "When young, people yearn for the affection of their parents. When aware of physical attraction, [they] yearn for the affection of the young and beautiful. When married, [they] yearn for the affection of their wives. When serving as an official, [they] yearn for the affection of their ruler. If [they] do not gain [the affection of their] ruler, [they] burn inside themselves. Great filial care is to yearn for the affection of one's parents for one's entire life. At the age of 50, we see this in Shun" 人少，則慕父母；知好色，則慕少艾；有妻子，則慕妻子；仕則慕君，不得於君則熱中。大孝終身慕父母。五十而慕者，予於大舜見之矣. According to Mengzi, Shun is to be praised for maintaining his desire for affection throughout his life. Even at fifty years old he still sought the care of his parents. Perhaps more important, Mengzi describes the feeling associated with officials failing to gain the attention of those they serve as *rezhong* 熱中, which I translated quite literally as "burn inside." Alternative translations include "uneasy," "perturbed," or "agitated"; and in contemporary Chinese the term can also mean "fervent desire." While Mengzi mentions this specifically within the relationship between officials and rulers, I see little reason to believe that such a feeling does not also pertain to the other relationships he lists as well. *Rezhong* 熱中, in this sense, is what occurs when desire for affection is frustrated. When we do not gain the attention of others we care about, we feel upset in the sense of being put out of sorts or disturbed. Shun, in this light, remained distraught for a long time. Rather than moving on to search for the affection of others, he continued to desire the affection of his family. While Mengzi is not entirely clear here about the conditions that render these feelings appropriate, he clearly praises Shun for his continued unease with his family's lack of reciprocating his care.

In synthesizing the sources discussed thus far, we see that *yuan* 怨 is associated with terms of care such as *ren* 仁 (humaneness), *xiao* 孝 (filial care), *qinqin* 親親 (treating family members familially), and *ai* 愛 (love). These terms suggest that we can only truly resent those we care about.[20] While primarily manifest in parent–child relationships, resentment extends to all "close" (*qin* 親) relationships, or relationships where one's well-being is vulnerable to the other's care. When significant breaches of trust occur, one should feel resentment. Resentment is not only an accusatory anger but also a frustrated desire for affection—a burning that approaches outrage or even indignation when harm is offered instead of affection. Etymologically, the English word "resentment" is related to sentiment.[21] We might build on the Confucian resources presented here to think of resentment as a kind of reevaluation of our sentiment for significant others. As in the case of Shun, resentment should lead to a renewal of our sentiment—a guarded renewal where our anger alleviates self-blame and also protects ourselves to the degree possible from the continued harm of those who should care for us. Resentment, we might say, is a retooling of our devotion to significant others and often involves sorrow over the disappointment of reconsidering the appropriateness of our devotion.

I mentioned previously that most passages in early Confucian texts that mention resentment do not endorse it, making statements such as, "The exemplary person does not resent *Tian* 天" 君子不怨天.[22] It is also worth noting that Mengzi's interlocutors in 6B3 and 5A1 assume that resentment is inappropriate, and, as such, the debate takes place in a context where Mengzi seems to be arguing against (or nuancing) a dominant view.[23] This naturally raises the question of how to understand those passages that discourage resentment in light of passages such as *Mengzi* 6B3 and 5A1. I believe there are several responses to this question. For one, it is possible that what we see here is a diversity of perspectives in the Confucian tradition; some thinkers endorse resentment although most do not. The *Xunzi*, for instance, argues for a less responsive, and more naturalistic, *Tian* 天, and therefore it provides far fewer reasons to resent *Tian* 天.[24] While this explanation lends a certain degree of explanatory power, it does not fully account for inconsistencies within individual texts such as the *Mengzi*, which sometimes discourages resentment and at other times encourages resentment.

Additionally, it is entirely plausible that the tension between endorsing and discouraging resentment is due to the wide semantic range of *yuan* 怨. In this regard, bearing a grudge (*yuanyi* 怨艾, in contemporary Chinese) against one's parents or *Tian* 天 is not encouraged; however, being aggrieved (*beiyuan* 悲怨) by their major offenses is encouraged. Mengzi, in this light, is playing on *yuan*'s 怨 semantic range. I believe a variation of this theory best explains what is going on at least in the *Mengzi*. More specifically, the best way to make sense of divergent views of *yuan* 怨 is to understand these texts as endorsing a kind of authenticity where our initial reactions to situations serve to signify the depth of our relationships with others involved in those situations.[25] *Mengzi* 5A1 supports this reading.

In 5A1 Mengzi explicitly casts *jia* 恝 ("indifferent") in opposition to *yuan* 怨. He argues that a filial son should not be indifferent to his parents. *Yuan* 怨, as such, is a genuine reaction to major offenses inflicted upon us by our family members. To fail to be *yuan* 怨 is to fail to be attentive to the significance of these relations. At the same time, however, this feeling of resentment should not extend to hatred (*yuanhen* 怨恨).[26] The filial son does not hate his parents or *Tian* 天. In this sense, while we should allow the initial sentiment of *yuan* 怨 to inform our responses to these situations, we should not let this sentiment extend to the point of hatred. Sentiments such as resentment, therefore, are not to be suppressed since they are a part of sincere relationships, but at the same time neither are they to be spurred on to the point of excess.[27] Like many of the other feelings, dispositions, or virtues discussed in the *Mengzi*, *yuan* 怨 can become excessive, and therefore one should strive to keep it in proper bounds. Similar to the way that cultivating a pure character (*lian* 廉 or *qing* 清) can lead to "inflexibility" (*ai* 隘 in *Mengzi* 2A9) or disconnection with one's family (*Mengzi* 3B10), *yuan* 怨 can also lead to dispositions that are destructive to the self and relationships. In short, genuine feelings such as *yuan* 怨 are recognized and accepted as a necessary part of meaningful relationships. At the same time, Mengzi recognizes the ill effects of *yuan* 怨, yet he defends its importance in reacting to harm offered by those who are supposed to care.

Importantly, this notion of *yuan* 怨 encourages a rereading of other passages in early Confucian texts such as *Analects* 5.23, 17.9, and *Mengzi* 2B13 where *yuan* 怨 can in fact be understood in a positive light.[28]

As we will see in the next section, resentment is also tied to a creative impulse where pent up desire leads to the composition of texts. These texts work to connect the author's resentment with the reader's possibility of remaking the world in a way desired by the author. At the same time, these texts serve to form communities of commiseration where readers share in the regret of the authors. Readers and authors console each other in meeting an untimely end and seek comfort in a world they wish was otherwise.[29]

Frustration and Literary Production

Another prominent endorsement of resentment occurs in Qu Yuan's 屈原 (c. 340–278 BCE) biography in the *Shiji* 《史記》. According to the text, Qu Yuan had been a loyal minister to the ruler of Chu 楚, only to be slandered in court, demoted in rank, and eventually banished from Chu. Before committing suicide by drowning himself in a river, Qu Yuan purportedly composed several poems including the "Lisao" 離騷—a poem that laments his demise in the Chu court.[30] The term *lisao* 離騷 plays on the character *li* 離, which can mean "encounter" as well as "leave behind." So the "Lisao" is a record of Qu Yuan's encounter with sorrow (*sao* 騷), as well as a record of his attempt to leave sorrow behind (evident in the spirit journeys Qu Yuan makes in the text and finally in his suicide).[31] By the time of the *Shiji*, the "Lisao" was a well-known poem, admired by many scholars who were frustrated with their failed attempts at government service.[32] The *Shiji* provides the following explanation of the composition of the "Lisao":

> Qu [Yuan] rectified the Way and was upright in his conduct. [He] was absolutely loyal and completely wise when serving his ruler; [but when] slanderers cut him off [from the ruler, he was], in essence, "obstructed." While trustworthy, [he] encountered doubt; and while loyal [he] was maligned. Was it possible [for him] to be without resentment? When composing the "Lisao," Qu [Yuan] created it on the basis of his resentment.

> 屈平正道直行，竭忠盡智以事其君，讒人閒之，可謂窮矣。信而見疑，忠而被謗，能無怨乎？屈平之作《離騷》，蓋自怨生也。[33]

Qu Yuan is depicted as an exemplary minister. He is trustworthy, loyal, and wise. Yet his desires were obstructed and frustrated. The character *qiong* 窮 is sometimes used in contrast with *tong* 通, where it signifies blockage, limitation, or exhaustion in contrast with circulation. In this case, Qu Yuan's communication with the ruler is blocked, but in a more general sense, his hope in creating a better world is frustrated. Sima Qian (c. 145–86 BCE), the primary author of the *Shiji*, expresses some ambivalence about the feeling of resentment, yet he endorses Qu Yuan's resentment inasmuch as it led to the production of the "Lisao." An alternative translation of the final line in the quote above reads, "[The 'Lisao'] was born of resentment" 蓋自怨生也. Indeed, in this passage Sima Qian recognizes the productive nature of resentment, and in other places of the *Shiji* he reinforces this idea.

In the concluding chapter of the *Shiji*, Sima Qian recounts the final charge he received from his dying father. He describes this charge as *fafen* 發憤, literally a release of discontent or frustration. His father, Sima Tan 司馬談 (d. 110 BCE), explained this idea by recounting how great people of the past created texts, including Kongzi composing the *Chunqiu*. He then invoked the image of the *lin* 麟 (as discussed in chapter 3) to explain that 400 years have passed since the coming of the *lin* 麟 and no one has recorded the deeds of good ministers and rulers. In other words, Kongzi composed the *Chunqiu* to note the worthy accomplishments of those that came before him, and Sima Tan saw this as his task some four centuries later. Unfortunately, Sima Tan was unable to finish it. As such, his dying request is for his son, Sima Qian, to complete the task. He tells Sima Qian, "Proclaiming [your] name to future generations in order to glorify your parents is the greatest act of filial care" 揚名於後世，以顯父母，此孝之大者.[34] In this light, the *Shiji* is an expression of Sima Tan's frustration, inherited by his son, and produced as an act of filial care (both concepts shown earlier to be related to *yuan* 怨).

Sima Qian goes on to explain that Kongzi appeared several hundred years after Zhou Gong 周公, and since Kongzi's appearance it has now been another several hundred years; thus the appearance of another great figure is due. Sima Qian clearly sees himself as such a figure—a figure charged with "continuing [the tradition of] the *Chunqiu*" 繼《春秋》.[35] Sima Qian goes so far as to associate his composition of the *Shiji* with the composition of the great texts of the past. He states,

The authors of the *Shijing* and *Shangshu* were in constrained circumstances, [yet] they desired to follow after the longing of their ambitions. Previously, [when] Xi Bo was imprisoned in Youli, [he] let flow [i.e., wrote] the *Zhouyi*. [When] Kongzi was stuck between Chen and Cai, [he] created the *Chunqiu*. [When] Qu Yuan was banished, [he] wrote the *Lisao*. [When] Zuo Qiu lost his sight, [he] put together the *Guoyu*. [When] Sunzi was punished with getting his feet cut off, [he] recorded the *Bingfa*. [When] Buwei was exiled to Shu, [he] passed down the *Lülan* to future generations. [When] Han Fei was imprisoned by the Qin, [he wrote] the *Shuonan* and *Gufen*. The 300 poems of the *Shijing* were largely composed when the sages and worthies gave vent to their frustrations (*fafen* 發憤). These people all had hopes that were stopped up and knotted. [Their hopes] were unable to flow on their paths. Therefore [these men] recorded the affairs of the past in thinking about the people of the future.

夫《詩》《書》隱約者，欲遂其志之思也。昔西伯拘羑里，演《周易》；孔子厄陳蔡，作《春秋》；屈原放逐，著《離騷》；左丘失明，厥有《國語》；孫子臏腳，而論《兵法》；不韋遷蜀，世傳《呂覽》；韓非囚秦，《說難》、《孤憤》；

《詩》三百篇，大抵賢聖發憤之所為作也。此人皆意有所郁結，不得通其道也，故述往事，思來者。[36]

As translated, this passage exhibits the imagery of obstruction and flow. In each of the cases mentioned, the desire of some great figure is impeded by the unfortunate circumstances of his age. Their desires finally find release in the composition of texts.[37] While Sima Qian explicitly mentions *fafen* 發憤 in relation to the *Shijing*, there is little reason to believe that *fa fen* 發憤 is not related to the production of the other texts as well. Notably, the *Lisao*, which was created on the basis of *yuan* 怨, is also brought into this context. *Fen* 憤 and *yuan* 怨 each entail pent up desire.

Analects 7.8 discusses *fen* 憤 as a precondition for learning—if students are not full of desire to learn, Kongzi explains, there will be nothing to let flow on the path of learning (*bufen buqi* 不憤不啟). In his commentary on this passage, Zhu Xi 朱熹 (1130-1200) defines *fen* 憤 as follows: "*Fen* 憤 means to have one's heart seek for a path [to fulfill a desire to learn] but not yet find it" 憤者，心求通而未得之意.[38] Zhu Xi's notion of *fen* 憤 aligns with the notion of obstruction. In this regard, *fafen* 發憤 is to find such a path or "to release" 發 one's desire.

The desire of the individuals described in this passage from the *Shiji* is a desire for the world to be different than it is—a desire for the world to accord with their *dao* 道. Since they are unable to transform their circumstances, they "record the affairs of the past in thinking about the people of the future" 述往事，思來者. In other words, when they create texts such as the *Zhouyi* and the *Chunqiu*, they intend these texts to become tools that others in the future might use to implement their *dao* 道. Interestingly, resentment or frustration in these contexts is a creative force.[39] These figures do not resign themselves to total defeat, nor do they pity themselves to the point of despair. Rather, their resentment serves as a constructive impulse in the production of texts that pass on tradition. In this light, we might even say that their resentment entails an element of hope—a hope circumscribed by the limitations of their times. Additionally, it is worth noting that resentment functions as more than a "remainder" or "residue" of encountering an unfortunate circumstance; rather it functions as a constitutive part of attempting to cope with misfortune.

At the same time, however, the hope entailed in *fafen* 發憤 is a mitigated hope. Indeed, there is something quite tragic about literature produced because the author is unable to realize his righteous desires in his current generation. Literary production in these circumstances is also tragic in the sense that the author will never truly know those he writes for (although his readers may in some sense be said to know him), nor will he see his desires come to fruit. Even if early Confucians believed in a larger teleological plan where their *dao* 道

would eventually be realized, their circumstances are still tragic in the sense that they will never *personally* experience life in the full flourishing of the *dao* 道.[40] Alternatively, if they did not believe in a teleological force eventually ushering in the *dao* 道, then the fulfillment of the *dao* 道 is contingent on unknown others in the future. As such, if these texts are not passed down to the right hands, there is no way for the *dao* 道 to be realized. In either view, the hope entailed in *fafen* 發憤 is a hope set in contrast to personal anguish, either because one will never live in an ideal society or because of the uncertain nature of transmitting the texts necessary to establish such a society. Resentment, in a larger context, is part of regret in the sense that it is a reaction to a world that one wishes was otherwise. Indeed, one wishes for loving parents, profound governors, and upright compatriots, among other things. Instead one encounters abusive parents, unprincipled governors, and corrupt ministers, and as such resentment encourages a reexamination of the world. As we will see in the next section of this chapter, resentment can also lead to transgression, in particular when the creation of texts rooted in resentment requires going beyond the bounds dictated by social norms.

Transgression

Mengzi 3B9 is interesting because it develops themes such as the moral agent's pent-up desire to transform the world and the creation of texts in response to frustration. It develops these themes by describing how the release of frustrated desire can lead to the transgression of rules or standards. In particular, Kongzi's creation of the *Chunqiu* is described as an act only appropriate for the ruler (*tianzi zhishiye* 天子之事也). However, Kongzi is compelled to break this rule for the sake of providing others an opportunity to realize his *dao* 道. In *Mengzi* 3B9 we see this idea applied to not only Kongzi but also to many of the other great sages of the past, as well as to Mengzi in his own age. Importantly, my argument here is not concerned with the nature of such a transgression. In other words, I am bracketing the question of whether or not these transgressions impact the integrity of the moral agent. Indeed, as discussed in chapter 1, there are many resources within the Confucian tradition to understand actions such as Kongzi's as justified or noninjurious to the moral agent's integrity. As such, as far as this chapter is concerned, I am interested simply in establishing the fact of transgression. Future chapters will build on this fact to demonstrate that early Confucians saw the world as conflictual in the sense of presenting moral agents with irresolvable value conflicts.

Despite the length of the passage, it is necessary to quote it in full.

> Gongduzi said, "Those unaffiliated with us all say that you are fond of rhetorical strategies; may [I] ask why?"

公都子曰：「外人皆稱夫子好辯，敢問何也？」

Mengzi responded, "How could I be fond of rhetorical strategies? [Rather,] I am compelled [to engage in them]. The world has been around for a long time. At times [it] is ordered, and at times [it] is chaotic. During the age of Yao, water flowed in the wrong direction, and all of the states were inundated. Snakes and dragons lived there, [but] the people had nowhere to settle down. Those living in the lowlands made nests [in trees], and those living in the highlands made caves [in mountains]. The *Shangshu* says, "The profuse waters warned me." The "profuse waters" referred to the floods. Yu was sent to manage the floods. He dug waterways so that [the water] could flow to the sea, [and he] pushed back the snakes and dragons so that [they] were relegated to the marshes. The water [thereby] followed the course of the earth, and flowed together forming the Jiang, Huai, Yellow, and Han rivers. Dangers and hindrances were then far away from human beings, and harmful animals were vanquished. After this, human beings were able to find flat land to live on.

孟子曰：「予豈好辯哉？予不得已也。天下之生久矣，一治一亂。當堯之時，水逆行，氾濫於中國。蛇龍居之，民無所定。下者為巢，上者為營窟。《書》曰：『洚水警余。』洚水者，洪水也。使禹治之，禹掘地而注之海，驅蛇龍而放之菹。水由地中行，江、淮、河、漢是也。險阻既遠，鳥獸之害人者消，然後人得平土而居之。

Yao and Shun passed away, and the Way of the sages deteriorated. Violent rulers came about, replacing [each other in succession]. [They] tore down the palaces and homes [of Yao and Shun] in order to build [private] lakes and moats; [as such] the people had nowhere to rest. [They] got rid of farmland in order to build [private] parks; and as such the people were unable to get food and clothing. Wicked theories and violent actions repeatedly came about; and with the increase in parks, lakes, and marshlands, wild animals came back. Then Zhou 紂 personally saw to plunging the world into great chaos. Zhou Gong 周公 assisted Wu Wang in punishing Zhou 紂 and attacking the city of Yan. For three years [they] rallied against their ruler. [They] pushed back Fei Lian to the edge of the sea and slaughtered him. Altogether they destroyed 50 states; and drove back tigers, leopards, rhinos, and elephants so that these wild animals stayed far away [from people]. The whole world greatly rejoiced. The *Shangshu* says, "Great and splendid; the plans of Wen Wang. A great inheritance; fiercely [employed] by Wu Wang. [Given] to assist and awaken us, [their] posterity. All of it so upright, nothing lacking."

「堯、舜既沒，聖人之道衰。暴君代作，壞宮室以為汙池，民無
所安息；棄田以為園囿，使民不得衣食。邪說暴行又作，園囿、
汙池、沛澤多而禽獸至。及紂之身，天下又大亂。周公相武王，
誅紂伐奄，三年討其君，驅飛廉於海隅而戮之。滅國者五十，驅
虎、豹、犀、象而遠之。天下大悅。《書》曰：『丕顯哉，文王
謨！丕承哉，武王烈！佑啟我後人，咸以正無缺。』」

The age deteriorated and the Way became obscure. Wicked theories and
violent actions came about. There were cases where ministers killed their
rulers and sons killed their fathers. Kongzi feared for the worst, so he
created the *Chunqiu*. [Creating] the *Chunqiu* is the affair of a king; this
is why Kongzi said, "Those who recognize me will do so because of the
Chunqiu. Those who fault me will do so because of the *Chunqiu*."

「世衰道微，邪說暴行有作，臣弒其君者有之，子弒其父者有
之。孔子懼，作《春秋》。《春秋》，天子之事也。是故孔子
曰：『知我者其惟春秋乎！罪我者其惟春秋乎！』」

Sage-rulers have not come about, the feudal lords are proud and self-
indulgent, and recluses level unbridled criticism. The words of Yang
Zhu and Mo Di fill the world. [In looking] at the teachings [offered]
throughout the world, if they are not in favor of Yang Zhu, they are
in favor of Mo Di. Yang Zhu [advocates] being self-indulgent; this is
to be without a ruler. Mo Di [advocates] impartial care; this is to be
without a father. Being without a father and without a ruler is to be a
wild animal. Gongming Yi said, "With bountiful meat in the kitchen
and healthy horses in the stalls, the people are emaciated—their starved
corpses lying in the wild. This leads wild animals to eat people." The
Way of Yang Zhu and Mo Di goes on without reprieve, and the Way of
Kongzi remains darkened. These wicked theories deceive the people and
obstruct humaneness and rightness. When humaneness and rightness
are obstructed, wild animals are led to eat human flesh, and before long
people will eat each other. Greatly fearing this, I protect the Way of the
former sages; opposing Yang Zhu and Mo Di; and casting aside extravagant speech so that wicked theories cannot come about. What comes
forth in one's heart [can] harm one's actions; and what comes forth in
one's actions [can] harm one's government. If the sages were to return,
[they] would not change what I have said.

「聖王不作，諸侯放恣，處士橫議，楊朱、墨翟之言盈天下。
天下之言，不歸楊，則歸墨。楊氏為我，是無君也；墨氏兼
愛，是無父也。無父無君，是禽獸也。公明儀曰：『庖有肥

肉，廏有肥馬，民有飢色，野有餓莩，此率獸而食人也。』楊
墨之道不息，孔子之道不著，是邪說誣民，充塞仁義也。仁義
充塞，則率獸食人，人將相食。吾為此懼，閑先聖之道，距楊
墨，放淫辭，邪說者不得作。作於其心，害於其事；作於其
事，害於其政。聖人復起，不易吾言矣。

In former times Yu suppressed the floods and thereby brought peace to
the world; Zhou Gong 周公 annexed barbarian lands and drove away
wild animals, thereby giving rest to the people; and Kongzi composed the
Chunqiu, thereby inspiring fear in rebellious ministers and unprincipled
sons. A poem says, "[I] attacked the Rong and Di tribes; and punished
Jing and Shu. As such, there is none that dare to strike me." Those whom
Zhou Gong 周公 attacked were those [who advocated] being without
fathers or rulers. I likewise desire to rectify people's hearts, to bring an
end to wicked theories, to resist indecorous action, [and] to cast aside
extravagant speech; thereby inheriting [the Way] of the three sages. [So]
how could I be fond of rhetorical strategies? I am compelled [to engage
in them]. Whoever uses their words to resist Yang Zhu and Mo Di is a
disciple of the sages.

「昔者禹抑洪水而天下平，周公兼夷狄驅猛獸而百姓寧，孔子
成《春秋》而亂臣賊子懼。詩云：『戎狄是膺，荊舒是懲，則
莫我敢承。』無父無君，是周公所膺也。我亦欲正人心，息邪
說，距詖行，放淫辭，以承三聖者；豈好辯哉？予不得已也。
能言距楊墨者，聖人之徒也。」

There is a lot happening in this passage. It begins with Mengzi making a distinction between being fond of rhetorical strategies (*haobian* 好辯) and being compelled to engage in rhetorical strategies (*budeyi* 不得已). The notion of being
compelled, or *budeyi* 不得已 (literally "cannot stop"), entails conflicting desires.
On the one hand, Mengzi does not want to engage in rhetorical strategies (for
reasons discussed later); on the other hand he feels he must. Indeed, according to
this passage, if he is to bring order to the world, he has no other choice. The Way
of the sages, manifest in values such as humaneness and rightness, is obstructed
(*chongsai* 充塞) by alternative theories that fill (*ying* 盈) the world. Mengzi,
desiring to unobstruct the Way of the sages, is left with no other means besides
rhetorical strategies.

The character I have been translating as rhetorical strategies is *bian* 辯.
Etymologically, *bian* 辯 is comprised of the character *yan* 言 placed between two
xin 辛 characters. The notion of *yan* 言 in early Chinese texts is multi-faceted.[41]
It is often translated as "words," and coincidentally it parallels the complexity of

the English term "words" (with significant differences). For my purposes, *yan* 言 refers to verbal or written language one uses to interact with other people. While much more could be said about *yan* 言, this general definition suffices to establish my point.

Xin 辛, in contemporary Chinese, means "toilsome," "bitter," and "grieved." In early China it had similar meanings. Xu Shen, in the *Shuowen Jiezi*, defines *xin* 辛 as "[feeling] bitter pain to the point that tears and sobs emerge" 辛痛即泣 出.[42] In the same passage he also connects *xin* 辛 with *zui* 辠, meaning a crime or offense. Contemporary scholars likewise recognize the "offending" aspects of *xin* 辛, explaining its earliest occurrences as a pictograph of a knife used to punish criminals.[43] When discussing characters with two *xins* 辛 Xu continues to highlight notions of offense and pain. The character *bian* 辡 ("incriminate" or "wrangle") Xu explains as "criminals accusing each other at court" 辠人相與 訟也.[44] The character *bian* 辨 ("discriminate" or "dispute") he glosses simply as "anxiety" 憂.[45] Finally, the character *bian* 辯 ("rhetorical strategies") he defines as "manage" or "control" 治.[46] Indeed, all five of these characters can convey some sense of transgression, distress, or need for order.

Other early Confucian texts highlight the transgressive nature of *bian* 辯. When Kongzi ordered the execution of Shaozheng Mao 少正卯 (c. 500 BCE), one of the reasons he provides for the execution is that Shaozheng Mao engaged in *bian* 辯. Kongzi further explains that Shaozheng Mao's "words and discourses served to conceal [his] iniquity, deluding the people of the state" 言談足飾邪 營眾.[47] In the "Zhengming" 正名 chapter of the *Xunzi*, Xunzi also asserts that a good ruler (*junzi* 君子) does not engage in *bian* 辨 (*bian* 辨 is often synonymous with *bian* 辯) because *bian* 辨 frequently involves twisting words and thereby creating confusion (*luan* 亂) in the state.[48] Instead, a good ruler "leads the people with the Way" 道之以道.[49] Other early texts likewise discourage *bian* 辯.[50]

Indeed, some of these texts assign negative connotations to *bian* 辯 similar to the negative connotations sometimes given to the English term "rhetoric," where rhetoric is associated with valuing persuasion above honesty. The best illustration of this is in the "Qujie Jie" 屈節解 chapter of the *Kongzi Jiayu*. The title "Qujie Jie" 屈節解 literally means "explaining the bending of rules (or standards)." In the second passage, Kongzi gathers his disciples together and explains that their home state of Lu 魯 is threatened by Tian Chang 田常 (c. 485 BCE), who had recently come to power in the state of Qi 齊. Kongzi, desiring to save Lu, suggests "bending the rules" 屈節 in order to preserve the state. Several of his disciples volunteer to negotiate with Tian Chang, only to have Kongzi refuse their invitations. Finally they nominate his disciple Zigong 子貢 (520–446 BCE) to go on the mission because Zigong knows how to employ the art of rhetorical strategizing (*yongbian* 用辯).[51] Kongzi consents. What follows is a long and convoluted narrative of Zigong traveling to various states and "persuading" 說 those in power to attack each other or to defend the state of Lu. In the end, Zigong is successful in preserving Lu from harm but only at the cost of destroying other states and yet strengthening others. In the closing line of the passage, Kongzi warns,

> My original desire was to ruin Qi and preserve Lu. Yet strengthening the state of Jin to impoverish the state of Wu, and allowing the state of Wu to be destroyed while the state of Yue becomes the dominant power [in the area, is due to] Zigong's art of persuasion. [Indeed,] beautiful words harm truthfulness, so be cautious of words!
>
> 夫其亂齊存魯，吾之始願。若能強晉以弊吳，使吳亡而越霸者，賜之說也。美言傷信，慎言哉！[52]

In this passage, Zigong bends the rules by means of *bian* 辯. His "beautiful words" 美言 manipulate others to take action that may not be in their best interest; however, their actions serve the interest of Zigong. Kongzi's ambivalent response to the situation works well to capture the necessary, yet transgressive, nature of *bian* 辯. If you want to preserve the things that matter in life while living in chaotic times, it turns out you must be willing to engage in the art of deception.[53]

In this light, when Mengzi explains that he is not fond of rhetorical strategies, he is saying that he does not take pleasure in the transgressive activities entailed in rhetorical strategies. At the same time, he is compelled to participate in such activities because it is the only way to protect that which matters to him. He is compelled to engage in transgressive activity for the sake of reestablishing the Way of the sages. Importantly though, Mengzi also sees himself following after the Way of the sages. In short, they too engaged in transgressive activities.

One of these transgressive activities is the overthrow of Zhou 紂 (1105–1046 BCE), the final ruler of the Shang dynasty. The passage explains that Zhou Gong 周公 and Wu Wang "rallied against their ruler for three years" 三年討其君. While overthrowing an evil ruler is justified in a number of early Confucian texts (including the *Mengzi*), it is rarely understood as an unproblematic event in that the act does not need to be explained.[54] Passage 3B9 complicates justification by using the notion of ministers killing their rulers in later times as a sign that "the times had deteriorated and that the Way became obscure" 世衰道微. Furthermore, "three years" 三年, the time that Zhou Gong 周公 and Wu Wang fought against Zhou 紂, is the same length of time a minister would normally mourn for his ruler at his ruler's death. Indeed, it seems that Mengzi alludes to a deep contradiction in the actions of Zhou Gong 周公 and Wu Wang. The final show of respect a minister offers his ruler becomes, in this case, a final display of insubordination. Notably, in the *Shiji*, Wu Wang engages in similar behavior, rushing off to fight Zhou 紂 instead of mourning the death of his own father, and in the *Analects* the musical performances that recount Wu Wang's overthrow of the Shang dynasty are described by Kongzi as "entirely beautiful but not entirely good" 盡美矣，未盡善也.[55] I say more about Wu Wang in chapter 6. Here I focus on Kongzi's transgressive act in 3B9—composing the *Chunqiu*.

The *Chunqiu* purports to catalogue the activities of the aristocracy from the state of Lu between 722–481 BCE. According to tradition, Kongzi composed the *Chunqiu* after realizing that he would not be able to personally implement his *dao* 道.[56] The *Chunqiu*, in this view, expresses the *dao* 道 of Kongzi in historical narrative. As the contemporary scholar Piotr Gibas explains, the *Chunqiu* is understood by many of Kongzi's followers as a kind of "oracle." Kongzi produces the oracle by interpreting the past, and then those in later times use the oracle to live well in the future. Gibas states, "[Kongzi] is, at the same time, both the reader of the future—the prognosticator who understands the portent—and the writer of the past—the narrator who explains it."[57] While historically speaking it is difficult to substantiate a connection between Kongzi and the *Chunqiu*, Mengzi clearly believed Kongzi to be the author. In *Mengzi* 3B9 he states that Kongzi wrote the *Chunqiu* in response to his chaotic age. The problem, however, is that composing the *Chunqiu* is "the affair of the king" 天子之事也. In other words, putting a text together like the *Chunqiu* requires royal permission or a proper office (*wei* 位) in the state, which Kongzi did not have. As such, Kongzi explains that he will be praised and blamed because of the *Chunqiu*.[58] He will be praised because the text preserves the Way of the sages, but he will be blamed for engaging in activity reserved for the king.

Admittedly, the line "[Creating] the *Chunqiu* is the affair of a king" 《春秋》，天子之事也 is ambiguous. An alternative rendering might say that "the *Chunqiu* [records] the affairs of the king." In this view, Mengzi is merely stating that the *Chunqiu* offers a history of the central states from the perspective of the state of Lu and not that Kongzi is transgressing his social station by taking upon himself the authority of the king. Commentators have debated the meaning of this line for quite some time. Gao Gong 高拱 (1512–1578) presents a fairly standard interpretation that reads this line in terms of recording the affairs of the king. He states, "The line about the affairs of the king refers to Kongzi illuminating the exemplary policies of Wen Wang and Wu Wang, and following the feudal lords in respecting the royal family. [It] does not refer to him assuming the authority of the king" 夫天子之事云者謂其明文武之憲章，率諸侯以尊王室。非謂其假天子之權也.[59] Indeed, many commentators go to significant lengths to refute the notion that "Kongzi, lacking a position in the government, took upon himself 242 years of royal authority" 無其位而託二百四十二年南面之權.[60] Interestingly, however, while most traditional interpreters refute the notion of Kongzi illicitly attaining royal authority, many of them still read *tianzi zhi shi ye* 天子之事也 as an explanation of the authority necessary to produce a text such as the *Chunqiu*. In their view, creating the *Chunqiu* does indeed require special authority; however, Kongzi, one way or another, had such authority.

One fairly common view in this regard, claims that Kongzi was the "uncrowned king" 素王, and therefore he had the authority to produce the *Chunqiu*. Parts of this view are found as early as the Han dynasty, when Ban Gu (32–92 CE) 班固 (quoting Dong Zhongshu 董仲舒) recorded, "In creating the *Chunqiu*, Kongzi first rectified the office of king, and then strung together the myriad affairs [of the world], [thereby] revealing the patterns of an uncrowned king" 孔子作春秋，先正王而繫萬事，見素王之文焉.[61] Later Han commentators such as Zhao Qi 趙岐 (c. 108–201) also state, "The age deteriorated and the Way became obscure during the era of decline in the Zhou dynasty. Kongzi feared that the upright Way would be destroyed so he created the *Chunqiu* by relying on the historical records in the state of Lu, and by arranging the regulations of an uncrowned king. [This] is called the affairs of a king" 世衰道微，周衰之時也。孔子懼正道遂滅，故作《春秋》因魯史記，設素王之法；謂天子之事也.[62] Because Kongzi was the uncrowned king, he possessed the authority necessary to compose the *Chunqiu*. As another traditional commentator states, "Although in identity the Master was a commoner; in his mission the Master was no commoner" 不然夫子之身則匹夫也；夫子之職則非匹夫也.[63]

While denying that Kongzi's act of creating the *Chunqiu* had any negative impact on Kongzi's character, these commentators still feel the need to account for Kongzi's action. Indeed, they may not see the composition of the *Chunqiu* as a transgression in the sense of violating ethical standards, but they do see it as a disruption of social norms that must be explained, and it is the fact of explanation that reveals the troubling aspects of *Mengzi* 3B9.[64]

Other passages in the *Mengzi* strengthen the notion of transgression in Kongzi creating the *Chunqiu*. The very next passage, 3B10, for instance, tells about Chen Zhongzi 陳仲子 (c. 300 BCE) who nearly went blind and deaf because he refused to eat anything "unrighteous" 不義 (discussed more fully in chapter 6). His quest to be pure (*lian* 廉), Mengzi explains, is not something a human being could actually accomplish. This is because being human entails living in a world where we cannot always ensure the appropriateness of every interaction. Although individual passages in early Chinese texts are sometimes randomly grouped together, other times they are grouped according to common themes, and this theme of necessary transgression is a primary contender for common themes among this section of the *Mengzi*.

A more explicit example of the problematic nature of Kongzi composing the *Chunqiu* is found in *Mengzi* 4B21. This passage starts out similar to 3B9 with Mengzi explaining that when the teachings of the former kings began to vanish, other paradigmatic people came forth to spread those teachings by creating texts based on the historical records of their states. Mengzi mentions several of these texts and then quotes Kongzi, saying, "I have usurped their significances" 其義則丘竊取之矣. While this line is somewhat ambiguous, in context, and largely accepted in the commentarial tradition, it refers to Kongzi composing the *Chunqiu*. In other words, when writing the *Chunqiu*, Kongzi illicitly took the significant aspects of these other texts and incorporated them into the *Chunqiu*. As Shuangfeng Rao 雙峯饒 (c. 1250) states, "The line 'I have usurped their significances' refers to the fact that in composing the *Chunqiu*, Kongzi enacted the rewards and punishments of a king, but he himself was a commoner. So he said 'usurp' as an expression of self-blame and self-deprecation" 『其義則某竊取之』方是孔子之春秋，以匹夫行天子賞罰。故曰『竊取』自咎自謙之辭.[65] In this light, Kongzi exceeded his social station by acting as a king. This occurred because the historical chronicle he produced spoke not only for his state (a position he did not hold) but also for all the states in the kingdom. Passages such as *Mengzi* 4B21 strengthen the theme of transgression in 3B9.

The commentaries on passages such as these establish a further connection between the *Chunqiu* and the transgression of rules or norms. This is particularly worth mentioning when interpreters connect the *Chunqiu* with the notion of *quan* 權, or moral discretion, which as we saw in chapter 1, entails transgressing established standards for the sake of implementing the *dao* 道. These associations are often quite explicit. Hu Bingwen 胡炳文 (1250–1333), for instance, calls the *Chunqiu* "the Sage's book of moral discretion" 聖人之權書.[66] In a more extended comment, Zhang Daheng 張大亨 (c. 1085) relates the *Chunqiu* to moral discretion in the context of *Analects* 9.30 and *Mengzi* 4A17 (both passages previously discussed in chapter 1). He states,

> Kongzi said, "There may be [those] that can travel the Way [with you], but are not yet able to establish [their] character with [you], nor yet able to employ moral discretion (*quan* 權) with [you]." Mengzi said, "For men and women not to touch when exchanging things accords with ritual propriety, [but] to extend a hand to assist one's drowning sister-in-law is a case of moral discretion (*quan* 權)." If not a worthy, [one] cannot employ *quan* 權; and if not a sage, [one] cannot fathom [it]. Because it is so difficult to fathom, [we can use] the *Chunqiu* to get to the bottom of it.
>
> 孔子曰『可與適道，未可與立，未可與權。』孟子曰『男女授受不親，禮也。嫂溺援之以手，權也。』權非賢者不能用；非聖人不能察也。以其難察，故《春秋》盡其辭焉。[67]

The *Chunqiu*, in this light, serves as a means for teaching its readers how to employ moral discretion. As we also saw in chapter 1, *quan* 權 is understood as a difficult activity to master, and so the *Chunqiu* provides the key. Practically speaking, *quan* 權 is about negotiating value conflicts, and the *Chunqiu* presents Kongzi's method of *quan* 權. In other words, the *Chunqiu* displays a process of sifting through the complexities of interpersonal exchange. It teaches its readers how to negotiate the difficulties of political interaction by showing how Kongzi judged the interaction of aristocrats over a 200-year span. It shows which people are worthy of emulation and which people are worthy of disdain. In short, it displays how we are to navigate our way through a world where choices are not always simple and where good is not always apparent. Interestingly, the *Chunqiu* is not only composed by means of Kongzi's transgression, but it also teaches its readers how to transgress.

The purpose of this section is to connect transgression with resentment and to show how the early Confucian texts endorse transgression as a legitimate means of regretting the condition of the world. Kongzi composes the *Chunqiu* to relieve his pent-up frustration with his times. Mengzi sees himself following after Kongzi by engaging in rhetorical strategies, and Sima Qian sees himself following after Kongzi in composing the *Shiji*. Each of these men understood their role as reestablishing the sagely Way. In speaking about the creation of the *Chunqiu* and the *Shiji*, Michael Puett refers to a "tragic possibility."[68] The language of "possibility" suggests an opportunity to reorder the world. The language of "tragedy" refers to the transgressive nature of this opportunity. In other words, the coming forth of these texts demonstrates that creating an ordered world is sometimes rooted in violating the very norms of order one seeks to create.

Conclusion

Several portions of this book touch on the recurring theme of saving someone from drowning. In 3B9, Mengzi compares his efforts of responding to Yang Zhu and Mo Di with Yu saving the kingdom from the floods. Because of Yu's hard work, which came at the expense of him serving someone that executed his father, people were able to live in accordance with the *dao* 道. Similarly, in Mengzi's view, his own involvement in the transgressive activity of rhetorical strategies would likewise create the opportunity to order the world. The traditional commentator, Chen Li 陳櫟 (1252–1334), ties these two activities together as follows: "In refuting Yang Zhu and Mo Di, Mengzi's efforts were not any less than [the efforts of] Yu in controlling the flood waters. Floods may drown people's bodies, [but] heterodox ideas ensnare and drown people's minds; and drowned minds are even worse than drowned bodies" 孟子闢楊墨，功不在禹治洪水下者。洪水溺人之身，異端陷溺人心。心溺之禍甚於身溺故也。[69] In Chen's view, the work of the sage is to save people from drowning, whether the drowning is literal or figurative. Interestingly, in the context of *Mengzi* 3B9, the work of saving people from drowning is transgressive work, and it is rooted in conflicting desires that seek on the one hand to realize the Way of the sages but on the other hand to avoid violating social norms. The notion of *budeyi* 不得已, which I explained earlier as "reluctance," reflects the ambivalent nature of transgression. It captures the tragic sensibility of resentment and regret. Zhu Xi, in speaking about *Mengzi* 4A17, explains *quan* 權 as "an action compelled by urgency" 急遽不得已之為.[70] Indeed, these are acts of exigent reluctance due to their transgressive nature.

Resentment is a feeling of frustration and anger we experience when those whose care we depend on offer harm in place of care. It is a natural response when our trust is significantly breached. Resentment signifies, to turn a phrase from Robert Douglas-Fairhurst, that values are threatened and norms are out of place. While Douglas-Fairhurst is talking specifically about the feeling of disgust (not unrelated to resentment), his analysis is effective in explaining resentment as well. He states, "[In] these contexts, expressions of [resentment] work like ethical sign-posts, allowing individual characters and their audience to check their bearings in a world where the line between good and evil, or right and wrong, starts to look simultaneously like a division and a continuum."[71] Indeed, resentment serves as an opportunity to regret the complex condition of the world.

Notes

1. Teng Zhixian 滕志賢, *Xinyi Shijing Duben* 《新譯詩經讀本》 (Taibei Shi 臺北市: Sanmin shuju 三民書局, 2011), 598–599. Hereafter, *Shijing.*

2. Xu Shen 許慎, *Shuowen Jiezi* 《說文解字》 (Beijing: Zhonghua shuju, 2004), 221.

3. Axel Schuessler, *ABC Etymological Dictionary of Old Chinese* (Honolulu: University of Hawai'i Press, 2007), 594; and Bernhard Karlgren, *Grammata Serica Recensa* (Stockholm: Museum of Far Eastern Antiquities, 1957), 83. I thank Newell Ann Van Auken for pointing this out and for her many other helpful comments on this chapter.

4. *Analects* 4.18 and 20.2. See also *Liji* 31.9/140/20.

5. *Kongzi Jiayu* 7.1/8/25.

6. *Xunzi* 4/13/19–4/14/1.

7. Similar sentiments are expressed in *Liji* 32.8/143/19–27, *Analects* 7.15, *Xunzi* 30.144.11–13, *Shuoyuan* 16.147/133/22, and Yi Zhongtian 易中天, ed., *Xinyi Guoyu Duben* 《新譯國語讀本》 (Taibei Shi 臺北市: Sanmin shuju 三民書局, 2006), 217.

8. Eric S. Nelson, "Recognition and Resentment in the Confucian *Analects*," *Journal of Chinese Philosophy* 40.2 (June 2013): 287–306.

9. Nelson, "Recognition and Resentment," 294, 295, 296, and 302.

10. Nelson, "Recognition and Resentment," 294.

11. Nelson, "Recognition and Resentment," 296.

12. See James Behuniak, *Mencius on Becoming Human* (Albany: State University of New York Press, 2005), 64–65; Philip J. Ivanhoe, "A Question of Faith." *Early China* 13 (1988): 153–165; Michael J. Puett, "Following the Commands of Heaven: The Notion of *Ming* in Early China," in *The Magnitude of Ming: Command, Allotment, and Fate in Chinese Culture*, ed. Christopher Lupke (Honolulu: University of Hawai'i Press, 2005), 60–61; Benjamin I. Schwartz, *The World of Thought In Ancient China.* (Cambridge, MA: Harvard University Press, 1985), 127; Edward Slingerland, Trans., *Confucius: Analects* (Indianapolis: Hackett, 2003), 168; and Maoze Zhang, "Confucius' Transformation of Traditional Religious Ideas," *Frontiers of Philosophy in China* 6.1 (2011): 31. For an alternative view of resentment in a comparative context see Kwong-loi Shun, "Resentment and Forgiveness in Confucian Thought," *Journal of East-West Thought* 4.4 (December 2014): 13–35.

13. For versions of this story see *Lienüzhuan* 《列女傳》 7.3, "Zhou You Xiusi" 周幽褒姒, and Ma Teying 馬特盈, ed., *Shiji Jinzhu* 《史記今註》 (Taibei 台北: Taiwan Shangwu yinshuguan 臺灣商務印書館, 1987), 129–131. Hereafter, *Shiji.*

14. *Shijing*, 594–601. The notion of frustration and sorrow in poetry is particular acute in the *Chuci* 《楚辭》, many of the poems written by men who saw themselves as followers of Kongzi.

15. It is also worth noting the upward direction of the discontent. Sons resent fathers, and younger brothers resent older brothers. Rarely is it the other way around.

16. I follow Bryan Van Norden on this. *Mengzi: With Selections from Traditional Commentaries* (Indianapolis: Hackett, 2008), 161. Interestingly, the *Shijing* is seen as endorsing resentment in other places as well including *Analects* 17.9. See also *Shiji*, 2504.

17. Franklin Perkins takes *yuanmu* 怨慕 as "angry longing" in *Heaven and Earth are not Humane: The Problem of Evil in Classical Chinese Philosophy* (Bloomington: Indiana University Press, 2014), 124. On page 255 fn. 19 he also cites several other translators' interpretations: Van Norden, "He was bitter over the fact that he did not receive the affection of his parents." Lau, "He was complaining and yearning at the same time." Legge, "He was dissatisfied, and full of earnest desire."

18. Ruan Yuan 阮元, *Shisanjing Zhushu* 《十三經注疏》 (Taibeishi 台北市: Dahua Shuju 大化書局, 1977), 2776.

19. There are several relevant parallels between *mu* 慕 and attachment theory. See, for instance, John Bowlby, *A Secure Base: Parent–Child Attachment and Healthy Human Development* (New York: Basic Books, 1988).

20. Something similar is suggested in *Analects* 4.3: "Only those who are humane are able to be fond of others and to detest others" 唯仁者能好人，能惡人.

21. "Resentment," *Oxford English Dictionary*, www.oed.com (accessed January 15, 2015).

22. For instance, *Mengzi* 2B13.

23. See, for instance, the interpretation of Shun's longing for the care of this parents in the *Lienüzhuan* 1.1/1/11–17.

24. Although Xunzi does endorse *yuan* 怨 in other contexts such as minister-ruler relationships; see *Xunzi* 27/129/8.

25. For more on the connection between *yuan* 怨 and authenticity, see Xu Bing 徐冰, "Xiaozhiyuan yu Xingshanlun de Jichu" 孝之怨与性善论的基础, *Zhexue Dongtai* 《哲学动态》 (December 2014): 46–51. Xu also provides a good overview of this debate in the commentarial tradition.

26. *Mengzi* 5A3 also states that the "humane person" 仁人 will not "remain resentful" 宿怨 with his brother.

27. This moderate view of *yuan* 怨 is supported, for instance, in *Shiji*, 2504. Winnie Sung argues for a similar view using a distinction between "momentary *yuan* 怨" and "harbored *yuan* 怨." "The View from Here, Looking Outward," unpublished manuscript.

28. For a rereading of *Mengzi* 2B13 see Michael D.K. Ing, "Review of *Heaven and Earth are not Humane: The Problem of Evil in Classical Chinese Philosophy* by Franklin Perkins," *Frontiers of Philosophy in China* 10.1 (2015): 153–158.

29. This is also a main thesis of Robert Ashmore, *The Transport of Reading: Text and Understanding in the World of Tao Qian (365–427)* (Cambridge, MA: Harvard University Press, 2010).

30. While the *Shiji* and most commentators assume Qu Yuan to be the author of the *Lisao*, there are a number of reasons to suspect that he is not the author. A more indepth discussion of this can be found in Galal Walker, "Toward a Formal History of the *Chuci*" (PhD diss., Cornell University, 1982), 22–108. A more recent discussion occurs in Gopal Sukhu, *The Shaman and the Heresiarch: A New Interpretation of the* Li sao (Albany: State University of New York Press, 2012), 1–38.

31. Part of the point of the poem is the inseparable nature of "leaving" and "encountering." The main character encounters sorrow in the act of leaving.

32. Not all Confucians admired the "Lisao." Yang Xiong 揚雄 (53–18 BCE), for instance, criticized it in his essay, "Fansao" 反騷. For portrayals of Qu Yuan in different periods of Chinese history see Laurence A. Schneider, *A Madman of Ch'u: The Chinese Myth of Loyalty and Dissent* (Berkeley: University of California Press, 1980).

33. *Shiji*, 2504.

34. *Shiji*, 3353. A similar phrase appears in the *Xiaojing*. Li Xueqin 李學勤, ed., *Xiaojing Zhushu* 《孝經注疏》, *Shisanjing Zhushu* 《十三經注疏》 Vol. 26 (Beijing北京: Beijing daxue chubanshe 北京大学出版社, 2000), 4.

35. *Shiji*, 3354. For Sima Qian as a Kongzi-like figure see Michael J. Puett, *The Ambivalence of Creation: Debates Concerning Innovation and Artifice in Early China* (Stanford, CA: Stanford University Press, 2001), 177–181; and Stephen W. Durrant, *The Cloudy Mirror: Tension and Conflict in the Writings of Sima Qian*

(Albany: State University of New York Press, 1995), 29. Durrant discusses contrary views on pages 31 and 72. See also Michael Nylan, "Sima Qian: A True Historian?" *Early China* 23–24 (1998–1999): 203–246.

36. *Shiji*, 3360. Similar language also appears in *Kongcongzi* 《孔叢子》 2.4/15/ 17–25.

37. For more on literary production in response to frustrated desire see Durrant, *Cloudy Mirror*, 13–14. This theme is also prominent in the "Jiuzhang" 九章 and哀 時命 "Ai Shiming" poems in the *Chuci*.

38. Zhu Xi 朱熹, *Sishu Zhangju Jizhu* 《四書章句集注》 (Beijing 北京: Zhonghua Shuju 中華書局, 2005), 95.

39. For more on *fafen* 發憤 see Durrant, *Cloudy Mirror*, 15. In *Analects* 7.19 Kongzi describes himself in terms of *fafen* 發憤.

40. For scholars that interpret *Mengzi* and the *Analects* in terms of a teleological plan see Ning Chen, "The Concept of Fate in Mencius," *Philosophy East and West* 47.4 (October 1997): 495–520; and Robert Eno, *The Confucian Creation of Heaven: Philosophy and the Defense of Ritual Mastery* (Albany: State University of New York Press, 1990), 82, 88. Alexander Huang also makes an interesting note in this regard: "Chinese tragic characters are *homo political* and *homo historien*, as they resort to Time, the future, when seeking comfort for injustice done in the past and when seeking to restore their names." "The Tragic and the Chinese Subject," *Stanford Journal of East Asian Affairs* 3.1 (2003): 65.

41. On the notion of *yan* 言 in early China see Zhenbin Sun, "*Yan*: A Dimension of Praxis and its Philosophical Implications," *Journal of Chinese Philosophy* 24 (1997): 191–208.

42. Xu, *Shuowen*, 309.

43. Fu Xu 徐復 and Wenmin Song 宋文民. *Shuowen Wubaisishi Bushou Zhengjie* 《說文五百四十部首正解》 (Jiangsu 江蘇: Guji chubanshe 古籍出版社, 2003), 420.

44. Xu, *Shuowen*, 309.

45. Xu, *Shuowen*, 219.

46. Xu, *Shuowen*, 309.

47. *Xunzi* 28/138/19–21. Similar language is used to describe Zhou 紂, the final ruler of the Shang dynasty: "[His] capacity for rhetoric was sufficient to conceal wrong-doing" 辯足以飾非; *Lienüzhuan* 7.2/64/3–4. The same phrase is used to describe Robber Zhi 盜跖 in *Zhuangzi* 29/86/22.

48. *Xunzi* 22/108/4–10. Xunzi does, however, consent reluctantly to debate in 5/20/ 12–21/2. On the synonymous usage of *bian* 辨 and *bian* 辯 see *Lüshi Chunqiu* 18.5/ 113/27–114/4 and *Kongcongzi* 4.1/47/21–48/1.

49. *Xunzi* 22/110/1.

50. See *Han Shi Waizhuan* 2.7; *Kongzi Jiayu* 10.17; *Hanfeizi* 《韓非子》 15/27/25–26; *Shangjunshu* 《商君書》 3/5/19–24; and *Lunheng* 《論衡》 1/3/5–6. The

Zhuangzi 《莊子》 endorses "a wordless form of rhetorical strategies" 不言之辯 and connects *bian* 辯 with the *Chunqiu* in 2/5/28–6/3. A. C. Graham talks about a group in early China known as sophists, or *bianzhe* 辯者. He describes them as "thinkers who delight in propositions which defy common sense, and consequently are derided as frivolous and irresponsible." He continues, "Confucians, Daoists and Legalists alike scorn them for wasting their time on abstractions." *Disputers of the Tao: Philosophical Argument in Ancient China* (Chicago: Open Court, 1989), 75. The *Lüshi Chunqiu* (4.2/18/20–21) also makes a related statement: "Those who engage in persuasion should be critical of others, and not seek to please them. Persuaders of this generation, [however,] are largely incapable of being critical, and so [they] resort to pleasing people. Not being critical, and instead resorting to pleasing [others], is [like] trying to save someone drowning by tossing him a stone, or trying to save someone sick by feeding him poison" 凡說者，兌之也，非說之也。今世之說者，多弗能兌，而反說之。夫弗能兌而反說，是拯溺而硾之以石也，是救病而飲之以堇也. See also *Lüshi Chunqiu* 4.5/21/20–21.

51. *Kongzi Jiayu* 37.2/63/15. Zigong is also mentioned for his ability to *bian* 辯 in the "Zhongni" 仲尼 chapter of the *Liezi* 《列子》 as well as the "Zhongni Dizizhuan" 仲尼弟子傳 chapter of the *Shiji*; the latter of which states, "Zigong [had] a keen mouth [that spoke] crafty words. Kongzi often denounced his rhetorical strategies" 子貢利口巧辭。孔子常黜其辯. *Shiji*, 2232; see also *Kongzi Jiayu* 38/66/4.

52. *Kongzi Jiayu* 37.2/64/14–16.

53. Much more could be said about the "Qujie Jie" chapter. The notion of *qujie* 屈節 seems to involve obscuring one's intentions, or using words in such a way that they do not clearly express one's intentions. This fits with Amy Olberding's description of Zigong's opacity in *Moral Exemplars in the* Analects: *The Good Person is* That (New York: Routledge, 2011), 162–179.

54. On the notion of regicide in the *Mengzi* see Justin Tiwald, "A Right of Rebellion in the *Mengzi*?, *Dao: A Journal of Comparative Philosophy* 7.3 (2008): 269–282. For a broader look on regicides and killings in the Spring and Autumn period see Newell Ann Van Auken, "Killings and Assassinations in the *Spring and Autumn* as Records of Judgments," *Asia Major* 27.1 (2014): 1–31.

55. *Analects* 3.25.

56. There are good reasons not to accept the traditional view that Kongzi authored (or edited) the *Chunqiu*. For the purposes of this project, however, I am not concerned with the historical accuracy of the traditional view. For a history of the *Chunqiu* see Michael Nylan, *The Five "Confucian" Classics* (New Haven, CT: Yale University Press, 2001), 253–306; and Newell Ann Van Auken, *The Commentarial Transformation of the* Spring and Autumn (Albany: State University of New York Press, 2016).

57. Piotr Pawel Gibas, "Waiting for the Unicorn: Perception of Time and History in Early Chinese Writings" (PhD diss., University of California, Berkeley, 2009), 35.

58. Modern scholars have questioned the praise and blame narrative with regard to the *Chunqiu*. The text, and its three main commentaries, may not have been composed with such a moralizing purpose. See Newell Ann Van Auken, "Could 'Subtle Words' have Conveyed 'Praise and Blame'? The Implications of Formal Regularity and Variation in *Spring and Autumn* (*Chūn qiū*) Records," *Early China* 31 (2007: 47–111).

59. Zhu Yizun 朱彝尊, *Jingyikao* 《經義考》, *Wenyuange Sikuquanshu Dianziban* 《文淵閣四庫全書電子版》 (Hong Kong: Digital Heritage Publishing, accessed September 2, 2014), 202.10.

60. Cai Mo 蔡模, *Mengzi Jishu* 《孟子集疏》, *Wenyuange Sikuquanshu Dianziban* 《文淵閣四庫全書電子版》 (Hong Kong: Digital Heritage Publishing, accessed September 2, 2014), 6.13.

61. Ban Gu 班固, *Hanshu* 《漢書》 (Beijing 北京: Zhonghua Shuju 中華書局, 2007), 565. See also *Lunheng* 39/188/7–12, 80/349/5–13; and *Zhuangzi* 13/34/20–21.

62. Sun Shi 孫奭, ed., *Mengzi Zhushu* 《孟子注疏》, *Wenyuange Sikuquanshu Dianziban* 《文淵閣四庫全書電子版》 (Hong Kong: Digital Heritage Publishing, accessed February 3, 2015), 6B6–7.

63. Yang Changru 楊長孺, *Chengzhaiji* 《誠齋集》, *Wenyuange Sikuquanshu Dianziban* 《文淵閣四庫全書電子版》 (Hong Kong: Digital Heritage Publishing, accessed September 2, 2014), 85.15–16.

64. Van Norden likewise feels the need to explain this part of 3B9: "Writing history is the prerogative of the Son of Heaven [i.e. the king], so Kongzi worried that he would be thought presumptuous for doing it. However, Kongzi felt that he had to speak out against wrongdoing." Van Norden, *Mengzi*, 85.

65. Hu Guang 胡廣, ed., *Mengzi Jizhu Daquan* 《孟子集註大全》, *Wenyuange Sikuquanshu Dianziban* 《文淵閣四庫全書電子版》 (Hong Kong: Digital Heritage Publishing, accessed September 2, 2014), 8.29.

66. Hu Bingwen 胡炳文, *Yunfengji* 《雲峰集》, *Wenyuange Sikuquanshu Dianziban* 《文淵閣四庫全書電子版》 (Hong Kong: Digital Heritage Publishing, accessed February 3, 2015), 4.5.

67. Zhang Daheng 張大亨, *Chunqiu Tongxun* 《春秋通訓》, *Wenyuange Sikuquanshu Dianziban* 《文淵閣四庫全書電子版》 (Hong Kong: Digital Heritage Publishing, accessed February 3, 2015), 3.4.

68. Puett, *The Ambivalence of Creation*, 210.

69. Qiu Jun 邱濬, ed., *Daxue Yanyibu* 《大學衍義補》, *Wenyuange Sikuquanshu Dianziban* 《文淵閣四庫全書電子版》 (Hong Kong: Digital Heritage Publishing Limited, accessed February 3, 2015), 77.9. See also *Liji* 35.15/153/26–28.

70. Li Guangdi 李光地 and Xiong Silü 熊賜履, eds., *Yuzuan Zhuzi Quanshu* 《御纂朱子全書》, *Wenyuange Sikuquanshu Dianziban* 《文淵閣四庫全書電子版》 (Hong Kong: Digital Heritage Publishing, accessed February 3, 2015), 16.29.

71. Robert Douglas-Fairhurst, "Tragedy and Disgust," in Sarah Annes Brown and Catherine Silverstone, eds., *Tragedy in Transition* (Malden, MA: Blackwell, 2007), 67. I replaced the word "disgust" with the bracketed word "resentment."

5

Irresolvable Value Conflicts in a Conflictual World

As I think back on what my father taught me,
I shed tears of blood day and night, and am nearly mad
*   with grief.*
I still have my old mother; ill with her old illness,
*   dependent on [me] to keep her alive a bit longer.*
I want to die, but cannot [die and] be a filial son.
I want to live, but cannot [live and] be a loyal minister.

我憶我父教我者，日夜滴血哭成顛。
我有老母病老病，相依為命生余生。
欲死不得為孝子，欲生不得為忠臣。

(ZHENG SIXIAO 鄭思肖 [1241–1318], *Tiehan Xinshi*
《鐵函心史》)[1]

CHAPTER 2 EXPLORED THE harmony thesis, which argues that when confronted with complex situations, the imaginative moral agent is able to tend to
all values at stake. Value conflicts, in this view, are epistemic, not ontological. In
other words, the world is understood as a place where tensions between values
can be resolved if the skills or other capacities of the moral agent are sufficient to
resolve them. Failure to tend to some value signifies a shortcoming of the moral
agent, not a problem with the possibilities afforded by the world.

Negative feelings such as grief and sorrow, however, still have a place in the
harmony thesis. They are important in responding to pain and suffering; however, the paradigmatic moral agent should never feel guilt. Toward the end of
chapter 2 I noted three points of criticism for the harmony thesis. Chapters 3 and
4 worked to develop the first point of critique, namely that regret, understood
as a sorrowful longing for things to be otherwise, is an apt description for moral
remainder or distress. This chapter as well as the next will develop the second
critique—that early Confucians saw irresolvable value conflicts as real possibilities. This chapter also touches on the third critique (explained more fully in

chapters 6 and 7) that the possibility of irresolvable value conflicts means that the moral agent's integrity is vulnerable to tragic circumstances.

In arguing that early Confucians recognized the possibility of irresolvable value conflicts, it will be helpful to distinguish between a strong claim of this sort and a more moderate claim that I wish to emphasize. I am not making the strong claim that Confucians believed that irresolvable value conflicts are a part of the inherent nature of values. Early Confucians did not believe that we live in a fractured world where values are necessarily at odds with each other. Yet they did believe in the possibility of value conflicts such that tragic circumstances could occur. For instance, early Confucians could conceptualize values such as communal welfare (*gong* 公) and personal welfare (*si* 私) or filial piety (*xiao* 孝) and loyalty (*zhong* 忠), and it may turn out that these values often conflict with each other—sometimes producing irresolvable value conflicts. However, they did not see these values in a relationship with each other that necessitates irresolvable conflict. Sor-hoon Tan expresses a similar thought in a comparative framework: "Although Confucianism resists a depiction of social life as fundamentally conflict-ridden, it does not deny that at any one time there could be conflicts that are beyond our abilities to resolve, and the best we could do is damage control. Confucian acknowledgement of the reality of conflicts, however, is different from some Western views that perceive conflicts as consisting in a clash of absolute moral duties, or categorical imperatives, that are in principle irreconcilable."[2] Building on this, we might say that early Confucians recognized the complexities of life such that even the highly skilled moral agent (i.e., a sage) could encounter a situation where the values at stake were incapable of being harmonized, but, at the same time, the Confucian moral agent does not see the world as necessitating conflict. The Confucian conflictual world is one of possible incongruity, where minor value conflicts may even be inevitable given the complexities of life, but values in the abstract sense are not thought to be in conflict in and of themselves. In this light, deep value conflicts such as those discussed in this chapter may rarely occur, but the fact that they can occur, and that they can occur for even the most profound people, is significant in forecasting the sentiments people have about the world they live in. Following Christopher Gowans, the possibility of tragic value conflicts "lends a very different, and far less sanguine, complexion to one's life."[3] This is because "there is no sphere of life that guarantees a safe haven from tragedy."[4] Indeed, tragic possibility can give way to a tragic sensibility about the world—a realization that we, human beings, cannot construct an invulnerable world.

The view that Confucians understand the world in terms of harmony is not new. Indeed, as discussed in places such as Li Chenyang's recent book, *The Confucian Philosophy of Harmony*, this is a dominant trend within the tradition itself.[5] Many scholars in the eighteenth, nineteenth, and twentieth centuries, however, connected narratives of harmony with discourses of orientalism such that harmony became the hallmark feature to differentiate China from "the West." In *The Ambivalence of Creation*, Michael Puett provides a useful overview of this discourse (speaking about harmony in terms of "continuity") by quoting Voltaire, Leibniz, and Hegel, as well as contemporary scholars such as Jacques Granet, David Keightley, and K. C. Chang.[6] To this list we might add Bertrand Russell, Derk Bodde, and Herbert Fingarette.[7] Max Weber's notion of Confucianism as "adjustment to the world" has been particularly influential.[8] His theory of adjustment essentially means that Confucians saw society as but a "special case" of the "cosmic order," and as such their goal was for "man [to] fit himself into the internally harmonious cosmos."[9] While Weber intended these notions of harmony to serve as a critique of the "iron cage" of Western modernity, more often than not these views served to reinforce claims of Western exceptionalism with regard to the development of things such as science, democracy, and human rights.

As recently as 2003, prominent philosophers such as Martha Nussbaum reiterated these views. Nussbaum essentially claims that democracy failed to develop in China because, among other things, "in Kongzi's China ... one would see all around one the evidence of the permanent differences among humans."[10] This is in contrast with notions rooted in Aristotelian (and protodemocratic) thought where "one thinks about what it would be like to be in the position of the vulnerable and suffering person ... and this is supposed to make one choose generous and considerate treatment."[11] In other words, Chinese people lacked the perspective from which they could see that any two people's roles could be reversed, maintaining instead a "fixed hierarchy."[12] Nussbaum calls this the "missing thought" and explains that life in a "feudal hierarchy" would likely preclude the missing thought.[13] As such, at least one major component of democracy is not found in traditional China.

While this discussion of Nussbaum may seem tangentially related to harmony and value conflicts, her claim that traditional China lacked notions similar to ancient Greek conceptions of pity aligns with claims about harmony in denying the possibility of tragedy in premodern China. For Nussbaum, pity in the sense of sympathizing with the misfortune of others is key to tragedy, and for many other scholars, seeing human beings at odds with the world is a central component of tragedy. The first of these views is impossible without the missing thought, and the second view is impossible if one's goal is to seek harmony with the cosmos. Karl Jaspers famously remarked with regard to China, "[Tragedy cannot occur] wherever man succeeds both in achieving a harmonious interpretation of the universe and in actually living in accord with it."[14]

The claim that China lacked tragedy is likewise tied up with notions of orientalism and western exceptionalism. Heiner Roetz explains, "In [tragedy's] aporetic rupture, the limits of ethical life are experienced in such an elementary way that they can subsequently be transcended. Tragedy, therefore, is significant for moral evolution. Its lack would be an indication of the unquestioned continuing existence of 'substantiality,' and it is in this sense that the Orient remains nontragic for Hegel."[15] Indeed, Hegel's lectures on the philosophy of religion bear out the idea that he believed China developed to a certain point, but never achieved the moral evolution of the West.[16] More recently, scholars such as George Steiner, Richard Seawall, and Jennifer Wallace reaffirm aspects of a non-tragic China.[17] John Morreall, a professor of religious studies at William and Mary, makes a representative statement in this regard: "In Chinese thought, too, the universe is a harmonious unity in which each part reproduces the whole. The human body is a microcosm of the universe—we know that our blood circulates, for example, because we know that rivers flow. The Chinese acknowledge that life has it[s] moments of need and pain, but those are just part of the harmonious whole, rather than something to be questioned, or, as in tragedy, something to be protested."[18]

In contrast with this, scholars of China such as Heiner Roetz, Alexander Huang, and Franklin Perkins argue for notions of tragedy in premodern China.[19] All three scholars are careful to distinguish subtle, but important, differences between tragedy in Confucian texts or Chinese fiction and Greek or Shakespearean tragedies. Tragedy as theatre may not be found in premodern China, but tragedy as a concept can be found in the sense of affirming a tension between human hopes about the world and human experience in the world.[20] Perkins's recent book, *Heaven and Earth Are Not Humane*, stresses the tension between human beings and *Tian* 天 (heaven) in several early Chinese texts. The *Mengzi*, Perkins explains, is particularly tragic in this sense. In talking about human nature (*xing* 性) and humaneness (*ren* 仁) in the *Mengzi* Perkins says,

> The heaven-derived *xing* 性 of human beings leads us to humaneness even though heaven itself is not humane, just as the *xing* 性 of Ox Mountain leads it to grow trees even though heaven itself is not wooded. In shifting the relevant ground for human action from heaven to our own nature, Mengzi makes the purposes of heaven irrelevant. The move from generic patterns of nature to the specific tendencies of kinds of things leaves Mengzi with a view that necessitates conflict. Barley naturally strives to grow, even though other things naturally strive against it. Human beings strive to bring peace and order to the world, even though other things and even the cycles of history strive against them. This striving against heaven's own cycles does not entail a rejection of heaven, because heaven itself generates these strivings. This kind of struggle is the very nature of life.[21]

In a way, human beings are at odds with *Tian* 天. We strive to order a world that works against us and may ultimately lie beyond our power to order. However,

Tian 天 itself, while worthy of resentment when impeding order, is also the same power that gave us the desire for order. As such, this conflict does not ostracize us to a point of "ontological homelessness" (to borrow from George Steiner), or stir up a "guilt of existence" (to borrow from Arthur Schopenhauer).[22] Perkins importantly notes, "Mengzi sees suffering as part of life but does not see life *as* suffering."[23] In other words, life may entail struggling against the given conditions of the world, but it is not constituted by struggle.[24]

Huang develops a similar account of tragedy in premodern Chinese dramas, adding that what distinguishes Chinese tragedy is "isolation of the tragic character" in combination with "the necessity and tyranny of Time."[25] In other words, rather than a kind of existential fear or torment connected with the subjective freedom of the individual, the tragic character in the Chinese case is ostracized from "interpersonal relationships" that largely define the self (enabling an alternative kind of "self-splitting," to draw from Nietzsche). This occurs in a context where Time (*shi* 時, discussed in chapter 3) limits the ways in which the tragic character can tend to his relationships. The result, building from Huang, is that the tragic character's relationships compel tragic actions, and, as such, the tragic character is isolated from these relationships in the very act of attempting to fulfill them.

As we will see, many of the vignettes in this chapter bear out the theories of Perkins and Huang. More specifically, tragedy in an early Confucian context is rooted in our inability to fulfill our desires to tend to all meaningful relationships. We are limited by our circumstances (*shi* 時) as well as the fact of our finite existence. Being human means being vulnerable to distress, disappointment, and the possibly of tragic conflict. Indeed, the texts discussed in this chapter demonstrate that a Confucian tragic sensibility, set in the context of a conflictual world, has been marginalized by many scholars. Some of these scholars constructed or reinforced narratives of harmony and the lack of tragedy in China in order to contribute to the discourse of modernization. Part of what I aim to accomplish in this chapter is a critique of these narratives, which then suggests a greater possibility for dialogue among cultures in thinking about tragedy.

Rethinking Value Conflicts—The Case of Shen Ming 申鳴

The *Han Shi Waizhuan* 《韓詩外傳》, a text purportedly compiled by Han Ying 韓嬰 (c. 200–c. 130 BCE) in the early Han dynasty, tells the following story:

> In the state of Chu there was a soldier named Shen Ming (fl. 480 BCE) who farmed a garden in order to provide for his parents. His filial

[reputation] spread throughout the state of Chu. [One day] the ruler summoned him [but] Shen Ming declined the invitation and did not go [to see the ruler].

His father asked, "The ruler wishes to employ you, why did [you] decline the invitation?"

楚有士曰申鳴，治園以養父母。孝聞於楚，王召之，申鳴辭不往。其父曰：「王欲用汝，何為辭之？」

Shen Ming replied, "How could [I] cast aside [my] role as son to become a minister?"

申鳴曰：「何舍為子，乃為臣乎？」

His father stated, "If you get a salary from the state, and have a position in the court, you will be happy; and I will not worry [about being taken care of]. I think you should go and serve [the state]."

其父曰：「使汝有祿於國，有位於廷，汝樂，而我不憂矣。我欲汝之仕也。」

Shen Ming responded, "As you wish." And so he went to the court and accepted the ruler's charge, thereby becoming a military general.

That year [they] encountered the chaos caused by Bai Gong, who killed the district magistrate, Zixi, and the general, Ziqi. Shen Ming took his troops and surrounded [Bai Gong].

Bai Gong told [his minister] Shi Qi, "Shen Ming is one of the bravest soldiers in the world, and now he leads the troops; what should [we] do about this?"

申鳴曰：「諾。」遂之朝受命，楚王以為左司馬。其年，遇白公之亂，殺令尹子西、司馬子期。申鳴因以兵之衛。白公謂石乞曰：「申鳴，\天下勇士也，今將兵；為之奈何？」

Shi Qi replied, "I have heard about how filial Shen Ming is. [Let's] use our troops to kidnap his father."

石乞曰：「吾聞申鳴孝也，劫其父以兵。」

[After doing this, they] sent messengers to Shen Ming saying, "If you side with us, then [we] will split the state of Chu with you. If you do not side with us, then [we] will kill your father."

使人謂申鳴曰：「子與我，則與子楚國；不與我，則殺乃父。」

Shen Ming wept, and responded saying, "In the beginning [I] was the son of [my] father, but now [I] am the minister of [my] ruler. Since it is already the case that I cannot be a filial son, why should [I] not be a loyal minister?" [And so he] seized the drumstick, sounded the military drums, and killed Bai Gong. His father, however, also died.

When the ruler returned [he] rewarded Shen Ming. [Despite his offer,] Shen Ming said, "To draw a salary from a ruler, but avoid the difficulties a ruler faces is not to be a loyal minister. However, to uphold the laws of a ruler by killing one's father is not to be a filial son. Two virtuous actions cannot both be completed; two virtuous reputations cannot both be established. How sorrowful! If I was to live under these conditions how could [I] be a model [for the other] soldiers in the world?" And so [he] slit his own throat and died.

The *Shijing* says, "Whether advancing or retreating there is only obstruction."

申鳴流涕而應之曰：「始則父之子，今則君之臣，已不得為孝子，安得不為忠臣乎！」援枹鼓之，遂殺白公，其父亦死焉。王歸，賞之。申鳴曰：「受君之祿，避君之難，非忠臣也；正君之法，以殺其父，又非孝子也。行不兩全，名不兩立。悲夫！若此而生，亦何以示天下之士哉！」遂自刎而死。《詩》曰：「進退惟谷。」²⁶

From the beginning, this story raises the issue of whether or not values such as caring for one's parents and serving the state are always capable of being harmonized. When approached by officials from the ruler's court, Shen Ming declines their invitation—fearing that he cannot be both a good minister and a good son. His father, however, disagrees with his decision and suggests that if Shen Ming served the court, Shen Ming would not only find personal satisfaction in gaining an influential position but would also then be able to provide for his father (because of his salary). This sets the stage by bringing to the fore values such as care for one's family members, delight in one's achievements, influence in society, obedience to one's parents, and loyalty to one's state. It is significant that Shen Ming and his father represent divergent views of value conflicts. Shen Ming's father believes that tensions between values in this case are harmonizable—by serving the state, Shen Ming serves his father. Notably, similar views are articulated in many other early Confucian texts. The *Xiaojing* 《孝經》, purportedly authored by Kongzi and his disciple Zengzi 曾子 (505–436 BCE), for instance, states, "Filial care begins with serving [one's] parents, continues in the service of [one's] ruler, and is completed when [one] establishes his individual character [such that it can be passed down to future generations]" 夫孝， 始於事親，中於事君，終於立身.[27] In this view, care for one's family is largely harmonized with service to one's state.[28] Vigorously serving one's ruler (or the principles that ought to be embodied by a ruler) is being filial. Shen Ming's view, on the other hand, is that filial care (*xiao* 孝) and loyalty (*zhong* 忠) can be brought into irreconcilable tension with each other. When brought into tension with each other, Shen Ming feels compelled to choose between values, and after choosing, he is left with such sorrow (i.e., moral distress) that he kills himself.

The two particularly important phrases in this passage are "two virtuous actions cannot both be completed" 行不兩全 and "whether advancing or retreating there is only obstruction" 進退惟谷 (also appearing in other texts as *jintui weigu* 進退維谷). Both phrases (the first supposedly coming from Shen Ming and the second added by Han Ying) articulate a view of irresolvable value conflicts. The character *xing* 行 in the first phrase can be understood in various ways. It can mean "virtue" (*dexing* 德行) as well as "path of action"; hence my translation as "virtuous action." Zheng Xuan 鄭玄 (127–200), an early commentator from the Han dynasty, explicitly ties *xing* 行 to virtue (*de* 德) in commenting on the *Zhouli* 《周禮》. He states, "*De* 德 and *xing* 行 are designations for the internal and the external. When within [one's] heart, it is *de* 德; when put into action, it is *xing* 行" 德行內外之稱。在心為德。施之為行.[29] As such, *xing* 行 is the application of virtue.

The early form of the character *xing* 行 seems to be a pictograph of a road or intersection; it also depicts the movement of feet.[30] Xu Shen 許慎 (c. 58–147) in the *Shuowen Jiezi* 《說文解字》 glosses *xing* 行 as "the feet of someone walking" 人之步趨也.[31] *Xing* 行 is associated with movement, flow, and circulation and in this regard can be contrasted with *qiong* 窮, which as we saw in the previous chapter is tied to blockage and leads to pent up anger or frustration (*fen* 憤). The line *jintui weigu* 進退惟谷 from the *Shijing* reinforces this notion. In this context, *gu* 谷, which means "valley" or "gorge," becomes a metaphor for blockage. Similar to the way steep valley walls prohibit physical movement, Shen Ming's situation prohibits him from tending to all values at stake in the situation. No matter what he does he will be blocked from realizing some value. Coincidentally, one of the earliest commentaries on the *Shijing* glosses *gu* 谷 in this poem as *qiong* 窮.[32]

The character *quan* 全 in the phrase *xing buliangquan* 行不兩全 is also significant. Most English dictionaries translate it as "to complete" or "to preserve," each of which can have different connotations. *Quan* 全 in the passage under discussion suggests some sense of completion as well as preservation. Shen Ming laments the fact that he cannot complete two tasks but also laments the fact that he cannot preserve the virtues he had up until that point cultivated in his life.

Early uses of *quan* 全 connect it with jade of a "pure color" 純色 or with *quan* 牷, a sacrificial animal of a single color.[33] In this light, *quan* 全 is associated with purity or unadulteration. The *Shuoyuan* 《說苑》 version of Shen Ming's story includes an important variation with regard to this point. When presented with the choice of defecting to the enemy's side or having his father killed, Shen Ming in part states, "Now it is already the case that I cannot become [my] father's filial son. As such, even if [I] am a loyal minister of the ruler how would I preserve myself" 今吾已不得為父之孝子矣，乃君之忠臣也，吾何得以全身?[34] The last two characters, *quanshen* 全身, I translated as "preserve myself." The idea here is that Shen Ming is concerned with maintaining or protecting aspects of his person. Exactly what this means is not entirely clear in the context of this passage. However, Deborah Sommer provides a useful insight with regard to *shen* 身 ("body" or "self"). In her work on conceptions of the body in early China, Sommer notes several characteristics of *shen* 身 (in contrast with other terms used for "body" such as *ti* 體, *xing* 形, and *gong* 躬). She explains, "[It] is the *shen* 身 body, person, or self that is self-aware and is the site of inner reflection and cultivation. . . . *Shen* 身 is the socially constructed self that is marked by signs of status and personal identity, and it is the accumulated corpus of a person's moral values, character, experience, and learning."[35] According to Sommer, *shen* 身 is often used to talk about the self in terms of cultivation and the accumulation of virtue.

Putting this together, we might surmise that *quanshen* 全身 means to preserve those moral aspects of the self gained through the work of self-cultivation. In this light, Xunzi explains, "The exemplary person works to cultivate his interiority—manifesting it externally. [He] works to accumulate virtue in his *shen* 身—utilizing it in following the Way" 君子務脩其內，而讓之於外；務積德於身，而處之以遵道.[36] Virtue, as such, is collected, stored in the self, and circulated beyond the self in implementing the *dao* 道. With regard to Shen Ming's story, Shen Ming sees his situation primarily in terms of moral injury. While he might lament leaving some value undone, his primary concern—indeed, that which causes him to suffer—is the harm done to himself in light of his accumulation of virtue in being a filial son and loyal minister. As such, *xing buliangquan* 行不兩全 might also be translated as "two virtues cannot both be preserved," meaning that filial care and loyalty, at least in Shen Ming's circumstances, cannot both be kept intact.[37] To put it into contemporary philosophical terminology, Shen Ming sees himself as having chosen between two evils, and, despite doing the best he could—doing what was right all things considered—he still felt a sorrowful distress that moved him to death.

A more extended explanation of *xing buliangquan* 行不兩全 as it relates to "completion" and "preservation" is that the virtues cultivated and collected by Shen Ming that allowed him to exert a moral influence in the world could no longer flow forth and they (as a part of him) were thereby harmed. In other words, circumstances can inhibit one's ability to circulate virtue in ways that not only prevent one from establishing a reputation that can be passed down to future generations but also inhibit one from relating with those immediate others that are meaningful in one's life, and this, as discussed more closely in chapter 7, harms the self. The notion of *xing buliangquan* 行不兩全 highlights themes of flow and obstruction in the context of filial care (*xiao* 孝) and loyalty (*zhong* 忠).

The tragic aspect of Shen Ming's story is that his virtue compels him into an irresolvable value conflict. At first Shen Ming declines the ruler's invitation to visit the court because he fears a conflict between his role as son and his would-be role as minister. He finally accepts the ruler's invitation however, because his father asks him to accept it. Shen Ming only appears at court and becomes a minister as an expression of his desire to care for his father. His filial piety, therefore, serves as the catalyst for the conflict. Ironically, his filial piety leads him into a situation where he can no longer be filial. The story of Shen Ming suggests that being virtuous can put the moral agent in situations where he can no longer maintain virtue. The values of filial piety and loyalty may not inherently produce irresolvable value conflicts, but, as the story of Shen Ming suggests, the possibility of conflict is real.

Value Conflicts in Chinese Literature

The anecdote of Shen Ming raises a number of relevant questions. Perhaps the most relevant is whether or not we should understand this story as a description of a good person who otherwise lacked the moral imagination of a sage, or as a description of a good person caught up in a genuinely tragic situation. One way to more fully argue for the later view is to demonstrate that even sages confronted similar situations. I make this argument in the next chapter. In this chapter, however, it is worth mentioning that Confucians have debated how to reconcile values associated with filial care and loyalty for over 2,000 years. Indeed, this vignette from the *Han Shi Waizhuan* is neither the first nor the last to discuss the tension between loyalty and filial care.[38] Some later texts specifically invoke the language of *zhongxiao liangquan* 忠孝兩全 ("preserving both loyalty and filial piety"), thereby directly referencing the Shen Ming story. Other texts discuss similar situations in terms of loyalty and trustworthiness (*xin* 信), humaneness (*ren* 仁) and justice (*yi* 義), or communal welfare (*gong* 公) and personal welfare (*si* 私), and other texts discuss the tension in terms of role conflicts or conflicts of commitments rather than virtues often associated with roles or commitments.

For the sake of establishing the prevalence of these tensions, I mention several anecdotes here and then elaborate on a few others that demonstrate the irresolvable nature of some value conflicts. In chapter 2 I discussed *Analects* 13.18, where a father stealing a sheep puts values like filial care in tension with values such as honesty or uprightness (*zhi* 直). Versions of this story appear in many other early texts where the conflict is discussed in terms of humaneness (*ren* 仁) and justice (*yi* 義) or filial care and trustworthiness (*xin* 信).[39] The *Analects* (15.9) also mention the possibility of humaneness conflicting with the preservation of one's life. In this situation, Kongzi explains, the humane person will "kill himself [in order to] fill out [his] humaneness" 殺身成仁. Mengzi likewise speaks about choosing between one's life and rightness or justice (6A10), as well as choosing between ritual propriety (*li* 禮) and starvation (6B1). The *Xunzi* recognizes that public justice (*gongyi* 公義) can come into tension with private desire (*siyu* 私欲), and in the "Way of the Son" ("Zidao" 子道) chapter, the author recognizes that obedience to one's father (discussed as *congming* 從命) can be detached from justice.[40] In this vein the *Xiaojing* advocates remonstrating (*jian* 諫 or *zheng* 爭) with one's father if his requests are not just.[41] The *Liji* 《禮記》 contains an entire chapter where Kongzi's disciple Zengzi asks about role conflicts in ritual performance—wondering, for instance, what to do when the death of a bride's mother or father conflicts with her wedding.[42] The *Liji* also recognizes the tension between prescribed ritual actions and the limitations of the young, the elderly or the sick—advocating that the moral agent "use discretion in conducting [rituals that involve these groups]" 以權制.[43] The *Kongzi Jiayu* 《孔子家語》 discusses the tension between humaneness and ritual propriety when a female neighbor wants to take shelter from a storm in single man's house.[44] It also discusses the tension between ritual propriety and friendship when Kongzi sponsors the funeral of an old acquaintance's wife, and his acquaintance violates ritual protocol.[45]

Texts that utilize historical narratives such as the *Zuo Zhuan* 《左傳》 tell about Yong Ji 雍姬 (c. 700 BCE) who was compelled to choose between the life of her husband and the life of her father when her husband was commissioned by the ruler to kill her father.[46] It also tells of Shen Sheng 申生 (d. 656 BCE) who chose to die rather than torment his father by revealing the treacherous plans of his father's favorite concubine.[47] In the *Guoyu* 《國語》, Shao Gong 邵公 (c. 840 BCE) protects the heir to the throne by allowing his own son to be killed in his place.[48] The *Lienüzhuan* 《列女傳》 contains an entire chapter on women of "character and righteousness" (節義), many of whom face value conflicts and choose to die rather than compromise their character.[49] The *Gongyang Zhuan* 《公羊傳》 discusses several instances where the *Chunqiu* describes officials violating the norms of their stations, explaining that the *Chunqiu* had to use language that revealed the improper nature of their actions, but in reality the *Chunqiu* found their actions appropriate (*shiyu er wenbuyu* 實與而文不與).[50]

Post-Han historical texts such as the *Houhanshu* 《後漢書》 tell of Zhao Bao 趙苞 (c. 177 CE) who was in a situation similar to Shen Ming, where his mother was captured by enemy troops, and he was forced to choose between serving his ruler (*zhong* 忠) and caring for his mother (*xiao* 孝).[51] One of the more famous examples of a value conflict occurs in Pei Songzhi's 裴松之 (372–451)

commentary on the *Sanguozhi* 《三國志》 where Cao Pi 曹丕 (187–226), heir to the throne, poses the following question to a group of guests at a banquet: "If your ruler and father both were extremely ill, and [you] only had enough medicine to save one, should [you] save your ruler or father" 君父各有篤疾，有藥一丸，可救一人；當救君耶父耶？[52] Most guests respond by saying that they would save their ruler. Bing Yuan 邴原 (one of the government officials known for his knowledge of Confucian texts, and an advisor to Cao Pi) was the only one to argue for saving his father.

The poetic texts in particular highlight value conflicts. A common theme in the *Shijing* is the righteous minister caught between gaining the attention of a ruler and violating the propriety of a minister. More specifically, the *Shijing* explores the disjuncture between the values of tradition and the wishes of one's father in the "Xiaopan" 小弁 poem (as discussed in chapter 4).[53] Many of the authors of the *Chuci* 《楚辭》 lament the tension between public service and personal integrity. The "Lisao" 離騷 engages this theme by depicting the main character leaving a world of disgrace and shame in pursuit of purity (a main character who struggles to find satisfaction even on his spirit journeys). The "Aishiming" 哀時命, purportedly authored by Zhuang Ji 莊忌 (c. 150 BCE), uses language similar to story of Shen Ming in lamenting his situation. Zhuang Ji states, "I am not well-received by this filthy age; and [I] do not know whether advancing or retreating is most appropriate" 身既不容於濁世兮；不知進退之宜當.[54] Later poets who saw themselves as followers of Kongzi (such as Tao Yuanming 陶淵明, c. 365–427) echo the tension found in the *Chuci* between serving the state and withdrawing from public service for the sake of preserving one's integrity.

Recently unearthed manuscripts with a Confucian influence stress the tension between values such as kindness (*en* 恩) and justice (*yi* 義), with the *Liu De* 《六德》 stating, "In ordering [the affairs] internal to the home, kindness covers over justice; [but when] ordering [the affairs] external to the home, justice cuts off kindness" 門內之治，恩掩義；門外之治，義斬恩.[55] The *Nei Li* 《內禮》, as discussed in chapter 2, also recognizes the potential conflict between the family and the state.

Later Chinese fiction also focuses on value conflicts. Pieces that contemporary scholars sometimes include in the category of tragedy include *Zhaoshi Guer* (*The Orphan of Zhao*) 《趙氏孤兒》, a thirteenth-century play where, among other things, a courageous doctor allows those in opposition to the royal family to kill his own child so that he can save the last remaining child of the royal family and stop the dissenters from killing other children. Coincidentally, *The Orphan of Zhao* is based off of the "Zhao Shijia" 趙世家 chapter in the *Shiji* 《史記》. In *Dou E Yuan* (*The Injustice to Dou E*) 《竇娥冤》, a fourteenth-century play, a woman named Dou E allows herself to be executed after Zhang Lü'er 張驢兒, a man attempting to take control of Dou E and her property, frames her for the death of his father. Finally, the *Hongloumeng* 《紅樓夢》, written by Cao Xueqin 曹雪芹 in the eighteenth century, is, in the words of Wang Guowei 王國維 (1877–1927), "[A] tragedy from the very beginning to the end."[56]

In the contemporary academic community, several scholars have written books on the tensions depicted in the early literature. Huang Jianyue 黄建跃, for instance, examines the various debates about *gong* 公 ("public interest") and *si* 私 ("self-interest") in pre-Qin Confucian thought.[57] And in 2008 Zhang Kunjiang 張崑將 authored a book that compares the relationship between loyalty and filial care as conceptualized in Tokugawa Japan and the thought of Wang Yangming 王陽明 (1472–1509).[58] Wolfram Eberhard, in his book, *Guilt and Sin in Traditional China*, combs through numerous Chinese short stories written in the late imperial period and lists roughly sixty suicides described in these stories that result from value conflicts.[59] Finally, in 2007, *Dao: A Journal of Comparative Philosophy* dedicated an issue (6.1) to explore the tension between filial care and justice.

Demonstrating the prevalence of value conflicts discussed in premodern Chinese literature does not, of course, mean that early Confucians saw value conflicts as irresolvable; however, it does demonstrate several related things. It demonstrates, for instance, that value conflicts were a reoccurring issue for Confucians. Even if value conflicts were seen as harmonizable, Confucians spent significant time thinking about how to harmonize them. Further, the period of time over which these issues were discussed demonstrates the enduring nature of these tensions. Reconciling filial care with loyalty was a problem in Warring States China as well as in late imperial China.

Irresolvable Value Conflicts

While value conflicts in many of the examples listed may have been seen as resolvable, there are a number of passages in the early texts that demonstrate that early Confucians saw some value conflicts as irresolvable. The *Han Shi Waizhuan* tells about Shi Tuo 石他, who was a scholar in the state of Qi 齊 when it was illegitimately conquered by Tian Chang 田常 in 481 BCE.

Tian Chang murdered Jian Gong and then offered an oath to the people of the state, saying, "If you do not make an oath [with me, I will] kill you and your families."

田常弒簡公，乃盟于國人，曰：「不盟者，死及家。」

Shi Tuo said, "When those in antiquity served a ruler, they [were willing to] die in the service of the ruler. To cast aside [one's] ruler in order to preserve [one's] parents is not [true] loyalty [to one's ruler]. To abandon [one's] parents to die in the service of [one's] ruler is not [true] filial care. I cannot [do either of these]. Not making an oath will kill my parents, but in following the crowd and making an oath [I will] betray my ruler. Alas! [I am] born in a chaotic age and cannot find the right course of action. [I have been] coerced by a violent man and cannot preserve [my] righteousness. How sorrowful!"

石他曰：「古之事君者、死其君之事。舍君以全親，非忠也；捨親以死君之事，非孝也；他則不能。然不盟，是殺吾親也，從人而盟，是背吾君也。嗚呼！生亂世，不得正行；劫乎暴人，不得全義，悲夫！」

And so [Shi Tuo] went and made an oath in order to save his father and mother; [and then he] withdrew and fell on his sword in order to die for his ruler. Those who heard about this said, "What a exemplary person! [He] accorded with his fate!" The *Shijing* says, "The people have a saying: Whether advancing or retreating there is only obstruction." This describes Shi Tuo.

乃進盟，以免父母；退伏劍，以死其君。聞之者曰：「君子哉！安之命矣！」《詩》曰：「人亦有言；進退維谷。」石先生之謂也。[60]

There are several similarities between this vignette and the story of Shen Ming discussed here. In both cases, Han Ying appends the line from the *Shijing* that describes obstruction regardless of what the moral agent does. No matter what, some righteous desire will not be fulfilled. Shi Tuo recognizes that even if he makes an oath with Tian Chang in order to save his parents and then kills himself in order to express his loyalty to his ruler, he is still, at the same time, casting aside his ruler in making an oath with Tian Chang and neglecting his parents by dying for his ruler. Both Shen Ming and Shi Tuo also conceptualize their circumstance in terms of a conflict between filial care and loyalty, and in both cases they commit suicide in dealing with the situation. This vignette also discusses terms such as *xing* 行 and *quan* 全. Shi Tuo laments the fact that he is born in chaotic times such that he cannot take appropriate action and that he is coerced by Tian Chang such that he cannot preserve his righteousness (*quanyi* 全義). While Shi Tuo is praised for accepting his fate, he is distressed by his inability to preserve his *yi* 義. The idea of *yi* 義, which I have translated here as righteousness, also suggests a notion of proper role-performance.

Jia Jinhua and Kwok Pang-Fei trace the etymology of *yi* 義 from oracle bones to the Han. They argue that early appearances of *yi* 義 refer to decorative clan emblems that come to signify a we-group.[61] By the Warring States, they explain that *yi* 義 comes to be understood as "a set of human obligations and ethical standards which fit one's role and status in the kinship group as father or son, elder or younger, lord or subject, or in other words, it is the conventional norms of right conduct concerning the relationship between an individual and his group."[62] Said with regard to Shi Tuo, the notion of "not being able to preserve [his] righteousness" 不得全義 can also be understood as "not being able to maintain the integrity of his roles" as son and minister. His devotion to relationships with his parents and his ruler renders himself vulnerable to unfortunate circumstances.

The *Xinxu* 《新序》 telling of the story casts Shi Tuo's decision in a different light. After realizing his predicament, Shi Tuo in part states, "Even if [I] make an oath [with Tian Chang] so that my parents do not die, it is not as good as withdrawing [from the oath] and killing myself in order to [remain] in ritual accord with my ruler" 故雖盟，不以父母之死，不如退而自殺，以禮其君.[63] The passage concludes with Shi Tuo committing suicide. In this telling of the story, Shi Tuo does not even try to tend to both values at stake. Rather, he weighs one against the other (cast in terms of care for one's parents and ritual propriety, *li* 禮) and determines it best to be in proper accordance with his ruler. This model of trading off values is significantly different from the harmony thesis and is discussed in greater detail later.

Interestingly, people with the surname *shi* 石 appear in several other stories in early Confucian texts where they encounter irresolvable value conflicts. The *Han Shi Waizhuan, Xinxu*, and *Shiji* (as well as the *Lüshi Chunqiu*) all tell of Shi She 石奢 (c. 500 BCE) who was "fair-minded and committed to honesty" 公而好直.[64] The ruler of Chu 楚 enlisted him as a sheriff, and soon Shi She was pursuing criminals. Unfortunately, one of the criminals he captured was a murderer that turned out to be his own father. Feeling caught between filial care and loyalty, he let his father go and confessed his act to the ruler. The ruler of Chu forgave him, but Shi She could not live with himself so he cut his throat and died in the Chu court. This vignette is reminiscent of two other vignettes in early Confucian texts—*Analects* 13.18, where Kongzi endorses sons and fathers covering up for each other's crimes (Han Ying specifically mentions this passage in the *Han Shi Waizhuan* version of Shi She's story), and *Mengzi* 7A35, where Mengzi says that if Shun's 舜 father had committed a murder, Shun would give up the position of king and flee to the oceanside with his father, "rejoicing for the rest of his days; living in delight, and forgetting the kingdom" 終身訴然，樂而忘天下. One major difference between these vignettes and the story of Shi She is that the main characters in these vignettes from the *Analects* and *Mengzi* do not seem to exhibit moral distress. Passages such as *Mengzi* 7A35 lead Stephen Angle to conclude that "classic Confucian treatments of moral conflicts say little or nothing about the agent's mixed emotions or difficulties"; and this, in part, allows Angle to argue for a harmonious resolution of value conflicts.[65] The story of Shi She, on the other hand, complicates this. Shi She, like Shi Tuo, is conflicted with mixed emotions. He wants to "remain partial to his father" 私其父 and "enact the laws of [his] ruler" 行君法. Before killing himself, he states, "It would not be filial to not remain partial to one's father, nor would it be loyal to not enact the laws of [one's] ruler. [Indeed,] it would be impure to live with a transgression worthy of death" 不私其父，非孝也；不行君法，非忠也；以死罪生，不廉也.

The *Han Shi Waizhuan* further challenges Angle's claim in another passage that discusses the notion of sons covering for their fathers. It states, "If sons cover up for their parents then justice does not attain its rightful place. If rulers punish the unjust then humaneness does not attain its acceptable place. Despite contravening humaneness and harming justice, the model to follow lies in between the two" 子為親隱，義不得正；君誅不義，仁不得受。雖違仁害義，法在其中矣.[66] While the final phrase is ambiguous, the rest of the passage clearly highlights the harms involved in sons covering up for their fathers and rulers punishing lawbreakers.[67] The *Han Shi Waizhuan* endorses these actions even though they entail harming values of humaneness and justice. In contrast with passages such as *Analects* 13.18 and *Mengzi* 7A35, parts of the *Han Shi Waizhuan* recognize the necessity of a less than harmonious solution in doing what ought to be done.

In my view, part of what we see in the *Han Shi Waizhuan* is a subtle criticism of the clarity with which agents are assessed in portions of the *Analects* and the *Mengzi*. *Mengzi* 7A35, in particular, seems to advocate a distress-free resolution in dealing with one's father after he murdered someone. However, when read alongside the story of Shi She, Mengzi's resolution seems to be impractical if not naïve. Stories such as Shi She's can be read as the lived experience of value conflicts as opposed to hypothetical possibilities argued for in parts of the *Mengzi* and the *Analects*. These stories reveal at the very least the difficulty, if not impossibility, of realizing notions of invulnerability and value harmony in difficult situations. In doing this, the *Han Shi Waizhuan* takes part in a longer tradition of Confucians criticizing passages such as *Mengzi* 7A35. Later Confucians such as Sima Guang 司馬光 (1019–1086), who famously wrote a text entitled *Doubting Mengzi* 《疑孟》, Su Zhe 蘇轍 (1039–1112), and Li Gou 李覯 (1009–1059) were all skeptical of Mengzi's notion of Shun happily assisting his father flee from punishment.[68]

Another story involving a protagonist with the surname Shi 石 comes from the *Zuo Zhuan*. In 719 BCE, Zhou Xu 州吁 assassinated the ruler of the state of Wei 衛, and sought to take his place as ruler. In an effort to legitimate this coup, Zhou Xu's advisor, Shi Hou 石厚 asked his father, Shi Que 石碏, for advice. Shi Que recommended that Shi Hou and Zhou Xu gain the endorsement of the king by meeting with the ruler of Chen 陳 since he was on good terms with the king. Once they set out to Chen, however, Shi Que sent messengers to Chen informing the ruler that Shi Hou and Zhou Xu had murdered the ruler of Wei and that the people of Wei wanted them detained. The Chen court detained Shi Hou and Zhou Xu until men from Wei arrived and executed them. The *Zuo Zhuan* actually explains that Shi Que personally ordered the killing of his son Shi Hou. At the conclusion of the story, the *Zuo Zhuan* quotes the exemplary person (presumably Kongzi), who praises Shi Que as a "true minister" 純臣, and states that he "destroyed [his] familial connection for the sake of great justice" 大義滅親.[69] In short, at least from the view of the *Zuo Zhuan*, Shi Que chose justice over parental care. He chose loyalty to his state over concern for his son. There is no harmonization of competing values for Shi Que. He chose one value to the detriment of the other.

The fact that several of these stories involve people with the surname Shi 石 is significant. *Shi* 石 literally means "rock," or refers to something "impenetrable." One would expect those named "rock" to be firm or invulnerable—reminiscent of *Analects* 17.7 where Kongzi says "[If something is] truly hard, then scraping will not penetrate [it]" 堅乎，磨而不磷 (discussed in chapter 1). In some sense, individuals such as Shi Tuo and Shi She are firm in terms of firmly accepting the consequences of their unfortunate situations, and Shi Que is firm in his principles as a minister. However, in other respects these stories offer implicit critiques of invulnerability. No one, even those known for their impenetrability, is invulnerable to tragic conflicts. These vignettes each reveal that devotion to other people can lead to tragedy. In the cases of Shi Tuo and Shi She their commitment to their ruler and to their parents distresses them to the point of death. The *Zuo Zhuan* is silent with regard to the emotional condition of Shi Que, but nowhere does the text endorse not feeling sorrow for the suffering of one's family.

The narrative aspects of early Confucian texts particularly highlight irresolvable value conflicts. The *Zuo Zhuan* also tells of Xu Ni 鉏麑 (d. 607 BCE), who was commissioned to kill a minister named Xuanzi 宣子 for incessantly remonstrating the ruler of the state of Jin 晉. After sneaking into Xuanzi's residence and observing him throughout the night, Xu Ni discovered that Xuanzi was a man of principle. Xu Ni was now caught between following his commission to kill Xuanzi and not harming someone worthy of admiration. The *Zuo Zhuan* recounts, "[Xu] Ni stepped back [from the situation] and sighed, saying, '[One who] does not forget to be respectful and reverent is a leader of the people [i.e., Xuanzi]. To harm the leader of the people is to be disloyal. [However,] to toss aside the commands of [one's] ruler is to be distrustful. Being either one of these is not as good as death.' [So he] hit [himself] on a hardwood tree and died" 麑退，歎而言曰「不忘恭敬，民之主也，賊民之主，不忠。棄君之命，不信。有一於此，不如死也。」觸槐而死.[70] While the *Zuo Zhuan* passage about Xu Ni and Xuanzi is similar to other passages discussed in this chapter, it is different from most of the previous passages in that Xu Ni kills himself to avoid having to choose between commitments. Where Shi She killed himself for letting his father go, and thereby neglecting the laws of the state, Xu Ni kills himself in order to be neither disloyal nor distrustful. These vignettes reveal a complex of views with regard to suicide in early China. In some cases, suicide is a means of tending to a particular value in the situation (e.g., dying for one's ruler as an expression of loyalty).[71] Within this view, some suicides can even be seen as part of an attempt to tend to all values at stake in a situation—yielding a painful, yet harmonious, resolution. In other cases, suicide is a response to the defilement entailed in a tragic situation (e.g., the case of Shi Tuo). Following this line of thought, suicide is justified when one's virtue is blocked such that one can no longer meaningfully engage in those relationships that partially constitute the self. Suicide may even be seen as the culminating self-sacrifice done to engender the admiration of meaningful others. These situations are especially tragic when the act of tending to relationships generates the value conflict, as in the case of Shen Ming.

Finally, in other cases, as illustrated by Xu Ni, suicide is a means of demonstrating one's commitment to all values entailed in a situation, combined with the realization that one will not be able to tend to each value. In other words, Xu Ni kills himself to illustrate the seriousness with which he regards values such as loyalty and trustworthiness. In his view, his death is warranted because he understood not only the significance of loyalty and trustworthiness but also because he understood that he could not be both loyal and trustworthy. His death, as such, is a means of avoiding transgression. This brief taxonomy of suicides in early Confucian texts is not exhaustive, but it reveals that the commitments entailed in relationships can compel harmful, if not tragic, actions, and in the case of voluntary relationships (such as the minister of a ruler), the tragic nature of these actions is heightened in the sense that the moral agent may very well have chose to not enter into the relationship in the first place had he known his fate.[72]

The Minister, the Ruler, and the Recluse

Similar to the passages already discussed, the story of Xu Ni illustrates a conflict between commitments: in this case, a commitment to support those individuals dedicated to the best interests of the people and a commitment to follow through on promises made to those in authority. The first commitment, we might say, comes from a desire that good people have to encourage that which improves society. The second commitment comes from a relationship (usually) voluntarily entered into—becoming a retainer or a minister of a ruler. This latter commitment is interesting in the context of value conflicts. The number of anecdotes that depict conflicts that stem in part from the relationship between ruler and minister suggest that this relationship is particularly problematic. The fact that one can choose to forgo the relationship—electing to serve another ruler, or no ruler at all—highlights the regrettable nature of many of these value conflicts. In other words, in theory these value conflicts are avoidable since one need not enter into the relationship, but once one does enter into the relationship one is obligated to perform the requests of the ruler. While a minister can remonstrate against the ruler when the ruler's requests are not appropriate, it still entails navigating conflicting values that otherwise one would not necessarily have to navigate. Said differently, the problem with serving a ruler is that it can create commitments that impel one to carry out bad actions, or at the very least, place one in a position to have to negotiate competing values or even face irresolvable value conflicts. It adds dimensions to values such as loyalty and trustworthiness into the mix of an already complex life. This is one reason that many early Confucian texts stress the carefulness the worthy minister exercises in meeting with those in power.

Analects 18.7 presents an interesting vignette with regard to the difficulty of serving a ruler. In this passage, Zilu 子路 (542 BCE–480 BCE), a disciple of Kongzi, traveled after his master as he moved from one location to another. While looking for Kongzi, Zilu came across an old farmer who criticized Zilu for not understanding how to farm. Yet when Zilu stood respectfully in the farmer's presence, the farmer responded by providing Zilu with food, lodging, and even company by introducing Zilu to his two sons. When catching up to Kongzi, and relating this experience, Kongzi explained that the farmer must be a "recluse" 隱者—a man of talent "hiding" his services from the court.[73] He sent Zilu back to see the farmer—presumably to gain some bit of wisdom from the recluse (a common motif in the *Analects*). Upon returning, however, the recluse was gone. In speaking about this experience, Zilu remarked, "[If one] does not enter into the service [of a ruler], there is no [chance for] justice. [The farmer] did not cast aside the standards [brought about when] the young and old [interact], [so] how could [he] cast aside the justice [brought about when] a ruler and minister [interact]? In desiring to keep himself clean, [he] brings chaos to orderly relationships. When an exemplary person enters into service, [he] enacts what is just. [I] now know why the Way is not implemented" 不仕無義。長幼之節，不可廢也；君臣之義，如之何其廢之？欲潔其身，而亂大倫。君子之仕也，行其義也。道之不行，已知之矣. Zilu's criticism of the farmer, in short, is that he chose personal purity over the chance to maintain or establish the broad set of relationships that organize society and enact the Way. The *dao* 道 is not implemented, in Zilu's view, because people choose self-preservation over making just actions that order society. Passages such as 18.7 highlight the tension discussed in chapter 1 between a desire for self-preservation and a desire to order the world. Zilu's view is that the exemplary person ought to serve a ruler even if it entails compromising personal purity; without such service there is no chance to implement the *dao* 道. Zilu's view is reminiscent of Michael Walzer's claim discussed in chapter 2, where involvement in politics entails at least a willingness to dirty one's hands.[74] While later thinkers mediate these desires in different ways (as discussed later), Zilu's view of entering into service as a kind of self-sacrifice plays out in his own death in 480 BCE when he insists entering a besieged city because "after having eaten [the ruler's food; i.e., accepting a salary], [one] does not avoid the troubles the ruler [encounters]" 食焉，不辟其難.[75] The *Liji* explains that after being killed, Zilu's body was diced and pickled.[76]

The tension between serving a ruler and becoming a recluse is played out in many early Confucian texts. Zilu's view that one ought to serve even if it costs one's integrity or life is not universally accepted. In contrast to this view, several texts endorse the exemplary person becoming a recluse.[77] *Analects* 15.7, for instance, praises Qu Boyu 蘧伯玉 (d. 484 BCE), an aristocrat from the state of Wei 衛, saying, "When the nation has the Way, [he] serves [it]. When it does not have the Way, [he] then finds it acceptable to tuck away and hide himself" 邦有道，則仕；邦無道，則可卷而懷之. More plainly, in *Analects* 8.13 Kongzi states, "When the Way is found in the world, [the exemplary person] reveals himself; when the Way is not found in the world, [he] then goes into reclusion" 天下有道則見，無道則隱. In other places Kongzi praises figures such as Bo Yi 伯夷 and Shu Qi 叔齊 (c. 1050 BCE) for leaving their positions and refusing to serve a new regime. Some contemporary scholars see Kongzi as central in founding a tradition in early China for resigning from service, retiring, or becoming a recluse.[78] Aat Vervoorn endorses these views and summarizes Kongzi's position as follows: "[The] gentleman serves in office as long as by doing so he can further the Way; once that becomes impossible he must resign to avoid moral compromise."[79]

Other passages in early Confucian texts argue that a truly exemplary person can serve even a corrupt ruler while maintaining his integrity. As discussed in chapter 1, *Analects* 17.7 makes this kind of argument—the exemplary person is impenetrable like hard stone or he is white like fabric resistant to dye. In this view, the exemplary person ought to serve since his integrity cannot be harmed. Some traditional interpreters synthesize these latter two views of reclusion by discussing the difference between a sage (*shengren* 聖人) and a worthy (*xianren* 賢人). Since a sage is capable of maintaining his integrity, he ought to serve regardless of the circumstances, whereas a worthy has not yet attained the excellence of a sage, and therefore he ought to retire from circumstances that compromise his integrity. In commenting on a passage about recluses in the *Analects* (14.37), Huang

Kan 皇侃 (488–545) states, "[If] scraped, the sage will not be penetrated, [or if] dyed, [he] will not be stained. There is nothing [the sage necessarily] finds permissible or impermissible. [However,] as for a worthy, [if he] departs from [service], it is to accord with the times. If the heavens and earth are plugged and blocked up, the worthy goes into hiding" 聖人磨而不磷，涅而不緇，無可無不可，故不以治亂為隔。若賢者去就順時，若天地閉塞，則賢人便隱。[80] While positions such as Huang's produce a more holistic reading of texts including the *Analects*, they also leave unresolved the problem that extremely few people are actually seen as sages, and therefore the vast majority of people in these situations would have to opt for reclusion.[81] In contrast to these views, positions such as Zilu's that advocate some kind of self-sacrifice and obligation to serve are not uncommon.[82]

Self-Sacrifice and Value Conflicts

One significant passage that highlights the theme of self-sacrifice when ministers confront value conflicts comes from the *Gongyang Zhuan* 《公羊傳》.[83] In this vignette, Zhai Zhong 祭仲 (743–682 BCE), a minister from the state of Zheng 鄭, is captured by Song 宋 troops. They threaten to destroy the state of Zheng unless Zhai Zhong expels the rightful ruler of Zheng and replaces him with the ruler's younger brother, Tu 突. The passage states:

> In the seventh month of the year, in fall, Zhuang Gong from the state of Zheng was buried. In the ninth month men of Song captured Zhai Zhong from Zheng. Who was Zhai Zhong? [He] was an official from the state of Zheng. Why wasn't he [explicitly] named [in the *Chunqiu*]? Because he is a worthy. Why was Zhai Zhong a worthy? Because he understood how to *quan* 權. How is it that he understood how to *quan* 權?
>
> In antiquity, the state of Zheng was located in Liu. The ruler of Zheng at that time was on good terms with Kuai Gong, and had an affair with Kuai Gong's wife. [The ruler of Zheng] thereby acquired the state [of Kuai] and relocated the state of Zheng—leaving Liu on the outskirts [of Zheng].

> 秋，七月，葬鄭莊公。九月，宋人執鄭祭仲。祭仲者何？鄭相也。何以不名？賢也。何賢乎祭仲？以為知權也。其為知權奈何？古者鄭國處于留。先鄭伯有善于鄶公者，通乎夫人，以取其國而遷鄭焉，而野留。

> When Zhuang Gong died and was buried, Zhai Zhong prepared to go to Liu for an inspection. The road, [however,] passed through the state of

Song, and the men of Song detained him [on his journey], saying, "For our sake [we want you to] expel Hu [the rightful ruler] and set up Tu [as the new ruler]."

[If] Zhai Zong did not consent to their request, the ruler [i.e., Hu], would certainly die, and the state would certainly be brought to ruin [by Song]. [If he] consented to their request, [Hu, the rightful] ruler, would thereby live instead of die; and the state would thereby be preserved instead of ruined. By prolonging things this way, Tu could later be expelled, and Hu could later return [to his position]. [If Zhai Zhong] was unable to bring this about, [he] would [certainly] be distressed, but in the end the state of Zheng would be preserved.

莊公死已葬，祭仲將往省于留。塗出于宋，宋人執之，謂之曰：「為我出忽而立突。」祭仲不從其言，則君必死，國必亡。從其言，則君可以生易死，國可以存易亡。少遼緩之，則突可故出，而忽可故反。是不可得則病，然後有鄭國。

Among those of antiquity who had the capacity to *quan* 權 there is Zhai Zhong. What is *quan* 權? To *quan* 權 is to go against the standard (*jing* 經), and yet bring about good. As for situations where *quan* 權 is employed, unless it involves [preventing] death or destruction, it is not used. There is a method to enacting *quan* 權. The individual [enacting *quan* 權] is demeaned and harmed in enacting it, [but he] does not injure others in enacting it. The exemplary person does not kill others so that he can live; or destroy others so that he can preserve himself.

古人之有權者，祭仲之權是也。權者何？權者反於經，然後有善者也。權之所設，舍死亡無所設。行權有道，自貶損以行權，不害人以行權。殺人以自生，亡人以自存，君子不為也。[84]

In this passage, Zhai Zhong is praised for his ability to *quan* 權. Carrying out his duties as a minister leads to his capture, where he is forced to choose between values such as preserving the lives of the people in the state (including the rightful ruler) and putting the rightful ruler on the throne. He decides to preserve the state at the cost of expelling the rightful ruler. While this maintains the possibility of reinstating the ruler, Zhai Zhong has still gone against the conduct a minister should follow when interacting with a ruler, and, as the passage states, if he is not able to bring Hu back to the throne, he will be personally distressed. The purported author of the passage, Gongyang Gao 公羊高 (c. 450 BCE), explains that *quan* 權 involves going against a standard (in this case, not putting the eldest son on the throne), but yielding a good result (i.e., preserving the state of Zheng from destruction). Those who employ *quan* 權 should not harm others; however, enacting *quan* 權 will "demean and harm oneself" 自貶損.

This last point is most relevant for our purposes. Tragically, Zhai Zhong's dedication as a minister, through no fault of his own, puts him in a position where he is compelled to transgress the standards associated with being a minister. While he is praised as a worthy, he also submits himself to deprecation by forgoing the standards associated with being a good minister in relation to a ruler. One of the early commentators on the *Gongyang Zhuan*, He Xiu 何休 (129–182), explains this with regard to *quan* 權. He states, "*Quan*權 means to weigh; and thereby differentiate the light from the heavy. In this case, Zhai Zhong understood that the state was 'heavy' and the ruler was 'light.' The exemplary person will take up the crime of expelling the ruler for the sake of preserving the state" 權者稱也。所以別輕重，俞祭仲知國重君輕。君子以存國取逐君之罪.[85] In this remark Zhai Zhong is praised as a worthy and as an exemplary person. Part of what makes him a worthy is his willingness to engage in transgression. As discussed in chapter 1, traditional commentators understand the notion of "going against the standard" 反經 in various ways. In the case of the *Gongyang Zhuan*, to go against the standard entails some kind of personal harm. Chapter 7 looks at the nature of this harm more closely.

Weighing Competing Values

He Xiu's interpretation of *quan* 權 is markedly different from interpretations that read *quan* 權 in terms of harmonizing competing values (as explored in chapters 1 and 2). Instead of *quan* 權 balancing competing values, *quan* 權 is understood as weighing values against each other—one value is "heavy" 重 and another is "light" 輕.[86] In this line of thought, one ought to prioritize the heavy value, which in Zhai Zhong's case is preserving the state; however, tending to the heavy value does not negate one's obligation to tend to the lighter value. While the *Gongyang* passage preserves the possibility of Zhai Zhong tending to this value at some point in the future (when Hu might return to the throne), He Xiu stresses that Zhai Zhong's actions nonetheless involve the crime of expelling the ruler. We might surmise that He Xiu understands this transgressionary aspect of the situation in terms of "going against the standard" 反經.

This theme of weighing competing values against each other is not only found in the *Gongyang Zhuan*. Mengzi also conceptualizes value conflicts in terms of weighing values at stake in a situation and prioritizing them. *Mengzi* 6B1 discusses conflicts between the value of ritual propriety (*li* 禮) and the values of eating (*shi* 食) and procreating (*se* 色). In the passage, Mengzi's disciple, Wuluzi 屋盧子, had recently been outsmarted in a debate with someone from the state of Ren 任. Mengzi explains how he should have responded when the person from Ren asked him whether ritual propriety was more "heavy" (*zhong* 重; i.e., important) than eating or procreating. Wuluzi's original response was that indeed ritual is more important. His interlocutor, however, proceeded to raise cases where eating or procreating was clearly more important than ritual—compelling Wuluzi to choose, for instance, between starving to death and eating food in a ritually inappropriate way. Mengzi begins by explaining that he largely agrees with Wuluzi that in a general sense ritual is more important than eating or procreating; however, specific situations actually give these concepts practical value. He instructs Wuluzi with a series of metaphors:

> If you do not align the bottom of things, but line up their tops, then even an inch of wood can be made as high as a tall building. Think about the notion that metal is heavier than feathers; how could that refer to one clasp of metal compared with one cartload of feathers? [If we] look at a case where eating is "heavy" and ritual is "light," in comparing the two [surely we'll] arrive at the conclusion that eating is heavy. [If we] look at a case where procreation is heavy and ritual is light, in comparing the two [surely we'll] arrive at the conclusion that procreation is heavy.
>
> Go back and respond to the person from Ren, saying, "[If you] twist your brother's arm and take his food, you'll be able to eat. [But if you] do not twist his arm, [you] will not eat. Would [you] be willing to twist it? [If you] climb your neighbor's wall and drag away his daughter, [you'll] get a wife. [But if you] do not drag her away [you] will not get a wife. Would [you] be willing to drag her away?"

> 不揣其本而齊其末，方寸之木可使高於岑樓。金重於羽者，豈謂一鉤金與一輿羽之謂哉？取食之重者，與禮之輕者而比之，奚翅食重。取色之重者，與禮之輕者而比之，奚翅色重。往應之曰：『紾兄之臂而奪之食，則得食；不紾，則不得食，則將紾之乎？踰東家牆而摟其處子，則得妻；不摟，則不得妻，則將摟之乎？』

Mengzi's point is that asking the abstract question of whether ritual is more important than eating is like asking whether metal is heavier than feathers. To actually determine which is more important, the abstract values must be put into concrete situations. Similar to the way in which eating is more important than ritual when starvation is on the line, treating one's brother in accordance with ritual is more important when merely gaining a meal is on the line (and neither would one drag away a neighbor's daughter merely to get a wife). In short, there are situations where ritual is "heavy" and situations where eating is "heavy" (although the latter may rarely occur).[87] It is notable that in 6B1 Mengzi does not argue for finding a way to realize both values, notwithstanding the fact that he does not rule it out. Instead, he suggests prioritizing values such that one tends to the value with the most importance. I suspect that the act of *quan* 權, tied with the capacity for wisdom (*zhi* 智; discussed in chapter 1), allows the cultivated agent to correctly prioritize values.

Importantly, passages such as *Mengzi* 6B1 also demonstrate that at least some early Confucians did not conceptualize values or value conflicts at a highly abstract level. While they often made generalizations about values such as ritual or justice, they felt that values were best compared in particular situations. Stated more strongly, early Confucians believed that values in an abstract sense could neither be brought into conflict with each other nor harmonized since specific situations give these concepts their practical value. So early Confucians could speak about general categories such as communal welfare (*gong* 公) and personal welfare (*si* 私), and it may turn out that these values often conflict with each other—sometimes producing irresolvable value conflicts; however, they did not see them as inherently conflicting with each other since the only way to compare them is in the concrete particulars of life. Further, when put into actual situations, the moral agent may be able to harmonize these values, and harmonizing them may be ideal, but passages such as *Mengzi* 6B1 suggest that harmony is not always a possibility and that the moral agent may need to prioritize them and then tend to one value when tending to two or more are not possible.

Conclusion

This chapter challenges narratives that describe early Confucian accounts of value conflicts in terms of harmony. In contrast with scholars such as Max Weber, Karl Jaspers, and Stephen Angle, I have shown that irresolvable value conflicts were seen as real possibilities by many early Confucian authors and that the possibility of irresolvable value conflicts means that these early Confucian authors saw the world in terms of tragic possibility. This tragic possibility does not mean that values *necessarily* conflict, nor that when they do conflict they necessarily conflict in irresolvable ways. Rather, tragic possibility preserves the chance for irresolvable conflict regardless of how "impenetrable" an agent might be. The significance of this possibility is that it shapes the kinds of hopes moral agents have about their world and their role in the world. For instance, it enables a greater sympathy for others because their misfortunes may be unavoidable. This notion of tragic possibility opens the door for fate to be as cruel to me as it is to you. Indeed tragic possibility means that vulnerability runs deep.

The passages discussed in this chapter also demonstrate that devotion to others can sometimes lead to tragic situations such that one can no longer maintain a virtuous relationship. It is in this sense that one's integrity, or one's confidence in the way in which one fits into the nexus of relations that partially comprise the self, is compromised. Yet the obstruction of interpersonal connection can also be reframed as a sacrifice one makes for the sake of devotion. I explore this more fully in chapter 7, but first I strengthen the arguments in this chapter by discussing irresolvable value conflicts with regard to sages.

Notes

1. Yang Jialuo 楊家駱, ed., *Tiehan Xinshi* 《鐵函心史》 (Taibei 台北: Shijie Shuju 世界書局, 1962), 26. Translation modified from Frederick W. Mote, "Confucian Eremitism in the Yuan Period," in *The Confucian Persuasion*, edited by Arthur F. Wright (Stanford, CA: Stanford University Press, 1960), 235.

2. "Between Family and State: Relational Tensions in Confucian Ethics," in *"Mencius": Contexts and Interpretations*, edited by Alan K. L. Chan (Honolulu: University of Hawai'i Press, 2002), 173–174.

3. Christopher W. Gowans, *Innocence Lost: An Examination of Inescapable Moral Wrongdoing* (New York: Oxford University Press, 1994), 224.

4. Gowans, *Innocence Lost*, 226.

5. Chenyang Li, *The Confucian Philosophy of Harmony* (New York: Routledge, 2014). Li does not spend much time discussing whether or not value conflicts are resolvable. Li does, however, argue for the possibility of irresolvable value conflicts in "Cultural Configuration of Values," *World Affairs* 12.2 (Summer 2008): 28–49; especially pages 32–36; and he argues for tragic value conflicts in "Does Confucian Ethics Integrate Care Ethics and Justice Ethics? The Case of Mencius," *Asian Philosophy* 18.1 (2008): 78.

6. Michael J. Puett, *The Ambivalence of Creation: Debates Concerning Innovation and Artifice in Early China* (Stanford, CA: Stanford University Press, 2001), 1–15.

7. For Bertrand Russell see *The Problem of China* (London: Allen & Unwin, 1922). For Herbert Fingarette see *Confucius: The Secular as Sacred* (New York: Harper & Row, 1972), 23 and 57. For Derk Bodde see "Harmony and Conflict in Chinese Philosophy," in *Studies in Chinese Thought*, 55.5 (Part 2 Memoir No. 75), edited by Arthur F. Wright (University of Chicago Press, 1953), 19–80; especially 46, 54, and 69. The following quote by Fingarette is especially relevant for this chapter: "The passage [*Analects* 13.18] could be a model one for posing the need for choice between two conflicting moral requirements. A Westerner would almost inevitably elaborate on it by emphasizing that in this case we do have knowledge (it is right to respect the law; it is right to protect one's parents; both are profound obligations), but when two profound duties conflict, *we* must choose. And it is in this necessity to make a

critical choice that lies the seed of tragedy, of responsibility, of guilt and remorse. But this way of seeing the matter, so obvious a possibility to us, is not even suggested by Kongzi. It is the very obviousness of this view of the matter that makes Kongzi's failure to show any recognition of it the more blatant. We could have no better proof than this that the problem of genuine choice among real alternatives never occurred to Kongzi, or at least never clearly occurred to him as a fundamental moral task. Kongzi merely announces the way *he* sees the matter, putting it tactfully by saying it is the custom in *li* 禮. There is nothing to suggest a decisional problem; everything suggests that there is a defect of knowledge, a simple error of moral judgment on the Duke's part." Fingarette, *Confucius*, 23. Henry Rosemont makes a similar point in "Notes from a Confucian Perspective: Which Human Acts are Moral Acts?" *International Philosophical Quarterly* 16.1 (1976): 55–57.

8. Max Weber, *The Religion of China: Confucianism and Taoism*, Translated and edited by Hans H. Gerth (New York: Free Press, 1968), 152.

9. Weber, *Religion of China*, 152–153.

10. Martha Nussbaum, "Golden Rule Arguments: A Missing Thought?" in *The Moral Circle and the Self: Chinese and Western Approaches*, edited by Kim-chong Chong, Sor-hoon Tan, and C. L. Ten, (Chicago: Open Court, 2003), 13. It is worth noting that Nussbaum is quite tentative in her conclusions.

11. Nussbaum, "Golden Rule Arguments," 8.

12. Nussbaum, "Golden Rule Arguments," 8.

13. Nussbaum, "Golden Rule Arguments," 13. Li Chenyang in *The Confucian Philosophy of Harmony*, page 7, provides two relevant quotes from Nussbaum's other work that have implications for Chinese thought: "Moral objectivity about the value of a person (or, presumably, an other source of moral claims) requires, evidently, the ability to see that item as distinct from other items; this in turn requires the ability to see it not as a deep part of an innocent harmony but as a value that can be contrasted or opposed to others, whose demands can potentially conflict with other demands." And: "For we must choose, it seems, between active harmonizing or ordering and open responsiveness, between being the makers of a consistent conflict-free world of value and being receptive to the rich plurality of values that exist in the world of nature and of history."

14. As quoted in Alexander Huang, "The Tragic and the Chinese Subject," *Stanford Journal of East Asian Affairs* 3.1 (2003), 58.

15. Heiner Roetz, *Confucian Ethics of the Axial Age: A Reconstruction Under the Aspect of the Breakthrough Toward Postconventional Thinking* (Albany: State University of New York Press, 1993), 98. Roetz traces parts of this discussion on pages 93–100. Jennier Wallace also draws on Hegel in discussing tragedy in Chinese literature: "Hegel was pinpointing something similar when he declared, in his Aesthetics, that 'truly tragic action necessarily presupposes either a live conception of individual freedom and independence or at least an individual's determination and willingness to accept freely and on his own account the

responsibility for his own act and its consequences' and that in Chinese drama 'there is no question of the accomplishment of a free individual action but merely of giving life to events and feelings in specific situations presented successively on the stage.' " Jennifer Wallace, "Tragedy in China," *The Cambridge Quarterly* 42.2 (2003): 103.

16. Hegel, for instance, in describing China states, "The individual is wholly without the power of personal decision and without subjective freedom." Georg Wilhelm Friedrich Hegel, *Lectures on the Philosophy of Religion*, edited by Peter C. Hodgson, translated by R. F. Brown, P. C. Hodgson, and J. M. Stewart, with J. P. Fitzer and H. S. Harris (Berkeley: University of California Press, 1984–1987), 250 n. 137.

17. See Wallace, "Tragedy in China" and Richard Seawall, "Absence of Tragedy in Asian Drama": http://www.britannica.com/EBchecked/topic/601884/tragedy/51130/Absence-of-tragedy-in-Asian-drama. On page 3 of *The Death of Tragedy* (New York: Knopf, 1961) George Steiner states, "Tragedy as a form of drama is not universal. Oriental art knows violence, grief and the stroke of natural or contrived disaster; the Japanese theatre is full of ferocity and ceremonial death. But that representation of personal suffering and heroism which we call tragic drama is distinctive of the Western tradition."

18. John Morreall, *Comedy, Tragedy, and Religion* (Albany: State University of New York Press, 1999), 62. On page 63, Morreall also states, "Like all cultures, the Chinese face mistakes, sickness, hunger, and death; but that does not prompt them to ask whether Heaven owes them something better. Without a philosophy of suffering, tragedy just does not get started in Chinese religions." To understand how tragedy became a hallmark of modernity see Joshua Billings, *Genealogy of the Tragic: Greek Tragedy and German Philosophy* (Princeton, NJ: Princeton University Press, 2014).

19. I discuss Perkins and Huang later. For others advocating tragedy in China see Yun-tong Luk, "The Concept of Tragedy as Genre and Its Applicability to Classical Chinese Drama," in *The Chinese Text: Studies in Comparative Literature*, edited by Chou Ying-Hsiung (Hong Kong: Chinese University of Hong Kong Press, 1986), 24.

20. This is building on Franklin Perkins, "Wandering Beyond Tragedy with Zhuangzi," *Comparative and Continental Philosophy* 3.1 (Spring 2011): 85.

21. Franklin Perkins, *Heaven and Earth Are Not Humane: The Problem of Evil in Classical Chinese Philosophy* (Bloomington: Indiana University Press, 2014), 149. In contrast to this see G. E. R. Lloyd, *The Delusions of Invulnerability: Wisdom and Morality in Ancient Greece, China and Today* (London: Duckworth, 2005), 87: "The cycles of *yin* 陰 and *yang* 陽, and the constancy of change, are accepted with equanimity. It would be absurd to fight against them."

22. George Steiner, " 'Tragedy,' Reconsidered," in *Rethinking Tragedy*, edited by Rita Felski (Baltimore: Johns Hopkins University Press, 2008), 30; Arthur Schopenhauer, *The World as Will and Representation*, translated by E. F. J. Payne,

vol. 1 (Mineola, NY: Dover, 1969), 254. Schopenhauer's notion of tragedy becomes important in early-twentieth-century discussions of tragedy in China. Wang Guowei 王國維 (1877–1927), in particular, argues that the *Hongloumeng* 《紅樓夢》 is a Schopenhauerian tragedy. See He Jinli, "'The Third Kind of Tragedy': How Wang Guowei Departs From Schopenhauer," in *Inter-Culturality and Philosophic Discourse*, edited by Yolaine Escande, Chenyang Li, and Vincent Shen (Newcastle upon Tyne, UK: Cambridge Scholars Publishing, 2013), 71–80.

23. Perkins, "Wandering Beyond Tragedy with Zhuangzi," 92. Perkins also stresses another difference: "If tragedy is absent in classical China, it is not due to a lack of pessimism but rather this missing valorization of the will, the celebration of . . . 'the titanically striving individual.'" Perkins, "Wandering Beyond Tragedy with Zhuangzi," 92.

24. Kristina Lindell makes a similar point in "Stories of suicide in ancient China," *Acta Orientalia* 35 (1973), 186. See also Lloyd, *Delusions of Invulnerability*, 110: "We certainly find, in Chinese writings of different types, greater acceptance of the inevitability of change. Although the fate of many great people is tragic in the sense of to be regretted, there was, with that acceptance, less occasion for heroics—where the individual strives, hopelessly, against the inevitable."

25. Huang, "The Tragic and the Chinese Subject," 61.

26. *Han Shi Waizhuan* 10.24/78/6–16. For more on the history of the *Han Shi Waizhuan* see James Robert Hightower, trans., *Han Shih Wai Chuan: Han Ying's Illustrations of the Didactic Application of the* Classic of Songs (Cambridge, MA: Harvard University Press, 1952), 1–10.

27. Li, Xueqin 李學勤, ed., *Xiaojing Zhushu* 《孝經注疏》, *Shisanjing Zhushu* 《十三經注疏》 Vol. 26 (Beijing北京: Beijing daxue chubanshe 北京大学出版社, 2000), 5. The term *lishen* 立身, which I translated as "establish his individual character," is difficult to translate. In the context of the *Xiaojing* it is explicitly tied to "proclaiming [your] name to future generations in order to glorify your parents" 揚名於後世，以顯父母 (the very same line Sima Tan recites to Sima Qian on his deathbed; as discussed in chapter four); *Xiaojing* 4. See also *Xiaojing* 16; *Mengzi* 5A4; *Da Dai Liji* 4.4/29/25; and *Lüshi Chunqiu* 14.1/69/13–16. It is also worth noting that the *Xiaojing* does recognize the possibility of value conflicts in *Xiaojing* 56–59.

28. Roetz describes specific conflicts between the family and state in *Confucian Ethics of the Axial Age*, 93–94; see also 94–100. Keith Knapp also traces the priorities given to the state and family in different periods of Chinese history in *Selfless Offspring: Filial Children and Social Order In Early Medieval China* (Honolulu: University of Hawai'i Press, 2005), 127.

29. Li, Xueqin 李學勤, ed., *Zhouli Zhushu* 《周禮注疏》, *Shisanjing Zhushu* 《十三經注疏》 Vol. 7–9 (Beijing北京: Beijing daxue chubanshe 北京大学出版社, 2000), 411.

30. Xu Fu 徐復 and Wenmin Song 宋文民, *Shuowen Wubaisishi Bushou Zhengjie* 《說文五百四十部首正解》 (Jiangsu 江蘇: Guji chubanshe 古籍出版社, 2003), 24.

31. Xu Shen 許慎. *Shuowen Jiezi* 《說文解字》 (Beijing 北京: Zhonghua Shuju 中華書局, 2004), 44.

32. Mao Heng 毛亨, ed., *Mao Shi Zhengyi* 《毛詩正義》 (Xianggang 香港: Zhonghua Shuju 中華書局, 1964), 1587.

33. For *quan* 卷 see Axel Schuessler, *ABC Etymological Dictionary of Old Chinese* (Honolulu: University of Hawai'i Press, 2007), 437. Zheng Xuan refers to *quan* 全 in the context of jade with a "pure color" 純色 in Li Xueqin, *Zhouli Zhushu*, 1312. See also *Liji* 11.27/72/27–28. The *Fayan* 《法言》 (12/32/3) echoes the connection between *quan* 全 and purity—associating it explicitly with *de* 德. The text states, "Why are black, red, and white oxen of a single color presented in the temple? Because the exemplary person preserves his *de* 德" 牛玄騂白，睟而角，其升諸廟乎？是以君子全其德.

34. *Shuoyuan* 4.14/28/15–16.

35. Deborah Sommer, "Boundaries of the *Ti* Body," *Asia Major*, 3rd series, 21.1 (2008), 303.

36. *Xunzi* 8/30/1. See also *Liji* 25.36/128/7: "To not fatigue one's body, nor disgrace one's self, can be called *quan* 全" 不虧其體，不辱其身，可謂全矣.

37. Wang Chong uses the phrases *bude liang li* 不得兩立 and *bude er quan* 不得二全 in a related sense in 25/105/10–14.

38. For a sample of these passages see Qian Zhongshu 錢鐘書, *Guanzhuibian* 《管錐編》 (Beijing 北京: Zhonghua Shuju 中華書局, 1999), 134–136. Qian also explicitly argues for understanding these as "tragic dilemmas" on page 134.

39. See *Han Shi Waizhuan* 4.17/30/10 and *Lüshi Chunqiu* 11.4/56/6–9.

40. *Xunzi* 2/8/16 and 29/141/19–142/5.

41. *Xiaojing* 56–59.

42. See the "Zengzi Wen" 曾子問 chapter.

43. *Liji*, 50.6/175/7.

44. *Kongzi Jiayu* 10.16/18/29–10.16/19/4.

45. *Kongzi Jiayu* 37.4/65/12–17.

46. Yang Bojun 楊伯峻, ed., *Chunqiu Zuo Zhuan Zhu* 《春秋左傳注》 (Beijing 北京: Zhonghua Shuju 中華書局, 2000), 142–144 ("Huan Gong" 桓公 15). Hereafter, *Zuo Zhuan*.

47. *Zuo Zhuan*, 288–300 ("Xi Gong" 僖公 4). See also Guoyu 4.10/50/22–4.10/52/13.

48. *Guoyu* 1.5/3/6–10.

49. See also the vignettes in the chapter titled "Zhen Shun" 貞順, as well as the stories about the wife of Zhounan 周南之妻, the wife of Dazi from Tao 陶荅子妻, the wife of Liuxia Hui 柳下惠妻, and the wife of Jieyu from Chu 楚接輿妻 in the second chapter ("Xian Ming" 賢明); the story of Zhuang Zhi, the maiden of Chu

楚處莊姪 in "Bian Tong" 辯通; and the stories about Nie Zheng's older sister 聶
政姊 and Wang Ling's mother 王陵母 in "Xu Lienüzhuan" 續列女傳. For more
on value conflicts in the *Lienüzhuan* see César Guarde-Paz, "Moral Dilemmas
in Chinese Philosophy: A Case Study of the *Lienü Zhuan*," *Dao: A Journal of
Comparative Philosophy* 15.1 (January 2016): 81–101.

50. Newell Ann Van Vuken, *The Commentarial Transformation of the* Spring and
Autumn (Albany: State University of New York Press, 2016), 197–198.

51. Fan Ye 范曄, ed., *Hou Hanshu* 《後漢書》 (Beijing 北京: Zhonghua Shuju 中
華書局, 1965–1973), 2692–3. In commenting on this vignette Myeong-seok Kim
states, "In my view, this story implies the following idea: human beings can sometimes be tragically torn between two seemingly incompatible obligations." "Choice,
Freedom, and Responsibility in Ancient Chinese Confucianism," *Philosophy East
and West* 63.1 (January 2013): 22.

52. Chen Shou 陳壽, ed., *Sanguozhi Jijie* 《三國志集解》 (Shanghai 上海: Shanghai
Guji Chubanshe 上海古籍出版社, 2009), 1103–1108.

53. Teng Zhixian 滕志賢, ed., *Xinyi Shijing Duben* 《新譯詩經讀本》 (Taibei 台
北: Sanmin Shuju 三民書局, 2011), 594–601. Hereafter *Shijing*. The "Simu" 四牡
poem expresses the tension between serving one's ruler and tending to one's parents
(*Shijing* 439–442).

54. Fu Xiren 傅錫壬, ed., *Xinyi Chuci Duben* 《新譯楚辭讀本》 (Taibei 臺
北: Sanmin Shuju 三民書局, 2011), 262.

55. Ding Yuanzhi 丁原植, *Guodian Chujian: Rujia Yiji Sizhong Shixi* 《郭店楚簡：
儒家佚籍四重釋析》 (Taibei 台北: Taiwan Guji Chuban Youxian Gongsi 台灣
古籍出版有限公司, 2004), 242. See also *Liji* 50.4/174/27; *Dadai Liji* 13.2/77/
9–11; and *Kongzi Jiayu* 26.2/50/10–12.

56. As cited in He Jinli, "'The Third Kind of Tragedy,'" 73.

57. Huang Jianyue 黃建跃, *Xianqin Rujia de Gongsizhibian* 《先秦儒家的公私之
辨》 (Guilin 桂林: Guangxi Shifandaxue Chubanshe 广西师范大学出版社,
2013). Erica Brindley has also published an article on the topic arguing that the tension between *gong* 公 and *si* 私 becomes more apparent in the mid to late Warring
States. "The Polarization of the Concepts *Si* (Private Interest) and *Gong* (Public
Interest) in Early Chinese Thought," *Asia Major* 26.2 (2013): 1–31. In Japanese see
Mizoguchi Yūzō 溝口雄三, *Chūgoku no Kō to Shi* 《中国の公と私》 (Tokyo
東京: Kenbun Shuppansha 研文出版社), 1995.

58. Zhang Kunjiang 张崑将, *Dechuan Zhongxiao Gainian de Xingcheng yu Fazhan: Yi
Bingxue yu Yangmingxue wei Zhongxin* 《德川忠孝概念的形成与发展：以
兵学与阳明学为中心》 (Shanghai 上海: Shanghai Huadong Shifan Daxue
Chubanshe 上海华东师范大学出版社, 2008).

59. Wolfram Eberhard, *Guilt and Sin In Traditional China* (Berkeley: University of
California Press, 1967). Meir Shahar and Robert P. Weller have also edited a book
titled *Unruly Gods: Divinity and Society in China* (Honolulu: University of Hawai'i
Press, 1996) that looks at deities worshipped in various periods of Chinese history

that are known for their capricious and even immoral activities. This demonstrates the plurality and complexity of views with regard to values in Chinese history. In contrast to this see Lloyd, *Delusions of Invulnerability*, 87: "Plenty of ancient Chinese texts speak eloquently of the fluctuations in human prosperity, but the Chinese did not feel threatened by envious gods."

60. *Han Shi Waizhuan* 6.12/44/18–22. Csikszentmihalyi discusses this vignette in *Material Virtue*, pages 4–6.

61. More specifically, *yi* 義 depicts a decorated axe; and Jia and Kwok point out several passages where *yi* 義 preserves this meaning in later texts (note also the *Liude* 《六德》 passage cited earlier in this chapter). Jinhua Jia and Pang-Fei Kwok, "From Clan Manners to Ethical Obligation and Righteousness: A New Interpretation of the Term *yi* 義," *Journal of the Royal Asiatic Society* 17.1 (January 2007): 35–38. Coincidentally, Eric Hutton reached conclusions similar to Jia and Kwok in his analysis of *yi* 義 in the *Xunzi*. "On the Meaning of *Yi* (義) for Xunzi" (Master's thesis, Harvard University, 1996). This notion of cutting or dividing as a means of signifying role relations relates to the discussion of *jie* 節 in chapter 7.

62. Jia and Kwok, "From Clan Manners," 39.

63. *Xinxu* 8.1/44/5–6.

64. *Han Shi Waizhuan* 2.14/10/19–26. Some texts use the name Shi Zhu 石渚 instead of Shi She. The *Lüshi Chunqiu* (19.2/121/3–9) version describes him as "fair-minded, honest, and without selfishness" 公直無私. It also casts Shi Zhu as someone both loyal (*zhong* 忠) and filial (*xiao* 孝). The *Shiji* describes him as "firm, honest, pure, and upright" 堅直廉正. Ma Teying 馬特盈, ed., *Shiji Jinzhu* 《史記今註》 (Taibei 台北: Taiwan Shangwu yinshuguan 臺灣商務印書館, 1987), 3125; hereafter *Shiji*. Csikszentmihalyi discusses this vignette in *Material Virtue*, 115–116.

65. Angle, *Sagehood*, 95.

66. *Han Shi Waizhuan* 4.17/30/10. On going against *yi* 義 as the right thing to do, see also *Shuoyuan* 13.33/108/14–21.

67. Csikszentmihalyi interprets this passage differently: "When applied to the case of Upright Gong, this passage implicitly argues for a balance between compassion and duty. For a son, model behavior may entail compromising one's righteousness out of feeling for one's parent. For a ruler, model behavior may entail compromising benevolence and executing the son out of a duty to maintain social order. For the *Han Shi waizhuan* it is the models of behavior, in an abstract sense, that are seen to ideally combine these two otherwise competing virtues." *Material Virtue*, 116.

68. For a brief discussion of this with regard to Sima Guang and Su Che see Chun-chieh Huang, "East Asian Conceptions of the Public and Private Realms," in *Taking Confucian Ethics Seriously*, edited by Kam-por Yu, Julia Tao, and Philip J. Ivanhoe (Albany: State University of New York Press, 2010), 83. For Li Gou see Hsieh Shan-yuan, *The Life and Thought of Li Kou (1009–1059)* (San Francisco: Chinese Materials Center, 1979).

69. *Zuo Zhuan*, 35–39 ("Yin Gong" 隱公 4). The *Lüshi Chunqiu* also tells a story about a Mohist who kills his son in 1.5/5/24–28. He is praised for enacting "great justice" 大義. See also *Shuoyuan* 5.28/38/9–16.

70. *Zuo Zhuan*, 658–659 ("Xuan Gong" 宣公 2). Alternative versions of this story appear in *Shuoyuan* 4.12/27/26–28 and *Guoyu* 4.56/74/1–6.

71. See, for instance, *Han Shi Waizhuan* 2.20/11/28–2.20/12/6.

72. For more on suicide in early China see Kristina Lindell, "Stories of Suicide in Ancient China." *Acta Orentalia* 35 (1973): 167–239; and Ping-Cheung Lo, "Confucian Views on Suicide and Their Implications for Euthanasia," in *Applied Ethics: A Multicultural Approach*, 4th ed., edited by Larry May, Shari Collins-Chobanian, and Kai Wong (Upper Saddle River, NJ: Prentice Hall, 2005), 624–641. For a related treatment of the topic in the *Xinxu* and *Shuoyuan*, see Charles Sanft, "The Moment of Dying: Representations in Liu Xiang's Anthologies *Xin xu* and *Shuo yuan*," *Asia Major* 24.1 (2001): 127–158. Sanft's article also cites several passages related to the larger theme of value conflicts.

73. The term *yinzhe* 隱者 ("recluse" or "hermit") entails not just hiding from society but hiding some kind of talent one can offer society. Early interpreters of the *Analects* often understood recluses as "worthies" 賢 rather than Daoists or proto-Daoists proposing views in contrast to Kongzi's. Robert Ashmore explores this in *The Transport of Reading: Text and Understanding in the World of Tao Qian (365–427)* (Cambridge, MA: Harvard University Press, 2010), 57–61, 75–76, and 83–85. In *Analects* 18.7, this appears to be the case until the end of the passage when Zilu criticizes the recluse.

74. Michael Stocker explains that "dirty hands remind us of the perhaps archaic view that the immorality of the world can irredeemably stain our acts and lives. They show that not only one's own immoralities, but also another's immoralities, can make it impossible to avoid doing what is immoral. They show, contrary to the Kantian theme, that our acts are not always fresh moral starts." "Dirty Hands and Ordinary Life," in *Cruelty & Deception: The Controversy Over Dirty Hands in Politics*, edited by Paul Rynard and David P. Shugarman (New York: Broadview Press, 2000), 35.

75. *Zuo Zhuan*, 1696 ("Ai Gong" 哀公 15). Edward Slingerland translates an alternative account of his death in *Confucius: Analects* (Indianapolis: Hackett, 2003), 116.

76. *Liji* 3.7/11/21–22.

77. Becoming a recluse could entail a variety of actions from refusing to serve a ruler, refusing to participate in politics (which often leads to farming for a living), or altogether leaving society behind. For more on recluses, see Aat Vervoorn, *Men of the Cliffs and Caves: The Development of the Chinese Eremitic Tradition to the End of the Han Dynasty* (Hong Kong: Chinese University Press, 1990); and Alan J. Berkowitz, *Patterns of Disengagement: The Practice and Portrayal of Reclusion in Early Medieval China* (Stanford, CA: Stanford University Press, 2000).

78. In *The Transport of Reading*, 85, Ashmore explains, "The choice between public service and eremitic withdrawal, in other words, is by no means to be conflated with a choice between the ethical worldview of classicism and its rejection; rather, that ethical choice was articulated for scholars of this period [i.e., 4th and 5th century CE] precisely in terms of that worldview." See also Frederick W. Mote, "Confucian Eremitism in the Yuan Period," in *The Confucian Persuasion*, edited by Arthur F. Wright (Stanford, CA: Stanford University Press, 1960), 202–240. Contrast this with Weber, *The Religion of China*, 229: "Asceticism and contemplation, mortification and escape from the world were not only unknown in Confucianism but were despised as paratism."

79. Vervoorn, *Men of the Cliffs and Caves*, 30.

80. Tang Yijie 湯一介, et al., eds., *Ru Zang* 《儒藏》 (Beijing 北京: Beijing Daxue Chubanshe 北京大學出版社, 2005), *Lunyu Yishu* 《論語義疏》, 265. Ashmore also quotes this in *The Transport of Reading*, 141. On page 143 Ashmore quotes Shen Linshi 沈鱗士 (419–503): "When the age is chaotic, it is fitting for the worthy to seclude himself and thereby preserve his life; and it is fitting for the sage to appear in order to enrich the things of the world" 世亂賢者宜隱而全生，聖人宜出以弘物.，故自明我道以救大倫. Translations are my own.

81. Vervoorn quotes Han Yu 韓愈 (768–824): "Therefore for scholars who want to put the Way into practice, if they do not obtain a position at court, there remain only the mountains and forests." *Men of the Cliffs and Caves*, 32.

82. These competing views are well-represented in the story of Shen Tudi 申徒狄, which is discussed in the introduction. Xunzi is actually quite critical of Shen Tudi in *Xunzi* 3/8/20–3/9/1.

83. For background on the *Gongyang Zhuan* see Joachim Gentz, *Das Gongyang zhuan: Auslegung und Kanonisierung der Frühlings- und Herbstannalen (Chunqiu)* (Wiesbaden: Harrassowitz, 2001). A basic introduction in Chinese can be found in Liu Shangci 劉尚慈, ed., *Chunqiu Gongyang Zhuan Yizhu* 《春秋公羊傳譯注》 (Beijing 北京: Zhonghua Shuju 中華書局, 2010), 655–701; and Xue Ke 雪克, ed., *Xinyi Gongyang Zhuan* 《新譯公羊傳》 (Taibei 台北: Sanmin Shuju 三民書局, 2008), 1–20; hereafter *Gongyang Zhuan*. In English, see Göran Malmqvist, "Studies on the *Gongyang* and *Guliang Commentaries*," *Bulletin of the Museum of Far Eastern Antiquities* 43 (1971): 76–222; 47 (1975): 19–69; 49 (1977): 33–215.

84. *Gongyang Zhuan*, 54–56 ("Huan Gong" 桓公 11).

85. As quoted in Csikszentmihalyi, *Material Virtue*, 122. Translation is my own.

86. He Xiu is not alone in this. Griet Vankeerberghen cites this as a common usage of *quan* 權 in "Choosing Balance: Weighing (*Quan* 權) as a Metaphor for Action in Early Chinese Texts," *Early China* 30 (2005), 67–71.

87. Li Chenyang has a good illustration of this in "When My Grandfather Stole Persimmons... Reflections on Confucian Filial Love," *Dao: A Journal of Comparative Philosophy* 7.2 (2008): 136–137.

6

The Conflictual World of the Sages

Kongzi said, "Dragons eat in clean water and swim in clean water. Hornless dragons eat in clean water but swim in dirty water. Fish eat in dirty water and swim in dirty water. Now, I have not risen to the level of a dragon, nor fallen as low as a fish. I suppose I am a hornless dragon."

孔子曰：「龍食乎清而游乎清，螭食乎清而游乎濁，魚食乎濁而游乎濁。今丘上不及龍，下不若魚，丘其螭邪。」

(*LÜSHI CHUNQIU*《呂氏春秋》 19.8/127/23–24)[1]

IN *THE HEIR and the Sage: Dynastic Legend in Early China*, Sarah Allan makes an intriguing claim about early Chinese narratives concerning the sages who founded the first dynasties in China. She frames these discussions in terms of a value conflict between "rule by heredity" and "rule by virtue."[2] According to Allan, the early rulers including Yao 堯, Shun 舜, and Yu 禹 are depicted as having to negotiate the tension between these values when passing the throne on to a successor or, in the case of the latter two, accepting the throne in becoming king. In each case, rule by heredity is the established norm; however, since the rightful ruler is not virtuous, the king breaks from the norm and passes the throne on to someone who is virtuous in an attempt to ensure that the people of the kingdom are treated humanely. For instance, in many retellings of Yao's reign, Yao recognizes that his son, Dan Zhu 丹朱, is not a good person and therefore offers the throne to his minister Xu You 許由. However, the virtuous person (Xu You in the case of Yao), recognizing that he is not the rightful heir, declines the throne and opts for a life of reclusion (or opts for suicide). The king then finds another virtuous person to accept the throne—Shun, for instance, accepts the throne from Yao. Allan emphasizes that the virtuous person who accepts the throne can still be regarded as a "usurper for having breached the hereditary right of the former ruler."[3] In other words, the person who finally assumes the throne is a "figure of mediation"—negotiating the values of heredity and virtue.[4] This person demonstrates that virtue ought to win out over heredity but only with remainder. In speaking of Yao passing on the throne, Allan states, "Xu You represents pure virtue and is contrasted with Shun, who is willing to compromise his integrity in accepting the throne."[5] She also explains, "Both men were regarded as [worthies] (*xian* 賢), but Shun's virtue was less because of his violation of the hereditary principle."[6]

In this chapter I build on aspects of Allan's thesis in exploring irresolvable value conflicts with regard to sages. In doing this I begin with portrayals of Yao, Shun, and other sages as compromised figures in a broad array of early Chinese (mostly non-Confucian) texts.[7] I provide this as a context for understanding the claims early Confucians make about sages. While on the one hand early Confucians stress the virtuous nature of sages and often resist the rhetoric of compromise and imperfection, on the other hand they do not totally reject the claims of the broader discourse. To refine this point I look more closely at the case of Wu Wang 武王 and show that many early Confucian texts were ambivalent about his violent overthrow of the Shang dynasty—in some stories he not only kills his ruler but illegitimately inherits the throne and forgoes the burial rites for his father. This example demonstrates the reoccurring theme of value conflicts between values such as loyalty and filial care or the conflict between desire to order the world and desire to maintain one's integrity. It also stresses that even sages encountered irresolvable value conflicts. The last section of this chapter looks at Kongzi—in particular the ways in which he was seen as a compromised figure. Building off chapter 4's discussion about transgression and Kongzi's creation of the *Chunqiu* 《春秋》, this chapter shows that value conflicts, as described in early Confucian texts, were sometimes seen as irresolvable for not only ordinary people but also for sages. In contrast to Yu Kam-por's claim that sages find ways of doing the right thing without violating any "moral constraints," we will see here the reoccurring theme of violation in the context of doing what is right.[8]

The Early Sages

The author of the *Shiji* 《史記》 frames Yao's decision on passing down the throne in terms of choosing between his son and the best interests of the kingdom.

> Yao knew that the unworthiness of his son, Dan Zhu, made him unfit for receiving the kingdom. [He] therefore weighed the possibility (*quan* 權) of giving [the kingdom] to Shun. If given to Shun, the kingdom would benefit, but Dan Zhu would suffer. If given to Dan Zhu, the kingdom would suffer, but Dan Zhu would benefit.

Yao remarked, "When it comes to it, I cannot allow the kingdom to suffer for the benefit of one person." So in the end, for the sake of the kingdom, he gave [the throne] to Shun.

堯知子丹朱之不肖，不足授天下，於是乃權授舜。授舜，則天下得其利而丹朱病；授丹朱，則天下病，而丹朱得其利。堯曰：「終不以天下之病而利一人」，而卒授舜以天下。[9]

Interestingly, this passage uses the notion of *quan* 權 in the context of weighing two values. Yao weighs the well-being of his son against the well-being of the kingdom. He chooses the well-being of the kingdom—referring to his son as but "one person" 一人.[10] Other texts reinforce this narrative, explaining that, not only did Yao skip over his oldest son, Dan Zhu, but he skipped over all of his sons (with Shun later repeating this process). The *Lüshi Chunqiu* states, "Yao had ten sons, [but] did not give [the throne] to his sons, and instead handed it to Shun. Shun had nine sons, [but] did not give [the throne] to his sons, and instead handed it to Yu. [This] is the utmost of impartiality" 堯有子十人，不與其子而授舜。舜有子九人，不與其子而授禹；至公也.[11]

In many accounts of Yao's story, however, Shun is not the first person to which Yao tried to give the throne. The *Shangshu* 《尚書》, for instance, states that Yao tried to pass the throne on to Siyue 四岳 (alternatively appearing as 四嶽 in the *Shiji*), a minister of works and advisor to Yao.[12] Siyue, however declined the throne and recommended Yao seek out Shun. More broadly recounted, however, is Yao's attempt to give the throne to Xu You. The *Shiji*, for instance, explains, "Yao yielded the kingdom to Xu You. [However,] Xu You did not accept [it], and ran in shame; [becoming] a recluse" 堯讓天下於許由；許由不受，恥之逃隱.[13] The *Shuoyuan* 《說苑》 actually states that after Xu You heard Yao's offer he "washed [his] ears and would not accept [it]" 洗耳而不受.[14] Xunzi likewise describes Xu You as someone who regarded "rightness as heavy, and benefit as light" 重義輕利.[15] Generally speaking, Xu You declined the throne because he felt that it was wrong to break the hereditary line. In this light, Yao is someone willing to deny his son his rightful position as ruler, and it is in this light that the *Lüshi Chunqiu* and the *Huainanzi* 《淮南子》 mention Yao's "reputation for being uncaring" 不慈之名.[16] The *Zhuangzi* states it in the most stark language, saying, "Yao killed his oldest son" 堯殺長子.[17]

Shun's willingness to accept the throne and then repeat the actions of Yao in not giving the throne to his son likewise complicates his moral standing. The same passages just quoted from the *Lüshi Chunqiu* and the *Zhuangzi* speak of Shun as "unfilial" 不孝; and another place in the *Zhuangzi* quotes one of those to whom he tries to give the throne: "[Shun] desires to pollute me with his shameful actions; and I am disgraced by it" 欲以其辱行漫我，我羞之.[18] Similar descriptives are used for the sage-figures Yu and Tang 湯. The *Zhuangzi* provides a useful summary in this regard.

Among those highly regarded in this age, there are none as [highly regarded as] Huangdi. But even Huangdi could not preserve his integrity—waging war in the outskirts of Zhuolu [lit. "dirty deer"] such that blood flowed for a hundred miles. Yao was uncaring, Shun was unfilial, Yu [worked so hard that] one side [of his body] was deformed, Wu Wang attacked Zhou 紂, and Wen Wang was imprisoned in Youli. These six figures are highly regarded in this age. [However,] if looked at more closely [we see that] they obscured their authentic nature and fought against their genuine dispositions. Their actions are indeed disgraceful.

世之所高，莫若黃帝，黃帝尚不能全德，而戰涿鹿之野，流血百里。堯不慈，舜不孝，禹偏枯，湯放其主，武王伐紂，文王拘羑里。此六子者，世之所高也。孰論之，皆以利惑其真而強反其情性，其行乃甚可羞也！[19]

Of course, these views are not uniform across early Chinese texts. The passage just quoted from *Zhuangzi*, for instance, comes from a dialogue between Robber Zhi 盜跖 and Kongzi, where the story serves as an alternative viewpoint to Kongzi's. Of the texts usually taken as Confucian, the *Mengzi* 《孟子》 works the hardest against these kinds of views, arguing that Yao and Shun did not necessarily breach the hereditary principle; rather, "[If] *Tian* 天 gives [the kingdom] to a worthy, [it] gives [it] to a worthy; [and if] *Tian* 天 gives [the kingdom] to a son, [it] gives [it] to a son" 天與賢，則與賢；天與子，則與子.[20] In other words, *Tian* 天 directs the process of passing the throne on to an heir, and sometimes it gives it to a worthy and sometimes it gives it to a son. Practically speaking, Mengzi explains that after Yao died, the people of the kingdom "did not follow Yao's son, and instead followed Shun" 不從堯之子而從舜也; meaning that Shun did not seek the position of ruler; rather, the people sought him out. When Yu died, the people sought out his son instead of his minister, and, as such, his son, Qi 啟, became the ruler.[21] Mengzi explains this as the workings of *Tian* 天, saying, "The worthiness or unworthiness of the rulers' sons is all [due to] *Tian* 天. [It] is not something human beings are able to bring about" 其子之賢不肖，皆天也；非人之所能為也. In Mengzi's view, the sages are not responsible for negotiating between the values of heredity and virtue. Rather, *Tian* 天 determines the heir, and, as such, sages are not explicitly responsible for forgoing any value.[22] In other places in the *Mengzi*, Mengzi likewise argues against narratives circulating in his time, stating, for instance, that Yi Yin 伊尹 did not purposefully degrade himself in order to become Tang's minister and that Wu Wang did not engage in bloody war campaigns.[23]

At the same time, Mengzi does not argue for unified perfectionism among sages such that each sage is paradigmatic in every way. He calls Boyi 伯夷, for instance, a sage of purity (*shengzhi qingzhe* 聖之清者) and Yi Yin a sage of responsibility (*shengzhi renzhe* 聖之任者); however, when asked if they compare to Kongzi, he responds, "No. From the beginning of humanity to now there is yet to be one [as great as] Kongzi" 否。自有生民以來，未有孔子也.[24] In other places he calls Boyi "obstinate" 隘 and admits that Zhou Gong 周公 made mistakes (*guo* 過).[25] In Mengzi's view, sages can exemplify one virtue or a series of virtues while falling short in others. As discussed in chapter 1, for Mengzi, only Kongzi is able to exercise each virtue at the right time because of his sense of discretion (*quan* 權). Therefore, "When appropriate to serve, [he] serves. When appropriate to stay, [he] stays. When appropriate to remain, [he] remains. When appropriate to move on, [he] moves on" 可以仕則仕，可以止則止，可以久則久，可以速則速.[26]

Boyi provides a particularly interesting example because Mengzi praises Boyi's purity but also criticizes his obstinacy. Like many stories of the early sages, there were probably several traditions circulating by the time of Mengzi, and it is sometimes difficult to reconstruct which tradition a particular thinker accepted. The earliest lengthy retelling of the Boyi story occurs in the *Shiji*.[27] In that story, Boyi is the son of the ruler of Guzhu 孤竹 and rightful heir to the throne. His father, however, wanted Boyi's younger brother Shuqi 叔齊 to inherit the throne. When the ruler died, Shuqi yielded the throne to Boyi; however, Boyi, not wanting to go against the wishes of his father (*fu ming* 父命), fled the state. Shuqi, recognizing that he was not the legitimate heir, also went into hiding. The two brothers then made plans to live out the rest of their days under the care of Wen Wang 文王—someone known for tending to the old and weak. When they reached Wen Wang, however, they discovered that he had died and that his son, Wu Wang, had taken over and was leading a rebellion against the ruler of the dynasty.[28] Boyi and Shuqi chastised Wu Wang for plotting to kill the ruler and for rushing into battle without fully mourning for his father. They explicitly questioned Wu Wang's humaneness (*ren* 仁) and filial piety (*xiao* 孝). Wu Wang's troops wanted to kill Boyi and Shuqi for their seeming insubordination; however, Wu Wang's advisor, Taigong 太公, convinced the troops to spare them because they were "righteous people" 義人.[29] Boyi and Shuqi then fled into the mountains and starved themselves to death to avoid participating in Wu Wang's new dynasty. They stated that they were "ashamed" 恥 of Wu's actions. If this is the account largely accepted by Mengzi, his criticism of Boyi as obstinate likely stems from Boyi's insistence to cling to righteousness (*yi* 義) or purity (*qing* 清) instead of adjusting to the circumstances. Mengzi intimates this is the case when he calls Kongzi the sage of timeliness (*shengzhi shizhe* 聖之時者). Mengzi labeling Boyi as obstinate is interesting because Mengzi, at least implicitly, questions the pursuit of purity. While in other places of the text (such as *Mengzi* 6A10) Mengzi advocates choosing righteousness even at the cost of one's life, there are other passages where he is critical of the pursuit, or perhaps the over-pursuit, of righteousness and purity.[30]

In 3B10 Mengzi discusses the example of Chen Zhongzi 陳仲子 (c. 300 BCE), an aristocrat from the state of Qi 齊. Similar to Boyi, Chen Zhongzi starved himself in order to maintain his "cleanliness" 廉, and, also similar to Boyi, Mengzi praised Chen Zhongzi and then went on to criticize his pursuit of cleanliness. Mengzi states,

> I certainly regard [Chen] Zhongzi as a truly outstanding individual. Nevertheless, is it possible for Zhongzi to be [truly] clean? Only an earthworm would be able to fully hold to [the principles he advocates]. Above ground an earthworm eats of the earth, and below ground it drinks from deep springs. Was the house that Zhongzi lived in built by Boyi, or was it built by Robber Zhi? Was the grain that [he] ate planted by Boyi, or was it planted by Robber Zhi? [He] cannot know which is the case.

> 吾必以仲子為巨擘焉。雖然，仲子惡能廉？充仲子之操，則蚓而後可者也。夫蚓，上食槁壤，下飲黃泉。仲子所居之室，伯夷之所築與？抑亦盜跖之所築與？所食之粟，伯夷之所樹與？抑亦盜跖之所樹與？是未可知也。

Mengzi continues by relating the following story:

> Zhongzi is a descendent from the house of Qi. His older brother, Dai, received a large salary from Gai. [Zhongzi] believed his older brother's salary to be unrighteous, and so [he] did not eat [his food]. [He] believed his older brother's house to be unrighteous, and so he did not stay in it. He avoided his brother, left his mother, and moved to Wuling. One day he returned, and his older brother happened to receive a live goose as a gift. Frowning, Chen Zhongzi asked, "What are you going to do with that noisy thing?"
>
> Some days later, his mother killed the goose, and presented it to Zhongzi for him to eat. His brother happened to come in from outside and said, "This is the meat of that 'noisy thing'!" [Zhongzi] ran out and threw it up. And so, if his mother [cooked for him, he] would not eat. But if his wife [cooked for him, he] would eat. When it came to his brother's house, [he] would not stay in [it]. But when it came to [his home in] Wuling, [he] would stay in it. As such, how could [Zhongzi] pursue his

principles? When it comes to Zhongzi, only an earthworm would be able to firmly hold to his values.

曰：「仲子，齊之世家也。兄戴，蓋祿萬鍾。以兄之祿為不義之祿而不食也，以兄之室為不義之室而不居也，辟兄離母，處於於陵。他日歸，則有饋其兄生鵝者，己頻顣曰：『惡用是鶂鶂者為哉？』他日，其母殺是鵝也，與之食之。其兄自外至，曰：『是鶂鶂之肉也。』出而哇之。以母則不食，以妻則食之；以兄之室則弗居，以於陵則居之。是尚為能充其類也乎？若仲子者，蚓而後充其操者也。」

Mengzi's criticism of Chen Zhongzi is more specific than his praise. Chen Zhongzi avoided his family in seeking to be pure, yet he neglected the fact that he could not maintain his own demands for purity since he could not know whether his house was built by someone good or bad or whether the food he ate was grown by someone good or bad. Bryan Van Norden makes a useful note on this passage when he states, "Zhongzi prides himself on his 'purity,' because he supposedly avoids benefiting from any ill-gotten gains. However, it is impossible to consistently follow this standard while living in human society, because one cannot verify the righteousness of everything one accepts."[31] Mengzi's specific point in this passage likely applies to cases of giving and receiving gifts; however, his larger point is that human beings are interconnected in ways that prevent us from attaining to the kind of purity sought after by Chen Zhongzi. Said somewhat differently, living a life in which one is physically healthy and engaged in relationships entails mediating expectations for purity. Stated in even stronger terms, Mengzi suggests that the absolutely pure life is not worth living.

In the broader context of the *Mengzi*, we might say that Mengzi believes that human beings ought to aim for purity and righteousness. He expresses admiration for those who are willing to give their lives to preserve their purity; he even argues that he would be willing to give his life for the sake of righteousness. However, he recognizes that the pursuit of purity has limitations and that accepting certain kinds of impurities is a necessary part of being human.[32]

Interestingly, the *Shiji* account of Boyi explains that Wu Wang's advisor, Taigong, persuaded Wu Wang's troops to spare Boyi and Shuqi from being punished for chastising Wu Wang. Taigong, unlike Boyi and Shuqi, supported Wu Wang's rebellion against the reigning king. As discussed in chapter 3, Taigong appears in a passage from the *Kongcongzi* 《孔叢子》 where Kongzi is presented with a gift from the ruler of Chu 楚. In gauging whether or not Kongzi will accept the gift, Kongzi's disciples ask him to compare Taigong with Xu You. The idea here is that Taigong was willing to serve those engaged in illicit political activities, while Xu You fled from Yao when illicitly offered the throne. If Kongzi sided with Taigong, his disciples could expect him to accept the ruler of Chu's offer. If Kongzi sided with Xu You, they could expect him to reject it. Kongzi responds: "Xuyou only bettered himself; [but] Taigong united and benefited the world" 許由，獨善其身者也。太公，兼利天下者也.[33] Kongzi goes on to say that there are no rulers around in his time that would recognize someone such as Taigong. He thereby implies that, while he sides with Taigong, the ruler of Chu's offer will not work out. However, Kongzi's point seems to be that Taigong is more praiseworthy than Xu You because Taigong sought to benefit the world, whereas Xu You privileged himself over the world.[34]

Passages such as these from the *Kongcongzi* suggest that in situations where the desire for personal purity conflicts with the desire for ordering the world, the sage should be willing to make personal sacrifices for the sake of the world. This notion of self-sacrifice appeared in the previous chapter where the author(s) of the *Gongyang Zhuan* 《公羊傳》 described Zhai Zhong 祭仲 (743–682 BCE) as someone who understood how to *quan* 權. In that passage, Zhai Zhong is said to be someone willing to "demean and harm himself" 自貶損 in order to bring about "good" 善.[35] This theme of self-sacrifice is highlighted in other early Confucian texts as well. Yang Xiong 楊雄 (53 BCE–18 CE), in the *Fayan* 《法言》, a text explicitly modeled on the *Analects*, addresses a question about whether or not sages are "crooked" or "bent" 詘.[36] Coincidentally, the English word "crooked" has implications similar to the Chinese character *chu* 詘. Both terms can literally refer to a bent or crooked object, or they can metaphorically refer to bending the rules or compromising one's character. Yang's questioner asks, "Do sages have [cases where they] are crooked 聖人有詘乎?" Yang replies that there are indeed cases where sages are crooked and goes on to say, "Zhongni [i.e., Kongzi] did not want to meet with Nanzi, and did not want to show respect to Yang Hu. [If] meeting with the unmeetable and respecting the unrespectable are not being crooked, then what is" 仲尼於南子，所不欲見也；陽虎，所不欲敬也。見所不見，敬所不敬，不詘如何? Yang's interlocutor then asks, "Duke Ling of Wei asked [Kongzi] about military affairs. Why didn't [Kongzi] bend [himself in this case]" 衛靈公問陳，則何以不詘? Yang responds, "When the self is made crooked, it is done to channel the flow of the Way. However, making the Way crooked in order to promote oneself is not done even if the world [could be gained]" 詘身，將以通道也。如詘道而信身，雖天下不為也.[37] The specifics of the figures mentioned in this passage need not concern us except to note that each of them was involved in illicit behavior, and associating with them risks being drawn into their activities or other people presuming that one supports their activities. Yang's primary point is that figures such as Kongzi "bent themselves" 詘身 in associating with some of these people, yet they did it for the sake of "channeling the flow of the Way" 通道. In this passage we see themes that came up in earlier portions of this book. The moral agent is concerned with flow (as opposed to obstruction or dissipation), for instance, and acts against his desire to preserve his integrity for the sake of enabling the Way to function in the kingdom. This latter concept we saw in terms of *budeyi* 不得已 discussed in chapters 1 and 4. When taken together these passages suggest the following idea: there are circumstances where one's desire to preserve one's integrity will conflict with one's desire to create a more ordered world. The moral agent can compromise his integrity as long as it primarily harms himself and as long as it is done for the benefit of others. This will, imaginably, be undertaken with a sense of reluctance.

The notion of benefit, profit, or gain (*li* 利) is central to self-sacrifice and requires some qualification. Prominently, the opening passage of the *Mengzi* is a critique of benefit. Some interpreters have read the passage as an expression of Mengzi's disdain for economic profit. However, when examined more closely and put into a larger context of other Confucian statements on benefit, Mengzi's criticism is not a blanket condemnation of economic profit. Rather, he argues for properly prioritizing economic gain and for recognizing that seeking benefit ought not to be done for selfish reasons. When asked by Liang Hui Wang 梁惠王 (400 BCE–319 BCE) whether Mengzi has come to benefit his state (*liwuguo* 利吾國) Mengzi replies,

> Why must you speak of benefit? Indeed, [one should] simply aim for having humaneness and rightness. [This is because if] the ruler says, "How will [I] benefit my state?" the officials will say, "How will [we] benefit our clans?" and the literati and people will say, "How will [we] benefit ourselves?" Everyone will jostle and compete over economic gain, and the state will be in danger. . . . If one prioritizes benefit above rightness, [the people] will not be satisfied unless [they] are seizing [things from others]. [On the other hand,] there has never been a case where someone is humane and casts aside his parents, or where someone is righteous and does not prioritize his ruler. You should simply speak of humaneness and rightness. Why must you speak of benefit?

> 王何必曰利？亦有仁義而已矣。王曰『何以利吾國』？大夫曰『何以利吾家』？士庶人曰『何以利吾身』？上下交征利而國危矣。。。。苟為後義而先利，不奪不饜。未有仁而遺其親者也，未有義而後其君者也。王亦曰仁義而已矣，何必曰利？[38]

This passage can be supplemented by another passage in the *Kongcongzi* set in the context of a discussion between Mengzi and Zisi 子思 (Kongzi's grandson and Mengzi's purported teacher or teacher's teacher):

> Mengzi asked, "In tending to the people what should be given priority?"

> 孟軻問「牧民何先？」

Zisi said, "First benefit them."

子思曰：「先利之。」

[Mengzi] said, "The exemplary person uses nothing other than humaneness and rightness to educate the people; how is it that [you] speak of benefit?"

曰：「君子之所以教民，亦有仁義而已矣，何必曰利。」

Zisi responded, "Humaneness and rightness are actually what is used to benefit the people. [If] those in leadership roles are not humane, then their subordinates will not attain to their [proper] place. [If] those in leadership roles are not righteous, then their subordinates will take pleasure in causing chaos. This is the result of not being beneficial. This is why the *Yijing* says, 'Benefit is the harmonization of rightness.' It also says, 'Benefit is used to comfort oneself and exalt [one's] virtue.' This is the result of benefit."

子思曰：「仁義，固所以利之也。上不仁，則下不得其所；上不義，則下樂為亂也。此為不利大矣。故《易》曰：『利者、義之和也』，又曰：『利用安身以崇德也』。此皆利之大者也。」[39]

Both passages are set in a context where Mengzi is suspicious of benefit. In *Mengzi* 1A1 he discourages Liang Hui Wang from prioritizing benefit because, once he prioritizes benefit, everyone else in the state will follow his example. When people contend with each other over benefit the state will be brought to ruin, and, implicitly, if the state is ruined neither profit nor the cultivation of virtues such as humaneness and rightness will be possible. In place of this, Mengzi argues that the ruler should prioritize humaneness and rightness. When people are humane, they will seek to provide the material needs of their parents. They will seek after economic gain for the benefit of others, and the state will be stable. Mengzi does not say it here, but other passages make it clear that Mengzi believes that humaneness is central to building a stable state.[40] The danger of benefit, according to this view, is not so much that benefit itself is bad but rather that prioritizing benefit leads people to disregard others and plunges the state into chaos.

The *Kongcongzi* passage makes the argument more explicit—humaneness and rightness are used to benefit the people. This passage employs an expansive notion of benefit to include not only economic gain but also moral development.[41] To be truly beneficial is to tend to multiple areas of self-cultivation. In this light, we might say that terms such as "benefiting the world" 利天下 can entail a broad sense of human flourishing. It suggests implementing the Confucian *dao* 道.

These passages take as a given that human beings have impulses to tend to our selves as well as impulses to tend to others. When we give priority to our other-regarding impulses, our self will be benefited in this process. While this entails tendencies that seem altruistic, this is not a kind of self-abnegation where the individual loses him- or herself to another; rather, these tendencies are set in a context where the self is partially constituted by relationships with other people. As such, benefiting others is benefiting oneself.

Following this view, being employed by the state ought to be a kind of service—rulers and ministers are public servants. Prioritizing the impulse to tend to other people creates the conditions for a stable state where the self is able to flourish. At the same time, it happens to be such that working for the state can be highly lucrative. It can also lead to fame and large followings. In the views of most early Confucian texts, too many public servants worked for the state in the hopes of personal gain. They sought to be rich and famous. In these situations, prioritizing one's self-regarding impulses encourages one to conspire with others who are likewise corrupt. These individuals thus were willing to benefit themselves at the expense of others.[42] Indeed, this is one of the problems with moral individuals meeting with corrupt leaders. These are situations where otherwise moral agents appear to be acting for their own benefit rather than the benefit of others. And this is why it is so important that they do not desire to engage in this behavior. Their reluctance is a sign that they still maintain the correct priorities—that they put their other-regarding impulses above their self-regarding desires.[43]

Much more could be said about benefit or *li* 利.[44] The point worth establishing here, however, relates to self-sacrifice in the context of irresolvable value conflicts. The examples provided from the *Mengzi* and the *Kongcongzi* suggest that we can tend to both our other-regarding impulses and our self-regarding impulses when we prioritize the former over the latter. Situations of irresolvable value conflict, however, often prevent the realization of both. Self-sacrifice, in these situations, occurs when other-regarding impulses are tended to at the expense of self-regarding impulses. In these situations one sacrifices the latter for the sake of the former. Something like this occurs in the passages I quoted at the outset of this book. The *Yantielun* 《鹽鐵論》 purports to describe a debate between a faction of government officials and Confucian scholars in the first century BCE. The officials charge that Confucians are self-serving—claiming that Confucians are willing to "demean the Way in order to seek the acceptance [of the ruling class who would employ them]" 貶道以求容.[45] The Confucians respond,

> An illustrious ruler is concerned when the world is not at peace or when the various states of his kingdom are not tranquil. Sages and worthies are concerned when there is no king on the throne and no head of the royal clans serving beneath the king, or when the world is disarrayed and chaotic.

This is why Yao worried about the floods and Yi Yin worried about the people. Guan Zhong submitted to arrest and Kongzi wandered around [seeking employment] because they worried about the misfortunes of the people and longed to calm their fears. [The great figures of the past] shouldered vessels and stands, suffered imprisonment, and [tired themselves to the point of] crawling along the ground in order to save the people.

The point is that when one chases after someone fleeing, he runs fast; and when one saves someone drowning, he gets wet. Now, it seems that the people of the kingdom have fallen in a filthy ditch. Even if one wanted to be without stain [in saving them], how could it be otherwise?

天下不平，庶國不寧，明王之憂也。上無天子，下無方伯，天下煩亂，賢聖之憂也。是以堯憂洪水，伊尹憂民，管仲束縛，孔子周流，憂百姓之禍而欲安其危也。是以負鼎俎、囚拘、匍匐以救之。故追亡者趨，拯溺者濡。今民陷溝壑，雖欲無濡，豈得已哉？46

The response to the officials' challenge is twofold. For one, the Confucians explain that the great figures of the past did not demean the Way; instead, they sought to advance the Way in the world. Second, these great figures advanced the Way at personal cost. Yi Yin served as a cook to gain the attention of Tang 湯, Guan Zhong submitted to arrest, and, as a later chapter of the *Yantielun* explains, Kongzi "traveled around the kingdom until his head was sun-burnt and his feet were wet, hoping to enlighten the rulers of his day" 孔子生於亂世，思堯、舜之道，東西南北，灼頭濡足，庶幾世主之悟.47 All of these men harmed themselves in different ways for the sake of benefiting the world. The next chapter will explore the nature of this harm in more detail. The point worth stressing here, however, is that there is something heroic but also unfortunate in the act of self-sacrifice. On the one hand, the moral agent must be firm in his commitment to benefit the world. On the other hand, this comes at a cost—one must compromise some values, virtue, or aspects of integrity.48 The harmony thesis leaves little room for this kind of self-sacrifice.

Wu Wang

Among those referred to as sages in early Confucian texts, Wu Wang presents the most difficulty for interpreters. As mentioned, Wu Wang was the son of Wen Wang and founder of the Zhou 周 dynasty. In approximately 1050 BCE he overthrew Zhou Xin 紂辛, ruler of the Shang 商 dynasty, and established a new line of authority. Early Confucian texts uniformly portray Zhou Xin 紂辛 as an evil despot. He is said to have overtaxed the people—spending money on indulgences like a lake of wine and a forest of meat (*jiuchi roulin* 酒池肉林), and taken pleasure in torturing people; he is said to have ripped out the heart of his uncle, Bigan 比干, to see what the heart of a good person looked like (among other atrocities). Zhou Xin 紂辛, in short, is the antithesis of a sage-ruler, and in many respects he deserved to be overthrown. Early Confucian texts largely depict the vanquishing of Zhou Xin 紂辛 and the establishment of the Zhou 周 dynasty as positive events. Indeed, the Zhou周 dynasty is idealized in much of early Chinese literature, and Wu Wang is often praised for his role in setting it up. The *Kongzi Jiayu* 《孔子家語》, for instance, says, "Wu Wang rectified himself in order to rectify his state, he rectified his state in order to rectify the world. [He] attacked those who lacked the Way, and punished those involved in wrongdoing. With one movement, he rectified the world and completed his work. When spring and autumn fulfill their times, all things attain their purposes. When rulers fulfill their Way, all people find order" 武王正其身以正其國，正其國以正天下，伐無道，刑有罪，一動而天下正，其事成矣。春秋致其時，而萬物皆及，王者致其道，而萬民皆治.[49] There are many similar passages like this in early Confucian texts. Yet other passages suggest that the establishment of the new dynasty came at a cost, albeit a necessary one.

Early Confucian texts find Wu Wang troubling in two respects. He violently overthrew the previous dynasty—punishing its ruler—and he engaged in unfilial conduct by not properly mourning his father and by illegitimately inheriting his older brother's role as ruler. The *Mengzi* describes how Wu Wang conquered the territory of the Shang.

> Zhou Gong 周公 assisted Wu Wang in punishing Zhou 紂 and attacking the city of Yan. For three years [they] rallied against their ruler. [They] pushed back Fei Lian [i.e., Zhou's 紂 general] to the edge of the sea and slaughtered him. Altogether they destroyed 50 states.
>
> 周公相武王，誅紂伐奄，三年討其君，驅飛廉於海隅而戮之。滅國者五十 。[50]

The key battle of Wu's campaign took place at Muye 牧野, where Wu's troops faced the Shang troops with Zhou Xin 紂辛 at their head. According to several early texts, the Shang troops turned on each other: "The foot soldiers on the front line reversed their spears and attacked those behind [until they fled] to the north. So much blood flowed that shields floated [like buoys]" 前徒倒戈，攻于後以北，血流漂杵.[51] When Zhou Xin 紂辛 saw the defeat of his troops he fled. The *Shiji* recounts the confrontation with Zhou Xin 紂辛 as follows:

> On the Jiazi day, Zhou's troops were defeated. Zhou fled, entering [his stronghold] and ascending the Lu Tower. He changed his clothes—wearing

jewels and jade; then [he] threw himself into a fire and died. Upon [finding his body] Wu Wang cut off Zhou's head and hung it along with the great white flag [signaling the end of the battle]. He then killed Daji [Zhou Xin's favorite consort], released Jizi from captivity, and erected a monument on Bigan's tomb.

甲子日，紂兵敗。紂走入，登鹿臺，衣其寶玉衣，赴火而死。周武王遂斬紂頭，縣之［大］白旗。殺妲己。釋箕子之囚，封比干之墓。[52]

Other texts recount similar narratives. Many of these stories highlight the virtuous nature of Wu Wang and, contrary to the account presented in the *Shiji*, stress that Wu Wang was able to conquer the Shang without much bloodshed. The *Xunzi*, for instance, explains that not only did Wu Wang engage in military campaigns but so did Yao, Shun, and Yu. However, "[They] all employed humane and just military force in carrying out [their activities] in the kingdom. This is why those nearby drew close to their goodness, and those far away longed for their virtue. Their troops did not stain their swords with blood, and the near and far flocked in obedience. [Their] virtue flourished because of this, and [they] administered [it] to the four quarters [of the world]" 皆以仁義之兵，行於天下也。故近者親其善，遠方慕其德，兵不血刃，遠邇來服，德盛於此，施及四極.[53] The *Xunzi* also stresses that these campaigns were not "wars" 戰 but rather were "punishments" 誅; as such they were appropriate actions of the righteous inflicted on the corrupt.[54]

The *Mengzi* states it in even stronger terms. While the *Shangshu* 《尚書》 says that in the battle of Muye the enemy's blood flowed so heavily their shields floated in blood (*xueliu piaochu* 血流漂杵), Mengzi states, "To completely trust the *Shangshu* is not as good as being without the *Shangshu* altogether. In dealing with the 'Wucheng' chapter [of the *Shangshu*] I take only two or three passages [as trustworthy]. The humane person has no enemies in all the world. [So if] the utmost humane person attacks the utmost inhumane person, how would the troop's blood flow [so as to float] their shields" 盡信《書》，則不如無《書》。吾於《武成》，取二三策而已矣。仁人無敵於天下。以至仁伐至不仁，而何其血之流杵也?[55] In these views, the humane person has little need to resort to physical violence since most people follow him because of his virtue (with the exception of the utmost inhumane). The very next passage of the *Mengzi* (7B4) continues this line of thought:

There are some who say "I am good at deploying troops; I am good at war." This is a great mistake. If the ruler of a state is fond of humaneness [he] will not have any enemies in the entire world. [When] militarily engaging those in the south, the northern tribes will complain. [When] militarily engaging those in the east, the western barbarians will complain. [They will all] say "Why have [you] saved us for last?" When Wu Wang attacked the Shang [he had] 300 war-chariots and 3,000 fierce warriors. [Yet] he said, "Do not fear. [I bring] peace. [I] am not an enemy of the people." [And the people] bowed their heads like [an animal] dropping its horn. "A punitive expedition" is another way of saying "rectify." When each unit desires to rectify itself what need is there for war?

有人曰：『我善為陳，我善為戰。』大罪也。國君好仁，天下無敵焉。南面而征，北狄怨，東面而征，西夷怨。曰：『奚為後我？』武王之伐殷也，革車三百兩，虎賁三千人。王曰：『無畏！寧爾也，非敵百姓也。』若崩厥角稽首。征之為言正也，各欲正己也，焉用戰？

The *Mengzi* (1B8) also softens Wu Wang's rebellion against Zhou Xin 紂辛, explaining that Wu Wang did not "murder his ruler" 弒其君; instead he "punished some guy named Zhou" 誅一夫紂.[56] In this light, Wu Wang did not commit regicide. These texts largely work to justify Wu Wang's military tactics. However, rather than simply justifying them on the basis of righteous warfare or the good of the masses in overthrowing a bad ruler, they also hold to the idea that bloodshed is problematic and that a subject should not kill his ruler. As such, they tell Wu Wang's story in a way that allows him to accord with their ideals.

Part of the attempt to do away with violence, except in the case of punishing the most inhumane people, may be due to the notion (repeated in the *Xunzi*, *Mengzi, Han Shi Waizhuan* 《韓詩外傳》, and *Shuoyuan*) that the humane person does not kill innocent others. Each of these texts contain some version of the notion that "enacting one [act] of unrighteousness, or killing one [person] without offense in order to obtain the kingdom is not something the humane person would do" 行一不義，殺一無罪，而得天下，仁者不為也.[57] I suspect that the impulse to recast the story of Wu Wang is to ensure that he accords with an ideal like this.

The problem with the texts that argue for a less violent Wu Wang, however, is that substantiating their arguments entails disregarding parts of Wu Wang's narrative advocated in other early Confucian or quasi-Confucian texts. The second telling of Wu Wang's story in the *Shiji*, for instance, highlights the gory nature of Wu Wang's victory. Upon confronting the dead body of Zhou Xin 紂辛, Wu Wang shoots it with three arrows and hacks it with his sword before cutting off the head. He then goes after Zhou Xin's 紂辛 concubines to find that they too had killed themselves, at which point he likewise shoots them with arrows, stabs them with his sword, and then displays their heads on banners too.[58] The *Hanshu*

《漢書》 adds that Wu Wang sacrificed the ears of his enemies in the Zhou 周 temple.[59] In perhaps the most gruesome account, the *Shizi* 《尸子》, an eclectic text originating in the Warring States, explains that "Wu Wang himself shot Wulai [one of Zhou Xin's 紂辛 ministers] in the mouth, and he personally hacked at Zhou Xin's 紂辛 neck. With his hands caked in blood, he ate [his] raw flesh" 武王親射惡來之口，親斫殷紂之頸，手污於血，不溫而食.[60]

Indeed, since at least the Western Han interpreters have been suspicious of attempts to clean up the image of Wu Wang. Jia Yi 賈誼 (201–169 BCE), for instance, in contrast to Mengzi, explicitly claimed that "Wu Wang murdered Zhou 武王弒紂."[61] Wang Chong 王充 (27–97 CE), in the Eastern Han, expressed skepticism about Wu Wang's troops not bloodying their swords.[62] Later, in the Song dynasty Su Shi 蘇軾 (1037–1101) penned an essay titled *Lun Wuwang* 《論武王》 in which he criticized Mengzi's effort to explain away the violence of Wu Wang's campaign. The essay begins and ends with the statement, "Wu Wang is not a sage" 武王非聖人.[63]

At the same time, many of the texts that argue for a more humane version of Wu Wang are themselves heterogeneous, and, as such, their views on this event are not uniform. Earlier I quoted *Mengzi* 3B9, for instance, that depicts a more protracted engagement with the Shang armies, and, as discussed in chapter 4, this passage situates this narrative in the context of transgression. From this angle, Wu Wang participates in a longer tradition of transgressions necessary for ordering the world. Additionally, texts such as the *Analects* also present conflicting views of Wu Wang.

Analects 3.25 states, "In speaking of the 'Shao' [musical performance] the Master said, '[It's] completely beautiful and completely good.' In speaking of the 'Wu' [musical performance, he said, 'It's] completely beautiful but not completely good'" 子謂韶，「盡美矣，又盡善也。」謂武，「盡美矣，未盡善也」. "Shao" is a musical performance associated with Shun and his rise to power. This musical performance is discussed in another passage of the *Analects* (7.14) where Kongzi, after seeing the performance of "Shao," remains captivated by it for three full months and remarks, "[I] never thought music could be as exquisite as this" 不圖為樂之至於斯也! The "Wu" musical performance reenacts Wu Wang's conquering of the Shang and the establishment of the Zhou 周 dynasty. Musical performances (*yue* 樂) in early China were not simply audio events. They also included actors and props, which in the case of "Wu" included swords and shields. This meant that music, or *yue* 樂, was performative and closer to modern notions of a play or musical. For this reason I tend to translate the term *yue* 樂 as "musical performance."[64]

Like many other passages of the *Analects*, passage 3.25 is not easy to interpret.[65] One of the earliest commentators on the *Analects*, Kong Anguo 孔安國

(c. 100 BCE), explains this passage as follows: "'Shao' is the name of Shun's music. [It] tells how [Shun] accepted the abdication [of Yao] because of [his] sagely virtue; therefore [it] is completely good. . . . 'Wu' is the music of Wu Wang. [He] obtained the kingdom by means of punitive military expeditions, and therefore [his music] is not completely good" 《韶》，舜樂名，謂以聖德受禪，故盡善。．．．。《武》，武王樂也。以征伐取天下，故未盡善。[66] Later interpreters build on this with Xing Bing 邢昺 (932–1010), for instance, stating, "Employing punitive military expeditions to gain the kingdom is not as good as obtaining it by means of abdication. This is why Wu Wang's virtue is not completely good" 然以征伐取天下，不若揖讓而得，故其德未盡善也. Xing Bing goes on to say, "Even though a minister replacing his ruler is done in response to *Tian* 天 and accords with the people's [desires] it is not as good as receiving [the throne] by abdication. This is why ['Wu'] is not completely good" 以臣代君，雖曰應天順人，不若揖讓而受，故未盡善也.[67] Both traditional interpreters take the passage as a statement about the problematic nature of punitive military expeditions in setting up a new dynasty. Assuming that these musical performances are meant to comment on the figures they depict, we might say that Wu Wang, in this view, is simply not as good as Shun, and this is because of Wu Wang's involvement in militarily overthrowing the previous dynasty. The contemporary scholar Edward Slingerland makes a relevant comment on this passage in his translation of the *Analects*. He states, "The idea is that one's moral character is apparent in the music one creates: Wu Wang found it necessary to resort to force in deposing Zhou Xin 紂辛—rather than obtaining the world through Wuwei 無為, as did Shun (*Analects* 15.5)—because of a slight flaw in his character that is revealed in his music and apparent to the subtle ears of Kongzi."[68] What we see in Slingerland's comment is a tension in the act of interpreting the text. On the one hand, figures such as Wu Wang are praised as great models, so the interpreter ought to understand them as such even in places where they are not explicitly praised in this manner. On the other hand, the sages are sometimes depicted as engaging in troubling activities and, in this case, described as lacking in goodness, which Slingerland explains in terms of a "slight flaw." My sense, however, is to take Wu Wang's actions not simply as a flaw or deficit in his character but rather as the unfortunate consequences of necessary action.[69]

According to the *Shiji*, Wu Wang's great-grandfather, Gugong 古公, skipped over his two oldest sons to name his third son heir.[70] The reason he did this is because he recognized the greatness of his grandson, Wen Wang (referred to as Chang 昌 in the story) and hoped to further his success. According to the text, Gugong states, "In my lineage there will be one who establishes [a new dynasty]. Is this not Chang" 我世當有興者，其在昌乎?[71] Hearing this, Gugong's two oldest sons tattooed their bodies, cut their hair, and fled the state—leaving the position of ruler to their younger brother. Because of this, Wen Wang's father became ruler of the Zhou 周 and then passed the position on to Wen Wang. Interestingly, Wen Wang, like his grandfather Gugong, skipped over his oldest son (Boyi Kao 伯邑考) to name a younger son heir (Wu Wang).[72] In other words, Wu Wang became the leader of the Zhou 周 only by means of two illegitimate forms of succession.

This troublesome aspect of Wu Wang's past becomes more apparent in the *Shiji* account of the confrontation between Wu Wang and Boyi and Shuqi. In contrast to Wu Wang, neither Boyi nor Shuqi accepted the position of their father. The *Shiji* explains that in their search for Wen Wang, Boyi and Shuqi came across Wu Wang who was "carrying the spirit tablets [of his father]" 載木主, and heading east to attack Zhou Xin 紂辛.[73] The "Tianwen" 天問 chapter of the *Chuci* 《楚辭》 casts this in even more grim terms, explaining that Wu Wang actually carried the dead body (*shi* 屍) of his father into battle.[74] The point either way is that Wu Wang rushed into battle and did not complete the mourning rites for his father.[75] Boyi and Shuqi mention this point, asking Wu Wang, "Your father is dead, but not buried; and yet [you] take up arms. Can this be called filial" 父死不葬，爰及干戈，可謂孝乎? The two brothers also criticize Wu Wang for attacking his ruler, asking if such activity can be considered humane. The author of the *Shiji* ends this portion of the story by explaining that Boyi and Shuqi were "ashamed of Wu Wang" 恥之. In the *Lüshi Chunqiu* account of the confrontation with Boyi and Shuqi these sentiments are expressed in their voices: "Rather than polluting ourselves in joining the Zhou 周, [we are] better off avoiding them and keeping our virtuous conduct clean" 與其並乎周以漫吾身也，不若避之以潔吾行.[76] The two brothers then head to Mt. Shouyang where they eventually starve to death. In the *Shiji* version of the story, Boyi and Shuqi compose the following poem before dying:

> [We] climb this westward mountain, and pick its wild ferns.
> [Wu Wang] uses violence to replace violence, not knowing he is wrong.
> The eras of Shen Nong, Shun, and the Xia have faded away and are gone;
>   where should we go?
> Alas, [we will] die; the waning of [our] fate.

> 登彼西山兮，采其薇矣。
> 以暴易暴兮，不知其非矣。
> 神農、虞、夏忽焉沒兮，我安適歸矣？
> 于嗟徂兮，命之衰矣！[77]

From the perspectives of Boyi and Shuqi there is clearly something wrong with Wu Wang. He uses violence to replace the violence of Zhou Xin 紂辛 and therefore is not humane. While it might be tempting to read this vignette in light of Mengzi's critique of Boyi (and Shuqi) as being overly fixated on purity, it is equally plausible to read it in light of Kongzi's, Kong Anguo's, or even Su Shi's views, namely that Wu Wang is not completely good. We might even extrapolate from this to say that Wu Wang's actions might even be all things considered good but at the same time they are lacking in some important senses. Indeed, we might read this as Wu Wang being involved in a series of irresolvable value conflicts. Similar to figures discussed in chapter 5, Wu Wang is compelled to choose actions that are neither loyal nor filial. Yet he does this because of his desire to order the world, despite his conflicting desire to keep himself pure. Indeed, it seems reasonable to take Wu Wang as a conflicted figure—one who did the best he could with the time he was given.

Kongzi

Similar to Wu Wang, Kongzi is also occasionally portrayed as a conflicted figure. Like Wu Wang, Kongzi engaged in or endorsed violent activities. While no early Confucian text portrays Kongzi as a pacifist, a few texts portray his involvement in what appears to be excessive violence. The opening chapter of the *Kongzi Jiayu* describes Kongzi's time as a minister in Lu 魯, where among other things he observed an improper musical performance. After the performance he ordered the decapitation of the dancers and the dismemberment of their bodies (*shouzu yichu* 手足異處).[78] In the following chapter, "Shizhu" 始誅 (literally "beginning with punishment"), Kongzi orders the execution of Shao Zhengmao 少正卯, an aristocrat from the state of Lu. After having him executed, Kongzi left his body on display for three days (*shiyuchao sanri* 尸於朝三日).[79] In the "Tangong" chapters of the *Liji* 《禮記》 Kongzi also endorses avenging one's family members if they were wrongfully killed—"Sleep on the straw mattress used for mourning, use [your] shield as a pillow. Do not serve as a government official. Do not share the same world with [the murderer]. If [you] happen to encounter [him] at the market or at court, attack [him] without returning [home to grab your] weapon" 寢苫枕干，不仕，弗與共天下也；遇諸市朝，不反兵而鬬.[80] While these texts do not explicitly critique Kongzi for these violent actions or ideas, later interpreters tend to dismiss actions, such as the execution of the dancers, as fictitious. Chen Tingjing 陳廷敬 (1638–1712), for instance, argues that the execution of the dancers did not happen, on the grounds that a sage would not punish someone before attempting to change them by means of instruction.[81] Since the dancers did not knowingly engage in inappropriate activities, and since Kongzi was a sage, the event, according to Chen, is spurious.

Interestingly, the execution of Shao Zhengmao also appears in several other early Confucian texts. None of them (except the *Jiayu*) mention his body being left on display, and the three accounts that go into detail (in the *Xunzi*, the

Shuoyuan, and the *Xinyu*) all situate the event in the context of Kongzi's disciples challenging his judgment.[82] Kongzi's defense of executing Shao Zhengmao
is twofold. First, he explains, Shao is guilty of some of the worst offenses anyone could perpetuate. Second, sage-figures such as Tang, Wen Wang, and Zhou
Gong likewise executed people. Kongzi's response is intriguing because he seems
to justify his action in light of the notion that an exemplary person does not kill
innocent people and that the sages of the past did need to execute others.

More frequently, Kongzi is depicted as navigating the tension between values
such as ritual propriety (*li* 禮) and sincerely expressing one's feelings for others.
The "Tangong shang" 檀弓上 chapter of the *Liji* tells of Kongzi encountering
the funeral of a previous acquaintance:

> When Kongzi was traveling to Wei [he] came upon the mourning rites
> for a person he had previously lodged with. [He] went in and wept to the
> brink of sorrow. Upon exiting [he] sent Zigong, to unbridle two horses
> from his carriage and leave them for the grieving family. Zigong remarked,
> "You've never given horses at the mourning rites for your disciples, isn't
> giving them to someone that [simply] housed you quite excessive?"

> 孔子之衛，遇舊館人之喪，入而哭之哀。出，使子貢說驂而賻
> 之。子貢曰：「於門人之喪，未有所說驂，說驂於舊館，無乃
> 已重乎？」

> The master replied, "When I went in to pay my condolences to him, [I]
> encountered such singleness of sorrow that tears fell from my eyes. I would
> not like to shed so many tears, and not act on the basis of them. Go unbri-
> dle the horses [and give them to the family]."

> 夫子曰：「予鄉者入而哭之，遇於一哀而出涕。予惡夫涕之無
> 從也。小子行之。」[83]

In this vignette, Zigong, the same disciple that questions Kongzi's execution of
Shao Zhengmao, questions Kongzi's request to present the grieving family with a
large gift. Kongzi explains that his gift matches the degree of sorrow he felt while
paying his respects.

In the *Analects* Kongzi is also depicted as greatly sorrowing over the death of
his favorite disciple, Yan Hui 顏回. At one point Kongzi even cries out, "*Tian*
天 has forsaken me" 天喪予![84] In the next passage his disciples question the
appropriateness of Kongzi exhibiting such deep sorrow for Yan Hui. Kongzi's
response is, "If not for him, then who should I feel great sorrow for" 非夫人之為
慟而誰為? Oddly, however, in the same chapter of the *Analects* Kongzi refuses

to provide his carriage for Yan Hui's outer coffin (*guo* 椁, appearing in other texts as *guo* 槨). In justifying his decision he explains how his own son, who had previously passed away, did not have an outer coffin and that he refrained from giving up his carriage because it was inappropriate for himself, as a member of the aristocracy, to walk on foot for the funeral. While this passage is in line with other statements Kongzi makes about the way in which ritual (*li* 禮) is meant to restrain the excessive impulses that often arise at the death of someone meaningful, it stands in stark contrast to the "Tangong Shang" passage.[85] In this light, it is quite reasonable for Zigong to refer to the fact that Kongzi has never given such a large gift when mourning for his disciples.

Another passage from the *Kongzi Jiayu* (that also appears in the "Tangong" chapters) relates to this:

> Kongzi had an old acquaintance named Yuan Rang whose mother died. Kongzi assisted him in acquiring wood for the outer coffin. Zilu remarked, "Master, I have previously heard you say that one should not have friends that are not as [good as] oneself; but if it should occur, don't be afraid to change [friends].[86] Master, you [seem] afraid [to do something about the situation]. Why [don't you] stop?"

> 孔子之舊曰原壤，其母死，夫子將助之以木槨。子路曰：「由也昔者聞諸夫子，無友不如己者，過則勿憚改。夫子憚矣。姑已，若何？」

> Kongzi replied, "[It is said that] whenever someone is in mourning, grovel and crawl to assist them. How much more so for an old acquaintance? [It] is not that [he is simply] a friend; [rather,] I am going [to assist] him [in mourning]."

> 孔子曰：「凡民有喪，匍匐救之，況故舊乎？非友也，吾其往。」

> When it came time to make the coffin, Yuan Rang climbed on the wood and said, "It's been a long time since I've given [myself] to music." Then he sang out, "Like the colors of a raccoon's head; a finely crafted artifact of your hand."

> 及為槨，原壤登木，曰：「久矣，予之不託於音也。」遂歌曰：「狸首之班然，執女手之卷然。」

> The Master covered up for him; pretending not to hear as he went past. Zilu said, "Master, you've bent the rules to a great extent, and lost your senses. Shouldn't [you] stop it?

夫子為之隱，佯不聞以過之。子路曰：「夫子屈節而極於此，
失其與矣。豈未可以已乎？」

Kongzi replied, "I have heard that family members never lose that which
makes them family, and that old friends never lose that which makes them
old friends."

孔子曰：「吾聞之，親者不失其為親也，故者不失其為故也。」[87]

In this passage, Kongzi assists Yuan Rang in acquiring an outer coffin for his
mother. Kongzi's disciple, Zilu, questions his participation because he believed
Yuan Rang to be an unseemly character.[88] Zilu's cause is justified when Yuan Rang
breaks into song. Not only are songs of this sort prohibited when mourning, especially when mourning for one's parents, but Yuan Rang climbs on the very wood to
be used for his mother's coffin in order to sing his song. Since Kongzi acquired the
wood, he becomes entangled in Yuan Rang's affair. Yet rather than distance himself from Yuan Rang, he covers for him and justifies his own involvement. Given
the passages cited earlier, this passage throws Kongzi's unwillingness to provide
an outer coffin for Yan Hui or his own son into further suspicion. Coincidentally,
as early as the Eastern Han, thinkers such as Wang Chong questioned Kongzi's
actions on this very point. In a chapter titled "Questioning Kongzi" ("Wen Kong"
問孔) Wang cites several of these passages and points out the following contradiction: "Kongzi took his feelings of generosity seriously in giving [horses] to an old
acquaintance, but took the neglect of ritual lightly in the burial of his son" 孔子
重賻舊人之恩，輕廢葬子之禮.[89] From Wang's view, Kongzi is inconsistent in
the ways he navigates the tension between ritual (*li* 禮) and the spontaneous feelings (*qing* 情) generated in situations such as these. Said differently, what we see in
these passages is a Kongzi who did not always tend to all values at stake. He sometimes chose his sentiments over ritual, much to the chagrin of his disciples. While
interpreters might synthesize these passages to resolve the inconsistency that Wang
Chong notes—appealing to a theory of *quan* 權, for instance—the issue remains
as to whether or not these views are uniformly held across early Confucian texts.
Indeed, as presented in the *Jiayu*, it seems as if Kongzi is compelled to choose
between his relationship with an old friend and associating with someone who
flaunts the prescribed mourning rites. While it is possible that Kongzi did the best
he could in tending to each value at stake, it is far from clear that he fulfilled all of
his related desires to tend to these values.

The Yuan Rang anecdote is also significant because of the way in which
Kongzi explains his actions. The notion that "family members never lose that
which makes them family and that old friends never lose that which makes them
old friends" 親者不失其為親也，故者不失其為故也 is worthy of reflection.

The idea seems to be that our obligations to others are not terminated simply because they behave poorly.[90] While this can have dangerous consequences as far as abusive relationships are concerned, a more charitable reading is that human beings ought to stick together through thick and thin; even if it entails being complicit in the other's unfortunate acts. We saw echoes of this in the discussion of Chen Zhongzi earlier in this chapter, and we will explore the interconnected nature of the self in the next chapter. However, in the Yuan Rang affair, we have Kongzi himself modeling what it means to be enmeshed in relationships that compel unfortunate consequences. Kongzi reveals that we cannot distance ourselves from others simply because values conflict. Indeed, Kongzi, or at least the Kongzi described in this passage, would see something wrong with someone who was unwilling to make compromises for the sake of his relationships. At the same time, the Yuan Rang passage reveals that we ought to be careful in selecting our friends and our acquaintances.

The second chapter of the *Han Shi Waizhuan* contains a related vignette.

> Kongzi encountered Cheng Benzi of Qi while in the region of Yan. [They] tilted the canopies [of their carriages] and conversed [with each other] all day. At one point [Kongzi] summoned Zilu and said, "Zilu, please give 10 rolls of silk to this gentleman." Zilu did not respond. A while later [Kongzi] again summoned Zilu, saying, "Please present 10 rolls of silk to this gentleman."

> 孔子遭齊程本子於郯之間，傾蓋而語，終日，有間，顧子路曰：「由，束帛十匹，以贈先生。」子路不對，有間，又顧曰：「束帛十匹，以贈先生。」

> Zilu curtly responded, "Previously I heard you, Master, say that [an exemplary] scholar does not meet people in the middle of the road, and that if a woman [wanted to] get married without a matchmaker, the exemplary person would not permit it."

> 子路率爾而對曰：「昔者、由也聞之於夫子，士不中道相見，女無媒而嫁者、君子不行也。」

> Kongzi said, "Isn't there a poem that says,
> 'There is lush grass in the field; fervent and moist with dew.
> Here is a beautiful person; with bright eyes and a mild face.
> By chance we meet; and my wish is fulfilled.'
> Indeed, Cheng Benzi of Qi is a worthy scholar of the kingdom. If I do not
>   present him with anything, until the end of my days [I] will not see

him [again]. [In matters of] great integrity [I] do not go beyond the bounds, [but in matters of] small integrity it is permissible to go in and out [of bounds]."

孔子曰：「夫詩不云乎！野有蔓草，零露漙兮。有美一人，清揚婉兮。邂逅相遇，適我願兮。且夫齊程本子，天下之賢士也，吾於是不贈，終身不之見也。大德不踰閑，小德出入可也。」[91]

In this vignette, Kongzi explains his less than appropriate interaction with Cheng Benzi. According to Zilu, scholars such as Kongzi do not meet with people in the middle of the road. In other words, meetings between aristocrats ought to occur in accord with ritual protocol (*li* 禮). This is a major theme in early Confucian literature, appearing frequently in texts such as the *Analects* and *Mengzi*. Visits to others often entail formalities such as arranging a fitting time and place to enable the planned activities. It also includes preparing gifts to be exchanged. In the case of Cheng Benzi, Kongzi's meeting occurs spontaneously, without many of the formalities of ritual. Interestingly, however, Kongzi does not justify his actions in a way that reconciles the competing values of companionship and ritual propriety. His response is essentially that he has long desired to meet someone like Cheng Benzi, and he may not have another chance to meet such a person. He recognizes his actions as an infraction, albeit a minor one. The terms he uses to explain himself include *xian* 閑 and *de* 德. The former refers to a piece of wood used to obstruct a path—stopping the movement of those traveling on the path. In the context of this passage it refers to the boundaries of proper action designated by a system of rules such as ritual. Moral agents ought to remain within these boundaries. This passage implies that when a moral agent transgresses the boundaries of proper action, he harms or lessens his *de* 德, which I translated as "integrity." *De* 德, as more fully explained in the next chapter, refers to a kind of moral force best understood as a power to encourage others to fulfill their roles in relationships. When one has cultivated high degrees of *de* 德 (sometimes described as *shengde* 盛德), it "orders" 治 society such that all people operate in unison with each other or in conjunction with the *dao* 道. *De* 德 is "integrity" in the sense of each aspect of the moral agent, and each part of society, cohere together to create a sound whole. This power is cultivated by observing the rules of ritual propriety—actions that maintain integrity in the sense of sustaining identity-conferring commitments that encourage social cohesion.

In this passage Kongzi expresses little discomfort with compromising small amounts of integrity. Perhaps he feels that the values realized by making such a compromise outweigh the loss of integrity or that the rules of ritual propriety are simply not applicable in situations of minor importance (although this contradicts his views in several other passages). In any event, this vignette speaks to the notion of irresolvable value conflicts. In short, minor compromises can be willingly made, although they are still compromises. While this passage suggests that the moral agent ought not transgress the boundaries of proper action when "great integrity" 大德 is at stake, other passages discussed in this and previous chapters suggest that larger compromises might have to be made, and in these circumstances the moral agent should engage in compromises with a sense of reluctance. The *Fayan* passage quoted earlier, for instance, addresses this issue with regard to Kongzi engaging in illicit meetings. The closing line reads, "When the self is made crooked, it is done to channel the flow of the Way. However, making the Way crooked in order to promote oneself is not done even if the world [could be gained]" 詘身，將以通道也。如詘道而信身，雖天下不為也.[92] What we see here is the notion that compromises can be made as long as they are not done for the sake of directly bettering one's social or economic circumstances. Building off this, it is reasonable to suspect that "great integrity" can be compromised but only when one's hand is forced, and even then one ought not to make these compromises lightly or willingly.

While largely regarded as an eclectic text, the *Lüshi Chunqiu* provides a relevant vignette of Kongzi assessing himself in light of his illicit meetings with others. The passage comes from the "Lisu" 離俗 chapter, which John Knoblock and Jeffery Riegel translate as "Departing from Conventional Conduct." It states,

> The head of the Ji Sun clan usurped the office of duke. Kongzi wanted to instruct him in the proper methods while disassociating [himself from the duke's actions]. But because [he] accepted a salary and attempted to persuade [him,] people in the state of Lu criticized Kongzi.
>
> Kongzi said, "Dragons eat in clean water and swim in clean water. Hornless dragons eat in clean water but swim in dirty water. Fish eat in dirty water and swim in dirty water. Now, I have not risen to the level of a dragon, nor fallen as low as a fish. I suppose I am a hornless dragon."
>
> In wishing to establish a great work, how can one accord with the plumb line? One who saves the drowning gets wet; and one who chases after someone fleeing [must] hurry.
>
> 季孫氏劫公家。孔子欲諭術則見外，於是受養而便說，魯國以訾。孔子曰：「龍食乎清而游乎清，螭食乎清而游乎濁，魚食乎濁而游乎濁。今丘上不及龍，下不若魚，丘其螭邪。」夫欲立功者，豈得中繩哉？救溺者濡，追逃者趨。[93]

While this passage might be reasonably challenged as "non-Confucian," it employs many of the images seen throughout this book and fits with the tenor of the passages mentioned earlier. In it Kongzi describes himself as a creature that eats in clean water but swims in dirty water. In the context of this passage, Kongzi's description might suggest that he is justified in accepting a salary (i.e., food) from the duke but that he also recognizes that politics entails interacting in a world of filth. In a more general sense, Kongzi simply states that he is not as pure as other people might be. The editors' comment at the close of this passage endorses this general idea. Stated in more direct terms, this passage shows that accomplishing some great work may entail getting wet or dirty. The discussion of *Mengzi* 3B9 where Kongzi usurped the role of the ruler in creating the *Chunqiu* 《春秋》 (see chapter 4) expresses this rather well. The creation of the *Chunqiu*, a text meant to pass on the Confucian *dao* 道 to future generations, is rooted in violating the very norms of order Kongzi seeks to create.

The theme of saving the drowning, and the consequences this has for the one doing the saving, has come up several times in this book. These images help to capture a core idea that emerges in several early Confucian texts, namely that Kongzi, and other great figures in early Confucian literature, compromised their integrity for the sake of others. Kongzi engaged in unbecoming activity not because he wanted to but because he needed to, and his relationships compelled such action.

Conclusion

The *Han Shi Waizhuan* contains the following description of Shun's activities:

> The *Shao* musical performance is not the pinnacle of musical performances [because it] involves axes and shields. Shun did not accord with ritual [because he] married [Yao's] two daughters [and did not inform his parents]. When [Shun] enfiefed Huangdi's 19 sons it did not model righteousness. In fleeing to the farmlands and weeping [Shun] did not accept his fate. View these from a human perspective and [they seem] right; [but] measure them from a normative perspective and [they seem] lacking.

> 韶用干戚，非至樂也；舜兼二女，非達禮也；封黃帝之子十九人，非法義也；往田號泣，未盡命也。以人觀之則是也，以法量之則未也。[94]

This passage mentions two ways of viewing these actions—the "human" 人 and the "normative" 法. Another way of conceptualizing these two perspectives is understanding the human as the authentic, natural, or spontaneous dispositions that most human beings feel in response to situations such as Shun's. The normative perspective refers to rules or standards dictated by ritual or law. When seen from the perspective of one's authentic dispositions, Shun understandably married Yao's daughters without informing his parents. However, when seen from a normative perspective, Shun did not accord with ritual.[95] Notably, this passage does not clearly state how the human and normative perspectives are reconciled. While the text unambiguously praises Shun in other places, it is not entirely clear that it endorses his behavior in the cases mentioned here. The passage does not say that the human perspective is to be valued above the normative perspective, nor does it say that sages are able to recognize the rare exceptions to the rule. Rather, my sense is to take this passage at face value as a claim about the complexities of moral life. Life is such that values sometimes conflict. The sage desires to fulfill all values, and he does the best he can in the situations he finds himself in. In the end, however, he cannot always tend to all values, and choosing one value does not discount the importance of the other values. Indeed, the *Han Shi Waizhuan* reveals that human beings, and even sages, fail to resolve value conflicts. This is not necessarily a problem with the ability of sages per se as much as it is a problem with the possibilities afforded by the world.

The passages in this chapter show that one characteristic that makes sages worthy of emulation is their ability to cope with the strain on their integrity in situations of value conflict. Said somewhat differently, a person who recognizes value in the world realizes that he or she may not be able to fulfill all values and may even need to harm some value; yet the individual who acts under the weight of the situation is a person worthy of our admiration. Such a person is marked by his or her engagement with other people despite the vulnerability of integrity. The next chapter investigates precisely how the moral agent's integrity is harmed in irresolvable value conflicts.

Notes

1. Translation modified from John Knoblock and Jeffrey Reigel, trans., *The Annals of Lü Buwei: A Complete Translations and Study* (Stanford, CA: Stanford University Press, 2000), 505–506.
2. Sarah Allan, *The Heir and the Sage: Dynastic Legend In Early China* (San Francisco: Chinese Materials Center, 1981), 12. Mark Edward Lewis addresses a similar issue in *The Flood Myths of Early China* (Albany: State University of New York Press, 2006), 72–85.
3. Allan, *Heir and the Sage*, 5.
4. Allan, *Heir and the Sage*, 37.
5. Allan, *Heir and the Sage*, 53.
6. Allan, *Heir and the Sage*, 49. Although later in her book she nuances her position with regard to specific texts. For instance, on page 124 she states, "[The] transformations in which Shun and Yu took the rule from Yao and Shun and in which

Tang and Wu committed regicide occur most frequently in the *Hanfeizi* and the *Guben Zhushu Jinian*. In the *Xunzi* and the *Mengzi*, heaven [Tian 天] changes the mandate and the people change their loyalties from one rule to the other. The *Mozi* stresses the low position of the founding minister. The *Zhuangzi* celebrates the integrity of the rule-refusers."

7. I came across many of the primary sources used in this section while reading Allan's *Heir and the Sage*.

8. Kam-por Yu, "The Handling of Multiple Values in Confucian Ethics," in *Taking Confucian Ethics Seriously: Contemporary Theories and Applications*, edited by Kam-por Yu, Julia Tao, and Philip J. Ivanhoe (Albany: State University of New York Press, 2010), 32.

9. Ma Teying 馬特盈, ed., *Shiji Jinzhu* 《史記今註》 (Taibei 台北: Taiwan Shangwu yinshuguan 臺灣商務印書館, 1987), 23. Hereafter, *Shiji*.

10. A move rhetorically similar to *Mengzi* 1B8 where Mengzi refers to Zhou Xin 紂辛, ruler of the Shang 商 dynasty, as "a guy [named] Zhou" 一夫紂.

11. *Lüshi Chunqiu* 1.5/5/15.

12. Sun Xingyan 孫星衍, ed., *Shangshu Jinguwen Zhushu* 《尚書今古文注疏》 (Beijing 北京: Zhonghua Shuju 中華書局, 2004), 28. Some scholars understand Siyue to be four people instead of one.

13. *Shiji*, 2171.

14. *Shuoyuan* 8.23/64/6.

15. *Xunzi* 25/121/7.

16. *Lüshi Chunqiu* 19.8/127/15; and *Huainanzi* 13/127/22.

17. *Zhuangzi* 29/89/15.

18. *Zhuangzi* 28/85/8.

19. *Zhuangzi* 29/88/4–6. Lewis lists a few other passages where sages are described as bad fathers in *Flood Myths*, 183 fn. 14.

20. *Mengzi* 5A6.

21. Some texts depict Qi as morally depraved. See Lewis, *Flood Myths*, 182 fn. 10.

22. This also helps explain Mengzi's resentment of *Tian* 天 in 2B13.

23. See *Mengzi* 5A7 and 7B3.

24. *Mengzi* 2A2.

25. See *Mengzi* 2A9 and 2B9. Passage 2A2 also discusses Kongzi's disciples as partial exemplars.

26. *Mengzi* 2A2.

27. For more on Boyi and Shuqi see Aat Vervoorn, "Boyi and Shuqi: Worthy Men of Old?" *Papers on Far Eastern History* 28 (September 1983): 1–22.

28. The *Shiji* uses the predynastic name for Wen Wang, which is Xibo Chang 西伯昌. However, it uses Wu 武 instead of the equivalent to Xibochang, which would be Xibohou 西伯侯.

29. *Shiji*, 2172.

30. Mengzi seems to use notions of "purity" or "cleanliness" 廉 synonymously with "righteousness" 義 in his description of Chen Zhongzi in 3B10 and 7A34.

31. Bryan W. Van Norden, trans., *Mengzi: With Selections from Traditional Commentaries* (Indianapolis: Hackett, 2008), 87.

32. Of course, given the notion of *quan* 權 articulated in chapter 1, this does not necessarily mean that Mengzi saw these impurities as damaging to one's integrity. Indeed, passages such as 3B10 can be understood as advocating that full purity is impossible *or* that true purity is a moderated form of purity—it is neither excessive nor deficient.

33. *Kongcongzi* 2.2/11/7–8.

34. Importantly, this passage should not be read as a condemnation of Xu You. He is not like Yang Zhu 楊朱, whom Mengzi describes as someone unwilling to remove even a hair from his body if it would benefit the world. Rather, Xu You likely valued both personal purity and the betterment of the world; however, he valued the former over the latter. Kongzi's criticism, as such, is that Xu You has misordered his priorities. Yao was a righteous ruler, so Xu You should have assisted him even if it meant making personal compromises.

35. Xue Ke 雪克, ed., *Xinyi Gongyang Zhuan* 《新譯公羊傳》 (Taibei 台北: Sanmin Shuju 三民書局, 2008), 54–56 ("Huan Gong" 桓公 11).

36. For more on Yang Xiong see David R. Knechtges, *The Han Shu Biography of Yang Xiong (53 BC–AD 18)* (Tempe: Center for Asian Studies, Arizona State University, 1982). For more on the *Fayan* see Michael Nylan, *Exemplary Figures: Fayan* (Seattle: University of Washington Press, 2013).

37. *Fayan* 8/19/1–4. For other endorsements of being crooked in early Confucian texts see *Shuoyuan* 16.96/130/5–16.109/130/32 and *Dadai Liji* 8.1/47/11–17. The *Daodejing* also famously endorses being crooked in 22A/8/3 and 1B/64/3.

38. *Mengzi* 1A1.

39. *Kongcongzi* 2.3/13/14–17.

40. See, for instance, *Mengzi* 1A5 and 4A14.

41. The "Daxue" 大學 chapter of the *Liji* makes a similar point in *Liji* 43.2/166/21–24.

42. Interestingly, the *Shuowen* defines *dao* 盜 ("thief" or "to steal") as "keeping things for [one's] personal benefit" 私利物也. Xu Shen 許慎, *Shuowen Jiezi* 《說文解字》 (Beijing 北京: Zhonghua Shuju 中華書局, 2004), 181.

43. Mengzi seems to make a similar point in 3B4 when his disciples question him for accepting payment from a less than righteous source. While Mengzi does not use the term "benefit" 利, he argues that we should not focus on profiting from our labor, but, when we work for others, we should be paid. Our "focus" or "commitment" 志, though, should not be on this payment.

44. For a more in-depth treatment of the topic see Carine Defoort, "The Profit That Does Not Profit: Paradoxes with 'Li' in Early Chinese Texts," *Asia Major* 21.1 (2008): 153–181.

45. *Yantielun* 2.5/16/3–4.

46. *Yantielun* 2.5/16/6–9.

47. *Yantielun* 10.4/75/28.

48. This discussion about benefit in the context of self-sacrifice softens Mengzi's criticism of "bending an inch to straighten a foot" 枉尺而直尋 in *Mengzi* 3B1. While in the end he does not endorse "bending oneself . . . to straighten others" 枉己者。。。直人, his primary issue in the passage seems to be with seeking benefit and not with the kind of self-sacrifice discussed here.

49. *Kongzi Jiayu* 8.6/11/26–28.

50. *Mengzi* 3B9.

51. Qu Wanli 屈萬里, ed., *Shangshu Shiyi* 《尚書釋義》 (Taibei 台北: Huagang Chubanbu 華岡出版部, 1956), 185.

52. *Shiji*, 96–97.

53. *Xunzi* 15/71/22.

54. *Xunzi* 15/71/17. Mengzi makes a related point in *Mengzi* 7B2. See also *Mozi* 5.3/34/16–5.3/35/8.

55. *Mengzi* 7B3.

56. For the significance of the term *shi* 弒 in early Confucian texts see Carine Defoort, "Can Words Produce Order? Regicide in the Confucian Tradition," *Cultural Dynamics* 12.1 (March 2000): 85–109.

57. *Xunzi* 8/28/9, *Han Shi Waizhuan* 6.23/47/22, *Shuoyuan* 5.7/33/8–9, and *Mengzi* 7A33.

58. *Shiji*, 109.

59. Ban Gu 班固, *Hanshu* 《漢書》 (Beijing 北京: Zhonghua Shuju 中華書局, 2007), 132–133. Hereafter, *Hanshu*.

60. *Shizi* 2.51/17/7. For more on the *Shizi* see Paul Fischer, *Shizi: China's First Syncretist* (New York: Columbia University Press, 2012). Some interpreters take these descriptions of Zhou Xin 紂辛 as part of a ritual sacrifice. See, for instance, Mark Edward Lewis, *Sanctioned Violence In Early China* (Albany: State University of New York Press, 1990), 208–209.

61. In building on this passage, Paul Goldin explains that the view of Wu Wang as "guilty of usurpation" was "the mainstream Han-dynasty view." Goldin also notes that *Mengzi* 1B8 is never cited in any Han dynasty text, and states, "If it shocks us today that as conservative a writer as Jia Yi called . . . Wu [Wang an] 'assassin,' it is only because of the outsize influence that *Mengzi* 1B8 has attained." Paul R. Goldin, "Mencius in the Han Dynasty," in *Dao Companion to the Philosophy of Mencius*, edited by Yang Xiao (New York: Springer, forthcoming).

62. *Lunheng* 25/105/5–14. Wang is also skeptical that there was so much bloodshed that shields floated.

63. Zeng Zaozhuang 曾棗莊 and Shu Dagang 舒大剛, eds., *San Su Quanshu* 《三蘇全書》 (Beijing 北京: Yuwen Chubanshe 語文出版社, 2001), 14.230. See also

Wang Yangming's 王陽明 (1472–1529) view that if Wen Wang were still alive he would have been able to "use goodness in handling Zhou" 善處紂, whereas Wu Wang had to "resort to evil" 縱惡. *Wang Yangming Quanji* 《王陽明全集》 (Shanghai 上海: Shanghai Guji Chubanshe 上海古籍出版社, 2014), 21.

64. For more on the role of musical performances in early China see Erica Brindley, *Music, Cosmology, and the Politics of Harmony in Early China* (Albany: State University of New York Press, 2012).

65. It is possible, for instance, that Kongzi is remarking on a particular performance of "Wu" and not speaking about it in general terms.

66. Tang Yijie 湯一介 et al., eds., *Ru Zang* 《儒藏》 (Beijing 北京: Beijing Daxue Chubanshe 北京大學出版社, 2005), *Lunyu Zhushu* 《論語註疏》, 56.

67. *Lunyu Zhushu*, 56.

68. Edward Slingerland, trans. *Confucius: Analects* (Indianapolis: Hackett, 2003), 28.

69. The *Simafa* 《司馬法》 contains an interesting line in this regard: "Those in antiquity took it as their standard to use humaneness as the root [of society] and to use righteousness to order society. But if the standard did not attain as desired, [they] then used authority. Authority comes forth from war, not from morally managing people. As such, if killing people leads to calming others, killing is permitted. If attacking a state [is necessary] to care for their people, then attacking is permitted. If warfare can prevent [other] wars, then although [one uses] war, it is permissible" 古者，以仁為本以義治之之為正。正不獲意則權。權出於戰，不出於中人。是故：殺人安人，殺之可也；攻其國愛其民，攻之可也。以戰止戰，雖戰可也. *Simafa* D1/45/3–4. The relevant point is that governing by humaneness and righteousness can be set against a backdrop of authority that comes forth by force.

70. Gugong is a title—"Ancient Duke." His name is Ji Danfu 姬亶父. Sometimes he is referred to as Gugong Danfu 古公亶父.

71. *Shiji*, 102.

72. See *Liji* 3.1/10/29–32 and *Huainanzi* 13/120/19–20. In some accounts this is justified by explaining that Boyi Kao died before he could assume the throne. See, for instance, *Shiji*, 1596.

73. *Shiji*, 2172

74. *Chuci* 3/9/17–18.

75. What counts as "hurrying into battle" seems to vary across texts. Some texts, for instance, describe Wu Wang as waiting two years, which would still be before he completed the three years of mourning for his father, but he would likely have buried his father by that time. See, for instance, *Shiji*, 105–106.

76. *Lüshi Chunqiu* 12.4/60/25–26. In this account, Boyi and Shuqi also accuse Wu of "engaging in war and killing for the sake of benefit" 殺伐以要利.

77. *Shiji*, 2173.

78. *Kongzi Jiayu* 1.2/1/11–25.

79. *Kongzi Jiayu* 2.1/2/9–18.
80. *Liji* 3.47/15/27–28.
81. Chen Tingjing 陳廷敬, *Wuting Wenbian* 《午亭文編》, *Wenyuange Sikuquanshu Dianziban* 《文淵閣四庫全書電子版》 (Hong Kong: Digital Heritage Publishing, accessed February 3, 2015), 24.18.
82. *Xunzi* 28/138/10–15; *Shuoyuan* 15.26/122/29–123/8; and *Xinyu* 3/5/25–6/5.
83. *Liji* 3.40/14/31–15/2. See an alternative version of the story in *Kongzi Jiayu* 43.13/87/18–20.
84. *Analects* 11.9.
85. For an example of Kongzi advocating restraint by means of ritual, see *Liji* 3.25/13/15–17. Zisi 子思 makes a similar point in *Liji* 3.32/14/4–6.
86. This line is a variation of what appears in *Analects* 9.25, which states, "Focus on loyalty and trustworthiness. Do not befriend those not like oneself. [If you] make mistakes, do not be afraid to change" 主忠信。毋友不如己者。過則勿憚改. In the context of the *Analects* these appear as a list of injunctions, not necessarily related to each other. I translate it here, however, in the context of the *Kongzi Jiayu*. Kongzi seems to defend himself in the *Jiayu* in two respects. He suggests that (a) we have obligations to tend to others when they mourn and (b) once we have entered into a relationship, we have obligations that are not easily left behind. Interestingly, the *Analects* passage is an injunction against forming friendships with those less virtuous than oneself. However, it may not apply to situations where someone who is already a friend becomes less virtuous or fails to continually cultivate virtue. As a relevant point of comparison, Marina McCoy addresses this very issue in the work of Aristotle. See Marina McCoy, *Wounded Heroes: Vulnerability as a Virtue in Ancient Greek Literature and Philosophy* (Oxford: Oxford University Press, 2013), 149–153.
87. *Kongzi Jiayu* 37.4/65/12–17. For an alternative version of the story see *Liji* 4.69/30/6–8. For other passages involving the breaking of ritual protocol in following sentiment see *Liji* 3.34/14/10–14 and 3.6/11/16–19; as well as *Hanshu*, 798. For a more in-depth discussion on the topic see Michael D. K. Ing, "The Ancients Did Not Fix Their Graves: Failure in Early Confucian Ritual," *Philosophy East and West* 62.2 (April 2012): 223–245.
88. Yuan Rang also appears in *Analects* 14.43 where Kongzi harshly criticizes him for not engaging in worthwhile activities.
89. *Lunheng* 28/130/4–27.
90. For an example of terminating a relationship see *Mengzi* 1B6. The *Xinxu*, on the other hand, endorses the notion that "a humane [person] does not lightly sever relationships" 仁不輕絕. *Xinxu* 3.5/14/22.
91. *Han Shi Waizhuan* 2.16/11/6–11. See alternative versions in *Shuoyuan* 8.25/64/19–24 and *Kongzi Jiayu* 8.13/13/7–11. The concluding phrase of the passage also appears in *Analects* 19.11, spoken by Zixia 子夏.

92. *Fayan* 8/19/3–4.
93. Translation modified from Knoblock and Reigel, *The Annals of Lü Buwei*, 505–506.
94. *Han Shi Waizhuan* 4.9/27/20–23. This notably contradicts other passages about "Shao" 韶 where, in *Analects* 3.25 for instance, Kongzi describes it as "completely beautiful and completely good" 盡美矣，又盡善也. The reference to Shun marrying Yao's two daughters not according with ritual propriety may be a reference to him not informing his parents before marrying them and/or a reference to marrying both of them as "wife" rather than one as wife and the other as concubine.
95. Of course, Mengzi attempts to reconcile these two perspectives in *Mengzi* 2A26 and 5A2.

7

The Vulnerability of Integrity

Kongzi remarked, "The people of Lu must save the drowning."

孔子曰「魯人必拯溺者矣」。

(*LÜSHI CHUNQIU* 《呂氏春秋》 16.6/96/1-2)

SEVERAL PARTS OF this book discuss imagery in early Confucian texts where the moral agent gets wet, dirty, or sullied in responding to complex situations. The previous chapters argued that some of these situations could be understood as irresolvable or tragic value conflicts. This chapter aims to explore the results of such conflicts. It investigates what it might mean for otherwise good people to get wet, dirty, or sullied. More specifically, it investigates the impact these situations have on the moral agent's integrity.

In exploring these issues we will see that while images of impurity appear frequently in early Confucian texts, notions of impurity are not connected with metaphysical conceptions of guilt or sin as they might be in parts of the Western philosophical or religious discourse. Rather, impurity is often associated with the improper permeation of social boundaries and the language of shame, or the language of dissipation and blockage with regard to one's ability to perform one's roles in relationships and cultivate virtues. In other words, in an early Confucian context the sullied moral agent is one whose connections to others have been compromised such that his ability to realize his relationships as a constitutive part of himself is diminished. This chapter argues that integrity in early Confucian texts is best understood as a power or charisma the moral agent exhibits to encourage others to attain to their roles in relationships. This power is obstructed or weakened in situations of irresolvable value conflict. To make this argument I begin with a description of the Confucian self understood as interconnected and communal. I then discuss the porous nature of this self with regard to the connections and boundaries that are seen to exist between the individual and others. In doing this I rely on Jane Geaney's notion of shame as well as the concept *jie* 節, which connotes boundaries or monitored points of connection that situate parts of things into larger wholes. *Jie* 節 is an important term for understanding how the individual is conceptualized in relation to other people and things in the world.

The majority of this chapter focuses on integrity, which I articulate in terms of *de* 德—a term sometimes translated as "virtue," "power," or "integrity." The notion of *de* 德 provides a way of conceptualizing the harm entailed in irresolvable value conflicts. It is not always mentioned explicitly in accounts of irresolvable value conflicts, and it is not exhaustive in explaining Confucian theories of integrity, yet the notion of *de* 德 provides the best explanation for understanding injuries to integrity in early Confucian terms.

Contemporary scholars often think about integrity in terms of purity, coherence, or soundness. In the Western philosophical tradition, figures such as Bernard Williams stress that integrity involves being true to one's character or maintaining identity-conferring commitments.[1] In this view, someone who firmly holds to his or her commitments in difficult circumstances is said to be someone of integrity. Other theorists such as Cheshire Calhoun highlight the social nature of integrity. According to Calhoun integrity is not simply the evaluation of oneself by oneself but also entails membership in "an evaluating community" where one is invested in the community's judgments.[2]

By the end of this chapter, we will see that Confucian conceptions of integrity, similar to those put forth by Williams and Calhoun, are concerned with identity-conferring commitments, but in a Confucian context one's identity is especially social. As such, integrity expresses a personal confidence one has in relation to his or her commitments as well as a relationship between the individual and the communities that evaluate the individual's moral standing. Integrity, in short, is about integration. It is about bringing the self into a state of wholeness, where wholeness occurs on a personal level (i.e., not being torn by conflicting commitments) and a communal level (i.e., incorporation into the community). More particularly with regard to Confucianism, and differing from Williams and Calhoun, integrity is also understood as a moral power that compels others to fulfill obligations that arise from relationships. It can be accumulated and exhausted such that the more integrity we have, the greater confidence we have in our moral standing in our communities. Integrity is about fostering relationships that contribute to an ordered world; it is about plugging into a network of relationships where one's accumulated goodness furthers the Confucian *dao* 道.

Implications of an Interconnected Self

It is uncontroversial to say that Confucians understand human beings as relational or interconnected beings. The contemporary scholar Tu Weiming describes the Confucian notion of the self as a "center of relationships." He states, "Confucianism conceives of the self neither as an isolated atom nor as a single, separate individuality, but as a being in relationship. . . . Each relationship contributes to the development and overall constitution of the self. The self, in this sense, is the sum of its relationships. At the same time, it is conceived of as a center of relationships which is not reducible to the relationships themselves."[3] In the introduction of this book I quoted Roger Ames, who makes a similar point. Another contemporary scholar, Herbert Fingarette, perhaps states the matter most strongly: "Where there are not at least two truly human beings, there is not even one."[4] For these scholars "relational" means social, dependent, interdependent, role-bearing, and/or encumbered (as opposed to unencumbered and separate). While most scholars agree on the generalities of terms such as "relational" or "interconnected," they often disagree on the details.[5] For the purposes of this chapter, these disagreements are mostly irrelevant, since these scholars largely neglect questions of vulnerability and integrity as they relate to their notions of interconnectedness or relationality.[6] However, it is worth stating that I accept David Wong's general observation that Confucian notions of the self "reject the conception of a self who is conceived apart from others and then subordinated to them. In its place stand selves who are not human apart from social relations, who become selves in relationship to others, and who should strive for a kind of autonomy that does not separate them from others but makes them worthy of others' trust."[7] I build on this in terms of what this means for the vulnerability of such selves—particularly with regard to the vulnerability of integrity.

The "Jiyi" 祭義 chapter of the *Liji* 《禮記》 tells of Yuezheng Zichun 樂正子春, (c. 430 BCE) a disciple of Zengzi 曾子 who injured his foot while walking down a flight of stairs. Even after his recovery he was troubled by the incident. When a disciple asked why, he responded in part, "Fathers and mothers give birth to children [with their bodies] completely intact. A filial son returns [his body] to them completely intact. 'Completely intact' means neither disfiguring one's body nor disgracing oneself. . . . To be filial is to neither disgrace oneself nor dishonor one's parents" 父母全而生之，子全而歸之，可謂孝矣。不虧其體，不辱其身，可謂全矣。。。。不辱其身，不羞其親，可謂孝矣.[8] Yuezheng Zichun was bothered because of the connection between harming himself and demonstrating filial care for his parents. This passage introduces several significant concepts. A filial son keeps himself completely intact as a way of honoring his parents. To harm his body or disgrace himself is to dishonor his parents. Later in this chapter I discuss notions of preservation (*quan* 全) and shame (*chi* 恥) as they relate to integrity. The point worth stressing here, however, is the social nature of the self and the body. Coincidentally, the *Lüshi Chunqiu* 《呂氏春秋》 version of this story concludes with the statement, "The body is not something one privately possesses. Indeed, [it] is the corporeal remains bequeathed by [one's] parents" 身者非其私有也，嚴親之遺躬也.[9] In this view, the body and self do not belong solely to one entity; instead, identity is at least partially the construct of one's lineage, and the permeability of the body and self are worthy of concern because of the broader implications—to disgrace oneself is to dishonor one's parents.

While there are passages in early Confucian texts that highlight the interconnected nature of parents and children, none of them state it as succinctly as the following passage from the *Lüshi Chunqiu*:

> A father and mother are related to their son; and a son is related to his father and mother. [They] are one body with two parts. [They] are made of the same *qi* 氣 but take different breaths. [They] are like the flowers and fruit of shrubs and bushes, or the root and core of trees and wood. Even if in different places, [they] still connect with each other. [Their] secret ambitions reach each other. They aid each other in sickness and affliction; and they sense each other's worries and concerns. In life they rejoice in each other; and in death they mourn for each other. This is what it means to be as close as flesh and bones.

> 故父母之於子也，子之於父母也；一體而兩分；同氣而異息。若草莽之有華實也，若樹木之有根心也。雖異處而相通，隱志相及，痛疾相救，憂思相感，生則相歡，死則相哀。此之謂骨肉之親。 10

Here, to be of the same flesh and bones is to be "one body with two parts" 一體而兩分. Parents and sons not only sympathize with each other's pain and celebrate each other's successes, but there is a sense in which the pain or success of one *is* the pain or success of the other. The *Baihutong* 《白虎通》, a later Han text, makes this point in a discussion about *Analects* 13.18 (the passage about a father steeling a sheep). It states, "Fathers and sons are one body, so their share of glory and shame fall on each other" 父子一體，　而分榮恥相及。11 In short, "the self" in these relationships is neither individualistic nor impenetrable but rather is enmeshed, permeable, and relationally constituted.

While the relationship between parents and their sons is of particular importance in Confucian thought, similar views of interconnection extend beyond this relationship. The well-known "Daxue" 大學 chapter of the *Liji* opens with a description of self-cultivation (*xiushen* 修身) that extends from the internal motivations of the individual to the family (*jia* 家), the state (*guo* 國), and the world (*tianxia* 天下). There may not be the same degree of interconnection among some of these relationships as between parents and sons, but passages such as those mentioned here attempt to demonstrate that the self is interconnected with others including one's siblings, spouse, friends, statesmen, and rulers.12 In these relationships one's success or failure is often tied to the success or failure of others. As Kongzi says in *Analects* 6.30, "The humane person, in wishing to establish himself, establishes others" 夫仁者，己欲立而立人.

There are several implications of the view just described. Most important, early Confucians stress the obligations that exist among people—obligations they believed to naturally emerge in relationships. In remarking on this, the contemporary scholar A. T. Nuyen states, "Being a *something* entails that I owe them certain things, such as benevolence, faithfulness, respect, loyalty, and so on. . . . It does not seem to make much sense to say that I am your friend but I owe you nothing. It does not make much sense particularly to the Confucians to say that I am a self, a person, but I owe nothing to others."[13] To be human is to have relationships, and relationships entail obligations. These obligations are not easily cancelled. As we saw in the previous chapter where Kongzi paid for the outer coffin of an old friend's mother (despite his old friend's irreverent behavior), "Family members never lose that which makes them family, and old friends never lose that which makes them old friends" 親者不失其為親也，故者不失其為故也.[14] While there may be circumstances where "major offenses" 大過 nullify the obligations that exist between two people (as discussed in chapter 2), passages such as those investigated in chapters 5 and 6 make clear the notion that our relationships can not only lead to difficulties in navigating conflicting obligations but can even lead us to becoming entangled in the problems of others. This means that the self is susceptible to the choices and actions of others.

A passage from the *Gongyang Zhuan* 《公羊傳》 explains, "Rulers of a state form one body. The shame of previous rulers is the shame of the current ruler; and the shame of the current ruler is the shame of previous rulers" 國君一體也；先君之恥猶今君之恥也，今君之恥猶先君之恥也.[15] In a broader context, human beings can be shamed by our associations with others. The groups we belong to do not simply reflect on us; they partially shape who we are, even if we did not participate in their decision-making processes.

Jane Geaney provides an incisive theory of shame in this regard. In contrast to theories of shame where shame is understood in terms of the gaze of other people (representing their judgments according to the norms of society), Geaney advocates a "boundary-blurring model of shame."[16] Geaney states, "The shamed human person in early China seems to be one whose personal boundaries have been blurred. This blurring occurs in relation to both social status and the body—the mouth, the eyes, the ears, and the entire porous surface membrane—all of which is potentially shameful insofar as it is vulnerable to restructuring."[17] Geaney explains that such restructuring occurs when the body's faculties (of sight and sound, for instance) or an individual's social status are improperly penetrated by other things in the world. With regard to the body she states, "Thus, a fluid movement of entering and exiting seems to characterize this barely controllable sensory process. Certain things enter the senses, and other things exit from them. Whatever enters the senses seems designed to fill (*sai* 塞) their holes."[18] She continues, "The images suggest that a person's senses are a network of desirous holes to be opened or closed—permitting or not permitting a fluid movement, which can either be plumb with its target, or seep outside the boundaries where it belongs."[19] According to Geaney, shame is what occurs when the individual cannot manage the process of penetration— allowing him- or herself to be improperly penetrated (or when the individual engages in the improper penetration of others). In this view, something like bad music is a threat because it fills the ears with bad sounds, which can lead one to take bad action. Allowing such music to penetrate one's body by means of one's ears is shameful, even if, as Geaney states, such penetration is barely controllable. Geaney's notion of shame highlights the ways in which the body stores virtues and serves as the point of connection between the individual and others.[20] This view suggests that a truly interconnected self is a self with managed connections such that boundaries between the roles people play are appropriately porous.

Coincidentally, the term *jie* 節, which is often translated as "integrity" (or "boundaries," "rules," or "rhythm"), is also employed in the context of boundaries and the appropriate porousness of the self with regard to sense perceptions and the performance of social roles. Etymologically, the *Shuowen Jiezi* 《說文解字》 glosses *jie* 節 as the nodes of a bamboo plant.[21] Similar to the way in which sections of a bamboo plant are divided and connected by *jie* 節, society ought to be structured by boundaries and connections that determine the proper bounds of interaction. *Jie* 節 can also refer to parts of a tally. When used as such, *jie* 節 often appears with *fu* 符, designating a tally usually constructed out of bamboo or jade. These tallies are used in multiparty commitments, where each party takes a piece of the tally as a voucher that they were part of the commitment. Each part of the tally is called a *jie* 節. Tallies are used metaphorically in texts such as the *Mengzi* 《孟子》 where Mengzi explains that Shun 舜 and Wen Wang 文王, for instance, came from different times and different areas, they even performed different acts, but are both considered sages. The relevant line reads, "Like matching two sides of a tally, the early sages and the later sages fit together as one" 若合符節，先聖後聖，其揆一也.[22] *Jie* 節, in this line of thought, is about parts of things forming a whole and also about human beings managing connections with others. *Jie* 節 is perhaps best understood metaphorically as a sluice gate, which creates boundaries and manages the flow of things from one part to another.[23]

The "Yueji" 樂記 and "Sheyi" 射義 chapters of the *Liji* uses *jie* 節 precisely in this way. In explaining the importance of *jie* 節 the "Yueji" states,

> People are unperturbed when originally created. This is the constitution of human nature endowed by *Tian* 天. The desires of human nature are stirred when aroused by external things. Things interact [with oneself]

and are perceived by one's faculty of awareness. Only then do likes and dislikes take shape. If these likes and dislikes are left without managed boundaries (*wujie* 無節) internally, the faculty of awareness will be drawn away by things externally. [After such a reaction] it is impossible to return [to the previous state] of the self, and the heavenly patterns [one was originally endowed with] are ruined. External things arouse human beings without end; and so if the likes and dislikes of human beings are left without managed boundaries (*wujie* 無節), then when things interact [with human beings], human beings will transform them [in accordance with their unrestrained desires]. When human beings transform things [in accordance with their unrestrained desires] they ruin their heavenly patterns and exhaust their desires.

> 人生而靜，天之性也。感於物而動，性之欲也。物至知知，然
> 後好惡形焉。好惡無節於內，知誘於外，不能反躬，天理滅
> 矣。夫物之感人無窮，而人之好惡無節，則是物至而人化物
> 也。人化物也者，滅天理而窮人欲者也。²⁴

The "Yueji" depicts human beings in the midst of a world full of interaction. The things we interact with constantly arouse us. A lack of managed boundaries leads to our desires being drawn out in unrestrained ways, and this, in turn, ruins the order of things given by *Tian* 天. The *Lüshi Chunqiu* states this in related terms, "*Tian* 天 created human beings, causing them to be selfish and full of desire. Desires have natural inclinations, and natural inclinations have managed boundaries (*jie* 節). The sages devised boundaries (*jie* 節) in order to stop desires such that people's natural inclinations would not overflow" 天生人而使有貪有欲。欲有情，情有節。聖人修節以止欲，故不過行其情也.²⁵ The notion of "overflowing" 過行 reveals a central problem with the lack of managed boundaries (*jie* 節). Namely, without *jie* 節 the natural inclinations of human beings flow beyond their proper bounds. Here, *jie* 節 suggests a notion of proper flow or restraint. Practically speaking, these *jie* 節 often refer to rituals (*li* 禮), which prescribe specific courses of action that shape the internal dispositions of the self.²⁶ Proper rituals, or *jie* 節, instituted by the sages, curb and manage the expressions of desire and the natural inclinations of human beings.²⁷

The "Sheyi" chapter claims that music acts as *jie* 節, or guides for rhythm and cadence for different social groups during ceremonies such as an archery contest. This then reflects the way in which these groups function as parts of a whole to direct society in cadence with the *dao* 道.

The cadences (*jie* 節) are as follows: The king takes the song "Zouyu" as his *jie* 節. The magistrates take the song "Lishou" as their *jie* 節. The officials and high officials take the song "Caipin" as their *jie* 節. And the scholars take the song "Caifan" as their *jie* 節. "Zouyu" [expresses] joy in having all court offices properly stationed. "Lishou" [expresses] joy in timely meetings [with the king]. "Caipin" [expresses] joy in according with court orders. "Caifan" [expresses] joy in not falling short in one's responsibilities. Because of this the king considers properly stationing officers as his *jie* 節, the magistrates consider meeting with the king as their *jie* 節, the officials and high officials take according with court orders as their *jie* 節, and the scholars take not falling short of their responsibilities as their *jie* 節. These songs, therefore, illuminate the focus of each party's *jie* 節 such that they do not fail in their assigned activities. They bring to a completion their efforts and establish their integrity. When integrity is established, the state is without the catastrophes of chaos and disorder. When efforts are completed the state is at peace. This is why it is said that the archery ceremony is the means by which to observe wide-reaching integrity (*shengde* 盛德).

其節：天子以《騶虞》為節；諸侯以《貍首》為節；卿大夫以《采蘋》為節；士以《采繁》為節。《騶虞》者，樂官備也，《貍首》者，樂會時也；《采蘋》者，樂循法也；《采繁》者，樂不失職也。是故天子以備官為節；諸侯以時會天子為節；卿大夫以循法為節；士以不失職為節。故明乎其節之志，以不失其事，則功成而德行立，德行立則無暴亂之禍矣。功成則國安。故曰：射者，所以觀盛德也。[28]

Jie 節 in this passage is perhaps best translated as "rhythm." Practically speaking, this passage describes the songs that play while each group of officers fires their arrows during the archery ceremony. What most likely happens during this portion of the ceremony is that one verse of a song plays while the group that corresponds with it takes their position, followed by several other verses, during which the members of those groups shoot their arrows. The different songs not only have different rhythms and durations, but also each conveys a particular lesson. By operating in conjunction with these songs, especially during periods of practice, each group learns the appropriate lesson. Each group also demonstrates an understanding of the lessons conveyed by the songs through acting at the right time in the ceremony. Here, *jie* 節 refers to the proper bounds of one's social position. Within the ceremony, the participation of each group of people is bounded by the performance of a particular song. Outside the ceremony each group of people is bounded by his or her particular social regulations—or *jie* 節. When all groups within the state function in accordance with these proper bounds, the state enjoys peace. When these boundaries are confused, there is chaos. *Jie* 節 is understood as rhythm in the ceremonial context in that each group moves in accordance with its song. When each group moves accordingly, the ceremony is performed properly. Likewise, when each group in society moves in accordance with their *jie* 節, society will enjoy its proper rhythm. Scott Cook sums this up nicely in his study of music and thought in early China. He states, "The sense of restraint is also an important connotation of the term [*jie* 節], but it is the type of restraint brought about through rhythmic application—that is to say, doing things at the proper time, alternating activities in the proper succession, and not dwelling upon or indulging in one thing beyond the proper limits of what is considered timely to such action or behavior."[29] *Jie* 節 entails exercising self-control in the performance of one's social roles.

In almost all of the passages under discussion, *jie* 節 refers to not simply divisions or boundaries but divisions or boundaries that function to situate and connect parts of things into larger wholes. When the connections are appropriately maintained, each unit integrates into a larger body that works to achieve an aim such as self-cultivation or the flourishing of society. When the flow between connections is properly managed, these parts operate in rhythm with the *dao* 道 and contribute to a synergy that leads to self-realization (often on a large-scale). *Jie* 節 understood as integrity highlights Geaney's notion of boundary-blurring or, perhaps more accurately in this case, gateway-penetrating. Integrity, or the way in which the parts fit and interact together to function in accordance with the *dao* 道, is compromised when the connecting gateway (*jie* 節) between two parts is inappropriately penetrated. When ministers do not appropriately perform their role or when fathers do not act fatherly, the integrity of all parties involved is threatened.[30] This understanding of integrity is communal and contingent on the proper performance of each part.[31]

Many of the examples under discussion describe the physical body as the point of penetration or the object susceptible to external forces. Yuezheng Zichun feared that his injury to his foot demonstrated a lack of filial concern for his parents. Other passages in early Confucian texts discuss the body as the site of collecting and storing a kind of virtuous power best understood as integrity. The "Xiang Yinjiuyi" 鄉飲酒義 chapter of the *Liji*, for instance, in part states, "When ritual incorporates the old and young into one body it is called integrity (*de* 德). Integrity is gained in the individual's body" 禮以體長幼曰德。德也者，得於身也.[32] Xunzi explains, "The exemplary person works to cultivate his interior so as to manifest it in [his] exterior. [He] works to collect integrity (*de* 德) in his body, and employ it in following the Way" 君子務脩其內，而讓之於外；務積德於身，而處之以遵道.[33] The *Shuoyuan* 《說苑》 explains the collecting of integrity in terms of caring for one's parents: "The exemplary person serves his parents and thereby accumulates integrity" 君子之事親以積

德.[34] The *Xiaojing* 《孝經》 ties several of these concepts together in its opening passage:

> Kongzi said, "Filial care is the root of integrity. . . . One's body, hair, and skin are received from one's parents. Do not dare to injure or abuse [them]. [This] is the beginning of filial care. Establish your character [lit. establish your self/body], enact the Way, and proclaim [your] name to future generations in order to glorify your parents. [This] is the culmination of filial care. Filial care begins with serving [one's] parents, continues in the service of [one's] ruler, and is completed when [one] establishes his character.

> 子曰：「夫孝，德之本也。．．．身體髮膚，受之父母，不敢毀傷，孝之始也。立身行道，揚名於後世，以顯父母，孝之終也。夫孝，始於事親，中於事君，終於立身。[35]

In these passages, integrity is something collected and stored in the body. The body not only holds but manifests integrity. In this light, the mutilation of the body as a way of destroying the integrity of a person and the integrity of his or her relations makes sense. Wu Wang 武王 attacking the body of Zhou 紂, as described in the previous chapter, is done not only to demonstrate his power over the former monarch but to dissipate the integrity of the Shang dynasty.[36]

The term I have been translating as "integrity" is *de* 德, and it merits further clarification.

De 德

"Integrity" is often the translation of terms such as *de* 德, *xing* 行, *yi* 義, *jie* 節, *qing* 清, and *lian* 廉. Many of these terms have featured prominently in this study, and many of these terms have a range of meanings that extends beyond "integrity." The term *de* 德, for instance, is also translated as "virtue," "generosity," and "power" (among other translations). In most early Confucian texts *de* 德 is a moral power accumulated by individuals who demonstrate their commitment to people they form relationships with or their commitment to virtues embedded in relationships. In what follows I tease out some implications of understanding integrity in terms of *de* 德. My purpose here is not to argue for a particular translation of the term as much as it is to describe how *de* 德 functions as an important concept in understanding irresolvable value conflicts in early Confucian thought. I proceed by providing a broad overview of *de* 德 in early Chinese literature before contextualizing *de* 德 within early Confucian texts. What emerges from this discussion is a particularly Confucian view of integrity.

Historically speaking, *de* 德 has a range of meanings, and not all of them are consistent with the characterization of *de* 德 as a moral force. In a more basic sense, *de* 德 entails an element of response or reciprocity. Several early texts quote a line from the *Shijing* 《詩經》, which says, "There are no acts of speech that go unanswered; and no *de* 德 that goes unrequited" 無言不讎，無德不報.[37] The *Mozi* 《墨子》 immediately follows this with another quote from the *Shijing*: "If [you] toss me a peach, [I'll] repay it with a plum" 投我以桃，報之以李.[38] Responses to *de* 德 can come from other people (including one's relatives, one's ruler, other officials, etc.) or other powers in the world, including the spirits of one's ancestors and *Tian* 天. In these contexts *de* 德 is often associated with its homophone *de* 得, usually translated as "obtain/attain," "gain," or "get." The "Yueji" chapter of the *Liji*, for instance, states, "When [one] attains to ritual and music, it can be said that [one] has *de* 德. *De* 德 is to attain" 禮樂皆得，謂之有德。德者得也.[39] Ritual and music are often associated with ordering relationships between human beings or between human beings and the spiritual forces of the world. The idea these passages express is that *de* 德 is about giving and receiving. When one gives something, it initiates a response. As one would expect, *de* 德 is sometimes explicitly associated with gift-giving and is occasionally translated as "generosity."[40]

While *de* 德 is often used in a moral sense where good deeds are repaid, it also appears in neutral, and sometimes in negative, cases. The *Shangshu* 《尚書》, for instance, describes the violent *de* 德 (*baode* 暴德) of Jie 桀, the evil tyrant of the Xia 夏 dynasty, and numerous other texts speak about *xiongde* 凶德, or "inauspicious *de* 德."[41] Confucian texts from the late Warring States period and after tend to employ *de* 德 in a positive sense. I say more about the role of *de* 德 in responding to "negative" feelings such as resentment (*yuan* 怨) later.

In several early texts, *de* 德 is associated with *dao* 道; most famously in the *Daodejing* 《道德經》 where *de* 德 is the "nourishing force" 畜 of all things in the world (*wanwu* 萬物), all of which were generated by the *dao* 道.[42] The *Guanzi* 《管子》, in a similar vein, explains that "*de* 德 is the abode of the *dao* 道" 德者道之舍, meaning that *de* 德 provides a means of manifesting the *dao* 道 in practical affairs.[43] *De* 德 in these contexts is associated with life, sustenance, and transformative power.

In many early Confucian texts, *de* 德 is a virtuous power. Several texts define virtues such as *ren* 仁, *yi* 義, *xin* 信, and *xiao* 孝 in terms of *de* 德.[44] The *Xiaojing*, as quoted earlier for instance, explains that filial care is the root of *de* 德 (*fuxiao dezhibenye* 夫孝，德之本也).[45] A recently discovered text from the Warring States period thought to have Confucian origins talks about six *de* 德 (*sheng* 聖, *zhi* 智, *ren* 仁, *yi* 義, *zhong* 忠, and *xin* 信), each of which are tied to a role in a relationship (ruler–minister, *junchen* 君臣; husband–wife, *fufu* 夫婦; and father–son *fuzi* 父子).[46] Another recently discovered text called the *Wuxing* 《五行》 begins with an explanation that when virtues such as *ren* 仁, *yi* 義,

li 禮, *zhi* 智, and *sheng* 聖 take shape within the moral agent, they are expressed in actions of *de* 德 (*dezhixing* 德之行).[47] In this sense, *de* 德 is an umbrella term for many significant Confucian concepts.[48]

Robert H. Gassmann and David Nivison provide a synthetic description of *de* 德.[49] Building on many of the accounts previously discussed, Gassmann explains that *de* 德 refers to a "power to obligate."[50] In other words, Gassmann argues that *de* 德 is a compelling force of attraction generated when someone does something for someone else. Gassmann states, "*de* 德 is the establishment of a dependency between two parties, the obligee and the obligor."[51] When a father does something for his son, for instance, the son will feel obligated to respond in kind to his father. Simply put, *de* 德 entails fostering a desire to fulfill obligations that arise from our relationships. In this light, Gassmann explains *de* 德 by using the language of "a socially accepted debt." In a Confucian context these social transactions are structured by rituals, which often determine not only the way in which the obligations are created but also the way in which the obligations are fulfilled. David Nivison makes an argument similar to Gassmann, defining *de* 德 as a "gratitude credit."[52] He says, "when you do something for me or give me something, [there] is a compulsion I feel so strongly that I come to think of it not as a psychic configuration in myself, but as psychic power emanating from you, causing me to orient myself toward you. That power is your *de* 德—your 'virtue' or 'moral force.' "[53] Moral force understood as gratitude credit means that *de* 德 is accumulated and expended in social interactions. These comments help to explain Kongzi's remarks in the *Analects* that one who is "*de* 德 will not be solitary; [he] will surely have neighbors" 德不孤，必有鄰; and that "governing with *de* 德 is like being the North Star—one stays in his place while all the other stars revolve around it" 為政以德，譬如北辰，居其所而眾星共之.[54] In the views of Gassmann and Nivison, *de* 德 is a charisma that stems from the creation or realization of obligations entailed in relationships. Early Confucians would stress the moral nature of this charisma.

De 德 understood as "moral force" can be contrasted with *li* 力, or physical force. Several early texts highlight this contrast by defining *li* 力 as a coercive force one might employ to prompt others to follow oneself. The *Mengzi*, for instance, explains how *li* 力 can enable a ruler to become a hegemon (*ba* 霸) but only *de* 德 can enable a ruler to become a true king (*wang* 王). After stating this general point, Mengzi explains in more detail, "[If one] obeys someone because of physical force, [he] is not obeying with [his] heart. Physical force is not sufficient [for true obedience]. [However, if one] obeys someone because of *de* 德 [he] will de delighted in his heart and sincerely obey; just like Kongzi's 70 disciples obeyed him" 以力服人者，非心服也，力不贍也；以德服人者，中心悅而誠服也，如七十子之服孔子也.[55] The point these kinds of passages make is that *de* 德 is not a force that coerces others into ordered relationships but rather is a force that attracts others to form ordered relationships such that they come to want to do it themselves. *De* 德 is a force of attraction such that people come to feel their motives for responsive action as their own.[56]

What the accounts of Gassmann and Nivison largely neglect is the connection between *de* 德 and notions of flow and dissipation. *De* 德, as mentioned in chapter 5, is often connected with *xing* 行; the latter can also mean "virtue" or "integrity." Both characters contain the foot radical on the left-hand side suggesting some relation to movement, and indeed one common meaning of *xing* 行 is "to move" or "to circulate."[57] The term *wuxing* 五行, mentioned earlier as "five virtues," also appears in texts (beginning mostly from the Han dynasty) in terms of "five phases," or the five elements that make up the world (water, fire, metal, wood, and earth). Each element is always in flux and transitioning to another element. *De* 德 is not as explicitly associated with movement as is *xing* 行; however, it is often conceptualized in terms of flow or movement. Mengzi, for example, quotes Kongzi saying, "The flow and movement of *de* 德 is quicker than official messengers delivering orders" 德之流行，速於置郵而傳命.[58] The *Han Shi Waizhuan* 《韓詩外傳》 talks about how the *de* 德 of paradigmatic figures reaches up to the heavens and down to earth (*de ji tiandi* 德及天地) and that it flows forth filling the sea (*de zeyang hu hainei* 德澤洋乎海內).[59] The *Zhongjing* 《忠經》, compiled by Ma Rong 馬融 (79–166), states that "when *de* 德 is abundant [it] flows and fills everywhere under the heavens; and is passed down to later generations" 盛德流滿天下，傳於後代.[60] In a similar vein, the *Shuoyuan* 《說苑》 talks about the way in which the *de* 德 of the Zhou 周 dynasty was cultivated by its rulers and handed down to successive rulers. It states, "The *de* 德 of the Zhou 周 began with Hou Ji, was nurtured by Gong Liu, was expanded by Da Wang, was completed by Wen Wang and Wu Wang, and was made manifest by Zhou Gong. [Their] *de* 德 was collected [until it] shot up [to the heavens]. Below the heavens [it] seeped into the springs. There was nowhere [it] did not reach" 夫周德始產于后稷，長於公劉，大於大王，成於文武，顯於周公，德澤上洞，天下漏泉，無所不通.[61] In these passages we see *de* 德 described as a force that moves and flows.

Early Confucian texts often discuss *de* 德 in terms of water and the flow of water. In the *Kongzi Jiayu* Kongzi tells his disciple that "*de* 德 flows like a spring" 德如泉流.[62] The *Dadai Liji* 《大戴禮記》, *Kongzi Jiayu*, *Shuoyuan*, and *Xunzi* each contain a vignette where Kongzi likens *de* 德 to water. In the *Dadai Liji* account, Kongzi says, "Water is something the exemplary person associates with *de* 德. [It] covers things without [thought for] personal interest, [and therefore] is like *de* 德" 夫水者，君子比德焉：偏與之而無私，似德.[63] The *Chunqiu Fanlu* 《春秋繁露》, a text attributed to Dong Zhongshu 董仲舒 (179–104 BCE), explains that "the *de* 德 of an ordered age moistens the grass and trees,

accumulating and flowing to the four seas" 治世之德，潤草木，澤流四
海.[64] In accounts such as the *Chunqiu Fanlu, de* 德 is a power that enriches both
human relationships and relationships between humans and phenomena in what
might be called the natural world. This is similar to the way *de* 德 is discussed as
a nourishing force in the *Daodejing* as mentioned earlier.[65]

The watery effects of *de* 德 are also discussed with regard to the body of those
who accumulate it. The "Daxue" 大學 chapter of the *Liji* states that "*de* 德 moistens the body" 德潤身.[66] Another chapter in the *Liji* explains, "Confucians are
those who have a washed body and bathed *de* 德" 儒有澡身而浴德.[67] In commenting on a passage from the *Analects*, the sixth-century commentator Huang
Kan 皇侃 says, "Those who study, practice, and work for a long time are moist
and wet (*ru* 濡) to the core of [their] bodies. This is why those who practice
for a long time are called Confucians (*ru* 儒)" 學習事久則濡潤身中。故謂
久習者為儒也.[68] Huang is purposely playing on the homonyms "wet" 濡 and
"Confucian" 儒. Interestingly, he associates the notion of wetness with the category of Confucian. While these passages can be taken as metaphors to explain
the refining or transformative nature of *de* 德 or of Confucian practices, there
are also ways in which these claims function literally. Mark Csikszentmihalyi
explains this in his book *Material Virtue: Ethics and the Body in Early China*.
After quoting a commentary on the *Mengzi*, which states that the sage's face is
"moist and lustrous" 潤澤, Csikszentmihalyi explains, "Cultivating the attributes
of benevolence [*ren* 仁], righteousness [*yi* 義], ritual propriety [*li* 禮], and wisdom [*zhi* 智] involved an actual physical transformation in the body. This cultivation alters the sage's interior state (*nei* 內), and changes in that state affect
external appearances (*wai* 外)."[69] Csikszentmihalyi also explains, "[The] virtues
had specific quasi-material correlates in the body, and as such they were subject to
physical processes such as accumulation, dissipation and disorder."[70] The physical
body is not only the site of cultivating and storing *de* 德 as previously mentioned,
but the accumulation of *de* 德 has literal effects on the body. This helps to explain
why preserving the body is so important for Confucians.

Some passages in early Confucian texts also speak about *de* 德 in terms of
wind. The *Shuoyuan*, for instance, discusses how human beings are vulnerable
to sound and how sound functions like wind. It explains that good sounds elicit
good responses from people and that bad sounds encourage bad responses. The
text states,

> In terms of things that penetrate [human beings] from the outside, none
> go as deeply as sound. [Of all things it] changes people the most. This is
> why sages rely [on sound]. [They] infuse it with *de* 德, and call it "music."
> Music is the wind of *de* 德. . . . When the sounds of the court and the

ancestral temple come into contact with people, [their] upright *qi* 氣 responds to it. When the sounds of sacrificial rites and proper demeanor come into contact with people, [their] harmonious *qi* 氣 responds to it. When the sounds of brutality and violence come into contact with people, [their] angry *qi* 氣 responds to it. When the sounds from the states of Zheng and Wei come into contact with people, [their] lascivious *qi* 氣 responds to it. This is why the exemplary person is careful with what he uses to motivate people.

凡從外入者，莫深於聲音，變人最極，故聖人因而成之以德曰樂，樂者德之風。。。雅頌之聲動人，而正氣應之；和成容好之聲動人，而和氣應之；粗厲猛賁之聲動人，而怒氣應之；鄭衛之聲動人，而淫氣應之。是以君子慎其所以動人也。[71]

According to the *Shuoyuan*, human beings are entities susceptible to the forces that penetrate the body. Sounds stir up our *qi* 氣, and, when infused with *de* 德, these sounds stir up the appropriate *qi* 氣. In addition to this passage, the *Analects*, of course, also likens the *de* 德 of the exemplary person to wind (*junzi zhi de feng* 君子之德，風).[72]

This passage from the *Shuoyuan* is also interesting because it suggests a connection between *de* 德 and *qi* 氣—when sounds enter our body, we respond to them by means of our *qi* 氣. Good sounds, which the text calls "music" 樂, are composed with *de* 德; and these sounds encourage good responses. Like *de* 德, *qi* 氣 is conceptualized in terms of reciprocity or cause and effect.

Qi 氣 is a concept of increasing significance in early China. By the end of the Han dynasty (c. third century CE), *qi* 氣 comes to be seen as the material energy that comprises the world, including human beings.[73] Before the Han, *qi* 氣 is discussed less frequently, especially in Confucian texts—appearing in only four passages of the *Analects* and three passages of the *Mengzi*. The earliest sources associate *qi* 氣 with wind or with steam coming from warming water, and in English *qi* 氣 is sometimes translated as "vapor."[74] By the time of the *Analects qi* 氣 is also associated with blood and the flow of blood.[75] Since *qi* 氣 is often connected with life and movement, some scholars translate it as "vital force" or "vital energy." *Qi* 氣 in this sense is pervasive and life-giving.

In the *Analects* Kongzi discusses *qi* 氣 as something that can be "steady" 定, "directed and vigorous" 方剛, or "faint" 衰.[76] Mengzi explains that "*qi* 氣 fills the human body" 氣，體之充也 and that our "will directs [our] *qi* 氣" 志，氣之帥也.[77] In other words, according to Mengzi, *qi* 氣 not only moves within the body but can be controlled or at least channeled and guided by our capacity to focus or exert effort. Human beings are capable of directing their *qi* 氣 in appropriate or inappropriate directions. In the *Kongzi Jiayu* Kongzi speaks about how *qi* 氣 directed by the will "fills [the space between] the heavens and the earth; flowing forth and filling the four seas" 志氣塞于天地，行之充于四海.[78] In a similar vein, Mengzi speaks about "nourishing" 養 one's *qi* 氣 to the point that it is "flood-like" 浩然 and "fills the space between the heavens and the earth" 塞于天地之閒. Mengzi adds that this flood-like *qi* 氣 is "created by means of collecting righteousness" 集義所生.[79] For Mengzi *qi* 氣 is associated with virtue. Importantly, in his study of *Mengzi* and the *Wuxing*, Mark Csikszentmihalyi notes that the Mawangdui commentary on the *Wuxing* discusses terms such as "the *qi* 氣 of humaneness" 仁氣, "the *qi* 氣 of righteousness" 義氣, and "the *qi* 氣 of ritual propriety" 禮氣.[80] In elaborating on the significance of this he states, "There is a progression in the degree to which the virtues are associated with *qi* 氣 in these texts: in the *Wuxing* any link is implicit, in the *Mengzi* there is a rudimentary theory, and in the *Wuxing* commentary the link is explicit and detailed."[81] What we see in these texts is the gradual association between *qi* 氣 and central Confucian virtues. Cultivating these virtues comes to be seen as the cultivation of *qi* 氣.

The parallels between *qi* 氣 and *de* 德 are clear. Both terms are associated with flow, virtue, reciprocity, and the nourishment of life, and both concepts require cultivation or accumulation in the process of moral development. Occasionally early Chinese texts make a more explicit connection. The "Neiye" 內業 chapter of the *Guanzi*, which some scholars take as a Confucian text, uses language similar to the *Mengzi* in describing the flow of *qi* 氣 between the heavens and the earth.[82] Shortly after this statement the text reads, "This *qi* 氣 cannot be stopped by force; [it] can only be pacified by means of *de* 德. . . Hold [it] firmly, and with seriousness. Do not lose [it]. [Only then] can it be called the culmination of *de* 德. With the culmination of *de* 德 and the emergence of wisdom all things attain [their proper place]" 是故此氣也，不可止以力，而可安以德。。。。敬守勿失，是謂成德。德成而智出，萬物果得.[83] The *Shuoyuan* also states, "Heaven and earth [each] have their *de* 德. When [they] combine, *qi* 氣 is created as well as the vital essence [of human beings]" 天地有德，合則生氣有精矣.[84] The contemporary scholar Wang Huaiyu, building on the work of several other scholars, explains the connection as follows: "[We] can take the most original meaning of *de* 德 as the potency for life originating in the intercourse (*gantong* 感通) of *yin* 陰 and *yang* 陽 forces (*qi* 氣) harbored in the blood of dead ancestors and the landscape of particular historical communities."[85] In Wang's view, *de* 德 not only functions similar to *qi* 氣, but *de* 德 is the potency of *qi* 氣 itself.

For the purposes of this project, we do not need to go as far as Wang in linking *de* 德 with *qi* 氣. Rather, the relevant point is that *de* 德 and *qi* 氣 are conceptualized along similar lines of thought. *De* 德, like *qi* 氣, is responsive, active, and always in flux. It is nourished and stored in the body of an individual, and it transforms the body of those who cultivate it. Importantly, *de* 德, like *qi* 氣, extends beyond the individual—reaching up to the heavens and extending to the four seas. It is also, however, interconnected with things beyond the individual, and, as such, *de* 德, like *qi* 氣, is subject to similar concerns—particularly concerns of preservation and dissipation.

The Dissipation and Preservation of De 德

In the "Yueji" chapter of the *Liji*, Zixia 子夏 (507–c. 420 BCE) is asked about "sounds that drown things out" 溺音. In other words, he is asked about music that dampens the moral inclinations of human beings by arousing inappropriate impulses. Zixia responds, "The sounds from the state of Zheng encourage excessive [lit. "overflowing" 濫] behavior and inundate one's sense of determination. The sounds from the state of Song [encourage] indulgence in women and drown one's sense of determination. The sounds from the state of Wei have a quick tempo and exhaust one's sense of determination. The sounds from the state of Qi are overbearing and perverse—puffing up one's sense of determination. These four sounds all spill into one's external expressions, and harm one's *de* 德" 鄭音好濫淫志，宋音燕女溺志，衛音趨數煩志，齊音敖辟喬志；此四者皆淫於色而害於德.[86] *De* 德, according to Zixia, is harmed when human beings are stirred to excesses, or when our sense of determination is overcome by sounds that arouse inappropriate impulses, which then manifest themselves in action. The water imagery is particularly interesting. This passage discusses our sense of determination, or ability to focus and direct our impulses, in the context of "drowning" 溺, "overflowing" 濫, and "spilling" 淫. When we cannot determine our actions and dispositions we lose control of ourselves. Mengzi speaks in similar terms in the passage quoted earlier when discussing how one's will (*zhi* 志) can direct one's *qi* 氣. He explains, "When one's will is concentrated it moves one's *qi* 氣; [but] when one's *qi* 氣 is concentrated it moves one's will" 志壹則動氣，氣壹則動志也.[87] The notion of *zhi* 志, which I translated as "will" or "sense of determination," refers to the ability of human beings to focus or to commit ourselves to a particular course of action. Our will can determine the direction our *qi* 氣 flows, or, if we are not careful, our *qi* 氣 can determine our sense of direction. In the later case, we end up following after basic desires for things such as sex and wealth without regard to their appropriate attainment. Xunzi summarizes this idea quite nicely, stating, "The exemplary person masters things; [while] the uncultivated person is mastered by things" 君子役物，小人役於物.[88]

The *Liji* and *Dadai Liji* purport to contain an exchange between Ai Gong 哀公 (r. 494–468 BCE) and Kongzi about governing. In explaining the problems with rulers of their time Kongzi states that far too many rulers "spill *de* 德 without end" 淫德不倦.[89] In other words, according to Kongzi many rulers slowly lose the power to engender obligations in others by giving reign to their selfish desires in pursuing sex (per the *Dadai Liji*) or wealth (per the *Liji*). In contrast to this, the "Chaoshi" 朝事 chapter of the *Dadai Liji* explains that "when the feudal lords practice ritual and music with each other, [their] integrity and virtue is cultivated such that [they] do not flow out of control" 諸侯相與習禮樂，則德行修而不流也.[90] Following a similar line of thought, the *Han Shi Waizhuan* explains that "The exemplary person is full of integrity, and yet is meek. [He] humbles himself in receiving others—traveling alongside them without flowing out of control. [He] responds to things and yet is not exhausted" 君子盛德而卑，虛己以受人，旁行不流，應物而不窮.[91] *De* 德, in this view, needs to be collected and channeled. If not properly tended to, *de* 德 can spill out or be "exhausted" 窮.

The term *qiong* 窮, which I translate as "exhausted," suggests a sense of weakening, fatigue, or dissipation.[92] As discussed in chapter 4, it can also suggest a sense of limitation or blockage.[93] The character *qiong* 窮 is comprised of the character *xue* 穴, meaning "cave" or "opening," and the character *gong* 躬, which refers to the human body. While it is likely that *qiong* 窮 uses *gong* 躬 for its sound rather than its graphic meaning, it is nonetheless thought-provoking to consider the possibility that *qiong* 窮 refers to the dissipation of things via openings in the human body. While there is little evidence to support such a reading, the appearance of *xue* 穴 as a part of the character suggests some notion of "perforation" or "egress." In a more general sense, as it relates to concepts such as *qi* 氣, *qiong* 窮 suggests a weakening in activity or a waning in flow. The goal for human beings is to cultivate the appropriate flow of things such as *qi* 氣—if *qi* 氣 flows too vigorously it spills out of control; if it flows too slowly it coagulates, weakens, or dissipates. In the *Analects* (16.7), Kongzi explains that as people grow old their *qi* 氣 "wanes" or "becomes faint" 衰. The *Shuoyuan* likewise talks about *qi* 氣 and dissipation in the context of growing old and dying. The text states, "There are five ways that people die. The sage is able to eliminate three of them, but unable to eliminate two of them" 民有五死，聖人能去其三，不能去其二.[94] The *Shuoyuan* then explains that people die from lack of food, lack of shelter, or because of physical violence, old age, or sickness. According to the *Shuoyuan*, a sage-ruler can eliminate the first three but not the last two. Of particular importance is the text's explanation of death due to sickness, which the text explains as "the exhaustion of vital *qi* 氣" 血氣窮也. If one's *qi* 氣 weakens, one's health weakens. The *Baihutong* also talks about death in terms of "the exhaustion of refined *qi* 氣" 精氣窮也.[95] The decline of *qi* 氣 is a decline in one's health and is often conceptualized as a lessening of vigor or energy.

De 德 is spoken of in similar terms—most often as "waning" 衰 or "thinning out" 薄. Many early Confucian thinkers explain the gradual collapse of the Zhou 周 dynasty, for instance, as "the waning of the Zhou dynasty's *de* 德" 周德衰.[96] The *Kongzi Jiayu* also states that "when *de* 德 is profuse there will be order; [but] when *de* 德 is thin there will be chaos" 德盛者，治也。德薄者，亂也.[97] The idea here is that high degrees of integrity ensure that people perform their roles in relationships and low degrees of integrity weaken those roles and contribute to a disorganized society. When integrity is thin, disorder will likely follow. The notion of "profuse *de* 德" 盛德 is reminiscent of Mengzi's notion of "flood-like *qi* 氣" 浩然之氣. Since most authors understand *de* 德 as a *moral* force, they do not speak about cultivating too much *de* 德 or fear that *de* 德 might become turbulent or flow out of control. At the same time they also recognize that *de* 德 can be spilt, weakened, or dissipated.

The early texts, in this light, often speak about "accumulating" 積 and "preserving" 全 one's *de* 德. As mentioned previously, the *Shuoyuan* states that "the exemplary person accumulates *de* 德 by serving his parents" 君子之事親以積德; and the *Xunzi* explains that the exemplary person "works to accumulate *de* 德 in his self/body, and uses it in following the Way" 務積德於身，而處之以遵道. The *Yantielun* 《鹽鐵論》 adds, "The Zhou 周 dynasty accumulated *de* 德 through each passing generation [until] there were none under the heavens that did not consider them their ruler. Because [of this they] were able to rule without exerting great effort" 周累世積德，天下莫不願以為君，故不勞而王.[98] The point these passages make is that integrity is something built up over time. Xunzi uses the same character, *ji* 積 ("accumulate"), to describe the collection of dirt or water, which when accumulated over time can become something as large as a mountain or a sea. He likens this to people who become sages by "collecting goodness" 積善.[99] Hence, in Xunzi's view the ability to "accumulate" 積 is significant in moral development. There are many other passages in early Confucian texts that stress the importance of "accumulating *de* 德" 積德.[100]

The term *quan* 全 appears in a number of places in this study. In chapter 5 I explained that *quan* 全 often means "preservation" and is tied to notions of purity. The *Shuoyuan* account of Shen Ming 申鳴 explains that Shen Ming felt caught between loyalty and filial piety. He questioned how he could "preserve himself" 全身 (literally, "preserve his body"). Earlier in this chapter I also quoted from the "Jiyi" section of the *Liji* where *quan* 全 is defined as "not fatiguing one's body, nor disgracing one's self" 不虧其體，不辱其身. Previous appearances of *quan* 全 have also associated it with *de* 德. In chapter 6, for instance, I quoted the *Zhuangzi* 《莊子》, which critiqued the early sage Huangdi 黃帝 for engaging in warfare, saying that he was "unable to preserve his integrity" 不能全德.[101] Other passages in early Chinese texts also connect *quan* 全 with integrity. The *Huangdi Neijing* 《黃帝內經》, a late Warring States or early Han medical text usually associated with Daoism, for instance, relates *de* 德 to *quan* 全, as well as with health. It states, "Those who are able to live beyond 100 years and not have their capacity of movement diminished are able to do so because their *de* 德 is preserved and not damaged" 所以能年皆度百歲，而動作不衰者，以其德全不危也.[102] In this view, *de* 德 is associated with vigor and life. One who maintains integrity is able to live a long life. While early Confucian texts do not contain such explicit statements about longevity and preserving one's integrity, we see similar themes in places such as the Shen Ming story, where the inability to "preserve" 全 one's self or one's virtues such as loyalty and filial piety is a cause worthy of death. Indeed, the notion of "two virtuous actions not both being preserved" 行不兩全 is ultimately the impetus for Shen Ming ending his own life. The *Shuoyuan* states a similar notion quite succinctly, saying, "The exemplary person enacts *de* 德 in order to preserve himself" 君子行德以全其身.[103]

Related to this are accounts of blockage or frustrated desire discussed previously in terms of *yuan* 怨. Resentment is often associated with *de* 德. The *Analects* famously discusses both concepts in the context of *bao* 報, or reciprocity. In passage 14.34 Kongzi is asked what he thinks about the notion that one ought to respond with *de* 德 (sometimes translated as "generosity") in situations where one has been treated with resentment. Kongzi answers, "Why would one respond with generosity? Respond to resentment with forthrightness, and respond to generosity with generosity" 何以報德？以直報怨，以德報德. Kongzi's point here is that we ought to respond in a manner similar to the actions we encounter. Said more abstractly, reciprocity is about responding in kind. If we encounter resentment we ought to respond to it with the genuine feelings it evokes. *De* 德 promotes impulses to respond in a virtuous manner. Interestingly, Kongzi is not depicted as being uniform on this point. The "Biaoji" 表記 chapter of the *Liji*, for instance, quotes Kongzi saying, "Responding to resentment with generosity is a [kind of] humaneness that enlarges the self" 以德報怨，則寬身之仁也; and the *Shuoyuan* quotes him saying, "The sage turns curses into blessings— responding to resentment with generosity" 聖人轉禍為福，報怨以德.[104] In each of these cases, *de* 德 is connected with *yuan* 怨. Jia Yi 賈誼 (200–169 BCE), in the *Xinshu* 《新書》, makes the connection more explicit. He explains, "Resentment is the opposite of generosity" 反德為怨. While the term "opposite" suggests a kind of opposition between the terms *de* 德 and *yuan* 怨, the character *fan* 反 also implies a sense of "turning over" such that "opposites" are not divided but rather remain connected to each other. A more colloquial translation of the phrase would be "Resentment is the flip-side of generosity." In other words, *de* 德 and *yuan* 怨 are two sides of the same coin.

Both *de* 德 and *yuan* 怨 are about the directed release of energy. They are also both about response, retribution, or reciprocity. *De* 德 is a kind of positive energy. It infuses others to perform their roles in relationships. It can be accumulated, preserved, and released. *Yuan* 怨 is also about a release of energy in the context of response. *Yuan* 怨, in short, is often a response to cruelty. It entails frustrated or pent-up desire. Whereas *de* 德 is about flow, *yuan* 怨 is about impeded flow or obstruction. As we saw in chapter 4, *yuan* 怨 can also function such that it unobstructs the flow of energy by encouraging the moral agent to transgress the boundaries of proper action. Kongzi took upon himself the role of the ruler in creating the *Chunqiu*, which, as discussed in chapter 4, was created on the basis of Kongzi's resentment. Transgression, in this sense, parallels acts of integrity inasmuch as integrity enables the coming forth of the Confucian *dao* 道.[105]

Yuan 怨 is associated with the release of pent-up energy (*fafen* 發憤) that can compel transgression. However, these transgressions are undertaken not for one's personal gain but for the sake of others. Coincidentally, David Nivison makes a similar point about self-sacrifice in his discussion of *de* 德. Nivison states, "These sacrifice contexts tell us more already about what *de* 德 is: it appears to be a quality or psychic energy in the king that the spirits can perceive and are pleased to see in him, and it appears to be something he gets, or something that becomes more evident in him when he denies or risks himself, [when he] does something for another."[106] According to Nivison, *de* 德 increases when the moral agent risks himself. Similarly, transgressions spurred on by resentment can be seen as attempts to establish the results of integrity in situations where actions of integrity failed to generate the appropriate response.

Conclusion

Integrity in an early Confucian context is associated with maintaining and monitoring boundaries. These boundaries include the physical body as well as more abstract concepts such as the proper limits of actions and dispositions associated with the roles of father, son, and minister. When boundaries are properly maintained, moral agents accumulate integrity that transforms their selves and encourages others to likewise perform their roles. When this occurs on a large scale, all parts of society integrate such that they operate in conjunction with the *dao* 道.

The accumulation of integrity is described as the moistening of the body. At the same time, getting wet can also describe the loss of integrity, as in situations where one transgresses the boundaries of proper role performance. Those who stay within these boundaries are often discussed as being "pure" (*qing* 清, *lian* 廉, or *yi* 義). As mentioned in chapter 6, however, figures such as Chen Zhongzi, Bo

Yi, and Shu Qi, who on the one hand are praised for being pure, are on the other hand criticized for being overly fixated on maintaining their purity. In short, there is something praiseworthy in compromising one's integrity for the sake of others. John M. Parrish expresses this with regard to the Western philosophical tradition when discussing "the deontological absolutist"—an individual unwilling to compromise his or her principles under any condition. He states, "The deontological absolutist cannot hold firm to her position unless she is willing to let the heavens fall if necessary rather than surrender her principles. There is also a certain callousness to her refusal—seen in the ruthlessness required to let the world go to hell in order to preserve her own integrity—that intuitively renders her position not just politically but also morally untenable."[107] In other words, the deontological absolutist sticks to his or her identity conferring commitments regardless of the results. Similarly, in a Confucian context, figures such as Chen Zhongzi maintain their purity at the expense of other goods.

In the *Kongzi Jiayu* Kongzi is depicted offering advice to Zizhang 子張 (c. 503 BCE) on becoming a government official. As a part of his advice he explains that a ruler ought not to lead from a position too "high" 高 or too "far away" 遠 from the people. Kongzi goes on to explain that the sagely rulers of antiquity "covered up [their] brilliance" 蔽明 and "hid [their] perspicacity" 撝聰 in order to start governing from the concrete conditions of the people in the kingdom (*yinqiqing* 因其情). Kongzi describes this with a metaphor: "Water of the utmost purity is sure to have no fish" 水至清即無魚.[108] In other words, attracting fish requires some mud in the water, and governing the people requires getting dirty. Kongzi's metaphor can be taken several different ways. In conjunction with chapters 1 and 2, this metaphor can be understood to demonstrate the necessity of *quan* 權—a flexibility that allows sages to adapt to various circumstances while still maintaining their integrity. Sages, therefore, learn to behave in ways that may seem to compromise their integrity, yet they actually maintain it. Given the broader context of this passage, this interpretation is most likely. Yet Kongzi's metaphor is not wholly inapplicable to the other contexts of leadership and relationships discussed in this book. In this sense, relationships entail compromises, and not all compromises can resolve the tension between integrity and necessity. In these views, taking exigent action still entails a cost. In these situations "two virtuous actions cannot both be completed" 行不能兩全, and one's integrity cannot be preserved. The sullied moral agent in these situations is one whose integrity has been violated such that his ability to realize his relationships as a constitutive part of himself is damaged. The imagery of getting wet in early Confucian texts can be good or bad. Getting wet can be about accumulating integrity or about tarnishing one's integrity in a difficult situation. Yet these early Confucians would support the notion, to borrow from Christopher Gowans, that we ought to recognize the complexity of the world and commiserate with those who confront such misfortune. Gowans states, "Rather than looking to punish, we should be vigilant in demanding of them what we should demand of ourselves: continued moral sensitivity, balance, and courage while engaging a world of distressing and occasionally tragic moral conflicts."[109]

Notes

1. See especially Bernard Williams, "Persons, Character, and Morality" and "Moral Luck," both in his *Moral Luck: Philosophical Papers 1973–1980* (New York: Cambridge University Press, 1981), 1–39. In addition to the scholars discussed in this chapter, see also Mark Halfon, *Integrity: A Philosophical Inquiry* (Philadelphia: Temple University Press, 1989); and Thomas E. Hill Jr., "Moral Purity and the Lesser Evil," *The Monist* 66.2 (April 1983): 213–232.

2. Cheshire Calhoun, "Standing for Something," *The Journal of Philosophy* 92.5 (May 1995): 254. Roger Ames and David Hall make a related statement with regard to integrity in an early Confucian context: "'Integrity' is more than being true to oneself. Since all selves are constituted by relations, integrity means being trustworthy and true in one's associations. It is effectively integrating oneself in one's social, natural, and cultural contexts. At a cosmological level, integrity is the ground from which self and other arise together to maximum benefit. It is not *what* things are, but *how well* and *how productively* they are able to fare in their synergistic alliances." *Focusing the Familiar: A Translation and Philosophical Interpretation of the Zhongyong* (Honolulu: University of Hawai'i Press, 2001), 33.

3. As quoted in Ping Cheung Lo, "Family as First Bulwark for the Vulnerable: Confucian Perspectives on the Anthropology and Ethics of Human Vulnerability," in *Religious Perspectives on Human Vulnerability in Bioethics*, edited by Joseph Tham et al. (New York: Springer, 2014), 63. Changed to reflect American spelling of "center." In other places Tu states, "[S]ociety is not conceived of as something out there that is being imposed on the individual. It is in essence an extended self." *Humanity and Self-Cultivation: Essays in Confucian Thought* (Boston: Cheng and Tsui 1998), 25.

4. Herbert Fingarette, "The Music of Humanity in the Conversations of Confucius," *Journal of Chinese Philosophy* 10.4 (December 1983): 340. See also Ambrose Y. C. King, "The Individual and Group in Confucianism: A Relational Perspective," in *Individualism and Holism: Studies in Confucian and Taoist Values*, edited by Donald J. Munro (Ann Arbor: Center for Chinese Studies, University of Michigan, 1985), 57.

5. For an overview of these positions see David B. Wong, "Relational and Autonomous Selves," *Journal of Chinese Philosophy* 31:4 (December 2004): 419–432. These notions of an interconnected self are similar to the kinds of interconnection argued for by

feminist thinkers including Judith Butler and Erinn Gilson. Gilson, for instance, argues, "An ethics of vulnerability necessitates an idea of the self as reciprocally constituted by others, always fundamentally interconnected and interwoven with the selves of others, permeable, and both mutable and in the process of altering." Erinn G. Gilson, *The Ethics of Vulnerability: A Feminist Analysis of Social Life and Practice* (New York: Routledge, 2014), 178.

6. Which is not to say that these scholars do not indirectly address issues of vulnerability in discussing topics such as self-cultivation (*xiushen* 修身).

7. Wong, "Relational and Autonomous Selves," 427.

8. *Liji* 25.36/128/6–7.

9. *Lüshi Chunqiu* 14.1/70/16–17.

10. *Lüshi Chunqiu* 9.5/47/9–11.

11. *Baihutong* 12/33/17.

12. For more passages on this kind of interconnection see *Baihutong* 12/32/12–15, 20/44/24–45/2; *Zhongjing* 3/3/33; *Yantielun* 10.3/72/4–21; *Zhuangzi* 18/48/20–21; and Ban Gu 班固, *Hanshu* 《漢書》 (Beijing 北京: Zhonghua Shuju 中華書局, 2007), 87; hereafter, "*Hanshu.*" See also *Lüshi Chunqiu* 2.4/9/24–10/8.

13. A.T. Nuyen, "Moral Obligation and Moral Motivation in Confucian Role-Based Ethics," *Dao: A Journal of Comparative Philosophy* 8 (2009): 3. Italics added.

14. *Kongzi Jiayu* 37.4/65/16–17.

15. Xue Ke 雪克, ed., *Xinyi Gongyang Zhuan* 《新譯公羊傳》 (Taibei 台北: Sanmin Shuju 三民書局, 2008), 77 ("Zhuang Gong" 莊公 4). It is worth noting that this passage makes this claim with a particular emphasis on the ruler-state relationship.

16. Jane Geaney, "Guarding Moral Boundaries: Shame in Early Confucianism," *Philosophy East and West* 54.2 (April 2004): 114 and 120. In addition to the sources Geaney sites on 133 fn. 2 see also Antonio S. Cua, "The Ethical Significance of Shame: Insights of Aristotle and Xunzi," *Philosophy East and West* 53.2 (2003): 147–202; and more recently, Thorian R. Harris, "Aristotle and Confucius on the Socioeconomics of Shame," *Dao: A Journal of Comparative Philosophy* 13.3 (September 2014): 323–342; and Bongrae Seok, "Moral Psychology of Shame in Early Confucian Philosophy," *Frontiers of Philosophy in China* 10.1 (March 2015): 21–57. For a related article on the topic of shame in the western philosophical tradition see Cheshire Calhoun, "An Apology for Moral Shame," *The Journal of Political Philosophy* 12.2 (2004): 127–146.

17. Geaney, "Guarding Moral Boundaries," 120.

18. Geaney, "Guarding Moral Boundaries," 122.

19. Geaney, "Guarding Moral Boundaries," 122.

20. The notion of storing virtues is similar to other theories of the body in early China where the body stores (*cang/zang* 藏) *qi* 氣 or other life-giving energies. John Major et al., for instance, discuss the notion of *wuzang* 五藏 in the *Huainanzi* in John S. Major et al., trans. *The Huainanzi: A Guide to the Theory and Practice of Government in Early Han China* (New York: Columbia University Press, 2010): 900.

21. Xu Shen 許慎, *Shuowen Jiezi* 《說文解字》 (Beijing 北京: Zhonghua Shuju 中
    華書局, 2004), 95. Hereafter, *Shuowen*. This also seems to be the usage of *jie* 節
    in the "Mao Qiu" 旄丘 poem from the *Shijing*: Teng Zhixian 滕志賢. ed. *Xinyi
    Shijing Duben* 《新譯詩經讀本》 (Taibei 台北: Sanmin Shuju 三民書局,
    2011), 97. Hereafter, *Shijing*." For *jie* 節 as a boundary of time see *Shiming* 1.1/2/30;
    see also 2.2/22/17.

22. *Mengzi* 4B1. See also *Mozi* 4.3/28/5.

23. I thank Tobias Zuern for suggesting this metaphor and for his many other helpful
    comments on this chapter.

24. *Liji* 19.1/98/30–99/3.

25. *Lüshi Chunqiu* 2.3/8/21–22. In this passage, the *Lüshi Chunqiu* advocates a view
    of human nature closer to *Xunzi* but highlights the broadly shared theme of sages
    creating boundaries for the proper attainment of desire.

26. Tobias Zuern makes an insightful comment that ties these passages together: "*Li*
    理 is made out of connected (*tong* 通) nodes/floodgates (*jie* 節) that are main-
    tained by *li* 禮, [which] helps set up and maintain [social] distinctions (*fen* 分)."
    Personal communication.

27. For more on ritual in this light see Michael D. K. Ing, *The Dysfunction of Ritual
    in Early Confucianism* (New York: Oxford University Press, 2012), 18–37. Wang
    Huaiyu also makes a relevant comment: "Ancient Chinese often compared the
    function of ritual to that of bamboo joints (*jie* 節), which perform the double func-
    tions of at once containing and promoting the growth of each division of the whole
    branch." Huaiyu Wang, "Piety and Individuality Through a Convoluted Path of
    Rightness: Exploring the Confucian Art of Moral Discretion via *Analects* 13.18,"
    Asian Philosophy 21.4 (November 2011): 407.

28. *Liji* 47.3/170/28–32.

29. Scott Cook, "Unity and Diversity in the Musical Thought of Warring States China"
    (Ph.D. diss., University of Michigan, 1995), 82 fn. 153.

30. Nathaniel Barrett articulates a Confucian theory of shame that relates to several
    of these ideas. Barrett claims that shame "is intimately tied to human fulfillment"
    (160) and that it arises in the context of the disharmony of values central to one's
    identity. Shame is also relational because "the experience of 'self-value' is inti-
    mately connected to the experience of 'other value'" (147). Nathaniel F. Barrett, "A
    Confucian Theory of Shame," *Sophia* 52.2 (June 2015): 143–163.

31. Coincidentally, *jie* 節 also appears in contrast to *quan* 權 in places such as the
    "Sangfu Sizhi" 喪服四制 chapter of *Liji* (50.2/174/21–23). In this passage, the
    author associates *jie* 節 with ritual (*li* 禮) and associates *quan* 權 with wisdom (*zhi*
    知). As discussed in chapter 1, *quan* 權 entails a sense of deviating from standard
    ethical action. In this regard, *quan* 權 is about exercising wisdom in going beyond
    proper boundaries.

32. *Liji* 42.6/169/6–7. Xu Shen in the *Shuowen* describes *shen* 身 as an image of the
    body. Xu Fu 徐復 and Song Wenmin 宋文民 add that it may also be the pictograph

of a pregnant woman. See *Shuowen Wubaisishi Bushou Zhengjie* 《說文五百四十部首正解》 (Jiangsu 江蘇: Guji chubanshe 古籍出版社, 2003), 242–243.

33. *Xunzi* 8/30/1.

34. *Shuoyuan* 3.4/19/16; see also *Shuoyuan* 9.23/75/24, 14.10/114/5–9, 17.17/143/25; and *Xunzi* 28/140/18.

35. Li Xueqin 李學勤, ed., *Xiaojing Zhushu* 《孝經注疏》, *Shisanjing Zhushu* 《十三經注疏》 Vol. 26 (Beijing北京: Beijing daxue chubanshe 北京大學出版社, 2000), 3–5. See also Yang Bojun 楊伯峻, ed., *Chunqiu Zuo Zhuan Zhu* 《春秋左傳注》 (Beijing 北京: Zhonghua Shuju 中華書局, 2000), 1087–1090 ("Xiang Gong" 襄公 24); hereafter, *Zuo Zhuan*.

36. In other places such as the *Shiji* 《史記》, Wu Zixu 伍子胥 unearths the body of his father's murderer and repeatedly stabs it as part of an effort to "wipe away great shame" 雪大恥 (*Shiji*, 2223). Sima Qian 司馬遷 (c. 145–86 BCE) also explains that living long enough to finish the *Shiji* entailed "living with disgrace" 苟活 because of his castration (*Hanshu*, 621). On this theme see also *Zuo Zhuan*, 1611–1618 ("Ai Gong" 哀公 2).

37. *Shijing*, 870–871.

38. *Mozi* 4.3/29/24.

39. *Liji* 19.1/98/27. Scott Barnwell notes, "Many texts and authors either define, explain or connect *De* 德 with *De* 得, such as the authors of the pre-Qin era texts *Zhuangzi, Guanzi, Hanfeizi, Liji, Heguanzi*; the *Xinshu* and the *Huainanzi* of the Western Han Dynasty; Xu Shen's *Shuowen Jiezi*, Yang Xiong's *Fayan* and Liu Xi's *Shiming* of the Eastern Han Dynasty; Wang Bi's commentary on the *Laozi* in the third century C.E.; and more. This connection is *not* found in Western Zhou bronze inscriptions, where, although both 德 and 得 appear on the same bronzes, there is no apparent relationship." "The Evolution of the Concept of *De* 德 in Early China," *Sino-Platonic Papers* 235 (March 2013), 33.

40. Wang Huaiyu highlights this aspect of *de* 德 in "A Genealogical Study of *De*: Poetical Correspondence of Sky, Earth, and Humankind in the Early Chinese Virtuous Rule of Benefaction," *Philosophy East and West* 65.1 (January 2015): 81–124. Vassili Kryukov critiques the idea of *de* 德 as gift giving in "Symbols of Power and Communication in Pre-Confucian China (On the Anthropology of *De*) Preliminary Assumptions," *Bulletin of the School of Oriental and African Studies* 43.2 (1995): 315–316.

41. Li Xueqin 李學勤, ed., *Shangshu Zhengyi* 《尚書正義》, *Shisanjing Zhushu* 《十三經注疏》 Vols. 2–3 (Beijing北京: Beijing daxue chubanshe 北京大學出版社, 2000), 552. See also Barnwell, "The Evolution of the Concept of *De* 德," 24–26.

42. *Daodejing/Laozi* 51A/17/13–16. See also the "Xici xia" 繫辭下 chapter of the *Yijing* 《易經》: "The great *de* 德 of the heavens and earth is called life/creation" 天地之大德曰生. *Zhouyi* 66/81/16. *Zhuangzi* 12/31/10 reads, "That by which things live/are created is called *de* 德" 物得以生，謂之德.

43. *Guanzi* 13/96/31. Robert H. Gassmann also makes a relevant comment in "Coming to Terms with *De* 德: The Deconstruction of 'Virtue' and an Exercise in Scientific Morality" in *How Should One Live?: Comparing Ethics in Ancient China and Greco-Roman Antiquity*, eds. Richard A. H. King and Dennis Schilling (Boston: Walter de Gruyter, 2011), 117: "If *de* 德 is established as the noun 'the power to obligate,' then the partner noun *dao* 道 should also be taken as denoting 'the power to lead.'"

44. In addition to the texts cited below see also *Liji* 49.11/174/9–14; *Kongzi Jiayu* 12/21/28–22/1; *Dadai Liji* 6.2/38/20–21; *Zhouyi* 66/84/4–10; and *Xinshu* 8.5/59/5–8.

45. Li, Xueqin 李學勤, ed., *Xiaojing Zhushu* 《孝經注疏》, *Shisanjing Zhushu* 《十三經注疏》 Vol. 26 (Beijing北京: Beijing daxue chubanshe 北京大学出版社, 2000), 3.

46. See Scott Cook, *The Bamboo Texts of Guodian: A Study and Complete Translation* (Ithaca, NY: Cornell University East Asia Program, 2012), 751–798.

47. Cook, *The Bamboo Texts of Guodian*, 485–487. See also Mark Csikszentmihalyi, *Material Virtue: Ethics and the Body in Early China* (Boston: Brill, 2004). The *Wuxing* also highlights the internal nature of *de* 德, which is significant but not entirely relevant for this study. See Csikszentmihalyi, *Material Virtue*, 149–156; and Kryukov, "Symbols of Power," 316. See also Xu Shen, *Shuowen Jiezi*, 217; and *Fayan* 10/26/7.

48. It is worth noting that these concepts are not necessarily reducible to *de* 德. In other words, *de* 德 does not necessarily operate as a kind of ur-value where values such as humaneness and righteousness can be translated into *de* 德 and then weighed against each other. Instead, *de* 德 functions as a way of identifying things that serve similar purposes—values that may or may not be reducible to each other.

49. Scott Barnwell also provides a useful summary of *de* 德 in the early Zhou: "*De* 德 is spoken of in texts of this period as something that can be present or absent, abundant or slight, high or low, bright or dark, good or bad, consistent or inconsistent. *De* 德 can be accumulated, or it can be distributed and spread abroad. It can be maintained or neglected, kept intact or dissipated. *De* 德 is something that can elicit changes in living things. It can be used by rulers to pacify a population and it can win the people's hearts and minds, making people turn to them for direction. It can be used to guide and transform others." Barnwell, "The Evolution of the Concept of *De* 德," 2.

50. Gassmann, "Coming to Terms with *De* 德," 117. Wang Huaiyu also uses the language of "grant and gratitude" in "A Genealogical Study of *De*," 91.

51. Gassmann, "Coming to Terms with *De* 德," 107.

52. Gassmann, "Coming to Terms with *De* 德," 107; and David S. Nivison, *The Ways of Confucianism: Investigations in Chinese Philosophy* (Chicago: Open Court, 1996), 32.

53. Nivison, *The Ways of Confucianism*, 25–26.

54. *Analects* 4.25 and 2.1.

55. *Mengzi* 2A3. See also *Analects* 14.33; *Shuoyuan* 6.3/40/6–7 and 5.3/32/7–8.

56. The *Hanfeizi* talks about this in terms of *wuwei* 無為 in 20/34/8–11.

57. It is worth noting, however, that some early appearances of *de* 德 do not have the foot radical.

58. *Mengzi* 2A1. See also *Liji* 25.34/127/10–13; *Kongzi Jiayu* 7.1/8/28–9/1; and *Dadai Liji* 11.3/69/1–2.

59. *Han Shi Waizhuan* 3.7/17/20.

60. *Zhongjing* 13/17/9.

61. *Shuoyuan* 11.6/87/4–5.

62. *Kongzi Jiayu* 35.2/61/2.

63. *Dadai Liji* 7.3/45/24–28. See also *Shuoyuan* 17.46/148/23–27; *Xunzi* 28/140/4–9; and *Kongzi Jiayu* 9.5/15/14–19. There are significant variations in these accounts. All of them go on to compare other values to water as well.

64. *Chunqiu Fanlu* 17.4A/84/18–20. Interestingly, and relevant for the discussion of *qi* 氣 in this chapter, this passage goes on to say, "Between the heavens and the earth there is the *qi* 氣 of *yin* 陰 and *yang* 陽. [It] universally soaks people, like water universally soaks fish" 天地之間，有陰陽之氣，常漸人者，若水常漸魚也.

65. For other examples of *de* 德 as a nourishing force see *Liji* 32.30/147/8–10; *Xunzi* 1/2/9–11; *Shuoyuan* 5.3/32/7–8; *Han Shi Waizhuan* 3.25/22/12–16; *Xinshu* 8.5/59/19–21; *Zhouyi* 29/35/17; *Baihutong* 18/39/9–16; and *Zhuangzi* 21/58/8–10.

66. *Liji* 43.1/165/4.

67. *Liji* 42.9/164/4.

68. As quoted in Csikszentmihalyi, *Material Virtue*, 17. Translation is my own. See also *Yantielun* 6.6/47/20.

69. Csikszentmihalyi, *Material Virtue*, 127.

70. Csikszentmihalyi, *Material Virtue*, 6.

71. *Shuoyuan* 19.43/172/11–17. The term *feng* 風 also has explicit musical connections.

72. *Analects* 12.19. See also *Liji* 32.30/147/16–18.

73. For a brief overview of *qi* 氣 see Zhang Dainian, *Key Concepts In Chinese Philosophy* (New Haven, CT: Yale University Press, 2002), 45–63. For a more in-depth account see Cai Fanglu 蔡方鹿 et al., *Qi* 《氣》 (Beijing 北京: Zhongguo Renmin Daxue Chubanshe 中国人民大学出版社, 1990); and Onozawa Seiichi 小野澤精一, Fukunaga Mitsuji 福永光司, and 山井涌 Yamanoi Yū, eds., *Ki no Shisō: Chūgoku ni okeru Shizenkan to Ningenkan no Tenkai* 《気の思想：中国における自然観と人間観の展開》 (Tōkyō 東京: Tōkyō Daigaku Shuppankai 東京大学出版会, 1978), especially pages 13–180.

74. Csikszentmihalyi, *Material Virtue*, 144. See also Harold David Roth, *Original Tao: Inward Training (Nei Ye) and the Foundations of Taoist Mysticism* (New York: Columbia University Press, 1999), 41.

75. See *Analects* 16.7.

76. *Analects* 16.7.

77. *Mengzi* 2A2.

78. *Kongzi Jiayu* 27.2/51/29.

79. *Mengzi* 2A2.

80. Csikszentmihalyi, *Material Virtue*, 211–212.

81. Csikszentmihalyi, *Material Virtue*, 212. Franklin Perkins sees the connection between *qi* 氣 and the virtues in the *Mengzi* more explicitly. In *Heaven and Earth Are Not Humane: The Problem of Evil in Classical Chinese Philosophy* (Bloomington: Indiana University Press, 2014), 147, he states, "The heart of shame and aversion that fills out into rightness [*yi* 義] is a configuration of *qi* 氣, which, when stimulated, moves to be the actual feelings of shame and aversion. If these dispositions are thwarted rather than made to flow—if the heart is left unsatisfied—then the vital energy itself will decline." On page 148 he continues, "Humaneness, rightness, and ritual propriety, in so far as they are internal and genuine, are forms of *qi* 氣, vital energies."

82. See, for example, Brook Ziporyn, *Ironies of Oneness and Difference: Coherence In Early Chinese Thought* (Albany: State University of New York Press, 2012), 131–132.

83. *Guanzi* 16.1/115/19–20.

84. *Shuoyuan* 18.12/153/25.

85. Wang, "A Genealogical Study of *De*," 90.

86. *Liji* 19.25/103/3–4.

87. *Mengzi* 2A2.

88. *Xunzi* 2/6/12–13.

89. *Liji* 28.1/135/3–12. See also *Dadai Liji* 1.3/5/16–17.

90. *Dadai Liji* 12.1/72/21–22.

91. *Han Shi Waizhuan* 2.17/11/14–15.

92. *Qiong* 窮 can be used positively as well to mean something like "thoroughly fathom." For the etymology of *qiong* 窮 see Xu Fu, *Shuowen Wubaisishi Bushou Zhengjie*, 220.

93. This is particularly true in contexts where *qiong* 窮 is contrasted with *tong* 通 or *da* 達.

94. *Shuoyuan* 16.172/135/19–23.

95. *Baihutong* 43/77/19.

96. See, for instance, *Yantielun* 8.2/57/23, 9.1/62/26; *Han Shi Waizhuan* 8.3/57/15; *Shuoyuan* 5.3/32/12; and *Kongzi Jiayu* 39.2/73/8. See also *Lüshi Chunqiu* 12.4/60/25.

97. *Kongzi Jiayu* 25.1/48/13. See also *Liji* 26.22/133/2–6.

98. *Yantielun* 8.2/58/4.

99. *Xunzi* 8/34/4–6.

100. *Shuoyuan* 5.7/33/15 and 9.23/75/24; *Han Shi Waizhuan* 7.6/50/13; *Dadai Liji* 13.3/79/1; *Kongzi Jiayu* 21.1/40/4 and 35.2/61/4; and *Shangshu*, 272.

101. *Zhuangzi* 29/88/4. In contrast to those who are not able to preserve their integrity, the *Zhuangzi* mentions others who are able to preserve their integrity in 12/32/11–23. See also *Zhuangzi* 15/41/24–26 and 5/14/17–15/11. While the *Zhuangzi* is undoubtedly critical of Kongzi and his followers, it is not always antagonistic. See John Makeham, "Between Chen and Cai: *Zhuangzi* and the *Analects*," in *Wandering at Ease in the Zhuangzi*, edited by Roger T. Ames (Albany: State University of New York Press, 1998), 75–100.

102. Yao Chunpeng 姚春鹏, ed., *Huangde Neijing* 《黄帝内经》 (Beijing 北京: Zhonghua Shuju 中华书局, 2009), 5.

103. *Shuoyuan* 16.145/133/18. See also *Xunzi* 1/4/16–21 and 9/40/14–16; and *Lüshi Chunqiu* 1.2/2/21–25.

104. *Liji* 33.7/148/18–19; and *Shuoyuan* 13.21/106/10. See also *Shuoyuan* 6.12/42/11–23.

105. *Han Shi Waizhuan* 1.25/5/30 states that being too pure can actually interfere with accumulating *de* 德: "Sharp mountains are not tall; and straight-flowing water is not deep. If one's humaneness is pure, one's *de* 德 will not be abundant" 山銳則不高，水徑則不深，仁礛則其德不厚.

106. Nivison, *The Ways of Confucianism*, 24.

107. John M. Parrish, *Paradoxes of Political Ethics* (New York: Cambridge University Press, 2007), 8.

108. *Kongzi Jiayu* 21/41/8–42/14.

109. Christopher W. Gowans, *Innocence Lost: An Examination of Inescapable Moral Wrongdoing* (New York: Oxford University Press, 1994), 234.

Conclusion

THE VALUE OF VULNERABILITY

"To be humane, one must have courage."

仁者 , 必有勇 。

(*ANALECTS* 14.4)

MAX WEBER CLAIMED that, "Completely absent in Confucian ethic was any tension between . . . ethical demand and human shortcoming."[1] In Weber's Confucian worldview, the exemplary moral agent is always capable of being fully moral. A failure to be moral is the fault of the agent, not the fault of the possibilities afforded by the world. While harmony theorists vary from Weber in a number of significant ways, the harmony thesis largely accords with this part of Weber's theory. For harmony theorists, value conflicts in a Confucian worldview are epistemic, not ontological, and since being moral is fully in our control, our integrity can be made invulnerable to external agencies. In short, while not always easy to achieve, especially for non-sages, we have the capacity to tend to all values at stake in any situation, and we can do this without significant moral distress. As such, we can unconditionally maintain our identity conferring commitments and preserve our ability to encourage others to fulfill their roles in relationships.

The purpose of chapter 1 was to show how those within the Confucian tradition put forth similar arguments. Chapter 2 not only contextualized the harmony thesis within the Western philosophical discourse of value conflicts but also demonstrated how the harmony thesis might be further developed in Confucian terms that accord with parts of the Western philosophical tradition. Chapters 3 through 7 provided an alternative reading of early Confucian texts. This reading called for recognizing the possibility of irresolvable value conflicts and the vulnerability of integrity. In this portion of the book I examine the implications of my reading. Particularly, I aim to spell out the value of vulnerability in activities such as learning (especially learning to be moral), caring for other people (and being cared for by other people), and trusting others (and being trusted). My argument is that vulnerability, as an inherent part of human life, is valuable in instrumental and intrinsic ways. Instrumentally it enables moral development, social formation, trust, and maturity. Intrinsically, vulnerability is a state of care or, more specifically, a basic attitude of interest where one cares *about* things. As I detail in this conclusion, a particularly Confucian account of vulnerability sees self-cultivation as a process of learning to transform this state of caring about things to actions and attitudes of properly caring *for* things.[2] In other words, we ought to expand (*tui* 推) our incipient tendencies to value things such that we come to care for things in morally appropriate ways. These actions and attitudes are guided by the ritual tradition. This Confucian account of vulnerability advocates developing optimal degrees of vulnerability by means of ritual practice. As such, instead of seeking to eliminate vulnerability or treat it as a threat to human flourishing, we ought to recognize the value of vulnerability in good human living. In substantiating this argument I articulate a uniquely Confucian view of vulnerability and then show how this view of vulnerability relates to goods such as moral development, care, and trust.[3]

A Confucian Theory of Vulnerability

Jonathan Chan provides one of the few attempts to directly address the topic of vulnerability in the context of Confucianism. In his article titled "Health Care and Human Vulnerability: A Confucian Perspective," Chan argues that Confucianism presents a robust explanation for the intuition that we have special responsibilities to at-risk groups.[4] Chan largely follows the practice of defining vulnerability in negative terms (as explained in the introduction of this book). He defines it not only as susceptibility to injury but also as receptivity to the "prejudices" or "unjust discriminations" of those in power.[5] The responsible society, according to Chan, ensures that everyone is capable of living a quality life free from harm and oppression. Chan relies on a capabilities theory developed by Amaryta Sen and Martha Nussbaum to discuss the threats to at-risk groups, including children, women, the mentally and physical handicapped, and the elderly. While Chan successfully articulates the ways in which Confucian ideas might inform the treatment of these vulnerable groups, his analysis does not avoid many of the shortcomings of understanding vulnerability in negative terms, including conceptualizing it as a marginal experience rather than as a condition central to human experience. Indeed, my sense is that early Confucian texts can articulate a more comprehensive sense of vulnerability that is not limited to at-risk groups, although tending to the specific vulnerabilities of these groups remains important.

In chapter 7 I discussed a Confucian notion of the self that took human beings as interconnected and porous entities. The body, in this view, is the storehouse of integrity as well as the site of interaction with other things in the world. With regard to this conception of the body, Tu Weiming explains, "The body, so conceived, is not a static structure to be observed, dissected, and analyzed as an object but should be seen as more akin to energy fields. It is like a moving stream rather than an island. The body made of *qi* 氣 is an open system, encountering, enduring, engendering, and transforming."[6] In this sense, the body is a vulnerable entity open and receptive to other entities in the world.

Judith Butler argues for a notion of the body with which many Confucians can relate. She states, "The boundary of who I am is the boundary of the body, but the boundary of the body never fully belongs to me."[7] Butler goes on to discuss vulnerability with regard to the body as "the feeling of aliveness."[8] In many senses, the feeling of aliveness captures a Confucian conception of vulnerability. For early Confucians, to be human is to be vulnerable. Said somewhat differently, to be alive is to be receptive to the affect of others.

The notion of *ren* 仁, which most scholars take as a central concept in early Confucian thought, expresses this idea of aliveness. As mentioned in chapter 2, the character is comprised of two parts—the character for "person" (*ren* 人) on the left and the character for "two" (*er* 二) on the right.[9] *Ren* 仁 can be explained as the connection between two (or more) people, and scholars often translate it as "humaneness," "human-heartedness," or even "co-humanity." Many early Confucian text discuss *ren* 仁 as a defining characteristic of human beings, playing on the semantic relationship between the characters *ren* 仁 ("humaneness") and *ren* 人 ("person" or "human").[10] Several texts define *ren* 仁 in terms of *ai* 愛, usually translated as "love" but also understood as "care." *Ren* 仁, in this light, is a sensitivity to the ways in which we ought to care for our connections to each other. It is a desire to care for others that can be cultivated or stamped out. This notion of *ren* 仁 is famously illustrated by Mengzi's example of seeing a child about to be harmed (2A6). In the context of explaining how good government is based on "having a heart that cannot bear [the suffering] of others" 不忍人之心, Mengzi explains that if we were to suddenly see a child about to fall into a well, we would "all have a heart [that felt] alarm, grief, and commiseration" 皆有怵惕惻隱之心. Mengzi claims that we would have such feelings even before reflecting on whether or not we liked the child. In other words, according to Mengzi, human beings have a prereflective tendency to be concerned about the condition of others. He goes so far as to say that anyone "lacking a heart of commiseration is not a human being" 無惻隱之心，非人也. In other words, to *be* human is to be vulnerable to the suffering of others; to be otherwise is to be unhuman or inhumane.[11] Mengzi's point in the context of this passage is that a good ruler will build on these compassionate impulses—he will learn to recognize them in situations where he acted appropriately and apply them to other circumstances. This is the basis for Mengzi's notion of "humane government" 仁政. His point for our purposes, however, is that *ren* 仁, understood as an openness to the suffering of others, is a defining characteristic of being human. As stated in *Mengzi* 7B16, "One who is humane is human" 仁也者，人也.[12]

While Mengzi defines *ren* 仁 in terms that fit with negative definitions of vulnerability, there are many other passages that put forth a more positive notion of *ren* 仁 as affectivity, openness, or the feeling of aliveness. In the *Analects* (4.3) Kongzi explains, "Only the humane person is able to embrace others and to despise others" 唯仁者能好人，能惡人. In this somewhat pithy remark, Kongzi argues that being *ren* 仁 is about experiencing and expressing the wide range of feelings associated with being human. What this suggests is that while human beings are born with the natural capacity to feel for others, we must carefully tend to this capacity in order to maximize its potential. Only the truly humane person is able to really love and to hate. Said differently, only the appropriately vulnerable person is able to establish genuine connections with others that allow for deep relationships of mutual feeling and mutual development.

The notion of *ren* 仁 is sometimes explicitly connected with life itself. The *Shuoyuan* 《說苑》, for instance, explains that "the humane person does not harm life" 仁人不害生.[13] The same text also contains a dialogue between Zigong 子貢 (520–446 BCE) and Kongzi, set in a context where Kongzi stops to observe the water of a large river. Zigong asks Kongzi about why he observes the water. Kongzi explains that water can be likened unto a number of important virtues, hence observing water provides insight into these virtues. In speaking about *ren* 仁 he states, "Wherever [water] reaches there is life, [and so it] is like *ren* 仁" 所及者生，似仁.[14] In this line of thought, *ren* 仁 is a sensitivity to life, and a virtue that fosters life itself.[15] Later Confucians such as Cheng Hao 程顥 (1032–1085) build on these kinds of passages to explain, "[*Ren* 仁] is best observed in the desire all things have to live" 萬物之生意最可觀.[16] In other words, *ren* 仁 is an inclination or even an enthusiasm for life. To be *ren* 仁 is to be sensitive to one's own life and to the lives of others. Cheng Hao, relying on medical texts with counterparts in early China, describes the lack of *ren* 仁 as a kind of numbness or an insensitivity.[17] These texts define the lack of *ren* 仁 as a medical condition where one loses feeling in one's arms, legs, or other parts of the body (similar to the contemporary way one might say that a leg or other appendage has fallen asleep). Cheng Hao states, "When an appendage of the body is afflicted such that it is unaware of pain or sensation, [we] call it 'not-*ren* 仁'" 人之一肢病，不知痛癢，謂之不仁.[18] In other words, when part of the body loses its ability to feel, it is no longer *ren* 仁. For Cheng Hao, however, this becomes a metaphor for the ways human beings lose the ability to feel for others. Similar to the English word "numbness," Cheng Hao uses "not-*ren*" 不仁 to describe physical as well as affective (or even moral) states of insensitivity.

Later Confucians also describe *ren* 仁 by using the term *gantong* 感通—a phrase originating in the *Yijing* 《易經》, which refers to the way in which things in the world interact with each other.[19] The contemporary scholar Wang Huaiyu, in an article titled "*Ren* 仁 and *Gantong* 感通: Openness of Heart and the Root of Confucianism," explains *gantong* 感通 as follows:

> *Gan* 感 has a wide range of meanings including affection, perception, sensation, reception, animation, inspiration, and sympathy, as well as influence, intercourse, and infection. As a verb, it can be used to express both the active and passive senses of "to move" and "touch" or "be moved" and "be touched." In general, *gan* 感 describes the action or process—mainly affective in nature—through which human, natural, and spiritual beings are interconnected. On the other hand, the major meanings of *tong* 通 are "to reach," "pass through," "open," and "transmit," and "to correspond," "communicate," and "interact," as well as "to comprehend." As a noun, *tong* 通 refers to "a passage," "a thoroughfare," or "a hole"—an opening or orifice that runs through and discloses the internal body of a thing. The core meaning boils down to an open way of transmission among different bodies and locations. Accordingly, the phrase *gantong* 感通 carries the literal meaning of "to open oneself to and be affected by."[20]

Although Wang does not use the term "vulnerability," it is clearly applicable to his notion of *gantong* 感通. Coincidentally, in other places Wang argues that *gantong* 感通 is key to understanding *de* 德, or integrity.[21]

While *ren* 仁 is a feeling of aliveness or a sensitivity to life, it does not entail an unlimited or unrestrained sensitivity. Indeed, early Confucians recognized the need to constrain this sensitivity in sometimes doing things such as harming life. In *Analects* 3.17, Zigong expresses a desire to do away with a ritual sacrifice in order to spare the life of a sheep. Kongzi responds, "You care about the sheep; [while] I care about the ritual" 爾愛其羊，我愛其禮. Kongzi, in other words, recognizes Zigong's concern for the animal but argues that ritual is also important. Rather than allowing Zigong's concern for life to void the sacrifice, Kongzi suggests that there are more important things than the life of a sheep. Coincidentally, in *Analects* 12.22 Kongzi also employs the notion of *ai* 愛 ("care"). Here he uses it to define *ren* 仁, explaining that *ren* 仁 is "caring for others" 愛人. While these two circumstances of Kongzi invoking *ai* 愛 are not likely related, the language of "care" 愛 in the context of preserving life, in combination with the fact that Kongzi defines *ren* 仁 as care, suggests that *ren* 仁 bears some relation to passage

3.17.[22] The *Han Shi Waizhuan* actually ties several of these terms together and explains how *ren* 仁 requires constraint. It states, "*Ren* 仁 is when care comes forth and emerges from [our] genuine dispositions. Rightness is when this care is constrained (*jie* 節) and patterned in appropriate [ways]. Ritual propriety is when care is exerted with reverence and respect" 愛由情出，謂之仁，節愛理宜，謂之義，致愛恭謹，謂之禮.[23] These passages argue that *ren* 仁 requires a kind of restraint or further guidance. Without this guidance *ren* 仁 risks interfering with other goods in life. Put in the language of vulnerability, our openness to others is not meant to be boundless. There are optimal degrees of vulnerability.

In *Analects* 12.1 Kongzi discusses *ren* 仁 in relation to the restraining power of ritual. When one of his disciples asks about *ren* 仁 Kongzi replies, "*Ren* 仁 is put into action when the self is restrained by means of the repeated practice of ritual" 克己復禮為仁.[24] In the view of this passage, ritual provides the means of properly expressing *ren* 仁. As I explain next, ritual enables *ren* 仁 by ensuring that one's sensitivity is neither excessive nor deficient. I have written extensively about ritual in the context of early Confucianism. In *The Dysfunction of Ritual in Early Confucianism* I argue that *li* 禮, usually translated as "ritual" or "rituals," have impressive and expressive functions. Rituals, in this view, serve to impress upon ritual performers proper dispositions such that their responses to the things they confront are neither drastic nor deficient.

This is well illustrated in the context of mourning the death of other people. The sentiments experienced at the death of a family member or friend are commonly discussed in early Confucian texts. For most people described in these texts, experiencing grief at the loss of a family member is an overwhelming event; however, for others the loss of a loved one may not evoke much grief at all. For the former group of people, the sentiments of grief can lead them to take all kinds of actions in an attempt to mourn the loss. They might refrain from eating food, neglect important responsibilities, or even physically harm themselves. Mourning rituals provide a series of practices that allow for the controlled expression of grief. Fasting, for instance, as a part of mourning is given a specific starting point and an ending point according to the funerary rites. Fasting, therefore, gives vent to the feelings of grief but does not permanently harm the health of the person fasting. The latter group of people, however, must be spurred to grief. For these people, the mourning rites serve to stir their feelings of grief, giving them a form of practices that enables them to more deeply experience the loss. Confucian mourning rites, for instance, advocate visiting the home of the deceased the same way one would visit them while alive—after searching the home and not finding them, the mourner confronts the loss of the relationship by crying and sobbing. In short, the sentiments of grief, manifest in mourning, are not to be excessive (*guo* 過) nor insufficient (*buji* 不及 or *buzhi* 不至).[25]

Rituals, therefore, encourage and allow for the proper expression of refined dispositions. While the practice of ritual may focus on particular ceremonies, a ritual attitude is meant to extend to the daily affairs of life. In *Analects* 12.1, Kongzi actually goes on to say, "If not [seen] in accordance with a ritualized attitude do not look [at it]; if not [listened to] in accordance with a ritualized attitude do not listen [to it]; if not [said] in accordance with a ritualized attitude do not say [it]; if not [done] in accordance with a ritualized attitude do not do [it]" 非禮勿視，非禮勿聽，非禮勿言，非禮勿動. Ritual, as such, is about cultivating the skills and virtues that enable one to respond appropriately to whatever one confronts in life.

The notion of *li* 禮 is often associated with *zhi* 治, which means "to order," "to organize," or "to manage." Rituals are about ordering the inner dispositions of people in the context of constant interaction. With regard to vulnerability, rituals cultivate optimal affectivity—they rein it in when excessive and encourage it when insufficient. Channeling water, which is etymologically related to *zhi* 治, is a reoccurring metaphor in early Confucian texts for understanding the functions of ritual. Similar to the way in which a levee not only shapes the direction of water flow but also enables the flow of water, ritual both shapes the dispositions of ritual agents and allows for the expression of their dispositions. Rituals do this by scripting proper interaction—they encourage actions that cultivate sensitivity when it is lacking and advocate actions that diminish sensitivity when excessive.

A passage from the *Kongzi Jiayu* 《孔子家語》 illustrates these effects of ritual with regard to *ren* 仁. In an early Confucian context, the mourning rites are carefully scripted. with one's actions dependent on how closely one is related to the deceased.

> Zilu wore the mourning clothing worn for mourning one's sister. He could have removed it [because the requisite time had passed], but did not remove it. Kongzi asked, "Why don't you remove [the mourning clothing]?"
>
> 子路有姊之喪，可以除之矣，而弗除。孔子曰：「何不除也？」
>
> Zilu replied, "I have few siblings, and cannot bear [the loss]."
>
> 子路曰：「吾寡兄弟，而弗忍也。」
>
> Kongzi responded, "No ordinary person could bear such a loss. [This is why] the early kings fashioned ritual. [They did it such that] those who exceeded the proper bounds could look back to the proper bounds and reach them; while those who fell short [of the proper bounds] could

stretch [for them] and move toward them." Upon hearing this, Zilu immediately removed the clothing.

孔子曰：「行道之人皆弗忍。先王制禮，過之者俯而就之，不至者企而望之。」子路聞之，遂除之。[26]

This passage illustrates the impressive functions of ritual. Zilu continued to wear the mourning clothing worn when mourning one's sister because he could not bear (*furen* 弗忍) her loss. Kongzi explains that not bearing the loss of a loved one is a common response, yet ritual was created to ensure that grief was neither excessive nor deficient. The usage of *ren* 忍 ("bear" or "endure") in this passage is worth noting. Besides being cognate with *ren* 仁, it also appears as part of the explanation for *ren* 仁 in passages quoted earlier such as *Mengzi* 2A6. In that passage, "not bearing" 不忍 the suffering of others was a key component of *ren* 仁. Later in the *Mengzi*, Mengzi also uses phraseology similar to the *Kongzi Jiayu* passage to talk about *ren* 仁 in terms of broadening the category of things one "cannot bear" 不忍.[27] Texts such as the *Baihutong* 《白虎通》 state the matter more directly. It explains, "To be *ren* 仁 is not to bear [the suffering of others]" 仁者，不忍也.[28] *Ren* 仁, therefore, is a sensitivity to the condition of things around us. The *Kongzi Jiayu* passage suggests that such sensitivity, however, must be managed by the dictates of ritual.

When taken together, these passages argue that human beings, as porous and open entities, are naturally affected by other things in the world. While on the one hand we ought to expand our sympathies—becoming more and more aware of things beyond ourselves, on the other hand we should strive for optimal degrees of vulnerability. Ritual provides a means of experiencing other people and other things in a context that encourages the appropriate degree of vulnerability. As Tu Weiming explains, "*Li* 禮 points to a concrete way whereby one enters into communion with others. . . . [It] is understood as a movement leading toward an authentic relationship."[29] Ritual enables genuine relationships by managing vulnerability, where "management" is understood not as eliminating vulnerability but rather as ensuring its appropriateness for any context.

This Confucian account of vulnerability contributes to broader conversations on the topic of vulnerability. Specifically, it does this in several ways. For one, it foregrounds the notion of vulnerability as an essential characteristic of human beings. To be human is to be vulnerable, and, as such, vulnerability is not simply a source for ethics and learning but a source for identity itself. Vulnerability shapes not only what we ought to do but who we are. Second, building on the work of vulnerability theorists such as Erinn Gilson, many Confucians would argue that vulnerability is good in instrumental ways; yet, differing from Gilson, many Confucians would argue that vulnerability is also intrinsically good.

Instrumentally it enables values such as morality, trust, and maturity. Intrinsically, vulnerability, understood in terms of *ren* 仁, is a kind of caring *about* things. To be vulnerable is to be in a state of care. Such a capacity is good in itself, although it is indeterminately good because it may turn out that such care is misdirected or inappropriate. Caring about things ought to be cultivated into appropriately caring *for* things by means of ritual practice. Said differently, and in distinction from scholars that equate vulnerability with risk, vulnerability is more than risk, which is wholly neutral. Rather, being vulnerable is to be a caring being, and while it may turn out that certain things are more or less worthy of care, the fact that we care at the very least merits our appreciation.

Confucian accounts of vulnerability also contribute to broader conversations about vulnerability by providing a robust notion of self-cultivation aimed to foster the optimal degree of vulnerability by means of ritual practice. One idea discussions about the positive notion of vulnerability tend to neglect is how vulnerability ought not only be managed but cultivated to an optimal degree.

The Value of Vulnerability

Amy Olberding makes an intriguing claim in writing about the role of grief in the *Analects*. She states, "The ethical potency of grief resides, for Kongzi, in the willingness to lead a life that *courts* certain species of pain in order to achieve higher order values, and these values reside in our relations with others."[30] According to Olberding, Kongzi advocates "leading a life that *promotes* grief." In other words, Kongzi demonstrates that human beings should live in such a way that they remain open to being affected by the loss of others—particularly those others who are close to them. Allowing for the possibility of loss enables us to realize important values that can only be realized by risking loss. Said in more positive terms with regard to vulnerability, vulnerability enables a series of values that can only be realized when we remain open to the affect of others. These values include moral development, social formation (and the realization of relationships), trust, and maturity. In this section I detail how vulnerability fosters these values starting with a brief discussion of learning since learning to be moral, social, trusting (and trustworthy), as well as mature, is predicated on a kind of epistemic vulnerability that enables the acquisition of these and other values. I also say more about the intrinsic value of vulnerability.

Learning is a significant concept in early Confucian thought. The *Analects* begins with the character *xue* 學 ("learning" or "to learn"), and Kongzi describes himself as someone "fond of learning" 好學.[31] Kongzi is also quoted as saying, "When the exemplary person learns the Way [he] will care for others" 君子學道則愛人.[32] Other passages more explicitly connect learning with humaneness.[33] In a practical sense, early Confucian learning entailed gaining skills of ritual, music, and archery (among other skills). It also entailed gaining knowledge of poetry, history, and politics (among other areas of knowledge). In all of this, learning is understood as moral development. The *Xunzi* 《荀子》 begins with a chapter on learning and stresses the dedication, focus, and introspection necessary to learn. Xunzi highlights the fact that learning is transformative—it "enters the ears, impacts the mindful heart, and spreads to the four limbs" 入乎耳，著乎心，布乎四體.[34] Learning is about "accumulating goodness" 積善 and is only complete when one becomes a "sage" 聖人. Xunzi concludes his discourse on learning by explaining that as one learns one develops a "firm grasp of integrity" 德操. He goes on to say that firmly grasping integrity allows one to develop a stable (*ding* 定) commitment to self-development such that one is able to respond (*ying* 應) appropriately to any situation. The final result is that one "becomes human" 成人. The notion of becoming human is a normative claim about the potential of human beings to, in Xunzi's terms, "participate in [the transformative process of] the heavens and the earth" 參於天地.[35] In other words, learning is a process of understanding the ways in which human beings can assist the natural forces of the world to create a flourishing environment. For these and other reasons contemporary scholars have sometimes explained Confucian programs of learning as *xue zuoren* 學做人, or "learning to be human," where human beings are understood as interconnected entities, or centers of relationships.

In this view, learning is a moral act, and the acquisition of skills like archery is about learning to be moral. The *Liji* 《禮記》 contains a chapter titled "Sheyi" 射義, which translates to "the significance [or meaning] of archery." This chapter explains the parallels between archery and moral performance. It states that archery has an internal and an external component—internally the archer learns to straighten his focus (*zhizheng* 志正); externally he learns to keep his body upright (*tizhi* 體直). Only after doing these things can the archer begin to think about hitting the target (*zhonggu* 中鵠). The chapter goes on to explain that each role in society has its metaphorical target—fathers have a "fatherly target" 父鵠, sons have a "sonly target" 子鵠, and rulers have a "rulerly target" 君鵠.[36] In acting in one's role of father, son, or ruler, one aims for the target. Archery, therefore, becomes a means of training people (men in particular) to fulfill their social roles—one cultivates the proper inner and outer comportment and then strives to properly perform one's roles in society. These roles are expressions of one's humaneness, and they contribute to a flourishing world. As such, the "Sheyi" chapter states that "archery is the Way of humaneness" 射者，仁之道也.[37]

These passages suggest that vulnerability functions in several respects with regard to learning. For one, human beings must be "completed" 成 in order to become fully developed human beings.[38] We require transformation beyond our current state. In this sense, we must be open to learning to be more than we currently are. Erinn Gilson speaks about a similar program of learning in terms of "epistemic vulnerability." Gilson explains, "Undoing ignorance involves cultivating the attitude of one who is epistemically vulnerable rather than that of a masterful, invulnerable knower who has nothing to learn from others or for whom others are merely vehicles for the transmission of information."[39] While Gilson uses the term "epistemic" she also stresses that this learning is affective and bodily. She goes on to say, "To be epistemically vulnerable, therefore, is not just to be open to new ideas, but to be open to the ambivalence of our emotional and bodily responses and to reflecting on those responses in nuanced ways." The epistemically vulnerable person is "open to altering not just one's ideas and beliefs, but one's self and sense of one's self."[40] Vulnerability, therefore, is a precursor for learning. If we are not open to changing ourselves, we cannot learn.

As Gilson explains, epistemic vulnerability provides reasons for reflecting on our responses. More broadly speaking, vulnerability motivates moral agents to reflect on what counts as meaningful. The possibility of harm can lead to a healthy reappraisal of tradition. Risk compels reflection, and when done on a communal level, guided by concern for ourselves and others, vulnerability provides the impetus for reconfiguring values in a changing world. When a community needs to change, vulnerability motivates those invested in the community to reconsider the contours of association. It also serves to identify new things of value that ought to be incorporated into the community. Vulnerability, in this light, provides the conditions for learning, including learning about what things in the world are worthy of value and how we ought to relate to those things.[41]

Vulnerability also enables ethics and moral development, which in a Confucian context is inextricably tied to the realization of one's relationships with other people and other things. With regard to the connection between ethics and vulnerability, Gilson claims, "If we are not vulnerable, we have no need for ethics, and it is precisely because we are vulnerable—can be affected and made to feel sorrow, concern, or empathy—that we feel any compulsion to respond ethically."[42] In other words, vulnerability provides motivation for responding to the concerns of others. It allows us to feel for (and with) others, and it encourages us to care for others. Early Confucians would largely agree with Gilson.

In an early Confucian context the self is enmeshed in relationships, which means that tending to relationships is also a process of self-discovery or self-development. In this context, vulnerability serves as evidence that we cannot be alone—we require others in cultivating ourselves. Indeed, this means that aspects of our self are tied to aspects of others and that the project of constructing a good society is necessary for personal development. In contemporary Chinese, the term for ethics is *lunli* 倫理, which is based on early uses of the two characters

that literally mean "ordered relationships." This suggests that the social aspects of
life are mapped onto the ethical aspects of life such that there is no "ethics" apart
from social relationships. We cannot learn to be ethical in isolation from others.
Xunzi makes a related point:

> In living life, human beings cannot be without community. [Yet] com-
> munities that lack distinct social roles will be contentious; and when con-
> tentious [they] will be chaotic; and when chaotic [they] will be ruined.
> Therefore, lacking distinct social roles is a great danger for human beings;
> and having distinct social roles is the root of well-being for all under
> heaven. This is why [good] rulers of people attend to the essentials of dis-
> tinct social roles. Those who enhance them, enhance the root of all under
> heaven; those who secure them, secure the root of all under heaven; [and]
> those who enrich them, enrich the root of all under heaven. In antiquity
> the early kings [created] distinct social roles and divisions—classifying
> and differentiating among things. [They] thereby initiated [divisions]
> between the beautiful and the disgusting; the thick and the thin; the
> relaxed or the joyful and the toilsome or the fatigued. [They] did not do
> this for the sake of being praised as unconstrained, magnificent, extrava-
> gant, or handsome. [Rather, they] illuminated the patterns of humane-
> ness (*ren* 仁) and followed its course.

> 人之生不能無群，群而無分則爭，爭則亂，亂則窮矣。故無分
> 者，人之大害也；有分者，天下之本利也；而人君者，所以
> 管分之樞要也。故美之者，是美天下之本也；安之者，是安
> 天下之本也；貴之者，是貴天下之本也。古者先王分割而等異
> 之也，故使或美或惡，或厚或薄，或佚或樂，或劬或勞，非特
> 以為淫泰夸麗之聲，將以明仁之文，通仁之順也。[43]

In Xunzi's view, human beings naturally group together. If groups lack distinct
social roles they inevitably end in chaos. On the other hand, groups with distinct
social roles can enrich each member of the group as long as these distinctions
accord with humaneness. When groups operate in accordance with humaneness,
they flourish. Said in broader terms, society should be organized on the basis of the
interconnections and compassions people have for each other. Humaneness is the
surest foundation for lasting social formation. When relationships are structured
on the basis of humaneness, all those involved in the relationship are enriched.

Put in the language of vulnerability, people naturally form relationships
and are inherently susceptible to those others in the relationships. Properly performing one's roles cannot be done without being vulnerable to others. Being

a good father requires one to be affected by one's children in ways one cannot fully control. Being a good friend requires one to be susceptible to being changed by one's friends. Vulnerability enables the realization of relationships that form larger structures of social order. In other words, vulnerability is foundational for society. Vulnerability opens up opportunities for deep engagement with other human beings. It provides motivation to care for others and lays the grounds for realizing the obligations entailed in relationships.

Vulnerability also enables trust, particularly, interpersonal trust.[44] Trust is more than simply relying on others to provide goods or services. While such reliance entails a degree of vulnerability, trust goes deeper—it requires believing that the person trusted cares for one's holistic well-being. As such, trust opens one's self up to harm in the form of betrayal, but it also allows for the development of meaningful relationships that play essential roles in the formation of society. When a child trusts a parent, he or she is able to explore other relationships and other areas of life, knowing that a parent's support will provide security for certain aspects of his or her well-being. Trust, therefore, fosters social development. It is also intrinsically valuable as a sign of respect. When we trust another, we demonstrate that the person trusted is an individual of worth.

In an early Confucian context, several terms capture aspects of trust, including *xin* 信, *ren* 任, *ze* 責, and *kao* 靠. The term *xin* 信 is especially relevant.[45] It is comprised of the characters "person" 人 and "words" 言 and is often described in the texts and by commentators as an ability to follow through on one's word. Hence it tends to be translated as "trustworthiness." Kwong-loi Shun, for instance, explains that *xin* 信 is "the quality of being worthy of trust, a quality that one attains through a history of matching one's representation of things to the way things are."[46] David Hall and Roger Ames define *xin* 信 as "the doing of what one says with earnestness."[47] *Xin* 信 is often discussed in the context of ministers serving rulers, and as such the focus of *xin* 信 is on becoming the kind of person worthy of handling important affairs. *Xin* 信, however, is also discussed as a virtue between friends. Kongzi's disciple Zengzi 曾子 (505–436 BCE), for instance, is said to have reflected on three questions daily. One of those questions is "whether or not [I have] been trustworthy in [my] interactions with friends" 與朋友交而不信乎.[48] In other passages, *xin* 信 is related to acting with sincerity, or *cheng* 誠 (which is graphically composed of the characters "words" 言 and "completion" 成).[49]

The contemporary scholar Cecilia Wee, in an article-length study of *xin* 信, provides a useful description of the concept as it appears in many early Confucian texts. Wee states, "The person of *xin* 信 has some capacity for reflection, since she does not rashly make commitments but considers first whether she can fulfill them. She possesses a sense of what is appropriate, since she is concerned to ensure that her words are appropriate to her future actions. At its heart, *xin* 信 is an expression of the care that one needs to take in one's transactions with others, and the responsibility that one must fulfill toward others."[50] According to Wee, *xin* 信 provides the basis for thoughtful relationships where those in the relationship are careful and honest about their abilities to fulfill their obligations.

For most of these examples, the focus of trust is on the one trusted, and this emphasis holds for many appearances of *xin* 信 in early Confucian texts. At the same time, there are other passages that discuss *xin* 信 in light of the person doing the trusting. Mengzi, for instance, warned rulers, "[If you] do not trust those who are humane and worthy then [your] state will be empty and vacuous" 不信仁賢，則國空虛.[51] In other words, not trusting the right people will lead to the ruin of one's state. *Xin* 信 is also employed as trust in more personal relationships, especially the relationship between friends.[52] In *Analects* 5.26, Kongzi asks his disciples Zilu and Yan Hui about their ambitions. Zilu explains, "[I] would like not to be upset if my friends borrow [my] carriage or coat, and ruin them" 願車馬、衣輕裘，與朋友共。敝之而無憾. Yan Hui, in an attempt to do one better than Zilu, replies, "[I] would like to not boast of my accomplishments, nor make [others] toil with labor" 願無伐善，無施勞. Kongzi recognizes what is going on. He understands Zilu's implicit desire for wealth as well as his desire to cultivate a kind of trust in his friends. He also recognizes Yan Hui's soft-handed rebuke of Zilu—not wanting to show off his wealth, nor placing undue tasks on others. Integrating his disciples' ambitions, and adding a personal thought about Zilu and Yan Hui, he replies, "[I would like to] ease the burdens of the old, trust my friends, and cherish the young" 老者安之，朋友信之，少者懷之. While this scene is a touching display of Kongzi's ability to care for his disciples in ways that mediate differences and also express his fondness for them, the point for our purposes here is that it also emphasizes the importance of trusting friends.

In the *Analects*, Kongzi also makes a broader point about trust. He states, "[I] don't know how someone without trust is able to do [it]. If a large or small carriage does not have a linchpin how could one drive it" 人而無信，不知其可也。大車無輗，小車無軏，其何以行之哉?[53] This passage invokes the metaphor of *xin* 信 understood in terms of the linchpin used for connecting horses to carriages. Without a linchpin the carriage does not move, and, without trust, society cannot move forward. Kongzi's point is that trust is a virtue that binds roles together. *Xin* 信 enables the functioning of society.

Interestingly, texts such as the *Analects* stress the importance of *xin* 信 but also recognize that it must be supplemented by other virtues in order to fully bring about the Confucian *dao* 道. *Analects* 17.6, for instance, states that *xin* 信 is one of five virtues required for enacting humaneness, and 17.8 explains that *xin* 信 can turn into a vice if not supplemented with proper learning.[54] Both of these passages highlight the relationship between *xin* 信 and vulnerability by relating *xin* 信 to humaneness and learning.[55]

Xin 信 grew in importance for Confucians in the Han dynasty, as figures such as Dong Zhongshu 董仲舒 (c. 179–104 BCE) and Ban Gu 班固 (32–92) included it along with humaneness, rightness (*yi* 義), ritual propriety (*li* 禮) and wisdom (*zhi* 智) in the category of virtues that human beings are born with and need to develop for full self-realization.[56]

Vulnerability enables maturity, particularly moral maturity. When meaningful things are at risk, people naturally worry about those things. In these situations we might be tempted to protect that which matters to us by shoring up our vulnerability. We might, for instance, work to strengthen that which is vulnerable or to eliminate that which threatens meaningful things, thereby aiming for a state of invulnerability. While in many situations invulnerability is a worthy goal, the mature agent is able to recognize when vulnerability is preferable to invulnerability. He or she discerns optimal states of vulnerability. As such, maturity is about learning to live with risk and ambiguity. It entails seeking after higher order values (such as healthy relationships and virtue) when lower order values (such as recognition or comfortable living) are at stake. Maturity involves coping with discomfort in the hope of gaining long-term rewards. Brene Brown, in her work on vulnerability, uses the language of "leaning in to the discomfort" to describe a mature way of dealing with vulnerability.[57] Rather than shutting oneself off when confronted with situations of potential harm, one accepts the unease of not being able to control aspects of these situations. Brown describes this as "wholeheartedness," which she defines as "facing uncertainty, exposure, and emotional risks, and knowing that [one is] enough."[58] For Brown, wholeheartedness is about coming to learn that one is worthy of love and connection, which then instills within oneself a sense of courage in maintaining one's vulnerability. Put into my language used here, maturity is cultivating an attitude of resilience in order to accept that meaningful things might be transformed in undetermined ways. It is about cultivating a confidence that one can endure the frustration of righteous desires and that one will be able to integrate negative experiences in ways that are healthy for oneself and for others. It is about believing that the relationships vulnerability enables are worth the risk.

In early Confucian texts, Kongzi is held up as a paradigmatic figure. He models several virtues, including maturity.[59] Readers are encouraged to admire Kongzi's ability to not only engage meaningfully with other people but to reengage in meaning-creating activities when denied optimal relations with those people. What makes Kongzi worthy of emulation is that he lives a fully engaged life. Such a life is worthy of emulating in the sense of seeking to imitate his devotion despite his pain. Said somewhat differently with regard to value conflicts, there is something admirable about someone who understands the weight of the values at stake in various situations, realizes that he or she may not be able to ful-fill all values, may even need to destroy some value, and yet acts under the weight of the situation. Maturity, in this view, involves fortitude when the obscuring of one's conscience becomes the price of making the best out of a bad situation.

Maturity is depicted in the narratives told about the lives of early Confucians such as Kongzi. Like many of the other concepts discussed in this study, there is no one Chinese term that corresponds to the notion of maturity, although the terms *cheng* 成 or *chengren* 成人 (literally, "becoming a complete person," and in contemporary Chinese, "an adult") display a similar range of meanings. From an early Confucian perspective, people should aim at becoming a "mature person" 成人. In the *Analects*, Zilu asks about the qualities of a *chengren* 成人. Kongzi replies that the mature person is wise (*zhi* 知) and without selfish desires (*buyu* 不欲) and that when "encountering benefit, [he] reflects on what is right" 見利思義, and when "encountering danger, [he is willing to] give his life" 見危授命.[60] The "Jiyi" 祭義 chapter of the *Liji* emphasizes the importance of making sacrificial offerings to one's parents after they die. In this context, it speaks about "the Way of the mature person" 成人之道, represented by the "filial son" 孝子 who deeply cared for his parents while alive and properly sacrifices to them after their death. When offering the sacrifices he is "careful and attentive, preoccupied [by thoughts of his parents]; [he appears] as if unable to bear [the weight of the sacrifices], as if [he's] about to drop them" 孝子如執玉，如奉盈，洞洞屬屬然，如弗勝，如將失之.[61] In these views, the mature person is able to attend to the important needs of others, even when such attention may come at personal cost. When sacrificing to one's deceased parents, the mature person remains vul-nerable to their absence in his life. The final lines of the "Jiyi" passage suggest that the filial son is in those moments still stricken by the loss of his parents such that he appears to be on the verge of collapse. From the perspective of the text, the vulnerability of the filial son is key to his maturity. The filial son confronts the sorrow of loss, and, we might imagine, as a mature person he integrates it into a broader performance of a meaningful life.

To be vulnerable is to have an impulse to care. While this impulse should be transformed by learning in order attain to the right degree in the right context, it is nonetheless intrinsically good in that vulnerability is a primitive state of care. I have already said quite a bit about early Confucian conceptions of *ren* 仁, which best captures this notion of care. It is worth noting here, however, that many early Confucian texts tend to speak of *ren* 仁 in two respects—*ren* 仁 is something naturally present in human beings, but it is also something achieved through the hard work of cultivation.[62] In *Analects* 7.30, Kongzi remarks, "Is *ren* 仁 far away? [If] I [simply] desire it, it is here" 仁遠乎哉？我欲仁，斯仁至矣. Famously,

Mengzi explains that *ren* 仁 is a natural characteristic of the mindful heart of all people (*ren renxin ye* 仁，人心也).[63] To care, therefore, is a natural proclivity of human beings, and to have a mind to care is a good thing. On the other hand, *ren* 仁 also requires cultivation. In the *Analects* (8.7) Zengzi says, "When one takes up the task of *ren* 仁, is it not heavy? Stopping only at death, is it not far 仁 以為己任，不亦重乎？死而後已，不亦遠乎? In this respect, *ren* 仁 is not easily achieved, and as texts such as the *Mengzi* make clear, if we do not tend to these incipient impulses to care, they will likely disappear.[64] The Confucian task of "learning to be human" *xue zuoren* 學做人, therefore, can also be understood as "learning to be humane" *xue zuoren* 學做仁. And, as explained earlier, the natural proclivities of *ren* 仁 must be guided by ritual to reach this optimal state. In this sense, *ren* 仁 is a kind of care that must be developed from a rudimentary state of caring *about* people and things to a more refined state of caring *for* people and things. *Ren* 仁 in its basic state serves as an attentiveness to one's own needs and to the needs of others.[65] *Ren* 仁 is a desire for meaning—a desire for oneself to mean something to another and a desire to find meaningful those whom one encounters through the service of care. Vulnerability is the state of this desire.

Conclusion

The purpose of this final chapter was to demonstrate the value of vulnerability in human experience from a Confucian perspective. Vulnerability enables values such as ethics, trust, and maturity in ways that striving for invulnerability otherwise preclude them. Confucian notions of the self foreground vulnerability as an inherent condition of being human. In an early Confucian context this involves recognizing that vulnerability is rooted in the body/self, which is seen as an entity interconnected and related to other people and things. Human beings, in this view, are not just causally interdependent but are ontologically interdependent. To be human is to be enmeshed in relationships where meaningful aspects of the self are constituted by (and vulnerable to) others. As such, vulnerability is an identity-conferring experience. Because of this, Confucians strive to create the conditions of optimal vulnerability through a program of ritual (*li* 禮). These are a robust series of practices aimed to encourage or limit vulnerability as appropriate. Rituals shore up the self to avoid excessive vulnerability but also open the self up to fully engage in meaning-making relationships.

Resituated in the more specific argument of this book, the vulnerability of integrity means that vulnerability runs deep. Our relationships with others can compel actions that go against our desire (and ability) to maintain identity-conferring commitments. The possibility of tragic value conflicts means that we cannot construct an invulnerable moral identity. Yet the fact that our integrity is susceptible to change, harm, or transformation also heightens our appreciation for the kind of moral self we are able to achieve. Indeed, part of the value of integrity stems from its vulnerability. The vulnerability of integrity engenders a kind of sorrow with regard to the limits of human capacity, but it also fosters compassion and poignancy in the creation of relationships that serve as the basis for a good life.

Notes

1. Max Weber, *The Religion of China: Confucianism and Taoism*, translated and edited by H. H. Gerth (New York: Free Press, 1968), 235–236.

2. My usage of the terms "caring about" and "caring for" differs from Nel Nodding's use of the terms in *Caring: A Feminine Approach to Ethics and Moral Education* (Berkeley: University of California Press, 1984).

3. The body of this book focused on the vulnerability of integrity. This part of the book, however, discusses vulnerability in a more general sense. In speaking in this general sense, I am not necessarily critiquing the harmony thesis. In many regards I am teasing out the implications of widely held views on Confucian self-cultivation, a topic that many have written on but have not used the language of vulnerability to explain. This highlights certain features that I believe have not been highlighted in other accounts of self-cultivation, even though these features are implied in many of those accounts.

4. Jonathan Keung Lap Chan, "Health Care and Human Vulnerability: A Confucian Perspective," in *Religious Perspectives on Human Vulnerability in Bioethics*, edited by Joseph Tham et al. (New York: Springer, 2014), 154.

5. Joseph Chan, "Health Care and Human Vulnerability: A Confucian Perspective," *Studia Bioethica* 4.2 (2011): 33. This article and the article that appears in *Religious Perspectives on Human Vulnerability in Bioethics* are largely the same.

6. Weiming Tu, "Pain and Humanity in the Confucian Learning of the Heart-and-Mind," in *Pain and Its Transformations: The Interface of Biology and Culture*, edited by Sarah Coakley and Kay Kaufman Shelemay (Cambridge, MA: Harvard University Press, 2007), 233.

7. Judith Butler, *Frames of War: When Is Life Grievable?* (New York: Verso, 2009), 54.

8. Butler, 55. Brene Brown makes a similar point: "Vulnerability isn't good or bad: It's not what we call a dark emotion, nor is it always a light, positive experience. Vulnerability is the core of all emotions and feelings. To feel is to be vulnerable." *Daring Greatly* (New York: Gotham Books, 2012), 33.

9. For a larger discussion of the etymology of *ren* 仁 see Huaiyu Wang, "*Ren* and *Gantong*: Openness of Heart and the Root of Confucianism," *Philosophy East and West* 62.4 (October 2012), 469–482.

10. See, for instance, *Liji* 33.7/148/22; 32.14/144/26; and *Kongzi Jiayu* 17.1/34/15.

11. Mengzi's claim is that human beings come into the world with such a disposition. This disposition can, however, be diminished and possibly even stamped out (see *Mengzi* 6A8). However, the purpose of passages such as *Mengzi* 2A6 and 1A7 is to argue that even the smallest amount of concern can be cultivated and broadened or redirected. Hence, in a case where someone seems not to care for other people or other important things, Mengzi would find ways to take the concern one has for other less significant things and broaden it to include more significant things. The case of those who physically or mentally seem incapable of caring is also relevant. As I go on to explain, *ren* 仁 is a sensitivity to life, even one's own life, and the desire for survival marks a basic degree of care. Further, the notion of vulnerability as susceptibility to harm does not stop being applicable in a Confucian theory of vulnerability, and a lack of awareness of harm does not mean that one is less vulnerable.

12. See also *Liji* 33.7/148/22. For an alternative view on the notion of *ren* 人 and *ren* 仁 see Robert H. Gassmann, "Understanding Ancient Chinese Society: Approaches to Ren 仁 and Min 民," *Journal of the American Oriental Society* 120.3 (July–September 2000): 348–359.

13. *Shuoyuan* 16.19/124/31.

14. *Shuoyuan* 17.46/148/24.

15. For other passages on *ren* 仁 and *sheng* 生 see Wang, "*Ren* and *Gantong*," 466–467. On the broader connection between caring for others and life see *Analects* 12.10 and *Han Shi Waizhuan* 7.27/56/12.

16. Zhu Xi 朱熹, ed., *Ercheng Yishu* 《二程遺書》 *Wenyuange Sikuquanshu Dianziban* 《文淵閣四庫全書電子版》 (Hong Kong: Digital Heritage Publishing, accessed September 29, 2015), 11.5.

17. For an example of medical texts using this language see Paul Unschuld and Hermann Tessenow, trans., *Huang Di Nei Jing Su Wen: An Annotated Translation of Huang Di's Inner Classic—Basic Questions* (Berkeley: University of California Press, 2011), Vol I, 650–652. See also the sources mentioned in Wang, "*Ren* and *Gantong*," 489 fn. 23.

18. Zhu Xi 朱熹, ed., *Ercheng Waishu* 《二程外書》 *Wenyuange Sikuquanshu Dianziban* 《文淵閣四庫全書電子版》 (Hong Kong: Digital Heritage Publishing, accessed September 29, 2015), 3.2.

19. *Zhouyi* 65/79/22.

20. Wang, "*Ren* and *Gantong*," 464.

21. Huaiyu Wang, "A Genealogical Study of *De*: Poetical Correspondence of Sky, Earth, and Humankind in the Early Chinese Virtuous Rule of Benefaction," *Philosophy East and West* 65.1 (January 2015), 91.

22. Outside the *Analects*, Mengzi, of course, explicitly uses the language of *ren* 仁 in the context of avoiding the sacrifice of an ox in *Mengzi* 1A7.

23. *Han Shi Waizhuan* 4.24/31/18.

24. For more on this passage see John Kieschnick, "*Analects* 12.1 and the Commentarial Tradition," *Journal of the American Oriental Society* 112.4 (October–December 1992): 567–576.

25. Joel Anderson discusses the related concept of "surplus vulnerability" as "the level of vulnerability being greater than is actually *necessary* to secure the related enrichment of autonomy." "Autonomy and Vulnerability Entwined," in *Vulnerability: New Essays in Ethics and Feminist Philosophy*, edited by Catriona Mackenzie, Wendy Rogers, and Susan Dodds (New York: Oxford University Press, 2014), 154.

26. *Kongzi Jiayu* 4.28/84/23–25.

27. *Mengzi* 7B31.

28. *Baihutong* 30/55/28.

29. Weiming Tu, *Humanity and Self-Cultivation: Essays in Confucian Thought* (Boston: Cheng and Tsui 1998), 24.

30. Amy Olberding, "I Know Not 'Seems': Grief for Parents in the *Analects*," in *Mortality in Traditional Chinese Thought*, edited by Amy Olberding and Philip J. Ivanhoe (Albany: State University of New York Press), 160.

31. *Analects* 5.28.

32. *Analects* 17.4.

33. See, for instance, *Analects* 19.6.

34. *Xunzi* 1/3/14. The next series of references come from various parts of the first chapter of the *Xunzi*.

35. *Xunzi* 8/34/2.

36. *Liji* 47.8/171/20–23.

37. *Liji* 47.11/172/1. See also *Analects* 1.7.

38. Roger Ames sometimes uses the language of "human becomings" in describing Confucian conceptions of the self. See Roger T. Ames, "What Ever Happened to 'Wisdom'? Confucian Philosophy of Process and 'Human Becomings,'" *Asia Major* 21.1 (2008): 45–68.

39. Erinn G. Gilson, *The Ethics of Vulnerability: A Feminist Analysis of Social Life and Practice* (New York: Routledge, 2014), 93. Marina McCoy also discusses epistemic vulnerability in *Wounded Heroes: Vulnerability as a Virtue in Ancient Greek Literature and Philosophy* (Oxford: Oxford University Press, 2013), 103–104.

40. Gilson, *Ethics of Vulnerability*, 95.

41. Gilson, *Ethics of Vulnerability*, makes a related point on pages 177–178: "Overall, we might summarize an ethics of vulnerability as one defined by responsiveness and a critical disposition. Such an ethic calls us to be responsive to our own vulnerability and to the vulnerability of others, but also to be critical of the norms that orient those responses."

42. Gilson, *Ethics of Vulnerability*, 11. There is debate about the relationship between vulnerability and obligations. See for instance, Mackenzie, 10–13.

43. *Xunzi* 10/43/9–13.

44. I am taking "trust" here in a normative sense. I found the following scholarship helpful for understanding trust in broader academic discourses: Annette Baier, *Moral Prejudices: Essays on Ethics* (Cambridge, MA: Harvard University Press, 1994); Cheshire Calhoun, "Standing for Something," *The Journal of Philosophy* 92.5 (May 1995): 235–260; John Mordechai Gottman, *The Science of Trust: Emotional Attunement for Couples* (New York: W. W. Norton, 2011); Margaret Urban Walker, *Moral Repair: Reconstructing Moral Relations after Wrongdoing* (New York: Cambridge University Press, 2006).

45. In what follows I highlight an idealized version of *xin* 信. For more on *xin* 信 see Cecilia Wee, "*Xin*, Trust, and Confucius' Ethics," *Philosophy East and West* 61.3 (July 2011): 516–533; and Whalen Lai, "On 'Trust and Being True': Toward a Genealogy of Morals," *Dao: A Journal of Comparative Philosophy* 9.3 (2010): 257–274.

46. Kwong-loi Shun, "*Zhong* (*Chung*) and *Xin* (*Hsin*): Loyalty and Trustworthiness," in *Encyclopedia of Chinese Philosophy*, edited by Antonio S. Cua (New York: Routledge, 2003), 886.

47. David L. Hall and Roger T. Ames. *Thinking Through Confucius* (Albany: State University of New York Press, 1987), 61.

48. *Analects* 1.4. See also *Mengzi* 3A4. For friendship in Confucianism see Xiufen Lu, "Rethinking Confucian Friendship," *Asian Philosophy* 20.3 (November 2010): 225–245; Tim Connolly, "Friendship and Filial Piety: Relational Ethics in Aristotle and Early Confucianism," *Journal of Chinese Philosophy* 39.1 (March 2012): 71–88; and Eric C. Mullis, "Confucius and Aristotle on the Goods of Friendship," *Dao: A Journal of Comparative Philosophy* 9.4 (December 2010): 391–405.

49. The *Shuowen Jiezi* 《說文解字》 glosses *xin* 信 as *cheng* 誠. Xu Shen 許慎, *Shuowen Jiezi* 《說文解字》 (Beijing 北京: Zhonghua Shuju 中華書局, 2004), 52. See also *Liji* 32.18/145/17–19; *Mengzi* 2A12; *Xunzi* 6/24/12 and 27/133/22; and *Shuoyuan* 10.33/84/23.

50. Wee, 523.

51. *Mengzi* 7B12.

52. There is debate about whether or not friends are seen as equals in early China. See Lu, "Rethinking Confucian Friendship," and Sor-Hoon Tan, "Mentor or Friend? Confucius and Aristotle on Equality and Ethical Development in Friendship," *International Studies in Philosophy* 33.4 (2001): 99–121.

53. *Analects* 2.22. This passage is understood in various ways. See Edward Slingerland, trans., *Confucius: Analects* (Indianapolis: Hackett, 2003), 15. See also *Analects* 12.7 and 19.10; as well as *Liji* 33.9/149/8–9.

54. See also *Xunzi* 3/9/19–10/4.

55. See also *Dadai Liji* 9.2/54/24–27.

56. See Ban, Gu 班固. *Hanshu* 《漢書》 (Beijing 北京: Zhonghua Shuju 中華書局, 2007), 564; and *Baihutong* 30/55/28–56/6. See also *Fayan* 3/6/24–25.

57. Brene Brown, *Daring Greatly* (New York: Gotham Books, 2012), 8.

58. Brown, *Daring Greatly*, 29.

59. For a specific account of moral maturity in the *Analects* see Amy Olberding, "Confucius' Complaints and the *Analects'* Account of the Good Life," *Dao: A Journal of Comparative Philosophy* 12.4 (2013): 417–440.

60. *Analects* 14.12. See also *Kongzi Jiayu* 18.3/36/17–19.

61. *Liji* 25.14/125/6–8. See also *Liji* 44/167/7–8 and *Dadai Liji* 4.5/30/24–31/4.

62. For more on this see Weiming Tu, *Humanity and Self-Cultivation: Essays in Confucian Thought* (Boston: Cheng and Tsui, 1998), 7–10.

63. *Mengzi* 6A11. Coincidentally, the earliest appearances of the English word "care" are in the context of grief and mourning, which share affinities with Mengzi's discussion of *ren* 仁 in 2A6 where feelings of "alarm and compassion" 怵惕惻隱 at seeing someone about to be harmed are evidence of *ren* 仁. See the *Oxford English Dictionary's* entry on "care."

64. See, for instance, *Mengzi* 6A8.

65. For the notion of attentiveness in relation to an ethics of care see Joan Tronto, *Moral Boundaries: A Political Argument for an Ethic of Care* (New York: Routledge, 1994), 127–137.

Bibliography

Allan, Sarah. *The Heir and the Sage: Dynastic Legend In Early China*. San Francisco: Chinese Materials Center, 1981.

Ames, Roger T. *Confucian Role Ethics: A Vocabulary*. Honolulu: University of Hawai'i Press, 2011.

Ames, Roger T. "What Ever Happened to 'Wisdom'? Confucian Philosophy of Process and 'Human Becomings.'" *Asia Major* 21.1 (2008): 45–68.

Ames, Roger T., and David L Hall. *Focusing the Familiar: A Translation and Philosophical Interpretation of the Zhongyong*. Honolulu: University of Hawai'i Press, 2001.

Angle, Stephen C. "No Supreme Principle: Confucianism's Harmonization of Multiple Values." *Dao: A Journal of Comparative Philosophy* 7.1 (2008): 35–40.

Angle, Stephen C. *Sagehood: The Contemporary Significance of Neo-Confucian Philosophy*. New York: Oxford University Press, 2009.

Ariel, Yoav, trans. *K'ung-ts'ung-tzu: The K'ung Family Masters' Anthology*. Princeton, NJ: Princeton University Press, 1989.

Ashmore, Robert. *The Transport of Reading: Text and Understanding in the World of Tao Qian (365–427)*. Cambridge, MA: Harvard University Press, 2010.

Athanassoulis, Nafsika. *Morality, Moral Luck and Responsibility: Fortune's Web*. New York: Palgrave Macmillan, 2005.

Baier, Annette. *Moral Prejudices: Essays on Ethics*. Cambridge, MA: Harvard University Press, 1994.

Ban, Gu 班固. *Hanshu* 《漢書》. Beijing 北京: Zhonghua Shuju 中華書局, 2007.

Barnwell, Scott A. "The Evolution of the Concept of De 德 in Early China." *Sino-Platonic Papers* 235 (March 2013): 1–83.

Barrett, Nathaniel F. "A Confucian Theory of Shame." *Sophia* 52.2 (June 2015): 143–163.

Beattie, Amanda Russell, and Kate Schick, eds. *The Vulnerable Subject: Beyond Rationalism in International Relations*. New York: Palgrave Macmillan, 2013.

Behuniak, James. *Mencius on Becoming Human*. Albany: State University of New York Press, 2005.

Bell, Daniel A., ed. *Confucian Political Ethics*. Princeton, NJ: Princeton University Press, 2008.

Berkowitz, Alan J. *Patterns of Disengagement: The Practice and Portrayal of Reclusion in Early Medieval China*. Stanford, CA: Stanford University Press, 2000.

Berthrong, John H. "Weighing the Way: Metaphoric Balances in *Analects* 9:30." In *Interpretation and Intellectual Change: Chinese Hermeneutics in Historical Perspective*, edited by Ching-I Tu, 3–18. New Brunswick, NJ: Transaction, 2005.

Berthrong, John, Shu-Hsien Liu, and Leonard Swidler, eds. *Confucianism in Dialogue Today: West, Christianity & Judaism*. Philadelphia: Ecumenical Press, 2004.

Bi, Lijun, and Fred D'Agostino. "The Doctrine of Filial Piety: A Philosophical Analysis of the Concealment Case." *Journal of Chinese Philosophy* 31.4 (December 2004): 451–467.

Billings, Joshua. *Genealogy of the Tragic: Greek Tragedy and German Philosophy*. Princeton, NJ: Princeton University Press, 2014.

Birrell, Anne. *Chinese Mythology: An Introduction*. Baltimore: Johns Hopkins University Press, 1993.

Bishop, Sharon. "Connections and Guilt." *Hypatia* 2.1 (Winter 1987): 7–23.

Bowlby, John. *A Secure Base: Parent-Child Attachment and Healthy Human Development*. New York: Basic Books, 1988.

Brindley, Erica. *Music, Cosmology, and the Politics of Harmony in Early China*. Albany: State University of New York Press, 2012.

Brindley, Erica. "The Polarization of the Concepts *Si* (Private Interest) and *Gong* (Public Interest) in Early Chinese Thought." *Asia Major* 26.2 (2013): 1–31.

Brown, Brene. *Daring Greatly*. New York: Gotham Books, 2012.

Butler, Judith. *Frames of War: When Is Life Grievable?* New York: Verso, 2009.

Cai, Fanglu 蔡方鹿 et al. *Qi* 《氣》. Beijing 北京: Zhongguo Renmin Daxue Chubanshe 中国人民大学出版社, 1990.

Cai, Mo 蔡模, ed. *Mengzi Jishu* 《孟子集疏》. *Wenyuange Sikuquanshu Dianziban* 《文淵閣四庫全書電子版》. Hong Kong: Digital Heritage Publishing, accessed September 2, 2014.

Cai, Qing 蔡清, ed. *Sishumengyin* 《四書蒙引》. *Wenyuange Sikuquanshu Dianziban* 《文淵閣四庫全書電子版》. Hong Kong: Digital Heritage Publishing, accessed February 3, 2015.

Calhoun, Cheshire. "An Apology for Moral Shame." *Journal of Political Philosophy* 12.2 (2004): 127–146.

Calhoun, Cheshire. "Standing for Something." *Journal of Philosophy* 92.5 (May 1995): 235–260.

Chan, Alan K. L., ed. *"Mencius": Contexts and Interpretations*. Honolulu: University of Hawai'i Press, 2002.

Chan, Joseph. "Health Care and Human Vulnerability: A Confucian Perspective." *Studia Bioethica* 4.2 (2011): 33–40.

Chen, Ning "The Concept of Fate in Mencius." *Philosophy East and West* 47.4 (October 1997): 495–520.

Chen, Shou 陳壽, ed. *Sanguozhi Jijie* 《三國志集解》. Shanghai 上海: Shanghai Guji Chubanshe 上海古籍出版社, 2009.

Chen, Tianxiang 陳天祥. *Sishubianyi* 《四書辨疑》. *Wenyuange Sikuquanshu Dianziban* 《文淵閣四庫全書電子版》. Hong Kong: Digital Heritage Publishing, accessed September 17, 2014.

Chen, Tingjing 陳廷敬. *Wuting Wenbian* 《午亭文編》. *Wenyuange Sikuquanshu Dianziban* 《文淵閣四庫全書電子版》. Hong Kong: Digital Heritage Publishing, accessed February 3, 2015.

Cheng, Chung-ying. *New Dimensions of Confucian and Neo-Confucian Philosophy.* Albany: State University of New York Press, 1991.

Chong, Kim-chong, Sor-hoon Tan, and C. L. Ten, eds. *The Moral Circle and the Self: Chinese and Western Approaches.* Chicago: Open Court, 2003.

Chou, Ying-Hsiung, ed. *The Chinese Text: Studies in Comparative Literature.* Hong Kong: Chinese University of Hong Kong Press, 1986.

Cline, Erin M. *Confucius, Rawls, and the Sense of Justice.* New York: Fordham University Press, 2013.

Coady, C. A. J. *Messy Morality: The Challenge of Politics.* Oxford: Oxford University Press, 2008.

Connolly, Tim. "Friendship and Filial Piety: Relational Ethics in Aristotle and Early Confucianism." *Journal of Chinese Philosophy* 39.1 (March 2012): 71–88.

Cook, Scott. *The Bamboo Texts of Guodian: A Study and Complete Translation.* Ithaca, NY: Cornell University East Asia Program, 2012.

Cook, Scott. "Unity and Diversity in the Musical Thought of Warring States China." PhD diss., University of Michigan, 1995.

Crank, John P., and Michael A. Caldero. *Police Ethics: The Corruption of Noble Cause.* Cincinnati: Anderson Publishing, 2000.

Csikszentmihalyi, Mark. *Material Virtue: Ethics and the Body in Early China.* Boston: Brill, 2004.

Cua, Antonio S. "The Ethical Significance of Shame: Insights of Aristotle and Xunzi." *Philosophy East and West* 53.2 (2003): 147–202.

Cua, Antonio S. *Moral Vision and Tradition: Essays in Chinese Ethics.* Washington, DC: Catholic University of America Press, 1998.

Cua, Antonio S, ed. *Encyclopedia of Chinese Philosophy.* New York: Routledge, 2003.

Culp, Kristine A. *Vulnerability and Glory: A Theological Account.* Louisville, KY: Westminster John Knox Press, 2010.

Defoort, Carine. "Can Words Produce Order? Regicide in the Confucian Tradition." *Cultural Dynamics* 12.1 (March 2000): 85–109.

Defoort, Carine. "The Profit That Does Not Profit: Paradoxes with 'Li' in Early Chinese Texts." *Asia Major* 21.1 (2008): 153–181.

Defoort, Carine, ed. *Contemporary Chinese Thought: Translations and Studies* 41.2 (2009–2010).

Ding, Yuanzhi 丁原植. *Guodian Chujian: Rujia Yiji Sizhong Shixi* 《郭店楚簡：儒家佚 籍四重釋析》. Taibei 台北: Taiwan Guji Chuban Youxian Gongsi 台灣古籍出 版有限公司, 2004.

Douglas-Fairhurst, Robert. "Tragedy and Disgust." In *Tragedy in Transition*, edited by Sarah Annes Brown and Catherine Silverstone, 58–77. Malden, MA: Blackwell, 2007.

Durrant, Stephen W. *The Cloudy Mirror: Tension and Conflict in the Writings of Sima Qian*. Albany: State University of New York Press, 1995.

Eberhard, Wolfram. *Guilt and Sin in Traditional China*. Berkeley: University of California Press, 1967.

Eno, Robert. *The Confucian Creation of Heaven: Philosophy and the Defense of Ritual Mastery*. Albany: State University of New York Press, 1990.

Escande, Yolaine, Chenyang Li, and Vincent Shen, eds. *Inter-Culturality and Philosophic Discourse*. Newcastle upon Tyne, UK: Cambridge Scholars Publishing, 2013.

Fan, Ye 范曄, ed. *Hou Hanshu* 《後漢書》. Beijing 北京: Zhonghua Shuju 中華書局, 1965–1973.

Felski, Rita, ed. *Rethinking Tragedy*. Baltimore: Johns Hopkins University Press, 2008.

Fineman, Martha, and Anna Grear, eds. *Vulnerability: Reflections On a New Ethical Foundation for Law and Politics*. Burlington, VT: Ashgate, 2013.

Fingarette, Herbert. *Confucius: The Secular as Sacred*. New York: Harper & Row, 1972.

Fingarette, Herbert. "The Music of Humanity in the Conversations of Confucius." *Journal of Chinese Philosophy* 10.4 (December 1983): 331–356.

Fischer, Paul. *Shizi: China's First Syncretist*. New York: Columbia University Press, 2012.

Fraser, Chris, Dan Robins, and Timothy O'Leary, eds. *Ethics In Early China: An Anthology*. Hong Kong: Hong Kong University Press, 2011.

Fu, Xiren 傅錫壬, ed. *Xinyi Chuci Duben* 《新譯楚辭讀本》. Taibei 臺北: Sanmin Shuju 三民書局, 2011.

Fu, Yashu 傅亞庶, ed. *Kongconzi Jiaoyi* 《孔叢子校釋》. Beijing 北京: Zhonghua Shuju 中華書局, 2011.

Gale, Esson M., trans. *Discourses on Salt and Iron: A Debate on State Control of Commerce and Industry in Ancient China*. Taipei: Ch'eng-wen Publishing Company, 1967.

Gandolfo, Elizabeth O'Donnell. *The Power and Vulnerability of Love*. Minneapolis: Fortress Press, 2015.

Gassmann, Robert H. "Understanding Ancient Chinese Society: Approaches to Ren 仁 and Min 民." *Journal of the American Oriental Society* 120.3 (July–September 2000): 348–359.

Geaney, Jane. "Guarding Moral Boundaries: Shame in Early Confucianism." *Philosophy East and West* 54.2 (April 2004): 113–142.

Gentz, Joachim. "Can We Be in Time to Lead a Good Life? Discourses on the Human Ability to Lead a Good Life Through Timely Action in Early Chinese Thought." Unpublished manuscript.

Gentz, Joachim. *Das Gongyang zhuan: Auslegung und Kanonisierung der Frühlings- und Herbstannalen (Chunqiu)*. Wiesbaden: Harrassowitz, 2001.

Gibas, Piotr Pawel. "Waiting for the Unicorn: Perception of Time and History in Early Chinese Writings." PhD diss., University of California, Berkeley, 2009.

Gilson, Erinn G. *The Ethics of Vulnerability: A Feminist Analysis of Social Life and Practice*. New York: Routledge, 2014.

Goldin, Paul R. "Mencius in the Han Dynasty." In *Dao Companion to the Philosophy of Mencius*, edited by Yang Xiao. New York: Springer, forthcoming.

Goldin, Paul R. "The Theme of the Primacy of the Situation in Classical Chinese Philosophy and Rhetoric." *Asia Major* 18.2 (2005): 1–25.

Gottman, John Mordechai. *The Science of Trust: Emotional Attunement for Couples*. New York: W. W. Norton, 2011.

Gowans, Christopher W. *Innocence Lost: An Examination of Inescapable Moral Wrongdoing*. New York: Oxford University Press, 1994.

Gowans, Christopher W., ed. *Moral Dilemmas*. New York: Oxford University Press, 1987.

Graham, A. C. *Disputers of the Tao: Philosophical Argument in Ancient China*. Chicago: Open Court, 1989.

Guan, Xihua 管锡华, ed. *Erya* 《尔雅》. Beijing 北京: Zhonghua Shuju 中华書局, 2014.

Guarde-Paz, César. "Moral Dilemmas in Chinese Philosophy: A Case Study of the *Lienü Zhuan*." *Dao: A Journal of Comparative Philosophy* 15.1 (January 2016): 81–101.

Guo, Jianxun 郭建勳, ed. *Xinyi Yijing duben* 《新譯易經讀本》. Taibei Shi 臺北市: Sanmin shuju 三民書局, 1996.

Halfon, Mark. *Integrity: A Philosophical Inquiry*. Philadelphia: Temple University Press, 1989.

Hall, David L., and Roger T. Ames. *Thinking Through Confucius*. Albany: State University of New York Press, 1987.

Harris, Thorian R. "Aristotle and Confucius on the Socioeconomics of Shame." *Dao: A Journal of Comparative Philosophy* 13.3 (September 2014): 323–342.

He, Yan 何晏, ed. *Lunyu Jijieyishu* 《論語集解義疏》. *Wenyuange Sikuquanshu Dianziban* 《文淵閣四庫全書電子版》. Hong Kong: Digital Heritage Publishing, accessed September 17, 2014.

Hegel, Georg Wilhelm Friedrich. *Lectures on the Philosophy of Religion*. Edited by Peter C. Hodgson; translated by R. F. Brown, P. C. Hodgson, and J. M. Stewart, with J. P. Fitzer and H. S. Harris. Berkeley: University of California Press, 1984–1987.

Henry, Eric. "The Motif of Recognition in Early China Author." *Harvard Journal of Asiatic Studies* 47.1 (June 1987): 5–30.

Hightower, James Robert, trans. *Han Shih Wai Chuan: Han Ying's Illustrations of the Didactic Application of the* Classic of Songs. Cambridge, MA: Harvard University Press, 1952.

Hill, Thomas E. "Moral Purity and the Lesser Evil." *The Monist* 66.2 (April 1983): 213–232.

Hsieh, Shan-yuan. *The Life and Thought of Li Kou (1009–1059)*. San Francisco: Chinese Materials Center, 1979.

Hu, Bingwen 胡炳文. *Yunfengji* 《雲峰集》. *Wenyuange Sikuquanshu Dianziban* 《文 淵閣四庫全書電子版》. Hong Kong: Digital Heritage Publishing, accessed February 3, 2015.

Hu, Guang 胡廣, ed. *Mengzi Jizhu Daquan* 《孟子集註大全》. *Wenyuange Sikuquanshu Dianziban* 《文淵閣四庫全書電子版》. Hong Kong: Digital Heritage Publishing, accessed September 2, 2014.

Hu, Guang 胡廣, ed. *Sishu Daquan* 《四書大全》. *Wenyuange Sikuquanshu Dianziban* 《文淵閣四庫全書電子版》. Hong Kong: Digital Heritage Publishing, accessed September 25, 2014.

Huang, Alexander. "The Tragic and the Chinese Subject." *Stanford Journal of East Asian Affairs* 3.1 (2003): 55–68.

Huang, Jianyue 黄建跃. *Xianqin Rujia de Gongsizhibian* 《先秦儒家的公私之辨》. Guilin 桂林: Guangxi Shifandaxue Chubanshe 广西师范大学出版社, 2013.

Huang, Yushun 黄玉顺. *Ruxue yu Shenghuo: "Shenghuo Ruxue" Lungao* 《儒学与生活—『生活儒学』论稿》. Chengdu 成都: Sichuan Daxue Chubanshe 四川大学出 版社, 2009.

Huang, Zongxi 黃宗羲, ed. *Mingru Xuean* 《明儒學案》 *Wenyuange Sikuquanshu Dianziban* 《文淵閣四庫全書電子版》. Hong Kong: Digital Heritage Publishing, accessed February 3, 2015.

Hunter, Michael. "Sayings of Confucius, Deselected." PhD diss., Princeton University, 2012.

Hutton, Eric. "On the Meaning of *Yi* (義) for Xunzi." Master's thesis, Harvard University, 1996.

Ing, Michael D. K. "The Ancients Did Not Fix Their Graves: Failure in Early Confucian Ritual." *Philosophy East and West* 62.2 (April 2012): 223–245.

Ing, Michael D. K. *The Dysfunction of Ritual in Early Confucianism*. New York: Oxford University Press, 2012.

Ing, Michael D. K. "Review of *Heaven and Earth Are Not Humane: The Problem of Evil in Classical Chinese Philosophy* by Franklin Perkins." *Frontiers of Philosophy in China* 10.1 (2015): 153–158.

Ivanhoe, Philip J. "Character Consequentialism: An Early Confucian Contribution to Contemporary Ethical Theory." *Journal of Religious Ethics* 19.1 (1991): 55–70.

Ivanhoe, Philip J. "A Question of Faith." *Early China* 13 (1988): 153–165.

Jia, Jinhua, and Pang-Fei Kwok. "From Clan Manners to Ethical Obligation and Righteousness: A New Interpretation of the Term *yi* 義." *Journal of the Royal Asiatic Society* 17.1 (January 2007): 33–42.

Jiang, Yihua 姜義華. *Xinyi Liji Duben* 《新譯禮記讀本》. Taibei Shi 臺北市: Sanmin shuju 三民書局, 1997.

Johnson, Mark. *Moral Imagination: Implications of Cognitive Science for Ethics*. Chicago: University of Chicago Press, 1993.

Keightley, David. "Early Civilization in China: Reflections on How It Became Chinese." In *Heritage of China: Contemporary Perspectives on Chinese Civilization*, edited by Paul S. Ropp, 15–54. Berkeley: University of California Press, 1990.

Kieschnick, John. "*Analects* 12.1 and the Commentarial Tradition." *Journal of the American Oriental Society* 112.4 (October–December 1992): 567–576.

Kim, Myeong-seok. "Choice, Freedom, and Responsibility in Ancient Chinese Confucianism." *Philosophy East and West* 63.1 (January 2013): 17–38.

Kim, Sungmoon. "Achieving the Way: Confucian Virtue Politics and the Problem of Dirty Hands." *Philosophy East and West* 66.1 (January 2016): 152–176.

King, Ambrose Y.C. "The Individual and Group in Confucianism: A Relational Perspective." In *Individualism and Holism: Studies in Confucian and Taoist Values*, edited by Donald J. Munro, 57–70. Ann Arbor: Center for Chinese Studies, University of Michigan, 1985.

King, Richard A. H., and Dennis Schilling, eds. *How Should One Live? Comparing Ethics in Ancient China and Greco-Roman Antiquity*. Boston: Walter de Gruyter, 2011.

Knapp, Keith Nathaniel. *Selfless Offspring: Filial Children and Social Order In Early Medieval China*. Honolulu: University of Hawai'i Press, 2005.

Knechtges, David R. *The Han Shu Biography of Yang Xiong (53 BC–AD 18)*. Tempe: Center for Asian Studies, Arizona State University, 1982.

Kramers, R. P., trans. *K'ung Tzu Chia Yu: The School Sayings of Confucius*. Leiden: Brill, 1950.

Kryukov, Vassili. "Symbols of Power and Communication in Pre-Confucian China (On the Anthropology of *De*) Preliminary Assumptions." *Bulletin of the School of Oriental and African Studies* 43.2 (1995): 314–333.

Lai, Whalen. "On 'Trust and Being True': Toward a Genealogy of Morals." *Dao: A Journal of Comparative Philosophy* 9.3 (2010): 257–274.

Lau, D. C. 劉殿爵, ed. *Bingshu Sizhong Zhuzi Suoyin: A Concordance to the Militarists* 《兵書四種逐字索引》. Taibei 台北: Taiwan Shangwu yinshuguan 台灣商務印書館, 1992.

Lau, D. C. 劉殿爵, ed. *Chuci Zhuzi Suoyin: A Concordance to the Chuci* 《楚辭逐字索引》. Xianggang 香港: Shangwu yinshuguan 商務印書館, 2000.

Lau, D. C. 劉殿爵, ed. *Hanfeizi Zhuzi Suoyin: A Concordance to the Hanfeizi* 《韓非子逐字索引》. Xianggang 香港: Shangwu yinshuguan 商務印書館, 2000.

Lau, D. C. 劉殿爵, ed. *Han Shi Waizhuan Zhuzi Suoyin: A Concordance to the Han Shi Waizhuan* 《韓詩外轉逐字索引》. Taibei 台北: Taiwan Shangwu yinshuguan 台灣商務印書館, 1992.

Lau, D. C. 劉殿爵, ed. *Huainanzi Zhuzi Suoyin: A Concordance to the Huainanzi* 《淮南子逐字索引》. Taibei 台北: Taiwan Shangwu yinshuguan 台灣商務印書館, 1992.

Lau, D. C. 劉殿爵, ed. *Kongcongzi Zhuzi Suoyin: A Concordance to the Kongcongzi* 《孔叢子逐字索引》. Xianggang 香港: Shangwu yinshuguan 商務印書館, 1998.

Lau, D. C. 劉殿爵, ed. *Kongzi Jiayu Zhuzi Suoyin: A Concordance to the Kongzi Jiayu* 《孔子家語逐字索引》. Taibei 台北: Taiwan Shangwu yinshuguan 台灣商務印書館, 1992.

Lau, D. C. 劉殿爵, ed. *Laozi Zhuzi Suoyin: A Concordance to the Laozi* 《老子逐字索引》. Xianggang 香港: Shangwu yinshuguan 商務印書館, 1996.

Lau, D. C. 劉殿爵, ed. *Lunheng Zhuzi Suoyin: A Concordance to the Lunheng* 《論衡逐字索引》. Xianggang 香港: Shangwu yinshuguan 商務印書館, 1996.

Lau, D. C. 劉殿爵, ed. *Lüshi Chunqiu Zhuzi Suoyin: A Concordance to the Lüshi Chunqiu* 《呂氏春秋逐字索引》. Xianggang 香港: Shangwu yinshuguan 商務印書館, 1994.

Lau, D. C. 劉殿爵, ed. *Mao Shi Shuzi Suoyin: A Concordance to the Mao Shi* 《毛詩逐字索引》. Xianggang 香港: Shangwu yinshuguan 商務印書館, 1995.

Lau, D. C. 劉殿爵, ed. *Mozi Zhuzi Suoyin: A Concordance to the Mozi* 《墨子逐字索引》. Xianggang 香港: Shangwu yinshuguan 商務印書館, 2001.

Lau, D. C. 劉殿爵, ed. *Shangjunshu Zhuzi Suoyin: A Concordance to the Shangjunshu* 《商君書逐字索引》. Taibei 台北: Taiwan Shangwu yinshuguan 台灣商務印書館, 1992.

Lau, D. C. 劉殿爵, ed. *Shuoyuan Zhuzi Suoyin: A Concordance to the Shuoyuan* 《說苑逐字索引》. Taibei 台北: Taiwan Shangwu yinshuguan 台灣商務印書館, 1992.

Lau, D. C. 劉殿爵, ed. *Xunzi Zhuzi Suoyin: A Concordance to the Xunzi* 《荀子逐字索引》. Xianggang 香港: Shangwu yinshuguan 商務印書館, 1996.

Lau, D. C. 劉殿爵, ed. *Zhuangzi Zhuzi Suoyin: A Concordance to the Zhuangzi* 《莊子逐字索引》. Xianggang 香港: Shangwu yinshuguan 商務印書館, 2000.

Lau, D. C. 劉殿爵, and Fong Ching Chen 陳方正, eds. *Gu Lienüzhuan Zhuzi Suoyin: A Concordance to the Gu Lienüzhuan* 《古列女傳逐字索引》. Xianggang 香港: Shangwu yinshuguan 商務印書館, 1993.

Lau, D. C. 劉殿爵, and Fong Ching Chen 陳方正, eds. *Guoyu Zhuzi Suoyin: A Concordance to the Guoyu* 《國語逐字索引》. Xianggang 香港: Shangwu yinshuguan 商務印書館, 1999.

Lau, D. C. 劉殿爵, and Fong Ching Chen 陳方正, eds. *Jiayi Xinshu Zhuzi Suoyin: A Concordance to the Xinshu* 《賈誼新書逐字索引》. Xianggang 香港: Shangwu yinshuguan 商務印書館, 1994.

Lau, D. C. 劉殿爵, and Fong Ching Chen 陳方正, eds. *Liji Zhuzi Suoyin: A Concordance to the Liji* 《禮記逐字索引》. Taibei 台北: Taiwan shangwu yinshuguan 台灣商務印書館, 1992.

Lau, D. C. 劉殿爵, and Fong Ching Chen 陳方正, eds. *Mengzi Zhuzi Suoyin: A Concordance to the Mengzi* 《孟子逐字索引》. Xianggang 香港: Shangwu yinshuguan 商務印書館, 1995.

Lau, D. C. 劉殿爵, and Fong Ching Chen 陳方正, eds. *Shiming Zhuzi Suoyin, Jijiupian Zhuzi Suoyin: A Concordance to the Shiming* 《釋名逐字索引，急就篇逐字索引》. Xianggang 香港: Shangwu yinshuguan 商務印書館, 2002.

Lau, D. C. 劉殿爵, and Fong Ching Chen 陳方正, eds. *Shizi Zhuzi Suoyin: A Concordance to the Shizi* 《尸子逐字索引》. Xianggang 香港: Shangwu yinshuguan 商務印書館, 2000.

Lau, D. C. 劉殿爵, and Fong Ching Chen 陳方正, eds. *Xinxu Zhuzi Suoyin: A Concordance to the Xinxu* 《新序逐字索引》. Taibei 台北: Taiwan shangwu yinshuguan 台灣商務印書館, 1992.

Lau, D. C. 劉殿爵, and Fong Ching Chen 陳方正, eds. *Xinyu Zhuzi Suoyin: A Concordance to the Xinyu* 《新語逐字索引》. Xianggang 香港: Shangwu yinshuguan 商務印書館, 1995.

Lau, D. C. 劉殿爵, and Fong Ching Chen 陳方正, eds. *Yantielun Zhuzi Suoyin: A Concordance to the Yantielun* 《鹽鐵論逐字索引》. Xianggang 香港: Shangwu yinshuguan 商務印書館, 1994.

Lau, D. C. 劉殿爵, and Fong Ching Chen 陳方正, eds. *Zhongjing Zhuzi Suoyin: A Concordance to the Zhongjing* 《忠經逐字索引》. Xianggang 香港: Shangwu yinshuguan 商務印書館, 1998.

Lau, D. C. 劉殿爵, and Fong Ching Chen 陳方正, eds. *Zhouyi Zhuzi Suoyin: A Concordance to the Zhouyi* 《周易逐字索引》. Xianggang 香港: Shangwu yinshuguan 商務印書館, 1995.

Lau, D. C. 劉殿爵, Ho Che Wah 何志華, and Fong Ching Chen 陳方正, eds. *Lunyu Zhuzi Suoyin: A Concordance to the Lunyu* 《論語逐字索引》. Xianggang 香港: Shangwu yinshuguan 商務印書館, 1995.

Lewis, Mark Edward. *The Flood Myths of Early China*. Albany: State University of New York Press, 2006.

Lewis, Mark Edward. *Sanctioned Violence in Early China*. Albany: State University of New York Press, 1990.

Li, Chenyang. "The Confucian Ideal of Harmony." *Philosophy East and West* 56.4 (October 2006): 583–603.

Li, Chenyang. *The Confucian Philosophy of Harmony*. New York: Routledge, 2014.

Li, Chengyang. "Cultural Configuration of Values." *World Affairs* 12.2 (Summer 2008): 28–49.

Li, Chenyang. "Does Confucian Ethics Integrate Care Ethics and Justice Ethics? The Case of Mencius." *Asian Philosophy* 18.1 (2008): 69–82.

Li, Chenyang. "When My Grandfather Stole Persimmons . . . Reflections on Confucian Filial Love." *Dao: A Journal of Comparative Philosophy* 7.2 (2008): 135–139.

Li, Guangdi 李光地, and Xiong Silü 熊賜履, eds. *Yuzuan Zhuzi Quanshu* 《御纂朱子全書》. *Wenyuange Sikuquanshu Dianziban* 《文淵閣四庫全書電子版》. Hong Kong: Digital Heritage Publishing, accessed February 3, 2015.

Li, Jingde 黎靖德, ed. *Zhuzi Yulei* 《朱子語類》. Beijing 北京: Zhonghua Shuju 中華書局, 1999.

Li, Ling 李零. *Qu Sheng Naide Zhen Kongzi: Lunyu Zonghengdu* 《去圣乃得真孔子：论语纵横读》. Beijing 北京: Sanlian Shudian 三联书店, 2008.

Li, Ling 李零. *Sangjiagou: Wo Du Lunyu* 《丧家狗：我读论语》. Shanxi 山西: *Shanxi Renmin Chubanshe* 山西人民出版社, 2007.

Li, Wai-yee. *The Readability of the Past in Early Chinese Historiography*. Cambridge, MA: Harvard University Press, 2007.

Li, Xueqin 李学勤. "Zhujian *Jiayu* yu Han-Wei Kongshijia Xue" 竹简〈家语〉与汉魏孔氏家学. *Kongzi Yanjiu* 《孔子研究》 (1987.2): 60–64.

Li, Xueqin 李學勤, ed. *Lunyu Zhushu* 《論語注疏》, Vol. 2. Taibei 台北: Taiwan Shufang 台灣書房, 2001.

Li, Xueqin 李學勤, ed. *Shisanjing Zhushu* 《十三經注疏》. Beijing北京: Beijing daxue chubanshe 北京大学出版社, 2000.

Liang, Tao. "Thinking Through the Notion of 'Relatives Covering for Each Other' in Comparison with 'Covering and Taking Responsibility for Their Faults.'" *Contemporary Chinese Thought* 56.3 (May 2015): 40–66.

Liao, Mingchun 廖明春, and Zhang Yan 张岩. "Cong Shangbojian *Minzhi Fumu* 'Wuzhi' Shuolun *Kongzi Jiayu Lunli* de Zhenwei" 从上博简〈民之父母〉"五至 说论〈孔子家语·论礼〉的真伪. *Xian-Qin, Qin-Hanshi* 《先秦，秦漢史》 (2006.1): 54–59.

Lindell, Kristina. "Stories of Suicide in Ancient China." *Acta Orientalia* 35 (1973):167–239.

Liu, Shangci 劉尚慈, ed., *Chunqiu Gongyang Zhuan Yizhu* 《春秋公羊傳譯注》. Beijing 北京: Zhonghua Shuju 中華書局, 2010.

Lloyd, G. E. R. *The Delusions of Invulnerability: Wisdom and Morality in Ancient Greece, China and Today*. London: Duckworth, 2005.

Lu, Liehong 盧烈紅, ed. *Xinyi Yantielun* 《新譯鹽鐵論》. Taibei 臺北: Sanmin Shuju 三民書局, 1995.

Lu, Ruirong 盧瑞容. *Zhongguo Gudai "Xiangdui Guanxi" Siwei Tantao: "Shi," "He," "Quan," Ququ," Gainian Suyuan Fenxi* 《中國古代「相對關係」思維探討—「勢」「和」「權」「屈曲」概念溯源分析》. Taibei 台北: Shangding Wenhua Chubanshe商鼎文化出版社, 2004.

Lu, Xiufen. "Rethinking Confucian Friendship." *Asian Philosophy* 20.3 (November 2010): 225–245.

Lupke, Christopher, ed. *The Magnitude of* Ming: *Command, Allotment, and Fate in Chinese Culture*. Honolulu: University of Hawai'i Press, 2005.

Ma, Chengyuan 馬承源, ed. *Shanghai Bowuguancang Zhanguo Chu Zhushu (Si)* 《上海博物館藏戰國楚竹書(四)》. Shanghai 上海: Shanghai Guji Chubanshe 上海古 籍出版社, 2004.

Ma, Teying 馬特盈, ed. *Shiji Jinzhu* 《史記今註》. Taibei 台北: Taiwan Shangwu yinshuguan 臺灣商務印書館, 1987.

Mackenzie, Catriona, Wendy Rogers, and Susan Dodds, eds. *Vulnerability: New Essays in Ethics and Feminist Philosophy*. New York: Oxford University Press, 2014.

Major, John S. et al., trans. *The Huainanzi: A Guide to the Theory and Practice of Government in Early Han China*. New York: Columbia University Press, 2010.

Makeham, John. "Between Chen and Cai: *Zhuangzi* and the *Analects*." In *Wandering at Ease in the Zhuangzi*, edited by Roger T. Ames, 75–100. Albany: State University of New York Press, 1998.

Malmqvist, Göran. "Studies on the *Gongyang* and *Guliang* Commentaries." *Bulletin of the Museum of Far Eastern Antiquities* 43 (1971): 76–222; 47 (1975): 19–69; 49 (1977): 33–215.

Mao, Heng 毛亨, ed. *Mao Shi Zhengyi* 《毛詩正義》. Xianggang 香港: Zhonghua Shuju 中華書局, 1964.

Mason, H. E., ed. *Moral Dilemmas and Moral Theory*. New York: Oxford University Press, 1996.

May, Larry, Shari Collins-Chobanian, and Kai Wong, eds. *Applied Ethics: A Multicultural Approach*. Upper Saddle River, NJ: Prentice Hall, 2005.

McCoy, Marina. *Wounded Heroes: Vulnerability as a Virtue in Ancient Greek Literature and Philosophy*. Oxford: Oxford University Press, 2013.

Mizoguchi, Yūzō 溝口雄三. *Chūgoku no Kō to Shi* 《中国の公と私》. Tokyo 東京: Kenbun Shuppansha 研文出版社, 1995.

Morreall, John. *Comedy, Tragedy, and Religion*. Albany: State University of New York Press, 1999.

Mote, Frederick W. "Confucian Eremitism in the Yuan Period." In *The Confucian Persuasion*, edited by Arthur F. Wright, 202–240. Stanford, CA: Stanford University Press, 1960.

Mullis, Eric C. "Confucius and Aristotle on the Goods of Friendship." *Dao: A Journal of Comparative Philosophy* 9.4 (December 2010): 391–405.

Nelson, Eric S. "Recognition and Resentment in the Confucian *Analects*." *Journal of Chinese Philosophy* 40.2 (June 2013): 287–306.

Ni, Peimin. "Practical Humanism of Xu Fuguan." In *Contemporary Chinese Philosophy*, edited by Chung-Ying Cheng and Nicholas Bunnin, 281–304. Malden, MA: Blackwell, 2002.

Nivison, David S. *The Ways of Confucianism: Investigations in Chinese Philosophy*. Edited by Bryan W. Van Norden. Chicago: Open Court, 1996.

Noddings, Nel. *Caring: A Feminine Approach to Ethics and Moral Education*. Berkeley: University of California Press, 1984.

Nuyen, A. T. "Moral Obligation and Moral Motivation in Confucian Role-Based Ethics." *Dao: A Journal of Comparative Philosophy* 8 (2009): 1–11.

Nylan, Michael. *Exemplary Figures:* Fayan. Seattle: University of Washington Press, 2013.

Nylan, Michael. *The Five "Confucian" Classics*. New Haven, CT: Yale University Press, 2001.

Nylan, Michael. "Sima Qian: A True Historian?" *Early China* 23–24 (1998–1999): 203–246.

Olberding, Amy. "Confucius' Complaints and the *Analects*' Account of the Good Life." *Dao: A Journal of Comparative Philosophy* 12.4 (2013): 417–440.

Olberding, Amy. "I Know Not 'Seems': Grief for Parents in the *Analects*." In *Mortality in Traditional Chinese Thought*, edited by Amy Olberding and Philip J. Ivanhoe, 153–175. Albany: State University of New York Press, 2011.

Olberding, Amy. *Moral Exemplars in the* Analects: *The Good Person Is* That. New York: Routledge, 2011.

Olberding, Amy. "Regret and Moral Maturity: A Response to Michael Ing and Manyul Im." *Dao: A Journal of Comparative Philosophy*: 14.4 (December 2015): 579–587.

Olberding, Amy, ed. *Dao Companion to the* Analects. New York: Springer, 2014.

Onozawa, Seiichi小野澤精一, Mitsuji Fukunaga 福永光司, and 山井涌Yū Yamanoi, eds. *Ki no Shisō: Chūgoku ni okeru Shizenkan to Ningenkan no Tenkai* 《気の思想：中国における自然観と人間観の展開》. Tōkyō 東京: Tōkyō Daigaku Shuppankai東京大学出版会, 1978.

Oxford English Dictionary. http://dictionary.oed.com, accessed March 1, 2016.

Pankenier, David W. "'The Scholar's Frustration' Reconsidered: Melancholia or Credo?" *Journal of the American Oriental Society* 110.3 (1990): 434–459.

Parrish, John M. *Paradoxes of Political Ethics*. New York: Cambridge University Press, 2007.

Perkins, Franklin. *Heaven and Earth Are Not Humane: The Problem of Evil in Classical Chinese Philosophy*. Bloomington: Indiana University Press, 2014.

Perkins, Franklin. "Wandering Beyond Tragedy with Zhuangzi." *Comparative and Continental Philosophy* 3.1 (Spring 2011): 79–98.

Puett, Michael J. *The Ambivalence of Creation: Debates Concerning Innovation and Artifice in Early China*. Stanford, CA: Stanford University Press, 2001.

Qian, Zhongshu 錢鐘書. *Guanzhuibian* 《管錐編》. Beijing 北京: Zhonghua Shuju 中華書局, 1999.

Qiu Jun 邱濬, ed. *Daxue Yanyibu* 《大學衍義補》. *Wenyuange Sikuquanshu Dianziban* 《文淵閣四庫全書電子版》. Hong Kong: Digital Heritage Publishing, accessed February 3, 2015.

Qu, Wanli 屈萬里, ed. *Shangshu Shiyi* 《尚書釋義》. Taibei台北: Huagang Chubanbu華岡出版部, 1956.

Roetz, Heiner. *Confucian Ethics of the Axial Age: A Reconstruction Under the Aspect of the Breakthrough Toward Postconventional Thinking*. Albany: State University of New York Press, 1993.

Roth, Harold David. *Original Tao: Inward Training (Nei Ye) and the Foundations of Taoist Mysticism*. New York: Columbia University Press, 1999.

Rosemont, Henry Jr. "Notes from a Confucian Perspective: Which Human Acts are Moral Acts?" *International Philosophical Quarterly* 16.1 (1976): 49–61.

Ruan, Yuan 阮元. *Shisanjing Zhushu* 《十三經注疏》. Taibeishi 台北市: Dahua Shuju 大化書局, 1977.

Russell, Bertrand. *The Problem of China*. London: Allen & Unwin, 1922.

Rynard, Paul, and David P. Shugarman, eds. *Cruelty & Deception: The Controversy Over Dirty Hands in Politics*. New York: Broadview Press, 2000.

Sanft, Charles. "The Moment of Dying: Representations in Liu Xiang's Anthologies *Xin xu* and *Shuo yuan.*" *Asia Major* 24.1 (2001): 127–158.

Schneider, Laurence A. *A Madman of Ch'u: The Chinese Myth of Loyalty and Dissent*. Berkeley: University of California Press, 1980.

Schofer, Jonathan Wyn. *Confronting Vulnerability: The Body and the Divine in Rabbinic Ethics*. Chicago: University of Chicago Press, 2010.

Schopenhauer, Arthur. *The World as Will and Representation*, translated by E. F. J. Payne, vol. 1. Mineola, NY: Dover, 1969.

Schuessler, Axel. *ABC Etymological Dictionary of Old Chinese*. Honolulu: University of Hawai'i Press, 2007.

Schwartz, Benjamin I. *The World of Thought in Ancient China*. Cambridge, MA: Harvard University Press, 1985.

Seawall, Richard. "Absence of Tragedy in Asian Drama." In *Encyclopedia Britannica*. http://www.britannica.com/EBchecked/topic/601884/tragedy/51130/Absence-of-tragedy-in-Asian-drama, accessed December 18, 2014.

Sellman, James D. *Timing and Rulership in Master Lü's Spring and Autmn Annals (Lüshi chunqiu)*. Albany: State University of New York Press, 2002.

Seok, Bongrae. "Moral Psychology of Shame in Early Confucian Philosophy." *Frontiers of Philosophy in China* 10.1 (March 2015): 21–57.

Shahar, Meir, and Robert P. Weller, eds. *Unruly Gods: Divinity and Society in China*. Honolulu: University of Hawai'i Press, 1996.

Shun, Kwong-loi. "Ethical Self-Commitment and Ethical Self-Indulgence." In *The Philosophical Challenge from China*, edited by Brian Bruya, 183–204. Cambridge, MA: MIT Press, 2015.

Shun, Kwong-loi. *Mencius and Early Chinese Thought*. Stanford, CA: Stanford University Press, 1997.

Shun, Kwong-loi. "Resentment and Forgiveness in Confucian Thought." *Journal of East-West Thought* 4.4 (December 2014): 13–35.

Slingerland, Edward, trans. *Confucius: Analects*. Indianapolis: Hackett, 2003.

Smith, Nick. *I Was Wrong: The Meanings of Apologies*. Cambridge, UK: Cambridge University Press, 2008.

Smits, Gregory. "The Intersection of Politics and Thought in Ryukyuan Confucianism: Sai On's Uses of *Quan*." *Harvard Journal of Asiatic Studies* 56.2 (December 1996): 443–477.

Sommer, Deborah. "Boundaries of the *Ti* Body." *Asia Major* 21.1 (2008): 293–324.

Stalnaker, Aaron. *Overcoming Our Evil: Human Nature and Spiritual Exercises in Xunzi and Augustine*. Washington, DC: Georgetown University Press, 2006.

Steiner, George. *The Death of Tragedy*. New York: Knopf, 1961.

Sukhu, Gopal. *The Shaman and the Heresiarch: A New Interpretation of the* Li sao. Albany: State University of New York Press, 2012.

Sun, Shi 孫奭, ed. *Mengzi Zhushu* 《孟子注疏》. *Wenyuange Sikuquanshu Dianziban* 《文淵閣四庫全書電子版》. Hong Kong: Digital Heritage Publishing, accessed February 3, 2015.

Sun, Xingyan 孫星衍, ed. *Shangshu Jinguwen Zhushu* 《尚書今古文注疏》. Beijing 北京: Zhonghua Shuju 中華書局, 2004.

Sun, Zhenbin. "*Yan*: A Dimension of Praxis and its Philosophical Implications." *Journal of Chinese Philosophy* 24 (1997): 191–208.

Sung, Winnie. "The View from Here, Looking Outward." Unpublished manuscript.

Tan, Sor-Hoon. "Mentor or Friend? Confucius and Aristotle on Equality and Ethical Development in Friendship." *International Studies in Philosophy* 33.4 (2001): 99–121.

Tang, Yijie 湯一介 et al., eds. *Ru Zang* 《儒藏》. Beijing 北京: Beijing Daxue Chubanshe 北京大學出版社, 2005.

Teng, Zhixian 滕志賢, ed. *Xinyi Shijing Duben* 《新譯詩經讀本》. Taibei 台北: Sanmin Shuju 三民書局, 2011.

Tessman, Lisa. *Burdened Virtues: Virtue Ethics for Liberatory Struggles.* New York: Oxford University Press, 2005.

Tessman, Lisa. *Moral Failure: On the Impossible Demands of Morality.* New York: Oxford University Press, 2015.

Tham, Joseph et al., eds. *Religious Perspectives on Human Vulnerability in Bioethics.* New York: Springer, 2014.

Tiwald, Justin. "A Right of Rebellion in the *Mengzi*? *Dao: A Journal of Comparative Philosophy* 7.3 (2008): 269–282.

Tronto, Joan. *Moral Boundaries: A Political Argument for an Ethic of Care.* New York: Routledge, 1994.

Tu, Weiming. *Humanity and Self-Cultivation: Essays in Confucian Thought.* Boston: Cheng and Tsui, 1998.

Tu, Weiming. "Pain and Humanity in the Confucian Learning of the Heart-and-Mind." In *Pain and Its Transformations: The Interface of Biology and Culture*, edited by Sarah Coakley and Kay Kaufman Shelemay, 221–241. Cambridge, MA: Harvard University Press, 2007.

Unschuld, Paul, and Hermann Tessenow., trans. *Huang Di Nei Jing Su Wen: An Annotated Translation of Huang Di's Inner Classic—Basic Questions.* Berkeley: University of California Press, 2011.

Van Auken, Newell Ann. *The Commentarial Transformation of the* Spring and Autumn. Albany: State University of New York Press, 2016.

Van Auken, Newell Ann. "Could 'Subtle Words' Have Conveyed 'Praise and Blame'? The Implications of Formal Regularity and Variation in *Spring and Autumn (Chūn qiū)* Records." *Early China* 31 (2007): 47–111.

Van Auken, Newell Ann. "Killings and Assassinations in the *Spring and Autumn* as Records of Judgments." *Asia Major* 27.1 (2014): 1–31.

Van Norden, Bryan W. *Virtue Ethics and Consequentialism in Early Chinese Philosophy.* New York: Cambridge University Press, 2007.

Van Norden, Bryan W., trans. *Mengzi: With Selections from Traditional Commentaries.* Indianapolis: Hackett, 2008.

Van Zoeren, Steven. *Poetry and Personality: Reading, Exegesis, and Hermeneutics in Traditional China.* Stanford, CA: Stanford University Press, 1991.

Vankeerberghen, Griet. "Choosing Balance: Weighing (*Quan* 權) as a Metaphor for Action in Early Chinese Texts." *Early China* 30 (2005): 47–89.

Vervoorn, Aat. "Boyi and Shuqi: Worthy Men of Old?" *Papers on Far Eastern History* 28 (September 1983): 1–22.

Vervoorn, Aat. *Men of the Cliffs and Caves: The Development of the Chinese Eremitic Tradition to the End of the Han Dynasty.* Hong Kong: Chinese University Press, 1990.

Walker, Galal. "Toward a Formal History of the *Chuci*." PhD diss., Cornell University, 1982.

Walker, Margaret Urban. "Moral Luck and the Virtues of Impure Agency." In *Moral Luck*, edited by Daniel Statman, 235–250. Albany: State University of New York Press, 1993.

Walker, Margaret Urban. *Moral Repair: Reconstructing Moral Relations after Wrongdoing*. New York: Cambridge University Press, 2006.

Wallace, Jennifer. "Tragedy in China." *The Cambridge Quarterly* 42.2 (2013): 99–111.

Walzer, Michael. *Arguing about War*. New Haven, CT: Yale University Press, 2004.

Walzer, Michael. *Just and Unjust Wars: A Moral Argument with Historical Illustrations*. New York: Basic Books, 1977.

Walzer, Michael. "Political Action: The Problem of Dirty Hands." *Philosophy and Public Affairs* 2.2 (1973): 160–180.

Wang, Huaiyu. "A Genealogical Study of *De*: Poetical Correspondence of Sky, Earth, and Humankind in the Early Chinese Virtuous Rule of Benefaction." *Philosophy East and West* 65.1 (January 2015): 81–124.

Wang, Huaiyu. "Piety and Individuality Through a Convoluted Path of Rightness: Exploring the Confucian Art of Moral Discretion via *Analects* 13.18." *Asian Philosophy* 21.4 (November 2011): 395–418.

Wang, Huaiyu. "*Ren* and *Gantong*: Openness of Heart and the Root of Confucianism." *Philosophy East and West* 62.4 (October 2012): 505–528.

Wang, Yangming 王陽明. *Wang Yangming Quanji* 《王陽明全集》. Shanghai 上海: Shanghai Guji Chubanshe 上海古籍出版社, 2014.

Weber, Max. *Politics as a Vocation*. Translated by H. H. Gerth and C. Wright Mills. Philadelphia: Fortress Press, 1968.

Weber, Max. *The Religion of China: Confucianism and Taoism*. Translated and edited by H. H. Gerth. New York: Free Press, 1968.

Wee, Cecilia. "*Xin*, Trust, and Confucius' Ethics." *Philosophy East and West* 61.3 (July 2011): 516–533.

Weingarten, Oliver. "Delinquent Fathers and Philology in *Lun Yu* 13.18 and Related Texts." *Early China* 37.1 (December 2014): 221–258.

Whitlock, Greg. "Concealing the Misconduct of One's Own Father: Confucius and Plato on a Question of Filial Piety." *Journal of Chinese Philosophy* 21 (1994): 113–137.

Williams, Bernard. *Moral Luck: Philosophical Papers 1973–1980*. New York: Cambridge University Press, 1981.

Williams, Bernard. *Problems of the Self*. New York: Cambridge University Press, 1973.

Wilson, Mark A. "The Emotion of Regret in an Ethics of Response." PhD diss., Indiana University, 2007.

Wong, David B. "Relational and Autonomous Selves." *Journal of Chinese Philosophy* 31.4 (December 2004): 419–432.

Wright, Arthur F., ed. *The Confucian Persuasion*. Palo Alto, CA: Stanford University Press, 1960.

Xu, Bing 徐冰. "Xiaozhiyuan yu Xingshanlun de Jichu" 孝之怨与性善论的基础. *Zhexue Dongtai* 《哲学动态》 (December 2014): 46–51.

Xu, Fu 徐復, and Wenmin Song 宋文民. *Shuowen Wubaisishi Bushou Zhengjie* 《說文五百四十部首正解》. Jiangsu 江蘇: Guji chubanshe 古籍出版社, 2003.

Xu, Shen 許慎. *Shuowen Jiezi* 《說文解字》. Beijing 北京: Zhonghua Shuju 中華書局, 2004.

Xue, Ke 雪克, ed. *Xinyi Gongyang Zhuan* 《新譯公羊傳》. Taibei 台北: Sanmin Shuju 三民書局, 2008.

Yang, Bojun 楊伯峻, ed. *Chunqiu Zuo Zhuan Zhu* 《春秋左傳注》. Beijing 北京: Zhonghua Shuju 中華書局, 2000.

Yang, Changru 楊長孺. *Chengzhaiji* 《誠齋集》. *Wenyuange Sikuquanshu Dianziban* 《文淵閣四庫全書電子版》. Hong Kong: Digital Heritage Publishing, accessed September 2, 2014.

Yang, Chaoming 楊朝明, and Lilin Song 宋立林, eds. *Kongzi Jiayu Tongjie* 《孔子家語通解》. Jinan 濟南: Qilu Shushe 齊魯書社, 2013.

Yang, Jialuo 楊家駱, ed. *Tiehan Xinshi* 《鐵函心史》. Taibei 台北: Shijie Shuju 世界書局, 1962.

Yao, Chunpeng 姚春鵬, ed. *Huangde Neijing* 《黃帝内经》. Beijing 北京: Zhonghua Shuju 中华书局, 2009.

Yi, Zhongtian 易中天, ed. *Xinyi Guoyu Duben* 《新譯國語讀本》. Taibei Shi 臺北市: Sanmin shuju 三民書局, 2006.

Yu, Jiyuan. *The Ethics of Confucius and Aristotle: Mirrors of Virtue*. New York: Routledge, 2007.

Yu, Kam-por, Julia Tao, and Philip J. Ivanhoe, eds. *Taking Confucian Ethics Seriously: Contemporary Theories and Applications*. Albany: State University of New York Press, 2010.

Yü, Ying-shih. "'O Soul, Come Back!' A Study in the Changing Conceptions of the Soul and Afterlife in Pre-Buddhist China." *Harvard Journal of Asiatic Studies* 47.2 (December 1987): 363–395.

Zeng, Zaozhuang 曾棗莊, and Dagang Shu 舒大剛, eds. *San Su Quanshu* 《三蘇全書》. Beijing 北京: Yuwen Chubanshe 語文出版社, 2001.

Zhang, Daheng 張大亨. *Chunqiu Tongxun* 《春秋通訓》. *Wenyuange Sikuquanshu Dianziban* 《文淵閣四庫全書電子版》. Hong Kong: Digital Heritage Publishing, accessed February 3, 2015.

Zhang, Dainian. *Key Concepts in Chinese Philosophy*. Translated and edited by Edmund Ryden. New Haven, CT: Yale University Press, 2002.

Zhang, Kunjiang 张崑将. *Dechuan Zhongxiao Gainian de Xingcheng yu Fazhan: Yi Bingxue yu Yangmingxue wei Zhongxin* 《德川忠孝概念的形成与发展: 以兵学与阳明学为中心》. Shanghai 上海: Shanghai Huadong Shifan Daxue Chubanshe 上海华东师范大学出版社, 2008.

Zhang, Maoze. "Confucius' Transformation of Traditional Religious Ideas." *Frontiers of Philosophy in China* 6.1 (2011): 20–40.

Zhang, Yunfei 张云飞. "Shengzhe Qinghuai—Sangjia zhi Gou Shijie" 圣者情怀——"丧家之狗"试解. *Kongzi Yanjiu* 《孔子研究》 4 (2010): 40–48.

Zhao, Wu 赵武. "Sangjiagou Shuojie" "丧家狗"说解. *Renwen Zazhi* 《人文杂志》 3 (2013): 19–25.

Zhu, Xi 朱熹. *Sishu Zhangju Jizhu* 《四書章句集注》. Beijing 北京: Zhonghua Shuju 中華書局, 2005.

Zhu, Xi 朱熹, ed. *Ercheng Waishu* 《二程外書》 *Wenyuange Sikuquanshu Dianziban* 《文淵閣四庫全書電子版》. Hong Kong: Digital Heritage Publishing, accessed September 29, 2015.

Zhu, Xi 朱熹, ed. *Ercheng Yishu* 《二程遺書》 *Wenyuange Sikuquanshu Dianziban* 《文淵閣四庫全書電子版》. Hong Kong: Digital Heritage Publishing, accessed September 29, 2015.

Zhu, Xi 朱熹, ed. *Lun-Meng Jingyi* 《論孟精義》, *Lunyu Jingyi* 《論語精義》. *Wenyuange Sikuquanshu Dianziban* 《文淵閣四庫全書電子版》. Hong Kong: Digital Heritage Publishing, accessed September 25, 2014.

Zhu, Xi 朱熹, and Lü Zuqian 呂祖謙, eds. *Jinsilu* 《近思錄》. *Wenyuange Sikuquanshu Dianziban* 《文淵閣四庫全書電子版》. Hong Kong: Digital Heritage Publishing, accessed February 3, 2015.

Zhu, Yizun 朱彝尊. *Jingyikao* 《經義考》. *Wenyuange Sikuquanshu Dianziban* 《文淵閣四庫全書電子版》. Hong Kong: Digital Heritage Publishing, accessed September 2, 2014.

Ziporyn, Brook. *Ironies of Oneness and Difference: Coherence In Early Chinese Thought.* Albany: State University of New York Press, 2012.

Zufferey, Nicolas. *To the Origins of Confucianism: The 'Ru' in Pre-Qin Times and During the Early Han Dynasty.* New York: Peter Lang, 2003.

Index